MANx
Traditional Furniture

A Catalogue of the Furniture Collections
of Manx National Heritage

Bill Cotton
May '93

by
Bernard D. Cotton

ISBN 0 901106 34 8

FRONT COVER:

The workshop of Richard Hugh Kaighin, joiner, of Kerrowglass, Michael.

The interior of John Kinnish's cottage near Ramsey.

Working drawings from Richard Hugh Kaighin's notebook.

A 19th century arm chair, combining elements of both joined & Windsor chair construction (Catalogue No. 60).

BACK COVER:

Round topped table, circa 1880 (Catalogue No. 148).

19th century cradle on a rectangular stand (Catalogue No. 229).

Manx National Heritage is a unique organisation within the British Isles, charged by the people of the Isle of Man and with the authority of government statute, to protect, present and promote all aspects of the Island's natural and cultural heritage.

First Published by Manx National Heritage, Manx Museum and National Trust, Douglas, Isle of Man, 1993

Designed by Dot Shop Limited, Douglas, Isle of Man.
Printed by Print Centres Limited, Douglas, Isle of Man.

LIST OF CONTENTS

PREFACE

Stephen Harrison
DIRECTOR : MANX NATIONAL HERITAGE

In portraying the story of a community's past, a museum makes best use of its skills and resources to present a balanced selection of items in its care. As with all selections, the importance of what is included is often overshadowed by the evidence provided by a large number of items which, for various reasons, do not find an immediate place on the public stage.

The most obvious victims of this inevitable scenario are the large-scale collection groups which have their own story to tell but which tend only to supply 'supporting actors' to the larger drama unfolding in the public galleries.

It is therefore always a great pleasure when circumstances combine to provide an opportunity to promote one of these collections to 'centre-stage'. From this position, the qualities and testimony of individual pieces can be allowed to speak with their own accent, in their own regional dialect, revealing their own secret subtleties and significance.

As with all languages, however, the passage of the centuries sometimes obscures the original meaning. In such cases, the usual recourse is to experts in philology, semantics, phonetics and historical grammar. In a way, these are all valid elements in the study of furniture. I am delighted to say that for this review of the Manx National Heritage furniture collection, we have been fortunate enough to have had the services of Dr. Bernard 'Bill' Cotton and his wife Gerry who, together, provided us with a fluent command of the expert elements required to decipher the language spoken by traditional furniture.

However, no matter how scientific and exhaustive an examination of a witness may be, the most telling points are revealed to the most sympathetic questioner. The empathy and experience which Bill Cotton brings to the study of traditional furniture is obvious to anyone who has seen him closely confined with a chair. As if suddenly re-empowered with speech, it slowly reveals secrets of the original wood, the skill of the country joiner, the position it occupied in the house, and its modifications and adaptations by generations of Manx men and women. Frequently, the piece of furniture opens a window onto a past lifestyle in which the hanging layer of smoke from the turf fire and the uneven earth floor in the cottage become significant ingredients in the vernacular tradition of household furniture.

Above all, this is a 'human' approach which never allows the science of academic enquiry to sever the essential relationship between vernacular furniture and people.

This is a crucial element of this work as far as I am concerned, particularly in view of the contribution made to this project by a lady named Abigail Faragher.

Abigail lived in an isolated Manx cottage at Earystane in the south-west of the Isle of Man. I had the very great privilege of knowing her, and spent many hours, with my colleague Walter Clarke, talking to her about her memories of the Island's past lifestyles and traditions. Indeed, until her death in 1988 at the age of eighty-one, Abigail still epitomised the qualities, and many of the realities, of a traditional way of life which for most Manx families disappeared two or three generations earlier.

Her pride and, in many ways, her values were reflected in her house and her furniture. Indeed, she recognised quite clearly the importance of her collection of family-owned and, in some cases, family-made furniture in terms of the story it might tell to subsequent generations. She also recognised the unique role a museum can play in this important process of transmission, and bequeathed her cottage, its entire contents, and a substantial endowment to Manx National Heritage.

As I watched the careful cataloguing work being undertaken by Bill Cotton I thought more than once of the delight I knew Abigail would have felt at having her family furniture considered by such an expert. She would have loved to have been there, but she would have kept shyly to a quiet corner, smiling to herself, as she did when we originally documented the contents of her cottage before her death.

She would, I am sure, be equally delighted that part of her bequest has made this catalogue possible. Her foresight, generosity and, above all, her love of things Manx has enabled Manx National Heritage to provide this further testimony to the Island's life and traditions.

INTRODUCTION & ACKNOWLEDGMENTS

Bernard D. Cotton.

The study of British furniture has, historically, been largely concerned with the work of metropolitan designers and craftsmen who made furniture for fashionable households. The furniture made for the working people who inhabited the cottages, farmhouses and artisan houses has generally been neglected and indeed has been thought by some historians to be unworthy of scholarly attention.

In recent years, however, the work of a handful of pioneering researchers and latterly members of the Regional Furniture Society, has revealed that Britain is blessed with many rich and diverse traditions of furniture making, the products of individual regions. This work has heralded the beginning of a most remarkable story of furniture design, in which many strands of information are brought together. They include the different traditions of regional architecture for which furniture was made, as well as the social life of the people who owned and used it. There is a proper interest, too, in the craftsmen who made local furniture, in the materials they used and above all in how a sense of regional identity has come to provide the focus for studying different traditions.

The task of documenting furniture in its traditional settings remains a priority, since it is patently true that furniture, unlike the architecture for which it was made, moves around. The dispersal of people and the trade in 'antiques' has done much in this century to displace the evidence of traditional furniture from its original context. If a full history of British vernacular furniture is to be written, the making of proper records is a matter of urgency.

Of the many regions of the British Isles which await the recording of their historic furniture, the islands off its coasts are amongst those which still offer an opportunity to study furniture and a traditional way of life in a sense which has now largely passed in other areas. Amongst these, the Isle of Man has long offered an alluring possibility for such a study and in 1991 I made an appointment with the Director of Manx National Heritage, Stephen Harrison, to consider how a survey of Manx furniture might be carried out. It was the extensive furniture collection in the Manx Museum which proved to be the key to mounting a proper study.

Seldom has one museum housed such a splendid and extensive collection of traditional furniture from a single region: cradles (of which the stands are unique in the British tradition); spinning wheels and devices of many varieties; joined arm chairs and side chairs dating from the 17th to 19th centuries; settles and long case clocks. These and other items of furniture in the collection are representative of much, if not all, of the furniture which was used in Manx cottages and farmhouses.

Further items in the Museum collection include fashionable mahogany and oak furniture brought from the British mainland to the Isle of Man by the many incomers who left furniture behind them, dating variously from the 17th to the 20th centuries. These items, too, play an important part in the furniture history of the Island.

The Museum collection also includes items of 17th century furniture from the historic seat of administration at Castle Rushen, and has other important collections of furniture located in other parts of the Island. These include an intact collection of furniture from a small fashionable country house, The Grove, near Ramsey, which represents the tastes of the lesser gentry during the 19th century. Of equal importance, and of greater rarity, is the cottage furniture which was used in Harry Kelly's cottage at Cregneash. This remains as an unparalleled survival of a traditional Island home with its original furnishings. The collections at the Grammar School and the Nautical Museum, both in Castletown, also add their important perspectives to the history of furniture in the Isle of Man.

Encouraging though the prospects were for a significant study of the Island's furniture, it is to the Manx National Heritage's Director, Stephen Harrison, that special appreciation must go. It was his vision and enthusiasm to see a complete record and analysis of the Museum's furniture collection made, that was the mainspring for the project. Throughout the work, his sympathetic encouragement and support in all matters have been of the highest order.

My sincere thanks must also go to Dr. Nigel Wright, Assistant Keeper of Social History at the Manx Museum, who became a good friend during the course of the project. In every sense his support and unstinting efforts to sustain and assist my progress have been outstanding.

Ms. Yvonne Cresswell and Dr. Larch Garrad, also Assistant Keepers at the Manx Museum, have always been helpful and their informed advice on the project requires special thanks. The technical staff of the Museum, particularly Jim Rogers, Geoff Mitchell,

Carola Rush, Tim Westfold and Kevin Kinnin all played important roles in recording the Museum collection, and particularly in the project of clearing the workshop buildings at Kerrowglass. Their cheerfulness and willingness to help at every turn is most appreciated.

The Trustees of Manx National Heritage are to be thanked, too, for their support. It was their agreement to provide finance for a survey of Manx furniture, and its ultimate presentation in the form of this catalogue and a special exhibition at the Manx Museum, which provided the vital impetus for this project.

In addition to recording the Museum collections, it was decided to make various appeals to Manx people and others living on the Island, asking those who owned traditional furniture to invite us to their homes to see and record it. This we did, with the help of Manx Radio and the Manx newspapers. Our sincere thanks go to them for their co-operation.

As a result of these appeals, many Islanders contacted us to offer help in various ways, particularly by allowing us to visit their homes. Amongst these, special thanks must go to Mrs. Corkish of Bride, who permitted us to measure her home, to take photographs and to tape record her important memories of Manx life. Mr. Richard Cowley of Kerrowglass was crucial in our search for Manx furniture, as well as identifying the workshop of Richard Hugh Kaighin, joiner, of Kerrowglass. The time we spent clearing and re-establishing this workshop, which we found complete with bench, tools and documentation, was a magical phase of the project. Those of us who took part in it became involved in a major discovery of a substantially intact workshop and contents, of a kind which elsewhere has largely been swept away.

Mrs. Ida MacDonald of Peel, Hugh Kaighin's niece, also generously helped us to fill in many aspects of his life, and allowed us to photograph furniture made by him. Above all, she allowed us to study the personal diary and other documents which he had kept for over twenty years and which revealed much about the life of a Manx furniture maker.

Other members of the Island community who deserve special thanks include Mr. Quiggin of Castletown, Mr. Reg Silletto, Dr. John Thorpe, Mr. and Mrs. Kinrade, Rev. and Mrs. Rex Kissack, Mr. Jim Roscow, Mr. Frank Cowin and Mr. Peter Hill-Heaton. Mr. Nicholas Somers, ISVA, provided professional guidance on the values of furniture in the Museum collection.

Of unique assistance to this project, in a completely different sense, has been the existence of the Folk Life Survey which is held in the Manx Museum archives. The Survey is conducted by volunteers who began interviewing Islanders in the 1940s, and continues into the present. This Survey provides a record which is probably unique in the British Isles, in such a comprehensive form. Its capacity to provide the kind of detailed information which only members of a community could give has aided this project in many special ways.

A further person, although now dead, has been of vital assistance to this project. Miss Abigail Faragher of Earystane, Colby, provided the Museum with her family house and smithy, as well as the furnishings. These have allowed valuable insights into the furniture of one farming household and how it was used, as well as providing many valuable items for the Museum collection.

My thanks, too, go to several regional museums for their help and co-operation in allowing me to record items of furniture in their collections which, in various ways, have made important contributions to my understanding of the furniture on the Isle of Man. These include the Highland Folk Museum, Kingussie, the National Museum of Scotland in Edinburgh and the Ulster Folk and Transport Museum in Belfast.

The resulting survey of Manx furniture has required a long period of research and recording on the Island between 1991 and 1993 which has included many voyages on the Isle of Man ferry, bringing a full accompaniment of lighting and photographic equipment to record and analyse each item of furniture in the Museum collection and in homes on the Island. Although the sun (sometimes) shone in the summer months, this work has often been done in inclement weather. Cold and wet, and sometimes foggy, the conditions have required a sense of humour and a determination to see the project through to its proper conclusion. The staunchest and ever good-tempered member of the team, who always worked hard and uncomplainingly, must be thanked most sincerely, namely my wife Gerry. She handled heavy photographic equipment, took light meter readings, moved furniture, measured it and took detailed notes for the record sheets, talked to people and did all the thousand and one things that field research requires. To her go my deep appreciation and thanks.

Finally, it should be said that further work recording furniture on the Island remains to be done. Some items of furniture mentioned in the Folk Life Survey records were not found at all; wooden stump beds or box beds, for example. Others were mysteriously in short supply, dressers particularly. This record is the beginning of the story, not the final word. If any Islander can help by adding more information about other items, so much the fuller will the eventual story of Manx traditional furniture be.

THE ISLE OF MAN
Location & Background

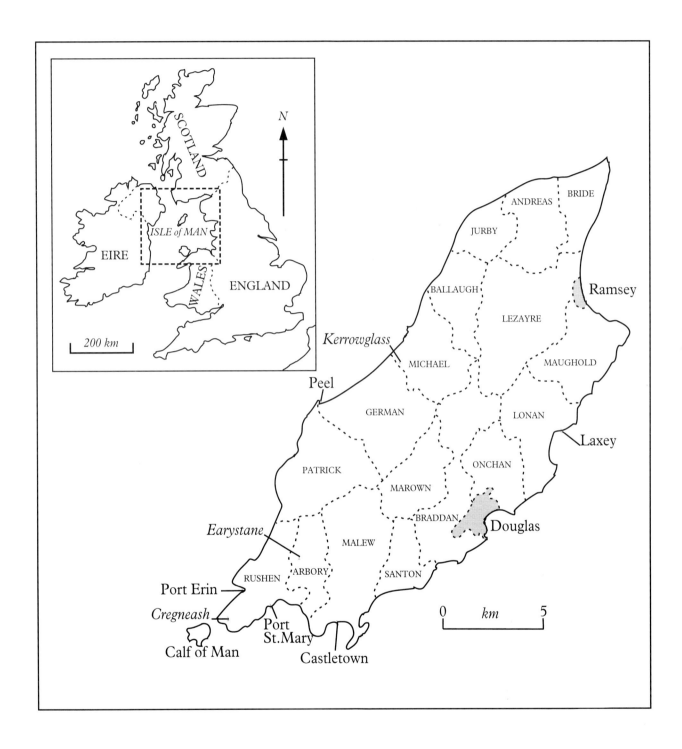

The Isle of Man occupies a central position in the British Isles, situated in the Irish Sea between the British mainland and Ireland. The Island is 33 miles long, north to south, and 13 miles wide, east to west, at its widest point.

Politically, the Isle of Man is a self-governing dependent territory of the British Crown and not part of the United Kingdom. It has its own parliament, Tynwald, dating back to the 10th century, making the Island probably the oldest parliamentary democracy in the world.

Traditionally, the Manx economy depended on agriculture, fishing, mining and trade, with tourism becoming an important industry by the end of the 19th century. Agriculture was small scale, with many of the population combining crofting with either fishing or mining.

MANX TRADITIONAL FURNITURE

An Introduction

Furniture history reflects, in a particularly intimate way, the social history of a place and its people. Long after the houses and the way of life for which the furniture was made have disappeared or been radically altered, furniture continues to offer evidence of past domestic life in an immediate and accessible way. Those who research regional traditions are generally deeply aware that in order to interpret furniture as part of the wider material culture of people's lives, it is necessary fully to record it, and then analyse its construction techniques, its decoration and the materials it is made from. Having created a full record, the next logical task is to put the furniture into categories - tables, chairs, dressers - and to examine their features in a way which enables us to recognise their regional characteristics. In the case of Manx furniture, it is often a matter of teasing out its antecedents from the traditions of the British mainland, or identifying furniture imported during the different phases of immigration to the Island, as well as from other outside contacts.

The purpose of the catalogue entries which follow these introductory essays is threefold: firstly, to provide a record of the major public collection of Manx furniture on the Island; secondly, to create a clear classification system which will enable comparisons to be made between items and thirdly to propose certain aspects of construction and design as salient descriptive features.

There is undoubtedly a great deal more traditional furniture in private homes on the Isle of Man; with the help of this publication it is hoped that many more items may be recognised by their owners and that they will bring information to Manx National Heritage at the Manx Museum so that the project of recording furniture on the Isle of Man can be continued.

In addition to recording and analysing furniture, however, the task of elucidating its social meaning is of equal importance. This is achieved by attempting to place the furniture within an historic context. In the case of Manx furniture, this necessitates an awareness of changes in the political complexion and administration of the Island over the past four centuries from which examples of furniture have been recorded.[1]

Probably more important to a full interpretation of a piece of furniture is an understanding of the houses for which the furniture was made, as the manufacture of furniture is closely linked to the domestic needs of

people and the architectural space into which it will fit. For this reason the traditional homes of crofters and cottagers on the Island are given priority in this catalogue. It is this aspect of Manx life, largely divorced from fashionable influences of British mainland culture until the second half of the 19th century, that best reveals its distinctiveness and richness. Every effort has been made to take these descriptions, of cottage construction, furniture and the traditional way of life, from the Islanders who spoke to the Manx Museum's Folk Life Survey over the years. Theirs is the surest testimony.

Finally, no study of regional furniture would be complete without proper recognition of the craftsmen who made it. Although there were a few specialist cabinet and clockcase makers on the Island from the end of the 18th century and the early - 19th century, the work largely fell to joiners, of whom there were many. These, often unsung, tradesmen were eminently skilled in many ways. We have been fortunate to be able to trace the life of one of these men, Richard Hugh Kaighin of Kerrowglass, in the parish of Michael. His workshop contents, examples of his furniture and above all his detailed diary and other records, have enabled us to understand the life of one of the Island's furniture makers in a way which has few parallels elsewhere in Britain. A description of his life and work is presented as a tribute to all the quiet and resourceful men and women of the Isle of Man who practiced self-sufficient and useful lives, and passed into history without similar record of their existence and work being made.

The colour illustrations on the following pages reveal some of the rich diversity of Manx traditional furniture - a full description of each item can be found in the main catalogue section.

The Manx National Heritage furniture collection owes much to the foresight and generosity of Miss Abigail Faragher. On pp. XIV - XV photographs of her furniture are shown together with views of her home at Earystane, near Colby, in the south of the Island.

The 'discovery' of the workshop of Richard Hugh Kaighin, provided a rare glimpse into the life and work of a typical joiner/crofter. The illustrations on p. XVI show his workshop and bench almost exactly as he left them on his death in 1945.

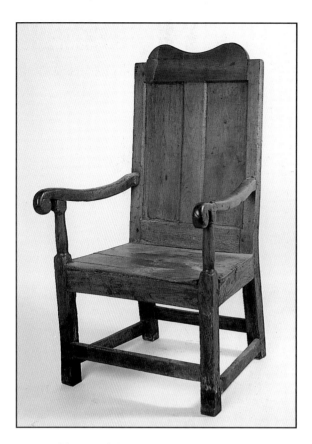

Plate 1; 19th century stick form Windsor chair, with ash arms and spindles, pine seat and legs.
(Catalogue No.66)

Plate 2; Mid-18th century oak arm chair.
(Catalogue No.11)

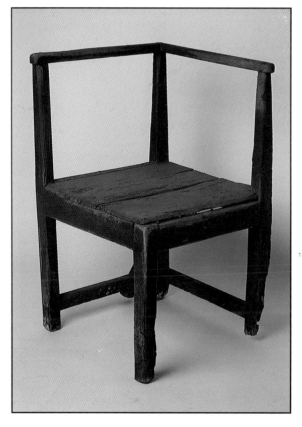

Plate 3; 18th century joined arm chair.
(Catalogue No.15)

Plate 4; Joiner-made oak corner chair, circa 1800.
(Catalogue No.86)

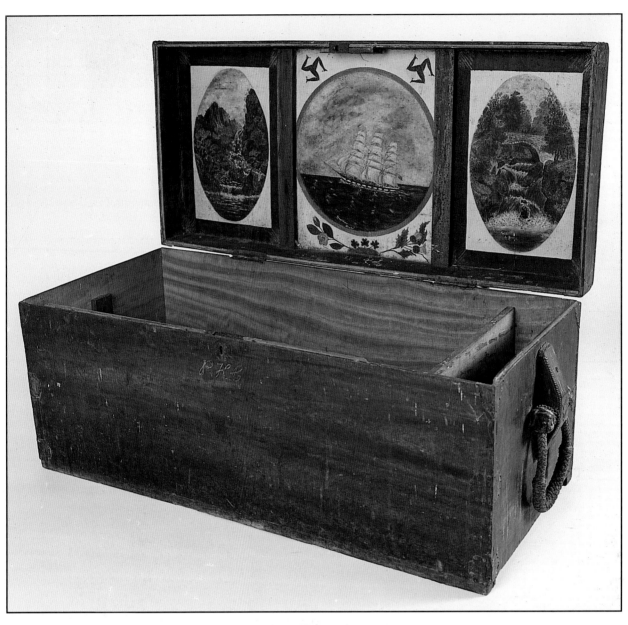

Plate 5; 19th century sea chest, with painted panels inside the lid.
(Catalogue N0.184)

Plate 6; Oak joined panelled chest, dated 1686, probably
Scottish in origin.
(Catalogue No.173)

Plate 7; Oak joined chest, circa 1640.
(Catalogue No.177)

Plate 9; Late-19th century stool with gorse stem legs.
(Catalogue No.124)

Plate 8; Late-19th century cradle which rocks on a rectangular
frame, a feature unique to the Manx cradles.
(Catalogue No.227)

Plate 10; 19th century pine rectangular stool.
(Catalogue No.119)

Plate 11; 19th century settle with curved, shaped ends. (Catalogue No.133)

Plate 12;
19th century great wheel.
(Catalogue No.233)

Plate 13; (bottom left)
Treadle operated bobbin-flyer
wheel for spinning wool or flax.
(Catalogue No.239)

Plate 14; (bottom right)
A hank or skein winder.
(Catalogue No.260)

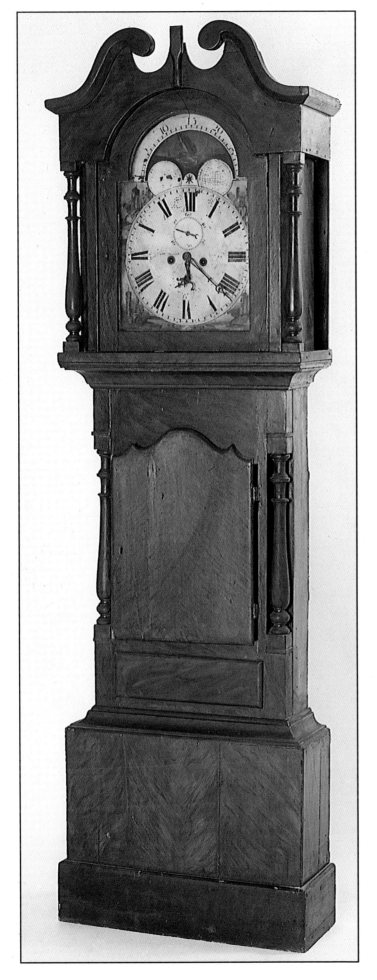

Plate 15; (left) A long case clock asssembled by Thomas Goldsmith of Douglas, circa 1850. The case probably came from the north of England, the movement from Birmingham. (Catalogue No.200)

Plate 16; (above) Long case clock, circa 1830. The clock has no assembler's name; however, the case is characteristic of cases made in Scotland. (Catalogue No.194)

Plate 17;
The main living room at Abigail Faragher's Smithy Cottage, Earystane, Colby.

Plate 18; (right)
An Austrian made clock movement, circa 1830, fitted into a later case, circa 1920.
(Catalogue No.190)

Plate 19;
Joiner-made chair of a common 19th
century Manx form.
(Catalogue No.40 B)

Plate 20;
A treadle operated bobbin-flyer spinning wheel with a distaff
attached for spinning flax.
(Catalogue No.190)

Plate 21;
The large bedroom at Smithy Cottage, Earystane, home of Abigail Faragher.

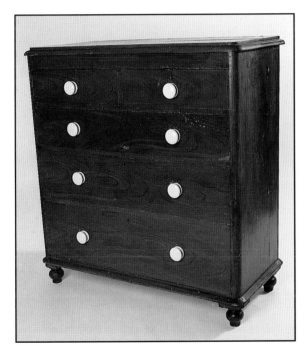

Plate 22;
19th century chest of drawers.
(Catalogue No.167)

Plate 23;
Wash stand, circa 1880, with Sicilian marble top.
(Catalogue No.211)

Plates 24 & 25; Interior views of Hugh Kaighin's workshop at Kerrowglass, in the parish of Michael.

The first written records of furniture in the Isle of Man are preserved in documents related to Manx customary law. These indicate that prior to the establishment of the Stanleys as Lords of Mann, one of the church's sources of income was the partial sequestration of the estates of deceased holders of Quarterland farms. This tithe was known as Corbes ('corpse present'). The Stanley's were concerned that this Church claim on an individual's estate might have detrimental effects on the payment of land rents, and in 1521 the twenty-four members of the House of Keys converted the Corbes to an itemised list of inalienable heirlooms. These passed to the deceased's eldest son and eldest daughter and were not considered part of the estate.

The following items of furniture were included to pass by right to the eldest son: "his best Board [table], his best stool . . . and his best Coffer." Among the effects to be passed to the eldest daughter only one item of furniture was included, ". . . the best Wheele and Cardes."[2] The use of the term 'best' is consistently applied to the furniture items, suggesting that others of a lesser quality would normally be present in such a household.

The list may be as much symbolic as utilitarian, since conventional male and female roles are represented in the kinds of furniture which were itemised. The man's seat and table symbolised his role as head of the house and provider. The only item of furniture inherited by the eldest daughter is the spinning wheel and carders for preparing wool for spinning, symbolising her role as the industrious woman of the house. Other items of necessary furniture, beds, stool, benches or display items are omitted from the list.

The fact that some prosperous households on the Isle of Man were endowed with much larger and more diverse collections of furniture than was indicated in the Corbes list, at least by the 17th century, is illustrated by references in 17th century wills. For example, the will of M. Christian (who died in 1637), lists . . . "Two carpett 20d, 3 standinge bedstockes, one truckle bed, one other old bedstocke one prest for clothes, one Cubbert. A table and frame with forme standing in the parlour. One chest 3/-. Wheel and Cards 22d".[3]

In 1663, a leading member of the Manx ruling elite, William Christian, popularly known as Illiam Dhone, was executed as a traitor - in 1651 he had led an uprising of Manxmen against the Countess of Derby and in support of a Parliamentary expeditionary force. Following the restoration of the monarchy in 1660 he was 'tried' and sentenced to death as a traitor. The extensive inventory of his estate at Ronaldsway illustrates a household which was well provided for with necessities and contained many comforts. His furniture included . . .

"In the parlour: 1 table and frame. 4 throne chaires. One Rowne table and frame. A blue stoule & chaire. 2 letther Chaires and leather Stoules.

Fig.i;
William Christian, popularly known as 'Illiam Dhone'; an inventory of his house contents in 1663 survives, revealing his comfortable furnishings.

In ye Clossett Chamber: A bed and Cloathes. One chist bound with Iron. One Boxe. 2 chaires & old stoule . . . 4 French Chaires. 5 blue stoules and chair. Ye best Bed and Cloathes." [4]

Notwithstanding the anachronistic spellings in this and other 17th century Manx inventories, these descriptions suggest that prosperous households were furnished with a similar range of furniture to their counterparts in England. Whether these furniture items were made on the Island, however, is open to doubt, since the production of joined furniture in the 17th century was the domain of specialist tradesmen. They were trained and affiliated to guilds, who retained exclusive rights over who could make and sell furniture. No 17th century joiner's, turner's or carver's guilds have been identified on the Isle of Man, and since training was dependent upon being apprenticed to such a guild member, it seems likely that most of the 17th century furniture items in Manx inventories were imported from Scotland and England. In the aforementioned case of William Christian of Ronaldsway, who also had estates in Lancashire, it is

Fig.ii;
Ronaldsway Farmhouse, home of the Christian family,
as depicted in a 1793 sampler.

probable that his furniture was imported from there, where there existed prolific schools of joiners.[5]

This sense of contiguity between the Isle of Man and Cheshire and Lancashire is reinforced by the writings of a contemporary of William Christian, namely William Blundell, a Lancashire gentleman. In 1648, he sought refuge on the Isle of Man from both sides in the English Civil War and wrote an illuminating account of the life of both rich and poor on the Island. He noted that there were four towns, Castletown, Douglas, Ramsey and Peel, although both Ramsey and Peel were little more than villages at the time. His impression of the Island folk was that the gentry and well-to-do merchants were very like people from Cheshire and Lancashire in their speech and behaviour, and that they lived in similar houses.

He wrote that the architecture in Castletown and Peel included stone houses which were built with two and three storeys, with slate roofs and outside stone stairs

like those used in barns. The houses of farmers and minor tradesmen were usually of one storey only and had thatched roofs of straw. Of the houses of the poorest, Blundell wrote that they were . . .

> "Mere hovels, compacted of stones and clay for the walls, thatched with broom, most commonly having only one room; very few have two, and further no upper room such as in towns are called 'lofts', nor any ceilings but thatch and bare rafters. Yet in this smoking hut doth the man, his wife and children co-habit and in many cases with the ducks and geese under the bed, the cockes and hennes over his head, his cow and calfe at the beds foot." [6]

The Manx National Heritage collection of furniture has a number of items of joined oak furniture dating from the 17th century, all of which were originally intended for wealthy households or for official use. These include two items which came from Castle Rushen: a large panelled press cupboard, or aumbry, which was used to hold the official rolls, and a massive

Fig.iii; The Rolls Cupboard, dating from the 17th century, was used to hold papers at Castle Rushen. (Catalogue No. 160).

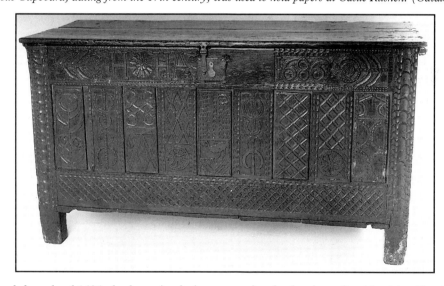

Fig.iv; A carved chest, dated 1686; the decorative devices suggest that the chest has a Scottish origin. (Catalogue No.173).

plank chest, with secure metal hinges and hasp (see Catalogue Numbers 160 and 174).[7] Both of these pieces are of Scottish design and it seems possible that they were brought to the Island from there.

Other furniture items in the Manx National Heritage collection dating from the 17th century are also of Scottish design. There are a number of joined arm chairs, including one dated 1685, which is closely paralleled by a chair recorded from the Whithorn area of south-east Scotland. A further item of Scottish

design is an elaborately carved chest, dated 1686, carrying Scottish decorative carving devices including the thistle emblem. The date of arrival on the Island of these items is not known, but their histories suggest that they have been on the Island since at least the 18th century.[8]

A second small group of furniture, also dating from the 17th century and present in the Manx National Heritage collection, include several joined chairs which are typical of those made in the Cheshire or south

Lancashire tradition, and which are North-West region or Welsh in design.

Additionally, the collection has three joined, panelled oak chests and an inlaid chest of drawers which are also of English design. Although one cannot categorically state that these items were not made on the Island, it seems more probable that these Scottish and English or Welsh styles of furniture were imported.[9]

Furniture dating from the 18th century is evidently scarce on the Isle of Man, and the items held in the Manx National Heritage collection are largely joined arm chairs with panelled or slatted backs (see chapter on Joined Chairs in the Catalogue section pp. 1-36). A number of these chairs appear to have been made on the Island, often from timber which has round mortice holes and which probably, therefore, came from shipwrecks, or from reclaimed house timbers. These important-looking chairs have close parallels with chairs held in the collections of the Ulster Folk and Transport Museum, Belfast, and both groups appear either to have been made in Scotland, or influenced by chairs from the Scottish tradition. Since many of these chairs date from the period when the Dukes of Atholl ruled the Island, this may explain the Scottish influence in the case of the Manx examples. Their survival may well reflect the Manx custom of inheritance of Corbes, as discussed earlier.

It is hard to believe that joined chairs of these kinds were made for other than the homes of the clergy,

farmers and perhaps the more prosperous fishermen and crofters on the Island. Scarce though they are, contemporary references to the lives of the poor in the 18th century generally paint a bleak picture. For example, Waldron (writing between 1720 and 1730) said that the houses of the peasantry . . .

"are no more than cabins built of sods, and covered with the same, except a few belonging to the better sort of farmers, which are thatched with straw . . . the greater part of them (the peasants) of both sexes go barefoot, except on Sunday or when they are at work in the field, and have then only small pieces of cow's or horse's hide to the bottom of their feet tied on with packthread, which they call carranes. Their food is commonly herrings and potatoes, or bread made of potatoes."[10]

John Wesley, who visited the Isle of Man in 1777 and 1781, gave another, gentler view of the Island and its people. He regarded it as . . .

"Shut up from the world; and having little trade . . . visited by scarce any strangers. The natives are a plain, artless, simple people: unpolished, that is, unpolluted; few of them are rich or genteel, the far greater part moderately poor and most of the strangers that settle among them are men that have seen affliction."[11]

It is not exactly clear what Wesley meant by this last comment, but the 'affliction' was most probably financial. It is true that in addition to its indigenous population other, often middle class, people came to

Fig.v;
A view of Castletown in the mid-17th century, as drawn by Daniel King, illustrating the stone houses as observed by William Blundell.

Fig.vi;
An oak joined chair dating from the mid-18th century, crudely made from re-used timbers. (Catalogue No.9).

the Island during the 18th century. Goods imported onto the Island attracted customs duties which were much lighter than those in England and this allowed those on small fixed incomes to live more comfortably than they could at home. This situation continued over many years and half pay Army and Navy officers joined them following the Napoleonic Wars, in the early years of the 19th century. Other immigrants came to avoid being pursued for debt, since the laws of the Isle of Man precluded their being pursued onto the Island. Amongst this group of incomers were those who dishonestly brought money with them, again to avoid English laws. After the Revestment, in 1765, came businessmen who developed various profitable small scale industries: brick-making, spinning, weaving, dyeing and brewing, while local entrepreneurs expanded into boat-building, brewing and fish-curing. Both groups were involved in banking and insurance and all spent welcome money with the tradesmen on the Island.

Since there is little evidence of a specialised cabinet making trade on the Island during the 18th century, it is possible that the small number of fashionable mahogany items held in the Manx National Heritage collection from this period were brought in by these immigrants from mainland Britain during the 18th century and the early years of the 19th century.

It is also from this source that items of fashionable furniture were gradually dispersed to the homes of prosperous Islanders. Mr. Edward Christian, of

Northop, Greeba, reporting to the Manx Folk Life Survey in 1963, said of furniture sales some 150 years ago that . . .

> "The first really good furniture was obtained from the sales of the household effects of some of the Scotch, English and Irish officers who retired here after the cessation of the French wars. That is how it started round Peel side anyway. People who were better off were going to the Sales and buying, and a lot of it was in the style of Chippendale and Hepplewhite . . . That's what I've heard - it was these retired people who first introduced it." [12]

Cabinet making as a distinct trade on the Island is first advertised in the Manx newspapers in the first years of the 19th century and continues to be so throughout the century. However, the exact nature of the items produced by Island craftsmen is unclear, and the Manx National Heritage collection appears not to contain any fashionable furniture items which could be attributed to them. It may be that their own limited production concentrated on items normally outside the scope of cabinet makers elsewhere and was augmented by furniture imported from the British mainland. An advertisement in the *Manx Advertiser* of 31 August 1811, for example, proclaims "On Sale. A few pairs of cart wheels, from four feet two inches to four feet eight high. For particulars, apply to Mr. George Woods, Cabinet Maker, Douglas." [13]

Fig.vii;
Douglas c.1800, a time when an increasing number of 'incomers' were making their home in the town, bringing fashionable pieces of furniture with them (detail from a painting by Warwick Smith).

Fig.viii;
A fashionable bureau-bookcase, probably made in Liverpool or Manchester in about 1840.
(Catalogue No.204).

The Grove in Ramsey (now The Grove Rural Life Museum), a small country house with decor typical of fashionable households of the first half of the 19th century in many parts of mainland Britain, is substantially furnished with items from Scotland and England, as well as from the owner's travels abroad. It is known that the house, initially a summer residence only, was largely furnished from an auction sale in Liverpool. These purchases were subsequently augmented by a few family heirlooms, when it became the sole permanent home of the widow of the Liverpool merchant who had enlarged it from a 'superior' cottage.

The Nautical Museum in Castletown also contains a small collection of fashionable 18th and early - 19th century furniture, including oak chairs, *circa* 1790,

It is traditional furniture dating from the 19th century, however, which forms the largest coherent group of Isle of Man furniture in the Manx National Heritage collection. This includes examples of joined chairs, stools, Windsor chairs, dressers, cradles, spinning wheels, round tables with three legs, oblong tables and benches, long case clocks, chests of drawers and storage chests. All of these items were made by the Island's joiners and carpenters and it seems clear from both the large number of surviving furniture items and the diverse functions they performed, that a largely self-sufficient farming, crofting and fishing economy provided, from the end of the 18th century, a stable, if modest, opportunity for Islanders to live in a way which previous generations had largely been denied.

Fig.ix;
The drawing room at The Grove, containing fashionable furniture from the first half of the 19th century.

made with mid-18th century design features, a mahogany Pembroke table fitted with tea caddies, and a desk dating from the late - 18th century which was modified in the early years of the 19th century to hold the files of a private bank, founded by its owner, George Quayle.

This all suggests that perhaps little cabinet making of fashionable furniture was available on the Island, and that the needs of prosperous households were largely supplied to them through importation of furniture from the British mainland. This situation could be perpetuated by the purchase of items of furniture from people leaving the Island and unwilling, or unable, to afford heavy transportation costs.

Even the houses of the poorest people seem to have been improved and extended by the beginning of the 19th century. By 1812, Thomas Quayle was able to record a Manx cottage as follows:
"The walls are about seven feet high, constructed of sods of earth. At each side of the door appears a square hole containing a leaded window. Chimney there is none but a perforation in the roof, a fire beneath. The timber forming the rafters is slender, coarse and crooked. It is thatched with straw secured by ropes of the same material attached to the wall by projecting stones, or to stones hanging from the end of ropes. From the end of the roof from which the smoke comes to the other end, the roof gently declines in height. If the means

Fig.x; Mrs. Gilrea outside her sod cottage at East Nappin, Jurby, 1897.

of the inhabitant enable him to keep a cow an extension of the roof covers a similar hovel accommodating the valuable inmate. The floor of both portions is hardened clay. The embers burn on a stone placed on the hearth without range or chimney . . . a partition separates the cottage into two rooms. Over the chamber is often a loft ascended by a ladder from the keeping room."[14]

Cottages and small farmhouses of this type were universally thatched on the Isle of Man. Straw (wheat, oat or barley) was the most common material used, although in the north of the Island marram grass ('bent') was used extensively. Other materials were also used, including ling, broom and rushes. Roofs of this type were held in place with hay rope, called 'suggane', which were tied to stone projections built into the eaves ('bwhid sugganes'), a method also utilised in many houses in Ireland and parts of western Scotland. [15]

The walling materials of the cottages varied too and, particularly in the north of the Island, crofts and other small buildings were often built merely of earth sods of puddled clay mixed with chopped straw or chaff. In 'A Tour through the Isle of Man' during 1797 and 1798 John Feltham comments on the cottages . . .
    "Thick as the cottages are, they do not strike the eye; the walls of the huts are seldom above seven feet high, composed of sods of earth, and the roofs thatched with straw, which soon becomes of a murky hue."[16]

An illustration of such a cottage can be seen in Figure x, the house of Mrs. Gilrea of East Nappin, Jurby. Miss I. M. Killip, Folk Life Survey Collector, commented on the photograph that . . . "these houses were literally dug out of the ground and when completed were not raised far above it. The late Mr. John Kneen of

Ballaugh who used to visit the Gilreas has said that their house was built out of sods dug out of the site itself . . . 'so that the ground sloped down to it and the house stood in a hollow'."[17]

Grace Quilliam, the previous Folk Life Collector, wrote that according to submissions made to the Survey the last puddled mud houses were built about 1860. She quotes a Mrs. Kneale of Ballagarrett, Bride, "going to Lark Hill to help puddle the mud mixed with chopped straw, (and) 'stramping' it with bare feet ready for the builders."[18]

Many other cottages and small farmhouses were built with stones set in clay - latterly lime mortar. Figure xiii shows such a stone-built thatched cottage. Mr. F. A. Comaish of Glen Wyllin recalled to the Folk Life Survey that "the mortar used was principally mud mixed with a tough hard grass that grew on dry banks and meadows. It was very tough and came out of the walls in good condition when the walls fell."[19]

Stone flags were used in Manx cottages, but earth floors were far more common. Grace Quilliam commented that,
    "the earthen floors were stamped down until they were dark and shining and were sprinkled with sand and swept with the efficient besom. . . the internal walls of cottages were whitewashed or colour washed, with ochre or umber being mixed with the whitewash."[20]

Mr. Cooper of Castletown, in his eighty-second year, spoke of the interiors of Manx cottages:
    "The windows were simple sashes, not made to open, with small panes of glass. Originally the joists of the loft were exposed, but were sometimes later covered with calico and papered. Floors were swept

Fig.xi; A mud walled cottage in Bride - photograph taken in 1953.

Fig.xii; Mr.Corkish of the Smeale, Andreas, collecting marram grass ('bent') from the Ayres in 1951.

with brooms made of ling, floors of earth beaten hard . . .The furnishings in my time, curtains, bedding, etc, were much as now. I never remembered seeing any carpets. There might have been a rug in front of the fire made of rags torn and stitched on canvas."[21]

Respondents to the Folk Life Survey had clear memories of the furniture used inside the traditional cottages. Mr. Comaish of Glen Wyllin, for example, recollects that . . .

"When you entered the kitchen by the front door on your right there was a wooden partition about two feet six inches; behind the partition there was a chair, then a table about five feet long, and two feet

six inches wide, square legged with a bar running the full length into the bedroom. There were usually two beds in this room which were used by the parents and female children. There was a loft over this room in which the male children slept. It was commonly called the cockloft and was reached by a shipladder going up out of the kitchen."[22]

Mrs. Kinrade of the Garey, Lezayre commented that "the furniture in the old Manx houses was only simple... the stuff would be made by the joiner."[23] Mr. Cooper of Castletown continued his recollections with a description of the 'simple' repertoire of furniture in a typical cottage . . .

"a round table, sometimes with shelf below, oblong table, arm chair and small chairs - locally made, dresser, shelves for crockery on top and row of drawers under the top, open underneath usually but sometimes with doors . . . bedroom, wooden stead with chaff bed and usual coverings, chair and table locally made."[24]

The kitchen was the main hub of family life. As Mr. Comaish of Glen Wyllin commented . . .

"the kitchen was living room, sitting room etc and the occupants hardly ever lived in any other room because farming in those times was all work from daylight in the morning to dark at night."[25]

Within the room itself the dresser took pride of place and it was usually positioned against the back wall of the kitchen . . .

"standing up against the back wall was the dresser. . . there was a grand display of old jugs, willow pattern plates, rosy basins. . . the dresser was the pride of the cottage."[26]

Fig. xiii; A stone walled crofter/fisherman's cottage, at Bride in the 1890s
- a fairly typical cottage, despite the posed nature of the photograph.

Fig.xiv; The Farmhouse Kitchen at the Manx Museum, with its traditional 19th century furniture.

Fig. xv; The cottage interior of John Kinnish, popularly known as 'Old Pete'.
Despite the fact that 'Old Pete' became something of a 'professional Manxman' after Hall Caine, a popular Manx novelist, based one of his characters on him, the cottage does retain an authentic feel.

Together with the long case clock, the dresser was often the tallest piece of furniture in the dwelling, which could create problems; whereas a long case clock could be let down into the puddled clay floor this was not an option for the dresser. . . "it was very high, fitting up under the joists."[27] One option was to have the dresser tailor made for a particular room. . .

> "Mr. Dugdale said they quite commonly had orders to make dressers for people - they made them for farmhouses and for cottages and the size varied to suit the house where they were to go."[28]

The traditional Manx cottage was heated with a peat fire, set on the floor of the kitchen, against the gable wall and surmounted by a canopy which covered the fire and the cooking area. This provided space or sitting and to the rear there could be a bread oven. A hearth of this type is known on the Island as a *chiollagh* and its presence was a characteristic feature of the traditional Manx home.[29] "It was fine and roomy inside the *chiollagh* and there were two chairs, arm chairs, one on each side of the fire, and you could sit there on the chairs" (Mr. Corkish, Ramsey).[30]

Figure xvi is a photograph of a typical Manx cottage interior, *circa* 1890, including a dresser to the right, whose style emanates from Ireland. The open fireplace shows the use of a cloth frieze below the mantleshelf and a bread oven to the rear of the fire, though this was only an occasional feature on the Island.

Although a number of photographs exist of the interiors of Manx cottages, few interiors were drawn to show the exact position of furniture in relation to the floor plan of the house. Such information can be crucial to our understanding of how the space within a dwelling was used, and adds to our understanding of the use and social significance of certain items of furniture.[31] A limited plan exists of Carmodil Cottage in Ballaugh, although only the position of the clock and dresser can be ascertained.

A drawing of Harry Kelly's cottage in Cregneash may be unique in showing all the furniture in a dwelling (Figure xviii). This cottage, complete with furniture, is owned by Manx National Heritage and is open to the public. The plan shows a two roomed cottage in which there is a blocked doorway to the rear, opposite the front door, originally intended to provide a through draught for the winnowing of grain. The drawing reveals that the cottage, when lived in by a man alone, had but one bed, a chest, dresser, round table, long case clock, an oblong table with two benches, one chair and one 'best' chair. Two cupboards were built, one on either side of the *chiollagh*.

This harmony between Manx cottage homes and the furniture which is so evocatively described by Islanders leads us to a further question - is there such a thing as a true Manx style of traditional furniture? This question, although understandable in terms of the need to evaluate the relative distinctiveness of the Island's

Fig.xvi; The interior of a cottage in Andreas circa 1900, with an Irish style dresser to the fore.

culture, inevitably leads us to more complex considerations of the Island's role in being at once independent, yet closely linked with the cultures from the adjacent British mainland.

The evidence so far suggest that at various points in the Island's history Manx joiners received information about furniture from different traditions on the British mainland. Scotland and England were the predominant influences in the 17th and 18th centuries. In the early -19th century, where the greatest evidence of extant Manx furniture exists, it is clear that many design influences came from other parts of the British Isles as well. These, too, were embraced and modified to produce 'Manx furniture'.

For example, influences from Wales are seen in the Manx dressers with cupboards in their bases and shelves above, as well as in the simple joined chairs.

Irish influence can be seen in the manufacture of Manx dressers with open bases. Furniture design from

England is clearly reflected in such items as oblong tables, boarded settles and lodging boxes. Yet other items of Manx furniture have design elements in which two or more countries are represented. For example, various Manx bobbin-flyer spinning wheels are of types common in England, Wales and Scotland. Great wheels too were made on the Isle of Man of a type which was common in many parts of Britain as well as in other European countries.

Manx cradles follow the influence of examples from England, Wales and Ireland, all of which are closely similar to each other, but with the exception that many Manx examples have a rectangular stand on which the cradle can rock. This does seem to be a unique Manx feature.

Yet other types of furniture - joined chairs, for example - have close similarities to particular traditions from the British mainland, but include some design elements which characterise them as Manx. For example, in some chair designs the use of relatively thin front legs,

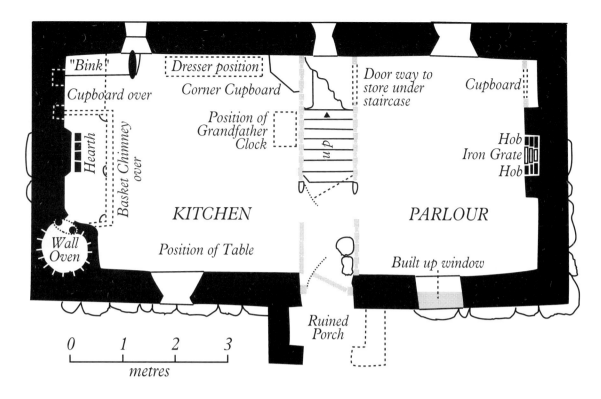

Fig. xvii; The ground floor plan of Carmodil Cottage, Ballaugh; only 3 pieces of furniture can be accurately positioned. The position of dresser, table and clock were shown by marks on the walls or floor.

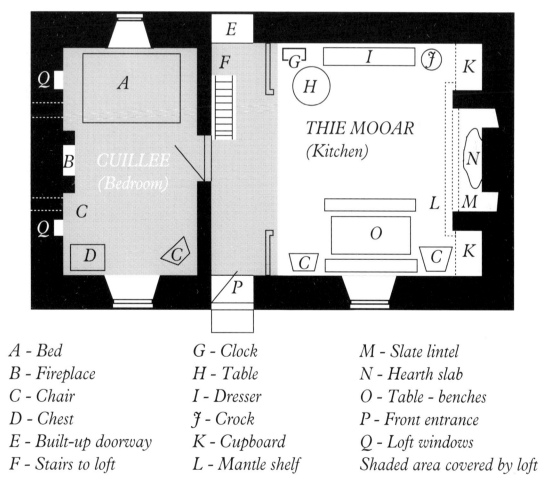

A - Bed
B - Fireplace
C - Chair
D - Chest
E - Built-up doorway
F - Stairs to loft

G - Clock
H - Table
I - Dresser
J - Crock
K - Cupboard
L - Mantle shelf

M - Slate lintel
N - Hearth slab
O - Table - benches
P - Front entrance
Q - Loft windows
Shaded area covered by loft

Fig. xviii; Ground floor plan of Harry Kelly's Cottage, Cregneash, marking the position of many pieces of furniture (taken from the Cregneash Village Folk Museum guide)

with corner moulding, is a significant revision from the conventional style elsewhere. The manufacture of joined chairs in pine, painted to simulate oak and with seats blackened to imitate a horsehair cover, also shows an unusual and characteristically Manx method of decoration. Other groups of traditional furniture on the Island were clearly directly imported from England and Scotland. These include long case clocks where the cases and mass produced movements were imported

Fig. xix;
A conventional Manx spinning wheel. (Catalogue No.245).

separately from the north of England and Scotland and 'united' by the Island's clockmakers.

Mass produced Windsor chairs from the High Wycombe centre of chair manufacture in Buckinghamshire were also imported. Windsors hand-made from hedgerow materials were common on the Island, following a pan-Celtic style of construction. Many innovative designs of these chairs were made; one of these, in the Manx National Heritage collection, illustrates a singular type of Windsor design, in which curved and bent sections are brought together to form what is a unique Manx interpretation of the Windsor form.

The answer as to whether there is a true Manx traditional style is therefore equivocal. What characterises the Manx furniture tradition is its capacity to absorb preferred parts of the British mainland traditions, and to make items which reflect these antecedents whilst at the same time offering constructional details which characterise them as Manx. The features which identify an item as Manx are now at least partially understood, and many of them are identified in the catalogue entries which follow these introductory essays. However, more

detailed analysis of styles and particularly of furniture measurements will establish the particular code of harmonies and decorative devices and enable a real understanding of the Island's furniture.

Furniture for more fashionable homes was both imported and made on the Island during the 19th century, and Manx National Heritage has two other collections of furniture which reflect the furnishings of this kind of home. The furniture from Miss Abigail Faragher's home at Earystane, Colby, mostly dates from the 19th century and was recorded *in situ* before its removal to the Museum. It is of a more fashionable, or at least commodious, nature than that usually found

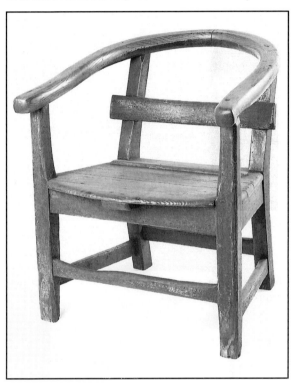

Fig. xx;
An unusual, Manx interpretation of the Windsor chair form. (Catalogue No.60).

in the traditional cottage homes on the Island, being appropriate to the larger farmhouses of that period. The individual items from the house are included in this catalogue in the chapters for chairs, chests of drawers, dressers, bedroom furniture and spinning wheels. The items are divided between those which were made locally by members of Miss Faragher's family and those which were imported to the Island from manufacturers who made mass produced items at relatively low cost.

The Grove at Ramsey is a small country house which had a farm attached and was owned continuously by the Gibb family from 1838 until 1976, when it passed to Manx National Heritage. The furnishings of the house represent the taste of the prosperous merchant class or lower gentry in the first half of the 19th century; it was altered very little by later, less prosperous generations of the family. Each room of the house, which is open to the public, is furnished in the authentic decor of the 19th century and it offers a rare insight into the furniture schemes of the period, including the use of fashionable mahogany and

Fig. xxi; The small bedroom at Abigail Faragher's Earystane home.

rosewood items. A separate description of the furniture in this house is given in a room-by-room inventory in Appendix I.

Manx National Heritage continues to collect furniture from all periods, including the 20th century, and holds a small but interesting group of furniture from this latter period. This aspect of the collection includes examples of wardrobes and other bedroom furniture from Miss Abigail Faragher's home. These show the influence of Art Nouveau designs and together they offer an unusually complete anthology of bedroom items from the early - 20th century. Other parts of the 20th century collection also come from Miss Faragher's home, and include a group of Lloyd Loom 'Lusty' chairs and imitations of these, as well as upholstered chairs dating from the 1950s. Two items, a hall table and a corner cabinet, show the influence of the Manx designer Archibald Knox.

As stated earlier, this publication is not designed to be the final word on Manx furniture but is merely a starting point. It is hoped that the interest aroused by the publication of the catalogue and its accompanying exhibition will alert people to the important information which furniture can hold; from the humblest chair to the finest long case clock - all have a story to tell.

REFERENCES

1. The Stanley family were granted the Isle of Man by Henry IV, in 1405. Originally 'Kings of Mann', the title changed to Lord of Mann with the succession of Thomas Stanley, the second Earl of Derby, in 1504. It was the rule of the seventh Earl that was the most significant in the Stanley regime. During the English Civil War (1642-1649) the seventh Earl was a staunch supporter of Charles I and was executed in England following an abortive attempt to place Charles II on the throne in 1651. After the Restoration in 1660 the Derbys were reinstated, with the eighth Earl. James Stanley, the tenth Earl, was the last of the Stanleys to rule the Isle of Man, after which the title passed to James Murray, Duke of Atholl in 1736, who was descended from a daughter of the seventh Earl of Derby.

   The Atholls ruled the Isle of Man for only thirty years, selling the Lordship to the British crown in 1765 ('the Revestment'). In 1793 the British government appointed the fourth Duke of Atholl as Governor, a position he retained until 1830.

2. Information from Mr. Jim Roscow.

3. Manx Museum Library; EW9. 1637. Information on the wills from Mr. Jim Roscow.

4. Anon, 'Unpublished Documents in the Manx Museum', *Journal of the Manx Museum*, Vol II, No. 38, 1930-34, p.170.

5. This is a subject which would repay further study; preliminary research by Mr. Jim Roscow suggests that the situation is by no means clear cut. For example, in a document dated 1699 there is a reference to 'Arthur Bridson, Carpenter a Bill of work done for making chairs and settles for our Honourable Lords £i.06.ii (Manx Museum Library; Bundle of Ingates and Outgates, Book of Charges, 1699).

6. Quoted in Stenning, E. H., *Portrait of the Isle of Man*, (Robert Hale, 1978), pp. 82-3.

7. The word 'Aumbry' (also Aumrey, Ambrey, Ambry) is a Scottish and northern English term, now largely obsolete except in some northern dialects. It is used to describe a repository for domestic utensils, either built-in, or as a separate piece of furniture. In Dr. Johnson's *Dictionary of the English Language* (1755), he wrote that an Aumbry was 'the place where plate, and utensils for housekeeping are kept; also a cupboard for keeping cold victuals a word still used in the northern counties, and in Scotland'.

8. Uncredited 'notes' at the beginning of the *Journal of the Manx Museum*, Vol. III, No. 43, June 1935, p. 21.

9. There is clear documentary evidence for the importation of furniture items. For example, on board the *Preston Merchant* in June 1700, among the "100 soaps, 2 gross bottles" and other assorted merchandise, are "1 dozen chairs" (Manx Museum Library, Bundle of Ingates and Outgates 1696 - 1704). Again, in July 1700 "1/2 dozen woodin chairs, [and] one small table . . ." were brought to the Island onboard the *Jane* of Castletown (Manx Museum Library, Bundle of Ingates and Outgates 1696 - 1704). Information from Mr. Jim Roscow.

10. Harrison, W. ed., *A Description of the Isle of Man*, by George Waldron gent, (Manx Society, Vol XI, 1865), p. 2 and p. 51.

11. Quoted in Kinvig, R. H., *The Isle of Man* (Liverpool University, 1975), p. 129.

12. Manx Museum Library - Folk Life Survey (hereafter FLS), C/27-K.

13. Manx Museum Library, Newspaper Microfilm, N44.

14. Quoted in Kniveton, G. and Goldie, M. *Tholtans of the Manx Crofter*, (Manx Experience, n.d.), p. 3.

15. Killip, I.M., "Thie Thooit Lesh Maidjyn Ayn: A Note on Manx Thatching Methods', *Journal of the Manx Museum*, Vol VII, 1966-76, pp. 157-160.

16. Airey, A. ed., *Feltham's Tour though the Isle of Man*, (Manx Society, Vol VI, 1861), p. 165.

17. Killip, I.M., 'Mrs. Gilrea of the East Nappin', *Journal of the Manx Museum*, Vol VI, No. 81, 1957-1965, Plate 277, p.232.

18. Quilliam, G.M., 'The Manx Museum Folk Life Survey', *IOMNHAS Proc.*, Vol V, No. 4, 1953-54, p. 407.

19. FLS/CFA-A.

20. Quilliam, G.M., 'The Manx Museum Folk Life Survey', *IOMNHAS Proc.*, Vol V, No. 4, 1953-54, p. 407.

21. FLS/CJH-A.

22. FLS/CFA-A

23. FLS/K/21.

24. FLS/CJH-A

25. FLS/CFA-A.

26. *Ibid.*

27. FLS/G/55.

28. FLS/D/6-A.

29. Williamson, K. 'Characteristics of the *Chiollagh* - Dominant Types and their Distribution', *Journal of the Manx Museum.*, Vol IV, No. 54, 1938-40, pp. 23-25.

    The author comments that "the development of the *chiollagh* can be traced through three different stages. The earliest known to us has a wattle and daub canopy . . . A later step was to board in the whole canopy at the front and sides with fairly wide planks cut to a suitable shape. Finally comes a culminating phase in which the *chiollagh* is actually no longer an open one, for the wooden canopy gives way to a funnel built of brick and supported on brick pillars".

30. FLS/C/104.

31. Drawings of house plans with furniture *in situ* are useful, since they reveal important aspects of the relationships between the different internal spaces of the home, how people used these spaces and the furniture they contained. Seen in this way, the home becomes more than a space in which mundane activities take place, but rather rooms take on the aspect of a stage in which pieces of furniture are the props which designate the place and form of many social events. For example, food preparation, sleeping, storing provisions and clothing, joining together with other family members and displaying precious possessions, all become dramatic events in which the themes of a particular culture's life are enacted.

    In this sense, identifying where furniture stood is important in enabling us to see how certain furniture items were used for special purposes at different times in the day, and where they fitted, quiescently, into the staged set of the home at other times. For example, tables used during the day for food preparation were usually stood under a window, and round topped tables might be stood in a particular corner of the parlour. Both alter their spatial relationships and enter into different symbolic moments when they have their positions altered at meal times and are drawn to the centre of the room or near to the fire.

    The movement of some furniture in this way contrasts with the fact that other items are rarely moved: the clock, the dresser and bed, for example the bed being used at night, forming the principal item of 'nocturnal' furniture. Because these latter items are relatively static, they appear in plan drawings as a part of the architecture, controlling the movement of people around them, and in this sense indistinct from the architecture.

    Mapping the different positions which movable furniture items have at appropriate times during a twenty four hour or other cycle is, therefore, about determining routine and particularly about important pivots in domestic life. Such plans also direct us to issues of furniture design, for little is casually achieved in the field of vernacular furniture.

    The dimensions, function, materials and weight of furniture items were closely related to the tasks to be engaged in and the space available for these in the home. This latter issue was observed by the joiners who made both the furniture and house woodwork, and this resulted in many different solutions being provided to accommodate different regional forms of houses. In single storey homes, for example, the limited floor space prompted the recognition that walls were as important an area for storage as the floor space.

    Individual styles and dimensions of furniture are ultimately given meaning through their relationship with other furniture items and the space allowed for them. Plan drawings, therefore, are important in showing furniture in the 'natural' or taken-for-granted position. One can then arrive at a sense of its relationship with architectural space, as well as an anthology of objects which simultaneously occupy the space of the home.

Fig. xxii; Studio photograph of Richard Hugh Kaighin (1864 - 1945); photograph taken c.1884.

RICHARD HUGH KAIGHIN
An Appreciation of a Manx Joiner

It is clear that joiners were largely responsible for producing the furniture for the Island's cottages and farmhouse homes, but seldom were these men specialist furniture makers. Rather, they were general woodworkers who turned their hand to a vast array of work as it presented itself. In self-sufficient communities which were based on farming and fishing, the skills which the joiner needed could include boat and cart building, spinning wheel making and repair, house joinery and the making of fences, gates, and all kinds of utensils needed on the farm and in the garden, such as harrows, wheelbarrows and ladders, as well as the making of furniture.

These skills could be combined with other work as a crofter, tasks which were merged effortlessly together. All were part of a way of life distinguished by an absence of hierarchy in the work to be done, which marked such men as different from those who toiled in highly specialised ways for a regular wage.

For the great number of these craftsmen, no record endures to open windows into their lives and allow us to see the integrated and unpretentious way in which they worked. Their lives are narratives which are usually only hinted at in the fragments of work which they left behind. However, the Isle of Man survey of furniture has been almost unbelievably fortunate in this respect. One response to the appeal which went out in the Manx newspapers asking Islanders to tell us of furniture in their possession, led directly to a major discovery, the location of an almost intact joiner's workshop. This dated from the late - 19th century and was complete with tools, tool chest, templates, bench and vices and many items of ephemera; bills and invoices speared on nails, long-dry tins of linseed oil, the heights of children written on the roof boards. To add to the picture, the joiner who worked in it, Richard Hugh Kaighin of Kerrowglass, Michael, left a personal diary extending from 1880, when he was sixteen years of age, until 1908. In addition to telling briefly of his work, day by day, he recorded his accounts and many fascinating details of his life such as the tending of his farm, the making of tools and the collection of shipwreck timber for his joinery work.[1]

A second diary also exists dating from 1921 until 1928, as does an exercise book in which Hugh Kaighin, as he was known, has copied the architect's specification for building two houses at Ramsey. In this book he kept working drawings for house and agricultural joinery, as well as the names of his cattle and other matters. Finally, his papers include a small, poignant notebook which he kept between 1933 and 1945, the year of his death, in which he tells of the trees which he grafted, and the varieties of fruit which he cultivated in his field hedgerows. These intimate details are heightened and personalised by a sepia photograph of him as a young man, taken in a photographer's studio in Ramsey. His

sensitive pose is made more evocative since he holds the first diary in his hand (Figure xxii). Happily, the account of Kaighin's life, so consistently given in his writing, includes details of his furniture making as well as the many other joinery and painting tasks which he undertook. Fortunately, too, seven items of furniture made by him have been recorded, and the making of several of these is described in his diary.

Hugh Kaighin's main diary, 315 pages long and bound between hard covers, was evidently seen by him as an important testimony to his life, which he intended as both a working record for himself and, one suspects, as a narrative for others to read. His account paints a picture of a man whose life was profoundly innocent and God-fearing. His Methodism persisted throughout his life and provided, by way of Sunday services and Chapel tea parties, rare interludes of leisure in a life of consistent labour. He remained unmarried and he mentions female and male acquaintances and close friends only very occasionally. His dedication to his parents and his unmarried sister, Christian, is clear, and taking his mother, and later his sister to market in Douglas on Saturdays is a regular event, mentioned throughout the diary. His early years were spent on his parents' farm at Rhenass, near Peel, before he left home to become an apprentice joiner, at the age of sixteen; his father paid an initial sum of £10 for his training. His diary opens in a portentous way, as if it were the beginning of his life; "I, Richard Hugh Kaighin went as an Apprentice to Thomas Harrison Ballacrane to learn for a Joiner on September 27th 1880. The agreement was that I were to serve three years and Father were to pay £10 to Harrison and Thomas Harrison were to give me meat and lodgings for the three years. The above Thomas Harrison failed in business after the £10 was paid and I had to leave in June 1882. About one and a half year of the time served."[2]

His training in joinery continued with his uncle, Willie Cowley, working on houses in Ballaquane Road, Peel, and living above a separate stone workshop which still stands in a small field behind the houses. It was this experience which provided the basis of Kaighin's woodworking skills; these he extended by working in Peel, Ramsey, and Onchan, on church and chapel repairs, fitting and making stairs, window frames, doors, and all the other skilled work of house joinery. Over the next thirteen years of working away from his family home, it becomes clear that he achieved a detailed knowledge of woodwork of many kinds, all of which enabled him to find work in many ways, and to provide for the woodworking needs of his local community.

As his experience grew, the nature of the entries in his diary alters, and leads us to see the expanding nature of his work. The first reference to furniture making, for example, occurs amongst notes on other joinery. On August 5th 1893 he wrote, "Making little table for kitchen window, making garden seat, salt box, making swing for May, [his niece] and finished and left Onchan."[3]

One glimpses in this entry an important aspect of the development of his woodworking skills, that after a decade working in his trade, his knowledge of the style, dimensions, and construction of many wooden objects had become part of a deep understanding which could be brought into use when needed and returned to the unconscious when the work was done.

In addition to house joinery and furniture making, agricultural woodwork comes seamlessly into the entries in his diary too. These tasks he did for his father, his brother, and other people in the locality of Peel, and particularly for those living near his father's farms at Rhenass and Kerrowglass. On December 2nd - 4th 1895, for example, he notes "At William Christian's, Lambfell. Making gates and swingletrees, also repairing gates etc. Paid Dec 4th 9/-."[4] Simple entries of this kind have the effect of obscuring the detailed knowledge which joiners needed to have in order to provide the correct shape and strength essential for utilitarian objects. Fortunately, Hugh Kaighin left a further notebook in which he itemised the specifications for building two houses in North Shore Road, Mooragh, Ramsey, with detailed drawings of a number of items of agricultural joinery, including a variety of swingletrees with a large and small design to be used with one or two horses and others for three horses. Interspersed among these designs are measured drawings for pick and scythe handles.

His drawings also include one for making a wheelbarrow of the sturdiest construction, with handles five feet long, a bed three feet one inch long, and a nineteen inch wheel and iron braces to strengthen the sides. A larger wheelbarrow, perhaps for transporting hay, gorse, or root crops, is also drawn in this book, as are sheep feeding troughs for turnips and cribs for hay.

A sense of the breadth of Kaighin's skills increases with each year's entries in this diary, and although he returns to Peel and Ramsey to undertake house joinery work for various employers, he is drawn back more and more to his father's land. His work used all of his skills, as a joiner and crofter, merging and separating, as they were needed. For example, in 1893 various notes read, "Dec. 26th and 27th. At Kerrowglass putting locks

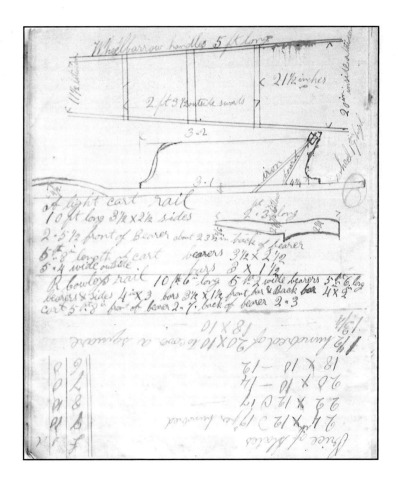

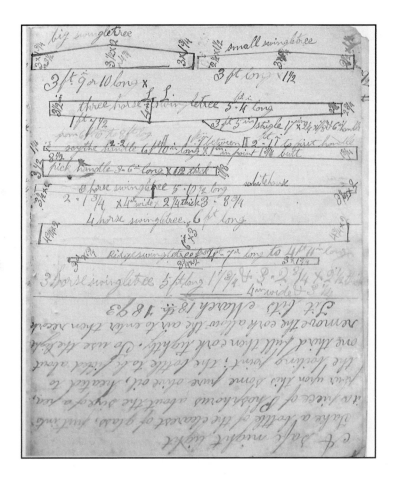

Fig. xxiii A & B; Drawings made by Hugh Kaighin of examples of his agricultural joinery work.

Fig. xxiv;
The farmhouse at Kerrowglass, Michael, begun in 1893;
Hugh Kaighin lived here until his death in 1945.

on doors, fixing window rollers and painting. Dec. 28th and 29th. Pulling turnips at Rhenass. Jan 1st and 2nd. Filling carts of turnips in Millers Field, Rhenass, and got all the turnips home for the season."[5]

These entries herald a major event in Kaighin's life; the building of the present farmhouse at Kerrowglass, begun in 1893, by his father, Hugh, on the site of an existing farm and buildings, two and a half miles from Rhenass. Here, to the new house which was completed in 1896, he would come to live as a crofter and joiner for the remainder of his life, working at first for his father and later on his own account. Here, too, he was eventually to die, in November 1945 in the back bedroom of the house just a few yards from his workshop.

The move to Kerrowglass from Rhenass is clearly noted in his diary, and in January 1896 his life is a flurry of activity as he gets ready for the move. In a breathless dash he writes, "Jan. 15th At Cowles Cottage, Ballaquane, Peel, sending material used to sink pump home . . . Jan 18th At Douglas choiceing chairs, carpets etc. for Kerrowglass," and on January 20 & 21st he writes, "Shifting goods from Rhenass to Kerrowglass." [6]

The purchases of furniture must have been of fashionable items for the parlour, for he was quite capable of making much of the furniture that was needed. A few days earlier he had written, "Dec. 31st 1895. Making table for Kerrowglass kitchen."[7] The final move from Rhenass seems to have taken place on June 1st 1896, when he notes ". . . and at Rhenass at night getting tool box."[8]

At the farm he set up his workshop in a small stone and slate stable, which had a feed and tack room adjoining and a hay loft above. This building stands just a few yards across the haggard (farmyard) behind the present farmhouse. He seems to have raised the roof to give it greater height, and the workshop must have been a considerable pleasure to him. Its wooden floor kept him dry underfoot, and it was well lit from a roof and gable window.

The door to his workshop is reached by a flight of stone steps, at the top of which a spectacular view of the surrounding landscape takes in the farm's land in the foreground and the sea beyond. In the far distance, on a clear day, the hills of Scotland can be seen. The Kaighin land stretched down to the sea edge, and provided Hugh Kaighin with a harvest of raw materials; kelp for his fields, stones for the gateways, and wood from shipwrecks and 'shore timber' for his joinery work. The workshop building is shown in Figure xxv and the scale drawing of it provides detailed information about its internal and external dimensions.

Fig. xxv; Hugh Kaighin's workshop at Kerrowglass, which he set up over a stable in 1897.

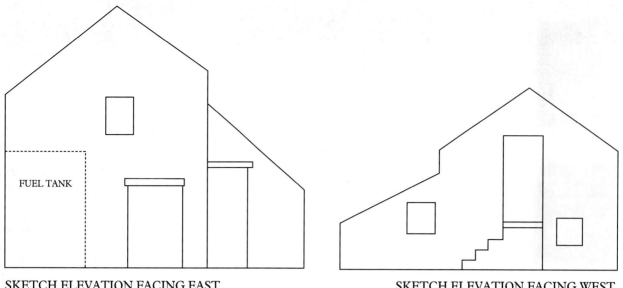

SKETCH ELEVATION FACING EAST   SKETCH ELEVATION FACING WEST

Hugh Kaighin's Workshop
Kerrowglass,
Kirk Michael,
Isle of Man.

(NDW 1992)

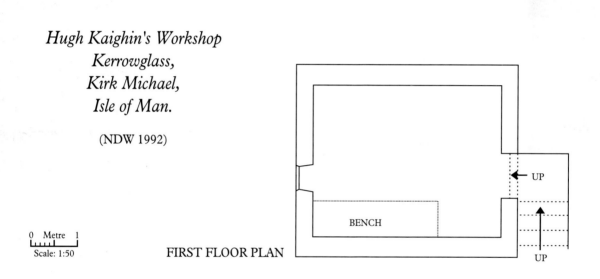

0 Metre 1
Scale: 1:50

FIRST FLOOR PLAN

Fig. xxvi; Measured drawings of Hugh Kaighin's workshop.

When the workshop was first looked at as part of the Isle of Man furniture survey in the Spring of 1991, tantalising glimpses of its contents were seen; a bench, vices, and tools. More recent things belonging to the present owner filled and covered much of the original workshop and its contents. Richard Cowley, a relative of Hugh Kaighin, agreed that a team from the Manx Museum should come to the workshop and clear it of all but the joiner's things. This uncovering of the workshop, both internally and externally, involved those who took part in an 'archaeological' task, with Richard Cowley moving heavy parts on his trailer. Others carried objects from the workshop to a store. In this way, the workshop gradually revealed its contents. To the left was Kaighin's fixed joiner's bench, complete with wooden vice. On the top lay many, but by now not all, of his woodworking tools, which were mixed with the other things that he used; paints, brushes, turpentine bottles, and linseed oil tins. His tool chest

lay on the floor and in the rafters above were packed templates, lengths of wood, and all those things which would come in useful one day. Hand-made tool handles for axes and spades still lay under the bench, further signs of the practical role which a joiner played in a farming community.

Many of the tools which lay on the bench are a particularly poignant survival, mostly stamped, as they are, with the name R. H. Kaighin. Some of them are recorded in his diary, on the days when he made them. For example, in January 1897 he notes, "1/2 day making two planes, a compass plane and a smoothing plane." In the margin he notes, "Jan 29th 2 smoothing plane bits 1/8d from V. Joughin." [9]

Hugh Kaighin's tool chest contained his collection of cardboard templates for joinery devices and motifs. Figure xxviii shows the front gate of Kerrowglass, made in 1893, with petal shaped apertures in its

Fig. xxvii; The interior of the workshop, showing Kaighin's bench, tool chest and many of his tools.

corners. The template for these is included in the illustration, and the top of the uprights has a profile similar to another template in the collection.

The hanging shelves shown in Figure xxixA which he mentions making as a wedding present for his brother, J. J. Kaighin, have a cornice moulding which follows the profile of another of the templates (Figure xxixB).

In addition to working at farming tasks and in his workshop at Kerrowglass, Kaighin also worked elsewhere. Some months after moving to Kerrowglass, on February 10th 1896, he was working at Patrick, and wrote, "Feb 10th to March 5th working for the Rev. Hugh Kinred, Patrick, making 2 pair of chest of drawers and study desk to stand with 17 drawers in and general repairs about and in the house."[10] This work was completed when he was aged thirty-two years, and probably at the height of his powers; it was evidently the only time that he made an item like the desk.

His versatility in making furniture and at the same time unselfconsciously merging this work with other tasks constantly punctuates his first diary. On August 1st 1896, he notes, "1/2 day making Kerrowglass picture frames. Putting glass in hen house and at Michael getting ginger beer etc. for Father."[11] His entries for picture frame making continue over the next few days,

and Figure xxx shows an example of one of the frames he made, with a photograph of the houses in Ballaquane Road, Peel, which he worked on in his early years with his uncle.

In addition to his joinery, Hugh Kaighin was clearly an adept painter and decorator. Increasingly, as he got older, he found local employment doing this work, painting houses, furniture and carts, which he also made. For example, on April 27th 1899 he notes, "At Ballacarnane painting cart for J. J. Cannel" and on the 28th, "ditto washing and painting little wheels, finishing cart."[12]

Painting furniture, too, fell within his normal work; on September 10th 1896 he records making a table for a Miss Quiggan, and on the 12th, "Making drawers for Miss Quiggan's table and painting table."[13]

In 1897, Kaighin's father was perhaps becoming unwell, and on January 6th Hugh begins the task of making a 'night chair' (commode) in mahogany. On the 8th he records going to Peel to get boards and hinges for the chair. His diary shows that he worked on it over several days, working it in with other farming tasks, and also finishing picture frames. He finally notes on January 30th "Polishing night chair and picture frames."[14]

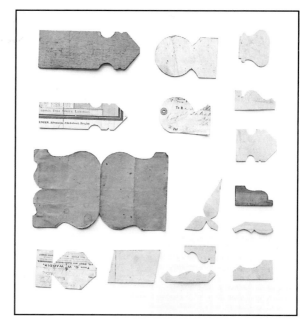

Fig.xxviii A & B;
The decorative garden gate at Kerrowglass Farm, illustrating the use of some of the templates from Kaighin's tool chest.

Fig.xxix B;
Cornice profile from the hanging shelves similar to one of the templates used by Kaighin.

Fig.xxix A;
The hanging shelves, made by Hugh Kaighin as a wedding present; made from pine and painted with staining varnish.

Fig. xxx; An oak picture frame made by Kaighin in about 1890, holding a photograph of the houses in Ballaquane Road, Peel, which he was involved in building when he was eighteen.

These records give important glimpses of Kaighin's knowledge and skills, although his experience of making chairs was rarely called on; it was only noted once more in his diary, and it may be that making the 'night chair' was the only time that he made this particular design. The chair remains in the possession of his niece. It is well made, with the competence of a skilled joiner who was working with a knowledge of the Island's joined chair designs.

By February 1897, Hugh Kaighin's diary shows that he is becoming increasingly involved in running the family farm, as well as working at furniture making and other joinery. Clearly his father became less able to work, and Kaighin's obligations to the farm and to his joinery work greatly increase. Throughout 1897 and 1898, he continued to make furniture; on November 17th 1898 he records "Cutting ash for bedstead."[15] On December 7th and 8th 1898 he notes "Making dresser" and on 14th & 15th, he records, "Ballacarnane setting (fixing) and painting dresser."[16]

Kaighin's work as a joiner was often supplied with timber from his farm's shoreline, and frequent references are made to this. On August 16th that year he notes, "2 carthouse doors of shore timber."[17] This may refer to wood washed up on the shore but on other occasions he refers to "shipwreck wood" or to particular ships. On the November 23rd 1896 he records "on shore, breaking *Orion*", presumably a ship of that name; the diary then records the use made of this timber - January 17th 1898, "E. H. Corkhill, Ballacregga, Making swingletrees of oak, *Orion* timber."[18] Kaighin may well have used reclaimed oak from this source in furniture making too, and on

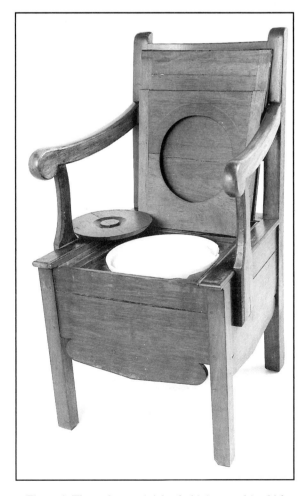

Fig.xxxi; The mahogany 'night chair' (commode) which Kaighin made for his father in 1897.

Fig. xxxii; A stool made by Kaighin, c.1900, with an elm top and hand-shaped pine legs, painted with red lead paint.

Fig. xxxiii; (Below) A pine chest painted and grained to simulate mahogany - made by Kaighin c.1900.

Fig. xxxiv; The inside of the chest, showing the till and hinging mechanism, using wooden pintles.

March 12th 1898, he notes "4 hrs finishing Uncle Willies table or washstand of oak with two drawers."[19]

Although his diary indicates that he made some items of furniture only once in his lifetime, Hugh Kaighin made other items of furniture, including stools, on many occasions. On February 6th 1899 he writes, "Footstools for Louisa. Making patterns for cart etc. etc."[20]

On another occasion, February 26th 1901, he writes in his diary, "Making stool for Gerty Caine's wedding present."[21]

One of the stools he made remains in family ownership, and is shown in Figure xxxii The legs of this stool, in common with other round sections he produced, have narrow, indistinct facets on their surfaces, showing that he did not have a lathe, but shaped round pieces using a draw knife. Many of the tools in his workshop with round handles would also have been made in this way.

Perhaps the most widely used item of storage furniture on the Island was the chest or 'chist'. These were usually made with nailed plank construction, a hinged lid, and corner uprights which extend below to act as

Fig.xxxv;
A pine lodging box made by Kaighin in about 1890.
Originally painted blue with an oak scumble over this.

Fig.xxxvi;
The interior of the lodging box, with two internal tills and
small drawers below.

feet. Chests of this type were made for food (meal) storage in outhouses. Others were made for use indoors, for the storage of linen and clothes, and as 'lodging boxes'.

Hugh Kaighin made both types, and on October 23/24th 1899, he notes, "P. Cannell, Skersdale, making calf rack and meal chist."[22] On Good Friday, April 13th 1900, he writes, "Cleaning and tidying close chist, getting turnips, hay and straw in."[23] This 'chist' is probably the one in Figure xxxiii, which is a commodious chest made for a bedroom at Kerrowglass. It is made in pine but painted in mahogany colour to simulate an exuberant wood grain. The inside has a small unlidded till. The top is made with a slight convex curve to add a decorative note to

an otherwise austere shape. The lid is hinged with wooden pintles, an archaic form of hinging, avoiding the use of metal (Figure xxxiv).

Kaighin made 'lodging' boxes as well; and one is shown in Figure xxxv. This is made of pine and has a coat of brown scumble over an earlier coat of blue paint. This box was clearly thoughtfully designed, with two open tills and small drawers below. A small piece of cloth for pins and needles is fixed into it and Kaighin wrote inside, "this box cost 6s 11 1/2d beside lock and labour." The box has strips nailed on the bottom to keep it off the floor, and the carrying handles are reminiscent of those used on seaman's chests (see pp.147-166 for more discussion concerning chests and boxes used on the Island).

Fig. xxxvii; A pine chest of drawers made for Kerrowglass Farm c.1900, painted to simulate mahogany.

Fig. xxxviii; The interior of the chest of drawers, showing the high technical qualities of its construction.

Probably the most complex items of furniture which Kaighin made were chests of drawers. His diary mentions three of these which he made for local people. A further example which he made for his own use at Kerrowglass is shown in Figure xxxvii. It is made in pine and painted on the outside in a similar style to the 'chist', with simulated mahogany graining. This chest has two small drawers at the top and three long ones below, all with locks. The turned feet and handles were probably bought from a hardware merchant.

The construction of this chest of drawers shows that Kaighin was both a knowledgeable and competent cabinet maker, as well as a joiner. The interior of the chest shown in Figure xxxviii indicates that he clearly knew the best conventions for making each piece. The side runners are rebated into the sides, rather than being nailed to them, and full dustboards run under each drawer except the bottom one, rather than having the cheaper alternative of half or no dustboards. The back boards have a central muntin, which makes a more stable structure, and the drawers are expertly dovetailed. (See pp 137-146 on chests of drawers for more detailed information about the use of these items on the Island).

The woods which Hugh Kaighin and other joiners on the Isle of Man used were both imported and home grown. A 19th century price list produced by the Douglas Steam Saw Mill and Timber Company Ltd. was found amongst Kaighin's papers and included both soft and hardwoods. Sweden and Canada (Quebec) are given as the source of the softwoods, under the headings: "Red Swedish deals and battens. Spruce deal and battens. Quebec pine deal. Pitch pine, sawn and cleft (hewn). White flooring boards."[24]

In addition to softwoods, a range of hardwoods was offered, priced by the cubic foot, and in the log. These included oak, ash, elm and birch. It is not clear from the list what the origin of these hardwoods was, but they are likely to have been mainly imported as little timber of sufficient size was then grown in the Isle of Man. The Douglas Steam Saw Mill offered to convert

logs to the customer's requirements, and advertised "sawing on the premises, by frame, deal, circular, and band saws; also planing, moulding and turnings."[25]

There is little doubt that Kaighin, in company with other joiners on the Island, bought the great majority, if not all, of his house joinery timbers from one of the wood merchants on the Island, and in Kaighin's case had it transported by rail to St. John's. Figure xxxix shows the woodyard of Quiggin & Co., established in 1821, as timber merchants and rope makers. This 19th century photograph shows the enormous quantities of baulks of timber which they imported and could convert to customers' orders.

In addition to the Swedish 'Red' wood, which was probably Scots pine, (*Pinus sylvestris*) imported from Scandinavia, 'Quebec' deals and white floorboards from Canada are also mentioned. This reference is probably either to Weymouth pine, (*Pinus strobus*), or White spruce (*Pinus glauca*). Pitch pine, (*Pinus rigida*) and spruce (*Pinus glauca*) are also mentioned separately on the list. Another term for pine used on the Island is 'yellow' pine, which is probably Weymouth pine, (*Pinus strobus*).[26] This wood is mentioned by a number of respondents to the Folk Life Survey. Killip, speaking in 1965 of eighty year old Mr. Fred Costain, joiner, of The Level, Colby, mentions that he made a chiffonier for himself. . .

"The wood used for this is yellow pine which was an extremely good wood for wear and durability, although it was a softwood, it would wear and weather well and would not warp. Window frames are often made of yellow pine. Red pine was also used but this was more resinous."[27]

In addition to imported woods, the Island produced some growing timber which Kaighin records felling or using for different purposes. Of these, larch seems to be the most common, and he records, for example, on September 1st 1896, "Felling larch trees" and "Dressing larch posts for beef house."[28] Larch was probably grown as a plantation wood on the Island, and since it grows quickly it may provide timber posts

Fig. xxxix;
Quiggins' timber yard, Douglas, c.1880.

within the lifetime of the planter. Kaighin certainly records planting larch, and on January 13th 1902, he writes, "R. Cannell Skersdale. Cutting down trees (to plant larch)."[29]

Kaighin used other softwoods, too, for making gates particularly, including pitch pine, and Scots pine. On March 10th 1902, he mentions "Making pitch pine gates."[30] He also mentions cutting sally (sallow probably in a Manx context *Salix cinerea* ssp. oleifolia) for firewood on a number of occasions and that he made a cattle shade from its branches. Kaighin also records felling and cutting sycamore for firewood.

He does not mention using sycamore for furniture making or other joinery, although other joiners did utilise this wood for furniture making, and a chest of drawers from Miss Abigail Faragher's home at Earystane, Colby has all its drawers lined with sycamore (see Catalogue No. 169, p. 144).

Another common hardwood, birch, both grew on the Island, and was also imported. Kaighin, however, seems not to have used this wood to any degree, and little mention is made of it; respondents to the Folk Life Survey similarly do not refer to it and it may be that it was used mainly for domestic turnery work. It was certainly used in spinning wheels and small domestic items on the Island. Kaighin mentions it only once, inconclusively, in his diary. On June 1st 1896, he notes, "Getting tool box and birch." [31]

Kaighin used oak for making furniture, although it is doubtful that this was grown on the Island, since

locally-grown oak was thought to be of an inferior kind. Mr. Fred Costain reported to the Folk Life Survey that "Spokes were often made of Irish and English oak. Manx oak was not serviceable, the majority of local oak being small and twisted."[32] Ancient bog oak was used on the Island, however, particularly for making turned parts for spinning wheels. Mr. J. C. Callister of Lhen Bridge, West Craig, Andreas, gave a particularly interesting account of this wood to the Folk Life Survey in 1957.

"The bog oak was a difficult wood to work with. It was apt to split. [Mr. Callister's] father had difficulty in finishing a suitable piece of oak for the block of the oak spinning wheel. When the men were widening the Lhen trench they were finding pieces of bog oak in it, and one of the men working there told about finding the oak trees in the turf ground. He said they would be in some places so thick and close together, lying lengthways and crossways, that they couldn't cut any turf, and they would have to go and look for another place and begin all over again."[33]

The oak which Kaighin used in his furniture making was probably all gleaned from wood washed up on the shore, or from shipwrecks. On January 17th 1898 he specifically mentions the name of the wreck, the *Orion*, from which he got oak to make swingletrees.[34] Ash was also felled and used by Kaighin equally for furniture and his agricultural work. Ash seems to have grown well on the Isle of Man, and again, speaking to the Folk Life Survey in October 1965, Mr. Fred Costain said, "The ash out of Colby Glen was good, also from Mount Murray; these trees grew in dry ground; trees growing in damp marshy ground were less sound."[35]

Of all the woods that Kaighin used, however, mahogany was the rarest, and he perhaps only worked with this timber once, in making the 'night chair' (commode) for his father.

The last entry in Hugh Kaighin's first diary is made on October 26th 1908, when he writes "Continued in new book (page 81)."[36] Above it, on October 11th, his father's death is noted in a curiously unemotional way, "Father died . . . at village getting shroud for father."[37]

At this time, Kaighin entered what was to be the second half of his life, living with his unmarried sister, Christian, and continuing his work as a crofter and joiner. The second diary he refers to has not been found, and there is a gap in his records until his account begins again on January 1st 1921, in a new small notebook bound in black cardboard covers. It continues until 24th August 1928, when he was aged 64, at which time he was evidently in good health and working as hard as ever. He recorded on the first day of his new diary, "Pulling and getting home 5 loads of turnips", and the last entry reads, "Wet jobs about, at Cronkbane getting load of thatch."[38]

During the period of this diary, there are no records of Hugh Kaighin making more complete furniture items, although he occasionally repaired or made new drawers for pieces. This lack of continuity in his furniture making probably reflects that by the early - 20th century mass produced fashionable furniture was widely available in furniture stores and through furniture catalogues, and the role of the local joiner as maker of utilitarian furniture was coming to an end.

This diary would have brought our knowledge of Hugh Kaighin to a close, were it not for the evidence of a further small notebook, without a cover. He kept this record from 1934 until April 10th 1945, eight months before he died in November of that year at the age of eighty - one. This last notebook was not a diary about his farm or joinery work as his others had been, but rather reflects a deep interest which he had in raising fruit trees, by grafting. He grew pears, plums and apples, in the hedgerows of his fields. These are shown on a map, and in his entries over a long period note and date the grafts he made, and the progress of the trees. For example, on April 11th 1938, he wrote in a vigorous hand, "Three apple grafts on plum tree bottom of meadow. June 18th 1938; 3 growing."[39]

The final entry in this remarkable document is made in a faltering hand on April 10th 1945 "4 apple grafts put on tree at hill water field."[40] This last note, made near the end of his life, seems typical of the man, and is a fitting epitaph to him. This and his other records show a man who worked hard all his life, at many times excessively so, combining an enormous range of skills, knowledge and industry. He evidently continued this learning process throughout his life, with his horticultural interest in the propagation of fruit trees becoming important to him in his declining years.

The remarkably good fortune in locating this record provides us with a wonderful insight into the life of one Manx joiner, furniture maker and crofter. Here is an example of a man who lived all of his life among his inter-related family groups within the Island community, often indeed bounded by the confines of the family farm. He provided members of the community with his competent and adaptable woodworking skills in a way which was both necessary and relevant to their lives. Furniture which he made, his workshop, his bench, and many tools in combination with his diaries and notebooks are his monument.

Richard Hugh Kaighin's life may seem restricted to some. Certainly during his lifetime many Islanders left the Island for 'greener pastures'. He left it only once, to have an operation in Liverpool. The unfolding narrative of his work and life, however, does not suggest that he felt restricted. Rather he led an uncomplaining existence in which work and the satisfaction of doing things well seem to have brought their own rewards.

He lived, too, at a time when non-conformist religion was a binding force, particularly in rural areas where chapels were built for each small community. His abstinence from alcohol, and a diet of hard work and largely home-grown food, seem to have kept him in good health throughout his full and active life. It is to him, as representative of the unsung men and women, who were fishermen, crofters, mothers and fathers, who knew the many skills of a trade, or the many tasks of their self-sufficient lives, that this account of one of their number is dedicated.

1908
Sept

17th & 18th W.D. Cannell roofing barn &c at Sherrisdale

19th Driving Christian to Lambfell & getting hay & straw in &c J.2. Cannells *close made*

Sunday 20th Kerrowglass Chapel twice hearing Rev. J.J. Heady Peel preaching (1st time)

21st ½ day W.D. Cannell at Sherrisdale roof ½ day at E.H. Cakill &c J.J. Kelly *timber getting*

22nd Door & frame & pig door & lintels for stockfield & setting & painting

23rd J.2. Cannells wall barrow repaired & Wm E.W Kaighins tumbling rake &c

24th Sherrisdale roof for Wm D. Cannell & door frame, door & lintels of fold house

25th 4 hrs W.D.C. ditto ½ day smithy & Peel &c

26th Wm E.W. Kaighin tumbling rake & mankiller rake new head on

Sunday 27th Kerrowglass Chapel twice hearing Joe Boyde Peel preaching

28th Reading, grinding tools &c digging potatoes

29the Making water gutter under road *Kerrowglass* between railway & haggard

30th Patching footrule, handle in pick & jobbing (not well)

October 1st & 2nd J.J. Kaighin Rhenass in harvest ½ day stacking

3rd Driving Christian to Douglas Market

~~Sunday~~ 4th Kerrowglass Chapel twice hearing J. Kinvig Greeba preaching

5th With Joe Garrett at Drain top field & cutting gorse &c setting Chapel stove *stones out of*

6th 7th, 8th, 9th & 10th with Joe Garrett draining top field 8 loads stones &c

Sunday *Father died* 11th Kerrowglass Chapel twice hearing R. Cowley W.P. preaching & at Village getting shroud *for father*

12th At Village ordering Coffin at J.D. Kelly & seeing sexton & parson &c At Peel twice for cards, death certificate, butchers meat & hearse &c

13th Tidying about for funeral 14th ditto about with cards &c at Michael

15th Fathers funeral a fine day preparing for horses

16th Digging potatoes & straw in at Stockfield painting new *doors at Lambfell*

17th Getting mares shoes removed & at Peel getting coals

Sunday 18th Wet day resting 19th W.D. Cannell at Sherrisdale spouts &c *General jobbing*

20th Philly Cannell Sherrisdale Roofing potato &c granary *house*

21st ditto 22nd thrashing with J. Caine Ballaquine

23rd P. Cannell door &c 24th Peel & Michael Christian at Douglas

Sunday 25th Kerrowglass Chapel twice hearing J. Crellin Peel preaching

26th 27th & 28th No 3 Ballaquane Road papering Parlour, part of sitting *room & kitchen*

Continued in New book (page 81)

Fig. xl;
The final page of Hugh Kaighin's first diary.

REFERENCES

1. On the fly leaf of his diary Richard Hugh Kaighin wrote the following verse:

   This book belongs to Richard Hugh Kaighin.
   If thou are borrowed by a friend
   Right welcome shall he be
   To read, to study, not to lend,
   But to return.

   Not that imparted knowledge doth
   Diminish learning Store;
   But books, I find, if often lent,
   Return to me no more.

   Read slowly, pause frequently,
   Think seriously, return duly,
   With the corners of the leaves
   Not turned down.

   R. Hugh Kaighin,

   February 22nd 1896.

2. The diary is in a private collection; p.1.

3. p. 11.

4. p. 27. Swingletree - in a plough or carriage, etc. a cross bar, pivoted at the middle, to which the traces are fastened, giving freedom of movement to the shoulders of the horse of other draught animal (Shorter OED).

5. p. 12.

6. p. 29.

7. p. 28.

8. p. 33.

9. January 30 1897; p. 45.

10. p. 30.

11. p. 38.

12. p. 76.

13. p. 40.

14. p. 45.

15. p. 69.

16. p. 69 and p. 70.

17. p. 51.

18. unpaginated section following p. 49 and p. 57.

19. p. 60

20. p. 73.

21. p. 100.

22. p. 82.

23. p. 88.

24. Papers in private collection.

25. *Ibid.*

26. 'Red Swedish' deals probably refers to Scots pine. 'Quebec pine' deals probably refers to Weymouth pine *(Pinus strobus)*. Another term for imported pine used on the Island is 'yellow' pine, probably also Weymouth pine, mentioned by a number of respondents to the Folk Life Survey. Weymouth pine may be known as such either in honour of a Captain Weymouth who was responsible for an early major import, or because Lord Weymouth planted it extensively at Longleat in the 18th century.

   It is always possible that Manx usage diverged from English, in part because there were direct imports well before the Manx language had been dominantly replaced by English (information from Dr. Larch Garrad).

27. FLS/C/171/B.

28. Diary, p. 40 and p. 46.

29. p. 112. The larch tree was introduced by the Dukes of Atholl as a plantation crop (information from Dr. Larch Garrad).

30. p. 114.

31. p. 33.

32. FLS/C/171/B.

33. FLS/C/59-H.

34. Diary, p. 57.

35. FLS/C/171/B.

36. Diary, p. 313.

37. p. 313.

38. Notebook/diary deposited in the Manx Museum Library, unpaginated.

39. Notebook deposited in the Manx Museum Library, unpaginated.

40. *Ibid.*

CATALOGUE INTRODUCTION

This catalogue includes all items of traditional furniture accessioned into the collections of Manx National Heritage.

The catalogue does not include the items of fashionable furniture in the Grove Rural Life Museum which are listed, along with other extra material, at the end of the catalogue sections in Appendix I.

The furniture has been grouped into sections, which appear as separate chapters. An introductory essay will discuss the items of furniture collectively, followed by the individual catalogue entries.

Each item is numbered consecutively.

All measurements are in centimetres (cms).

ABBREVIATIONS

FLS   The Manx Folk Life Survey, followed by an individual reference. The survey, housed in the Manx Museum's Library, is an ongoing oral testimony archive established in the 1940s.

No.   refers to the Catalogue Number of each item.

hh.   maximum height (e.g. chair back, cradle hood).

h.   height (with chairs this refers to seat height).

w.   width.

d.   depth.

A Glossary of terms used in the catalogue entries is located after the Appended material

JOINED CHAIRS

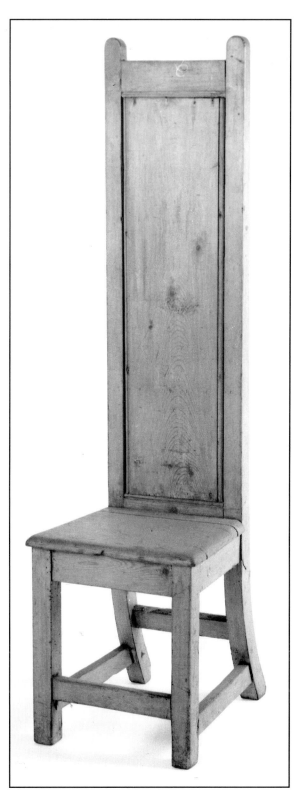

CHAPTER 1

JOINED CHAIRS

The largest single cohesive group of furniture recorded on the Isle of Man is of joined chairs. The earliest examples of these, dating from the 17th and 18th centuries, show design features of chairs from Scotland, the North-West of England, particularly Lancashire and Cheshire, and also, in a less pronounced sense, from Wales. Indeed, many of the joined chairs in the Museum dating from this period were evidently imported from those regions. Other examples were made on the Island in the 18th and 19th centuries, with some design features persisting and others changing over time.

Examples in the Manx National Heritage collection which emanate from the North-West region of England include a similar arm and side chair, (Nos. 6 and 7) *circa* 1700, which have narrow vertical splats in the back, turned back uprights, front legs, and connecting stretchers. Within 17th century North-West and Welsh regional traditions, the construction of wooden seats and the lower parts of the chairs is extremely conventional in style, with two major constructional types represented: (a) a flat panelled seat nailed to the seat frame: and (b) a flat panel rebated into an outer frame, as in the case of the arm and side chairs described above. This latter method of seat construction was also commonly used in Scottish chairs of the same period.

Turned legs, and central cross stretchers which had a variety of turnery devices, were also typical in both traditions, as are rectangular side and rear stretchers. The use of turned back uprights occurs in chairs from both the English and Scottish traditions, and is an absorbtion of this style from fashionable Restoration chairs, *circa* 1670, which were made in London. These usually had cane seats and backs, whilst some other varieties had both plain and ornate vertical wooden splats, the inner ones less decorative than the outer two, or central panels set between two outer vertical splats. These fashionable styles, too, were translated into the vernacular tradition, in Scotland and the North-West of England.

A further chair (No.8), has stylistic features which are typical of a major group of back stools from the North-West of England *circa* 1670. This chair has a panelled back and a nailed wooden seat. The semi-circular top rail is vigorously carved with foliar forms in a manner which epitomises chairs of this type. Unusually, this example has urn-shaped finials to the back uprights, in a tradition where pyramidal finials were conventional. This is one of a pair believed to have been owned on the Island by Bishop Thomas Wilson (1663 - 1755),

and a script below the seat gives a history of its ownership.

Two other oak back stools in the Museum collection (Nos. 3 and 4), dating from *circa* 1690, also have wooden seats which rebate into the seat rails, with simple turned front legs and crudely carved front stretchers, cross rails, and back uprights. These chairs have some generic features of chairs from the North-West region, but the relatively simple turnings and free style carving mitigate against this origin and the chairs are probably Scottish.

A further exceptionally large panel-backed side chair (No.1) which may have been made for ceremonial purposes is, again, reported to have belonged to Bishop Wilson, and its construction and design point to it being of Scottish manufacture. Another armchair (No.2) *circa* 1690, also exhibits Scottish design features.

The largest number of joined chairs held in the Museum collection are, however, made with either one or, more commonly, two framed vertical panels in the back; the panels are either raised and fielded, or alternatively flat to the front. Probably the earliest chair of this type (No.5) reinforces the Scottish contribution to joined chairs on the Island. This is a decoratively carved, joined armchair, with the initials 'MC' and the date 1685 carved on it. A number of features indicate that this chair is of Scottish origin, probably from the South-West region. These include the use of alternate concave and convex decorative gouge carving on the vertical back stiles. A further example of a Scottish chair showing this distinctive decorative form is shown in *Oak Furniture, the British Tradition*, V. Chinnery, 1979, p. 467, Fig. 4: 112. The use of vertical narrow panels in the back, sharply raised in their centres with flat, rather than chamfered edges, is also a Scottish constructional feature. See the Scottish carved and panelled chest, No. 173 which has panels of this type.

The use of a broad top rail and raised carving is a further device used on Scottish chairs, as is the use of flat shaped arms which have under-cut devices underneath each end. A number of joined chairs from the South-West area of Scotland have been recorded with variations of these devices. An example from the small port of Whithorn, on the west coast of the Scottish mainland, (Figure 1.1) although without carving, has similar constructional features to the Museum's example (Figure 1.2), including the use of a broad top rail with the date 1710 carved in relief, as well as similarly shaped arms. Other joined panelled back chairs in the Museum collection were made with similar designs at various times between the first years of the 18th century and the first half of the 19th century. Of these, one (No. 14) is dated Mar. 19 1723, and has the initials J. C. carved in the top rail. This chair, although plain in style, is more sophisticated in its manufacture than others recorded on the Island, and has a raised and fielded panel in the

Fig 1.1; A joined oak chair dated 1710, from Whithorn, south west Scotland. National Museum of Scotland collection (KN7).

back which is decoratively arched at the top. The design mitigates against it being Welsh or English, and it is probably also Scottish in origin. A further large oak armchair which has two panels composing the back, set level with the surrounding frame, and reeded decoration, has a brass plate screwed to the back which claims that the chair formerly belonged to the Earl of Derby in 1745.

A group of panelled chairs in the Museum collection (Nos. 9 - 13) dating from the mid-18th century, form a cohesive subgroup of joined chairs.

These are all plain, uncarved chairs with various turning forms to the front legs, and panels composing the backs. Chairs in this group have interesting parallels to similar chairs held in the Ulster Folk and Transport Museum, Belfast, some of which are closely similar in design. These chairs, too, were probably brought to Ulster by Scottish immigrants during the plantation settlements of the 18th century. Alternatively, chairs of this type from both Ulster and

Fig 1.2; (No. 5) An oak joined chair, carved, and dated 1685. This chair has constructional similarities with the chair in Figure 1.1, and both probably originate from the south west region of Scotland.

the Isle of Man could also have been made locally, following the patterns of Scottish chairs. Figure 1.3 shows an example from the Ulster Folk and Transport Museum collection, *circa* 1750, made in oak. This chair is closely similar to No. 9 from the Isle of Man, which similarly is made in oak (Figure 1.4). In this case, however, the chair shows evidence of being made from reclaimed timbers, a practice which was not uncommon in other items of Isle of Man vernacular furniture. It may be that this example was made on the Island. Plain joined chairs with panelled backs continued to be made into the 19th century in a similar way to those made in the 18th. Examples of this type were often made from reclaimed timber which probably came from buildings or ships, and often have ambiguous mortice holes (Nos. 19-22). Chairs in this group exhibit many of the features of chairs made fifty or more years previously, but their simplified construction and finishing techniques, as well as the lack of turned parts, point to them being made by general carpenters and joiners who on occasion also made furniture.

It was chairs made by these tradesmen, who during the whole of the 19th century also made the ubiquitous simple joined chairs with cross rails, which are the most common chairs on the Island.

These chairs were produced with simple square frames using joinery techniques including standard sawn and planed parts, mortice and tenon joints and nailed wooden seats. Closely similar chairs were also widely made in Scotland during the 19th century, in the

Glasgow and Kilmarnock furniture making traditions in which common furniture was produced for Scottish Lowland homes. Other examples were made in Wales, during the 19th century, in the South Wales furniture making tradition, where oak was the preferred wood. That such chairs were within the province of joiners is confirmed by contributors to the Folk Life Survey, and Mr. Fred Costain, who was a joiner in Colby, reported in 1965 when he was eighty years of age that "The joiners made plain wooden armchairs, some of them rocking chairs. The armchairs had stretchers

Fig.1.3; An oak joined chair, circa 1750, collected in Ulster, which forms part of a larger group of joined chairs from the province which show Scottish influence. U F T M Collection, Belfast

underneath and the back had plain flat uprights with an attempt at simple carving on the middle one. They also made kitchen chairs with open backs and one bar across and occasionally two bars or the back might be slightly curved." (FLS/C/17/B).

Within the basic design of chair described by Mr. Costain, different types were made, including commode chairs, upholstered armchairs, rocking chairs, children's chairs (often of a commode type), armchairs and side chairs. These chairs offered robust seats which in many cases continue in use until the present day. Although closely similar in their design and construction a limited number of options were provided in terms of their decoration, the woods used, and surface finishes.

In practice, the majority of chairs in this group were

made with two or three plain cross-rails forming the backs. These could be either straight or, for an extra cost, slightly curved or hollowed in front. Occasionally decorative back designs were produced; No. 44, for example, where the back has cross frame devices which reflect house joiners' devices, particularly those found in porch construction. An example of a joined chair on rockers which is upholstered (No. 45) has a padded back and seat made of oilcloth filled with meadow grasses. This chair offers a rare inclusion of extra comfort in an otherwise austere type, and it may be

Fig.1.4;An oak joined chair, circa 1750, from the Isle of Man, made from reclaimed timber and showing Scottish design characteristics as well as having close parallels with the chair in Figure 1.3

that it is the design referred to as an "ancient padded invalid chair, locally made" by Mrs. Janie Griffin of Ballaglonney, Fleshwick, in reporting to the Folk Life Survey in 1967. (FLS/G/44).

Within arm chair design, the device most commonly used to relieve the otherwise severely square form is that of shaped and scrolled arms, usually the only curvilinear feature (Figure 1.5). The use of this arm type may reflect a continuation in the use of an arm design which was common in the 17th and 18th centuries, and particularly in the panel back chairs of that time.

Fig 1.5; The interior of a 'Southside' farm in the late - 19th century - the scrolled arms relieve the square form of a traditional kitchen chair.

Occasionally, turned under-arm supports at the top of the front legs were used as an embellishment, but since this addition required the specialist services of a wood turner, the cost made it a rare feature (No. 48, for example).

Within the basic form of these 19th century joiner-made chairs, a number of variations in overall dimensions, tapers on leg profiles, as well as different intervals between back cross-rails and leg stretchers, point to makers working with templates which were individual to them. A classification of the Island's workshops may be developed as a result of these features, as more examples are located.

In common with much furniture on the Isle of Man, chairs were made with imported woods and in softwoods, mainly pine as well as straight grained imported oak. The surface finishes used on chairs often show evidence that they were stained with mahogany varnish or painted with red lead paint to simulate mahogany. Often these original finishes are overpainted with later paint, black or brown being the most common colours. Occasionally, examples of Manx joined chairs were also painted and grained to appear as oak and the wooden seats painted to simulate black upholstery fabric. (Nos. 33 A-D).

A further group of joiner-made chairs produced on the Island during the first quarter of the 19th century show a fusion of the simple rectilinear form of Manx chair, but with the influence of fashionable 18th century styles. These include chairs whose back designs use motifs from Thomas Chippendale's designs, and include examples with both fretted and unfretted vertical splats set below a curved top rail (Nos. 52 A-C and 58). Other chairs show the characteristically high curved top rail and stylised wheatsheaf fretted splat which was illustrated in a more sophisticated form, in George Hepplewhite's *Cabinet Maker's and Upholsterer's Guide* of 1788. Yet other chairs have square backs with vertical reeded splats, which reflect an interpretation of designs popularised by Thomas Sheraton in his *Cabinet Maker's and Upholsterer's Drawing Book* of 1793 and 1802 (No. 54 B).

Regional chairs which were influenced by fashionable designs in this way are common in many parts of Britain and establishing regional origins for them is often difficult. However, within the chairs of this type recorded on the Isle of Man, some features do seem distinct to them. These include the use of a beading on the front leg corners, combined with a general reduction in the dimensions of the seat, front leg, and stretcher size in relation to the larger, conventional, back dimensions.

Catalogue No: **1.**

Item: Joined side chair.

Date of Manufacture: Second half of 17th century

Significant Accession Details:
Said (1922) to have belonged to Bishop Wilson, and to have come from St. German's Cathedral.

Description: A turned and joined oak back stool dating from the second half of the 17th century. The chair has unusually large dimensions, and may have been made for a ceremonial purpose. It has turned back uprights and an arched top rail, in the manner of certain Scottish chairs recorded from this period. The back has a framed raised fielded panel, decorated with mouldings around the edges of the framing and around the arched top, which also has small foliar carvings. The front and rear legs are turned with similar motifs to each other, and the front and back turned stretchers also have similar turning devices. The side leg stretchers are square in form. The seat is a replacement in pine, and the original seat may have been upholstered and set on the seat frame.

Woods: Primary: Parts are clearly oak. Other areas cannot be determined observationally.

Applied Surface Finish:
Thick coats of oxidised black varnish.

Dimensions: 102.5 hh 61 h 63 w 42 d.

Noteworthy Construction Details: Pegged construction.

Damage/Repairs/Replacement: The later pine or birch seat is now loose. Back turning has had burn marks, now partially removed. Original turned feet missing. Seat may have originally been upholstered.

Catalogue No: **2.**

Item: Joined armchair.

Date of Manufacture: *Circa* 1690.

Description: A turned and joined oak armchair dating from the second half of the 17th century. This chair has turned back uprights terminating in turned knob finials, and an arched and carved top rail supporting four vertical splats between itself and a lower cross rail. The seat is framed and panelled, and the front legs are turned with alternate bell-shaped turnings between rectangular blocks. The scrolled curved arms are congruent with those made for joined armchairs during this period. The style of this chair has strong Scottish features, including the particular seat form, turned back legs, turned front legs, framed and panelled seat, and the use of plain vertical splats with an arched top rail above.

Woods: Primary: Oak.

Dimensions: 109 hh 71 h 63 w 43 d.

Noteworthy Construction Details:
All pegged construction.

Damage/Repairs/Replacement: Right seat support replaced. New under-seat support.

Catalogue No: **3.**

Item: Back stool or side chair.

Date of Manufacture: Circa 1690

Significant Accession Details:
From the Christian family of Ballayonaigue, Bride. Q.C. cut on back may refer to a member of the Christian family.

Description: An oak back stool dating from the second half of the 17th century, with generic features of chairs made in the North-West region of England as well as in Scotland. These features include the use of a framed and panelled seat with the front legs morticed into it, one of a small group of possible seat forms from those areas. This example is unusually complex in its decorative mode, with moulded decoration which is free-hand carved. The vasiform splat offers a classical allusion. The stylised carved tulips which are included as part of the back design offer a common fashionable reference to the tulip, relating to the accession of William of Orange to the English throne in the last quarter of the 17th century. The broad flowing shape of the front stretcher echoes the shape of the top rail and, in a similar way to cane seated chairs from the Restoration period, offers a highly fashionable mode of design. The plain turned front legs are surprisingly bereft of turnery motifs common to this style of chair, and the 'Braganza' carved foot, believed to have been imported from Spain in the 16th century, offers a further fashionable reference.

Woods: Primary: Oak.

Dimensions: 114 hh 70 h 46 w 36.5 d.

Damage/Repairs/Replacement: Clumsy repair with section of wood screwed to break in back right leg. Break in left leg. Back stretcher missing. Chair strengthened with old metal brackets.

Catalogue No: **4.**

Item: Back stool.

Date of Manufacture: Circa 1690.

Description: An oak back stool dating from the second half of the 17th century. This chair has a framed panelled seat similar to that of chair No.2, which is a common form in Scottish chairs of this period and is also associated with the North-West region of England, particularly Lancashire and Cheshire. This example is unusual in having two plain vertical splats in the back with a pronounced gap between them, but without evidence of another splat having been present. The top rail and the front leg stretcher have foliate carving of a fashionable 17th century design which, in both cases, has sustained some removal of top parts of the design. The chair legs have been lowered with the removal of the turned feet, and the equivalent height from the back legs.

Woods: Primary: Oak.

Dimensions: 102 hh 66 h 45 w 31 d.

Noteworthy Construction Details:
Originally pegged construction.

Damage/Repairs/Replacement: Some of the carving on the top rail has been removed, and the front stretcher carving also has had some alteration to its original form. Turned feet missing on the front legs. Old iron nails in joints to hold them firm.

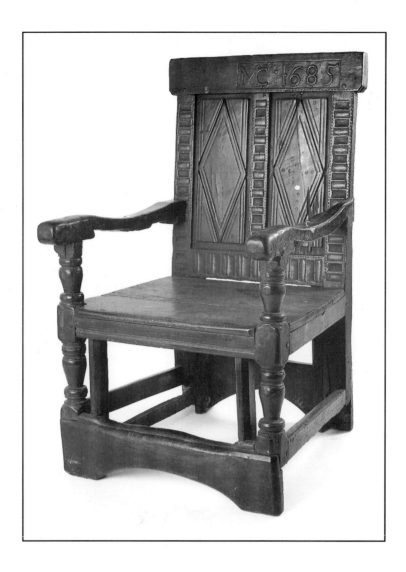

Catalogue No: **5** (See Fig. 1.2).

Item: Dated panel-back armchair.

Date of Manufacture: Circa 1685 (dated).

Significant Accession Details:
Bequeathed by Miss Christian, 1905, (NB. carved initials MC), Baldromma, Maughold.

Description: A joined armchair dated 1685 with clear design details which relate this example to Scottish chair designs, possibly from Kirkcudbright. In conformity with the majority of joined furniture made in the 17th century tradition, this chair is principally made in oak. However, it includes two carved pine back panels which appear original to the chair. Although it has design features which are entirely congruent with chairs made in England, particularly in the leg and under-arm turnings, the inclusion of pine parts is sufficiently unusual to indicate that this chair was made outside England, perhaps on the Isle of Man but more probably in Scotland. The gouge-carved decoration which appears on the three vertical stiles and the bottom stile is composed of a series of alternate concave and convex motifs, and represents a Scottish decorative carving motif, an alternative form to the English nulling which is composed of a series of concave arched gouge carvings. See *Oak Furniture, The British Tradition*, V. Chinnery, 1979, p.467, Fig 4: 112, for a further chair from the South-West of Scotland, dated 1681, which also shows the alternate concave and convex nulling decoration. The shape of the arms is interesting, and show the influence of Dutch or German design. This general form of arm has thicker sections at both rear and front, which are shaped and indented below. The form was also used for rush seated turned ladder-back chairs on the Continent. The front leg support stretchers are intact, although the feet of the chair are removed to the lower surface of the stretchers and it has been raised with two broad sections of wood nailed across the front and back. Four roughly shaped uprights, connected by cross stretchers, are also nailed below the seat to further support the higher level of the chair.

Woods: *Primary:* Oak with pine panels.

   Secondary: Replaced pine seat, lower plinth and nailed supports.

Applied Surface Finish: Dark stain.

Dimensions: 103 hh 64 h 66 w 51 d.

Noteworthy Construction Details: Pegged construction.

Damage/Repairs/Replacement: Replacement pine seat. Additions to front and back legs to raise it off the floor. Back stretcher missing.

Catalogue No: **6.**

Item: High backed armchair.

Date of Manufacture: Circa 1700.

Description: A walnut armchair with stylistic features which relate it to the 17th century North-West of England or Welsh chair-making traditions, where wooden seated chairs were made in large numbers and with great variety in back designs. The chair reviewed here has a back comprised of vertical splats, the inner ones plain and the outer ones moulded. The back is surmounted by an elaborate fretted crest rail, which is now broken. The chair is dark in colour, as is usual in this tradition where black staining varnishes were used.

Woods: *Primary:* Walnut.

Applied Surface Finish: Original dark staining varnish.

Dimensions: 117 hh 83 h 53 w 42 d.

Noteworthy Construction Details: Pegged construction.

Damage/Repairs/Replacement: Damage to cresting rail. Front section of seat missing. Old blacksmith's repairs.

Catalogue No: **7** A & B.

Item: Two back stools.

Significant Accession Details:
Said to have been given to donor's forebears by Bishop Claudius Crigan (1784 - 1813).

Date of Manufacture: Circa 1700.

Description: Two oak back stools with stylistic features which relate them to the North-West of England or Welsh chair-making traditions, where wooden seated side chairs were made in large numbers and with great variety in back designs. These chairs have backs composed of vertical splats, the inner ones plain, the outer ones moulded. The back is surmounted by an elaborate fretted crest rail, which is now broken. These chairs also have plain vertical inner splats and moulded outer ones, and the uprights are sawn rather than turned. The back legs are turned above seat level in the manner of cane backed and seated chairs from the Restoration period. The chairs are dark in colour, as is usual in a tradition where black staining varnishes were used.

Woods: *Primary:* Oak.

Applied Surface Finish: Original dark staining varnish.

Dimensions: 111 hh 69 h 45 w 36 d.

Noteworthy Construction Details:
Pegged construction. Many segments made from cleft oak.

Damage/Repairs/Replacement: Damage to cresting rail.

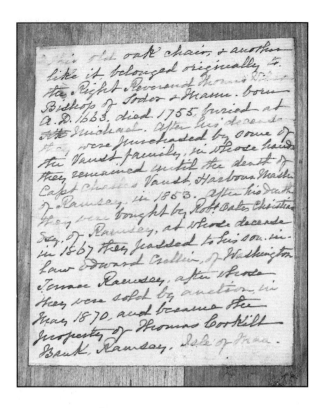

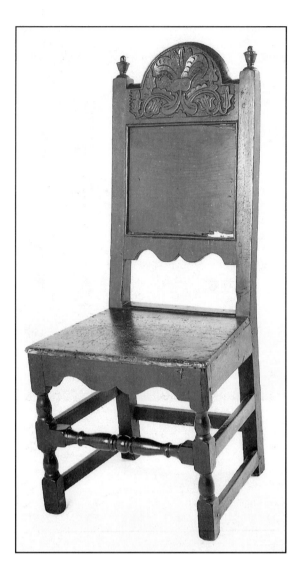

Catalogue No: **8.**

Item: Back stool.

Date of Manufacture: Circa 1670.

Significant Accession Details:
Descended through various families from the original ownership of Bishop Wilson (1663 - 1755). See photograph of recorded provenance on under-side of chair seat.

Description: An oak back stool of North-West origin, dating from the late 17th century. The design of this chair has strong stylistic links with chairs made in Cheshire and south Lancashire during the late - 17th and early - 18th centuries. The use of turned legs and central front cross stretchers in this form, and in combination with the use of rectangular side and rear stretchers, is characteristic of chairs from the North-West tradition. The adoption of a semi-circular curved top rail with a forward chamfered edge and robust foliar carving is also characteristic of a significant sub-group of chairs made within this tradition.

The urn-shaped finials on the back uprights are, however, unusual in a chair of this design, being more commonly found in association with chairs with vertical splats to the back (No. 6) or on fashionable cane-backed London made chairs from the Restoration period, from which the influence appears to have entered the vernacular tradition. Chairs of this type usually have pyramidal finials.

The seat is a later replacement, the original probably having been oak with a small overhang around the side and front edges. The overall dark appearance of the chair is entirely congruent with chairs from the North-West tradition where they were habitually stained with a black varnish. The chair has an unusually exact provenance to its ownership, given in both a hand-written and a typed biography glued beneath the seat, which claims the ownership of two similar chairs from that of Bishop Wilson until its last private owner.

Woods: *Primary:* Oak.

    Secondary: Replaced pine seat.

Applied Surface Finish: Dark staining varnish, probably its original finish.

Dimensions: 104.5 hh 65.5 h 45 w 36.5 d.

Noteworthy Construction Details: Panel chamfered on back. Signs of use of curved-bladed plane to remove excess wood.

Damage/Repairs/Replacement: Damage to lower back panel. Pine seat is a replacement. Has had a stuffed-over seat at some point, with nail marks evident on seat and stretchers.

Catalogue No: **9.**

Item: Joined armchair.

Date of Manufacture: Circa 1750.

Significant Accession Details:
Said by the donor to have been made by her great-great-grandfather (1755 -1825), a Craine of Squeen, Ballaugh.

Description: An oak joined and turned armchair dating from the mid-18th century. This chair is part of a generic group of panelled armchairs which were made on the Isle of Man from the late - 17th century and continued in production in various forms until the 19th century. This example is crudely made from reclaimed timber, with an oak frame and pine raised fielded panels. The seat, also in pine, is a replacement. The turnings are crudely executed and the arms, now mutilated at the ends, are unusually straight and lacking the flowing curves characteristically used in chairs of this type. The construction and production detail combined with the use of reclaimed timbers suggest, therefore, that this example was made within the Manx joined chair tradition, but probably by a house joiner or carpenter. This chair has features which strongly relate it to Scottish chair designs, including the use of two narrow vertical raised fielded panels in the back and the particular decorative shaping to the top rail.

Woods: *Primary:* Oak.

   Secondary: Pine panels (reclaimed timber).

Dimensions: 119 hh 81 h 60 w 42 d.

Noteworthy Construction Details:
Through pegging at joints.

Damage/Repairs/Replacement: Replaced seat and left bottom rail. Arms foreshortened. New part in middle of right front leg. Pegs missing on left side, and whole chair very loose at the joints.

Catalogue No: **10.**

Item: Joined armchair.

Date of Manufacture: Circa 1750.

Description: An 18th century joined and turned chair made of ash with a sycamore seat and front rail. This chair shows the characteristics of 17th and 18th century joined chairs, particularly from Scotland, with two framed and raised and fielded panels in the back, and turned front legs and front stretcher. The quality of the work indicates that this chair was made by a joiner trained in the use of moulding planes to create decorative effects around the edges of the panel stiles. The turnery devices are congruent with motifs used in the 18th century, and may indicate the use of a specialist turner in the production of the chair. Present evidence suggests that this chair is one of a number recorded on the Isle of Man which are part of the same generic group.

Woods: *Primary:* Ash.

   Secondary: Sycamore seat and front seat rail.

Applied Surface Finish: Residues of red lead.

Dimensions: 107 hh 69.5 h 64 w 44 d.

Noteworthy Construction Details:
All pegged construction.

Damage/Repairs/Replacement: Break at bottom of back left leg and left side stretcher.

Catalogue No. **11.**

Item: Joined armchair.

Date of Manufacture: Circa 1750.

Description: An oak joined armchair. The square framed base of this chair presents the chronologically latest design feature and dates the chair to the mid-18th century, with the *retardataire* features of scroll-shaped arms which are more typical of those found on 17th century chairs, particularly in metropolitan examples from the Restoration period. The shaped top rail fits between the uprights in the manner of some other Manx chairs of the period.

Woods: *Primary*: Oak.

Dimensions: 109 hh 72 h 62 w 40 d.

Noteworthy Construction Details:
Pegged, with reinforcing strut from front to back under seat. Raised fielded panels on rear - flat on front. Seat made from quarter-sawn oak.

Damage/Repairs/Replacement: Repairs to left front leg.

Catalogue Number: **12.**

Item: Joined armchair.

Date of Manufacture: Circa 1700.

Significant Accession Details: Said to have been used by John Wesley on one of his vists to the Island (1777 or 1781).

Description: This chair adopts the turnings and leg stretcher configuration of back stools from the North-West region of England, *circa* 1700. The back is unusually plain for a chair of this social significance. The gouge-carved eponymous 'Braganza' front feet are a fashionable design feature used in the late - 17th century, and believed to have been transmitted from Iberia. The chair has the appearance of being made within the turnery and joinery conventions of the 17th century. The plain back design has the demeanour of some Scottish chairs from late in the century, and this many be its place of origin. This, however, does not obviate the possibility of its being a Manx made chair, incorporating both North-West English and Scottish influences.

Woods: *Primary*: Oak.

Secondary: Pine panel. Right back leg ash.

Dimensions: 111 hh 73.5 h 60 w 45 d.

Noteworthy Construction Details:
Pegged at all joints. No under-seat support. No pegs driven through tenons underneath. Back panel not chamfered at back.

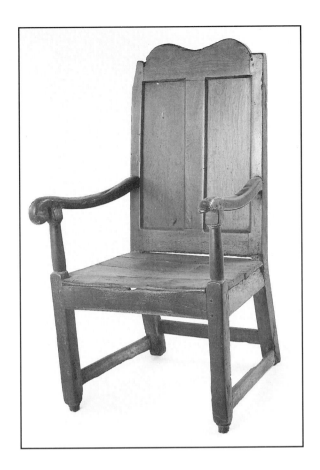

Catalogue No: **13.**

Item: Joined armchair.

Date of Manufacture: 18th century.

Description: This chair forms part of an identifiable group of panelled armchairs recorded on the Isle of Man which show characteristics of joined furniture made during the 17th and 18th centuries. With some modifications in design and use of woods they continued to be made into the 19th century - for further comment, see description of No. 10. This example has a framed back with flat panels where the shaped top rail fits between the back uprights, and chamfered inner edges to the stiles. The scrolled arms are made in the manner of those associated with metropolitan chairs from the Restoration period. These are supported on square legs which have plain turnings below the arms. The legs originally had turned feet. The front stretcher, now missing, was rectangular in section rather than turned. This chair has features found in some Scottish chairs, including the use of a framed back with flat panels.

Woods: *Primary*: Oak.

     Secondary: Pine seat.

Applied Surface Finish: Coats of later paint.

Dimensions: 107.5 hh 70 h 62 w 41 d.

Noteworthy Construction Details:
Square-pegged at joints. Stiles made from cleft oak and chamfered at the inner front edges.

Damage/Repairs/Replacement:
Front stretcher and end of right arm missing.

Catalogue No: **14.**

Item: Joined armchair.

Date of Manufacture: Chair carved, dated and initialled, 'Mar 19 1723 J.C.', its approximate date of manufacture.

Significant Accession Details: Donated by the Kermode family of Claghbane, Maughold.

Description: A joined armchair made within the conventional form of wainscot chairs from the 17th and early - 18th centuries. The turned front legs, arms, and stretcher form are suggestive of those made in the North-West region of England. The raised and fielded panel in the back has an arched and chamfered top. The top rail is positioned within the two uprights and is typical of English chairs of this type. The carved date (1723) is approximately the date of its production, and it is probable that this chair is Scottish in origin. Many of the segments, e.g. cross stretchers, are cleft. This, too, is unusual in the English tradition, where sawn sections were usually preferred.

Woods: *Primary*: Oak. Panels and stretchers made out of cleft wainscot..

Dimensions: 121 hh 79 h 63 w 41.5 d.

Noteworthy Construction Details:
Pegged at all joints. Top rail set between the back uprights.

Damage/Repairs/Replacement: Later strengtheners on back. Right side seat stretcher broken and reinforced.

Catalogue No: **15.**

Item: Joined armchair.

Date of Manufacture: First half of 18th century.

Significant Accession Details: An ancestress of the donor was housekeeper to the Earl of Derby at Peel Castle, and received the chair when the place was given up. A silver plate screwed to the back of the chair is inscribed "Formerly belonged to the Earl of Derby. 1745".

Description: This chair forms part of a distinct group of joined chairs recorded in the Isle of Man, which were made in various forms over a long period of time from the late - 17th until the 19th century. This example has a joined frame into which the back panels are fitted level with the stiles. The central stile is reeded, as are the tops of the two outer panels and around the periphery of the panels below. The silver plate screwed to the back, dated 1745, represents the approximate date of its production. The arms are created with outer angular shapes in the manner of *caqueteuse* chairs, which suggests an awareness of the fashionable 17th & 18th century form of chair design which originated in France and was adopted in both Scotland and various parts of England. The front legs are square in section with columnar turnings below the arms which are similar to those shown on chair No. 10.

Woods: *Primary:* Oak.

   Secondary: Pine seat (later replacement).

Dimensions: 111 hh 73 h 64.5 w 42 d.

Noteworthy Construction Details:
Through-pegged at joints with round pegs. Panels rabetted into frame with decorative central stile. Unexplained holes in some timbers, suggesting re-use of timbers.

Damage/Repairs/Replacement: Replaced pine seat. Later supports to arm back.

Catalogue No: **16.**

Item: Joined armchair.

Date of Manufacture: Largely 17th century (date 1709 carved in top rail) with later additions.

Description: An oak joined armchair of 17th century origin. This chair has had considerable alteration, with oak wing projections and arms being later additions, possibly in the 20th century. The carving, although of considerable age, was executed by a craftsman who lacked the skills typical of 17th century carvers. The foliar carving may coincide with the date of 1709, and represent a commemoration rather than production date. The basic chair frame is congruent with chairs made in the North-West region of England in the 17th century, particularly in the form of the turnings used in the front legs and the incurved terminals to the rear posts. However, the shape of the top rail and the front leg and stretcher turnings also have strong parallels in Scottish chairs. The use of a rope support for a seat cushion is somewhat unusual in both the North-West and Scottish traditions, where oak plant seats are usual. The use of decoratively turned lower leg stretchers, turned in the manner of the front stretcher, is a more usual feature of Scottish chairs.

Woods: *Primary:* Oak.

   Secondary: Rope seat supports.

Applied Surface Finish: Later coats of dark varnish.

Dimensions: 110 hh 76 h 66.5 w 44 d.

Noteworthy Construction Details:
All pegged construction. Unexplained patches in back uprights..

Damage/Repairs/Replacement: Side 'wings' and arms are later additions. Carving and date also later additions.

Catalogue No: **17.**

Item: Joined armchair.

Date of Manufacture: Circa 1700.

Significant Accession Details: Juan Nan (Watterson) family chair, Ballahane. It is claimed that John Wesley preached from it.

Description: An oak armchair which takes its inspiration from the general form of joined chairs, *circa* 1700, which were made in the Isle of Man from the 17th and 18th centuries. This example, however, was made within the tradition of agricultural joinery in which segments of cleft or, as in this case, reclaimed wood were shaped with a side-axe and draw knife as the principal edged tools, and where rudimentary mortices were created, probably with auger and twybil or chisel. The tenons were also probably created with a combination of side-axe and draw knife. The seat stretchers show nail marks which indicate that the chair has had a succession of fabric or leather seats rather than wooden ones.

Woods: *Primary:* Oak, probably reclaimed wood.

  Secondary: Leather seat.

Dimensions: 99 hh 65 h 58 w 41 d.

Noteworthy Construction Details:
Pegged construction. Chair made from cleft timber. Side-axe marks on back legs.

Damage/Repairs/Replacement: Front stretcher is a later replacement. Back seat rail is an addition.

Catalogue No: **18.**

Item: Joined back stool.

Date of Manufacture: Circa 1700.

Description: An oak joiner-made back stool which dates from the late - 17th or early - 18th century. The square rectilinear form is typical of seating from that period, and the use of four flat, vertical back splats below a shaped top rail is typically found in a group of chairs from the North-West region of England. This chair differs, however, from the North-West examples in being made from cleft rather than sawn sections, and it is probable that it is of Manx origin. The seat, which is now missing, was pegged and later nailed to the seat frame.

Woods: *Primary:* Oak.

  Secondary: Leather seat.

Applied Surface Finish: Vestiges of red lead paint.

Dimensions: 94 hh 56 h 46.5 w 39.5 d.

Noteworthy Construction Details:
Large pegs at joints. Seat had been pegged and later nailed.

Damage/Repairs/Replacement: Seat missing. Loose in leg joints.

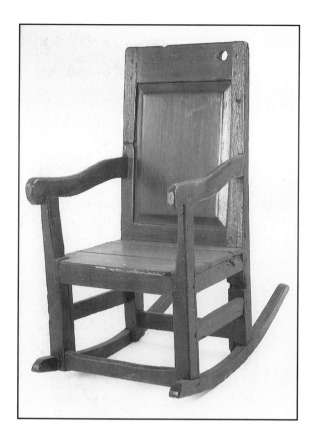

Catalogue No: **19.**

Item: Joined armchair on rockers.

Date of Manufacture: Oak chair, frame probably early - 19th century. Later back panel and seat.

Significant Accession Details: In the possession of the Kneale family of Kerrowgarroo, where it was known as "the nursing chair."

Description: A joined armchair on rockers. The frame and arms of the chair are in oak, and many unexplained holes and mortice marks suggest that it is made of reclaimed timber. The chair has been dismantled at some point, and a later raised and fielded panel made of pine has been fitted into the back. A replacement pine seat has also been added. The design of the chair is of 18th century origin, and follows in the tradition of joined armchairs from the late - 17th or early - 18th centuries. However, the chamfered arm supports and the use of original rockers indicate a chair made in the 19th century and with later additions. This design shows features common to Scottish chairs, particularly in the use of a simple framed back and one large raised fielded panel.

Woods:　*Primary:* Reclaimed hardwood, probably oak.

Applied Surface Finish: Later coats of paint.

Dimensions: 94 hh 61.5 h 50.5 w 37.5 d.

Noteworthy Construction Details:
Seat supports and arms morticed through the back posts. Front under-arm supports cut back to level of seat.

Damage/Repairs/Replacement: Replacement seat and back panel, in pine.

Catalogue No: **20.**

Item: Joined armchair.

Date of Manufacture: 19th century chair of earlier style.

Description: A pine joined chair, made during the first half of the 19th century with the characteristic square frame of many joiner-made chairs from the Isle of Man tradition. This chair includes a decoratively shaped top rail and a low framed and panelled back, in the manner of chairs made in the 18th century. In contrast, the arms reflect the 'Grecian' or 'Swan's Neck' swept arm, albeit in an unsophisticated form, which was fashionable during the first quarter of the 19th century, and continued in use in provincial traditions until the middle of the century.

Woods:　*Primary:* Pine.

Applied Surface Finish: Initial coat of red lead based paint. Later coat of green paint under seat, and brown paint over the exterior frame.

Dimensions: 103 hh 59 h 72 w 48.5 d.

Noteworthy Construction Details:
Pegged construction.

Damage/Repairs/Replacement: Excessive wear on front stretcher.

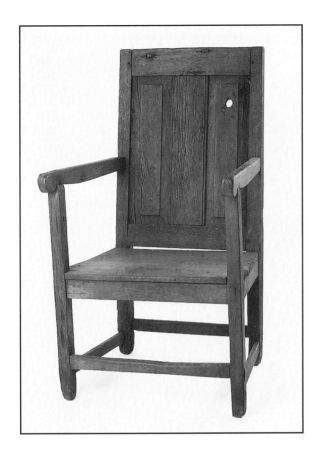 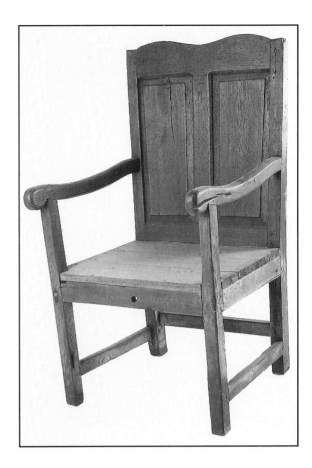

Catalogue No: **21.**

Item: Joined armchair.

Date of Manufacture: Late - 18th/early - 19th century.

Significant Accession Details: Billie Paie's chair, from his ruined house at Sulby Claddagh.

Description: An oak joined armchair. This chair has design features of joiner's work dating from the late - 17th and early - 18th centuries in its use of a square joined frame, and framed raised and fielded panels in the back. However, the generally low technical standards used in its production suggest that this is a *retardataire* design made by a joiner, dating from the late - 18th or early - 19th century, using reclaimed timbers and adopting the form of earlier joined chairs. The design shows features common to Scottish chairs, particularly in the use of two narrow vertical raised fielded panels in the back design.

Woods: *Primary*: Oak.

      Secondary: Pine replacement seat.

Dimensions: 103 hh 68 h 60 w 41 d.

Noteworthy Construction Details:
Many parts of this chair are made from reclaimed cleft timber.

Damage/Repairs/Replacement: Unexplained holes in back fitted with square pegs. Later filling of sawdust and glue compound. Right and left seat rails, and side and back stretchers are replacement.

Catalogue No: **22.**

Item: Joined armchair.

Date of Manufacture: Circa 1800.

Significant Accession Details: Said (1938) to have come from Billy Paie's ruined house on Sulby Claddagh.

Description: A joined armchair made in oak, with a replaced seat in pine. This chair has features of 17th and 18th century joined woodwork, including framed and raised fielded panel construction. However, the unsophisticated technical processes involved in its construction, allied with the use of reclaimed timber and of simple, sawn segments throughout, suggest that in common with a group of other joined chairs recorded in the Isle of Man this chair is probably of early-19th century origin. The top rail fits between the back uprights, and the chamfers on the lower edge of the rail form a continuous bevel with those on the edges of the middle stile and the lower cross-stile. The right arm was made from a cleft branch of oak, and has seasoning splits which follow the line of the medullary rays. The front stretcher is absent, and the seat is made of replaced pine boards. A number of unexplained round mortice holes have been plugged in the back, and an unplugged hole can be seen in the front under-seat stretcher. This design shows features common to Scottish chairs, particularly in the use of a simple framed back and two raised, fielded panels.

Woods: *Primary:* Reclaimed oak.

      Secondary: Replaced pine seat.

Dimensions: 137 hh 94 h 71 w 52 d.

Noteworthy Construction Details: Pegged construction. Double square pegs at seat joints. True mitre in top of panel. Joints not through pegged. No turnery work used.

Damage/Repairs/Replacement: Replaced pine seat. Replaced right arm and back stretcher.

Catalogue No: **23.**

Item: Armchair with vasiform splat.

Date of Manufacture: Circa 1780 - 1820.

Significant Accession Details: Believed by the donor who had 'owned it for many years' to have belonged to the Christian family of Balladromma, Maughold.

Description: An oak chair of sturdy elegance which embodies 18th century design elements. The frame of the chair is made in the manner of many joiner-made chairs from the Isle of Man, but this example has refinements which indicate that it may have been made by a cabinet maker. These include the use of square form legs which are turned below the arms with a common 18th century turnery motif. The arms are elegantly swept, and terminate in delicately shaped ends. The back legs are swept up and outwards from the seat, and surmounted by a shaped top rail which owes its design reference to 18th century fashionable chair designs, particularly those by Thomas Chippendale. This vernacular interpretation of fashionable chair design is continued in the classically shaped but unfretted splat which comprises the back design.

Woods: Primary: Oak.

Dimensions: 100 hh 63 h 67 w 46 d.

Noteworthy Construction Details:
All pegged. Tenons of side seat frame, and arms, pass through the back legs. Under-seat support mortices through back and front seat supports.

Damage/Repairs/Replacement: Pedestal broken at base.

Catalogue No: **24.**

Item: Armchair with cabriole legs.

Date of Manufacture: Circa 1780.

Description: This unusually elegant chair has a conventional vasiform splat and top rail associated with the 1730 - 1750 period of chair design. The cabriole shaped under-arm supports and front legs articulate with the scroll shaped arms to create flowing lines from all angles of perspective. Although cabriole legs were used in the English furniture tradition from *circa* 1710, this particular form is more related to an awareness of French style; cabrioles of this type appear in the English repertoire *circa* 1750. Given that this chair represents a vernacular interpretation, with a necessary time lag in the diffusion of the style it is probable that it dates from the period 1760 - 1780.

Woods: Primary: Mahogany.

Dimensions: 112 hh 70 h 70 w 49 d.

Noteworthy Construction Details:
Pegged joints.

Damage/Repairs/Replacement: Right arm has loose joint to back. Under-seat strut missing. Loose seat. Corner brackets missing on front legs, and original joint pegs replaced with 20th century screws.

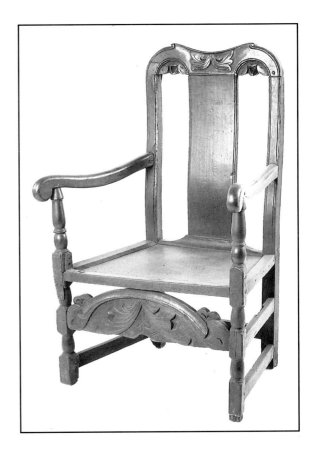

Catalogue No: **25.**

Item: Armchair with vasiform splat.

Date of Manufacture: First half of the 18th century.

Description: This joined chair, made of oak with an elm seat, is a vernacular interpretation incorporating two forms of chair design. The back has legs and a vasiform shaped splat which are curved in profile, in the manner of fashionable chairs associated with the walnut period of furniture making (1670 - 1725). The yoke shaped top rail is unusual in being mitre jointed to the top uprights. Typically, in conventional design terms, this form of back was combined with the cabriole form of front legs, with pad ball-and-claw feet. In this example, turned front legs are used, in the manner of joined chairs from the 17th century tradition. However, the turning devices used in this chair were actually common during the 18th rather than the 17th century. The removable seat form is unusual, composed of a frame onto which the seat boards are nailed, and which then fits into the chair seat frame, resting on four corner stays. The seat rails are unusually deep, and may have been intended to offer extra structural support to the legs which lack cross stretchers at the front and back. This appears not to have been very effective, and the right front leg has split away from the right hand seat rail tenon.

Woods: *Primary*: Elm with oak seat.

            Secondary: Pine (replaced) cross struts below seat.

Dimensions: 103.5 hh 61.5 h 69 w 48 d.

Noteworthy Construction Details:
Arm supports mortice through the arms, and arms and seat rails mortice through back legs. Yoke rail tenon jointed to back uprights. Splat asymmetrical in profile.

Damage/Repairs/Replacement: Turned feet missing to front. Old repair to back left leg. Front right leg split at cross rail joint.

Catalogue No: **26.**

Item: Joined armchair with central splat.

Date of Manufacture: *Circa* 1700.

Significant Accession Details: Said by donor (1922) to have been used by Bishop Wilson (1663 - 1755).

Description: An oak joined chair, *circa* 1700, in which a number of elements from different stylistic traditions are present, including the use of turned front legs, a panelled and frame seat, and foliar carving as part of the top rail and arched front stretcher. These are features found as decoration on 17th century joined chairs from Scotland, as well as from the North-West region of England. The elegant swept arms are typical of those used in metropolitan turned chairs dating from the Restoration period. The carved back legs, yoke shaped top rail and curved central splat reflect a further, and stylistically later, tradition from the fashionable chair making traditions of the walnut period (1670 - 1725), when Dutch designs influenced English chair makers in producing chairs with this back form, usually in veneered and solid walnut. See No. 25 for a further example of this form of design amalgamation. This chair has carved 'Braganza' style feet, and therefore represents a synthesis and re-interpretation of both regional and metropolitan design elements.

Woods: *Primary*: Oak.

Applied Surface Finish: Original stain.

Dimensions: 100 hh 65 h 67 w 43.5 d.

Noteworthy Construction Details:
Legs rhomboid in section, to accommodate the angles of the leg stretchers. Arms do not mortice through back posts. Seat made of one panel section. Pedestal (replaced) in two pieces.

Damage/Repairs/Replacement: Replaced pedestal. Some metal work repairs. Damage to front feet.

Catalogue No: **27.**

Item: Kitchen chair.

Date of Manufacture: 19th century.

Description: A joiner-made chair of rectilinear style common in the Isle of Man. The back legs are swept to the rear, below seat level. The front legs are square in section without the commonly found taper to their front elevation, and connected by a front stretcher which has much wear. Several coats of paint and oak scumble finish are residually present. The pine seat is nailed to the seat frame. The two back cross rails are straight, and set equidistantly apart in the back.

Woods: *Primary:* Pine.

Applied Surface Finish: Oak scumble over red lead or mahogany paint, and black painted seat.

Dimensions: 89 hh 44 h 45 w 39 d.

Noteworthy Construction Details:
Pegged construction with seat nailed to frame.

Damage/Repairs/Replacement: Residues of paint layers unevenly exposed.

Catalogue No: **28** A - C.

Item: Three side chairs.

Date of Manufacture: 19th century.

Significant Accession Details: From Harry Kelly's cottage, Cregneash.

Description: A group of three joiner-made chairs of basic rectilinear form, with sawn back uprights and two cross rails in the back. The legs are connected by stretchers, and the wooden seat is nailed to the seat frame. A taper to the front legs begins below the front leg stretcher, and probably indicates a particular workshop preference which is also commonly found in Welsh chairs of this type. These chairs have straight top and stay rails which represent a more basic craft technology than those made with curved or 'hollow' rails, and further confirms this style as the most fundamental design of Manx chair construction and design.

Woods: *Primary:* Pine.

Applied Surface Finish: Later coats of brown paint.

Dimensions: A. 81hh 40 h 46 w 39 d.

B. 81 hh 40 h 46 w 39 d.

C. 81 hh 40 h 46 w 39 d.

Noteworthy Construction Details:
Pegged construction. Does not have under-seat support. Cross rails and splat flush with uprights and uncurved.

Catalogue No: **29** A & B.

Item: Two kitchen side chairs.

Date of Manufacture: Circa 1820.

Description: Two oak joiner-made chairs of basic rectilinear form, with two back rails, slightly hollowed to the front. The wooden seat is nailed to the seat frame and has a thin cross rail nailed accross it to the rear, to hold it in place.

Woods: *Primary:* Oak.

Dimensions: A. 86 hh 44 h 44.5 w 38 d.

B. 86 hh 44 h 44.5 w 38 d.

Noteworthy Construction Details:
Joints pegged. Seat nailed.

Damage/Repairs/Replacement: A. One under-seat support missing. B. Back board of seat replaced. Back plinth missing from seat.

Catalogue No: **30.**

Item: Kitchen side chair.

Date of Manufacture: Circa mid-19th century.

Significant Accession Details: Family connections with Old Laxey.

Description: A joiner-made chair of basic rectilinear form. The taper profile to the front legs is pronounced and unusual, as is the large interval between the back top rail and the lower cross rail.

Woods: *Primary:* Pine.

Applied Surface Finish:
Initial coat of red lead with black paint over this.

Dimensions: 79 hh 43 h 46.5 w 38.5 d.

Noteworthy Construction Details:
Cross rails set flush with front uprights. Pronounced taper on side face of back legs, and on front and sides of front legs.

Damage/Repairs/Replacement:
Erosion to lower back legs.

Catalogue No: **31.**

Item: Side chair.

Date of Manufacture: 19th century.

Description: A joiner-made chair of basic rectilinear form, with saw-back uprights and two straight cross rails forming the back. The front legs show a pronounced taper, beginning one third of the way down on the inner faces of the legs. The front stretcher is replaced and has lap joints fixing it to the legs. The wooden seat is nailed to the seat frame. The chair was painted to simulate mahogany, and has been painted with black over this.

Woods: *Primary:* Pine.

Applied Surface Finish:
Initially simulated as mahogany, with later black paint.

Dimensions: 86 hh 44 h 45 w 39 d.

Noteworthy Construction Details:
Square pegged joints. Back struts flush with uprights on front face.

Damage/Repairs/Replacement: Replaced front stretcher using exposed lap joints. Worn side stretchers.

Catalogue No: **32.**

Item: Side chair.

Date of Manufacture: *Circa* 19th century.

Description: A typical Manx joiner-made chair in pine. This example adopts a lighter form than is usual, and is made in a more costly wood, oak. The back uprights are splayed outwards, creating a lively design. All of the leg stretchers are, unconventionally, set at the same level. The back has two cross rails of the same depth, and the wooden seat is nailed to the seat frame, with the rear of the seat held in place with a flat cross section.

Woods: *Primary:* Oak.

Applied Surface Finish: Painted.

Dimensions: 89 hh 44 h 49.5 w 39 d.

Noteworthy Construction Details:
Square pegged at joints. The leg stretchers are set at the same level as each other. The back rails flush with the back uprights.

Damage/Repairs/Replacement:
Gap in seat filled with putty.

Catalogue No: **33** A - D.

Item: Four side chairs.

Date of Manufacture: 19th century.

Description: Four joiner-made chairs of simple rectilinear form, with nailed flat seats and box form stretchers connecting the legs. The rear posts are swept backwards, and joined by two equally sized cross rails. The seats are flush with the seat rail edges and moulded around. The chair frames are finished in simulated oak grain, and the seats are painted black to simulate black fabric. These chairs have a simplicity of style which, combined with effective painting techniques, epitomises the ability of vernacular furniture-makers to create aesthetically pleasing furniture based on simplicity and an economy of materials and manufacturing processes.

Woods: *Primary*: Pine

Dimensions: A. 86 hh 44 h 46 w 37 d.

B. 86 hh 44 h 44.5 w 37 d.

C. 86 hh 44 h 46 w 37 d.

D. 87 hh 44 h 45 w 37d.

Noteworthy Construction Details:
Pegged construction at all joints.

Catalogue No: **34.**

Item: Child's armchair.

Date of Manufacture: Circa 1850.

Significant Accession Details: Said to have been made *circa* 1858 by Jimmy Watterson, 'Jimmy the carpenter', for donor's father in Rushen Parish.

Description: A joiner-made child's chair of basic rectilinear form, with curved back uprights and two cross rails. The flat arms are scrolled to the front and nailed to the sides and back uprights. The lower legs are not joined by stretchers. Circular saw marks under the seat indicate its manufacture in a mechanised workshop.

Woods: *Primary*: Pine with ash legs.

Secondary: L. & R. seat stretchers probably birch.

Dimensions: 56 hh 35 h 39 w 30 d.

Noteworthy Construction Details:
All joints pegged. Ladders set back from uprights.

Damage/Repairs/Replacement: Damaged left arm.

Catalogue No: **35.**

Item: Child's commode chair.

Date of Manufacture: Circa 1850.

Significant Accession Details:
From Lambfell Farm, German.

Description: A child's commode chair of a standard square backed form, commonly made by joiners on the Isle of Man. The example has the refinements of a pronounced curve to the back legs to create greater comfort, and unusually slender arms. The hole in the seat, made to hold a chamber pot, is cut through a recessed section of the seat, suggesting that a seat cover should have fitted into this space. However, no hinge marks are apparent.

Woods: Primary: Oak.

            Secondary: Pine seat.

Applied Surface Finish: Mahogany simulation with later coats of black paint over this.

Dimensions: 46 hh 31.5 h 35 w 29 d.

Damage/Repairs/Replacement:
No evidence of a hinged seat. This chair may have had a loose seat originally, which is now missing.

Catalogue No: **36.**

Item: Child's rocking commode chair.

Date of Manufacture: 19th century.

Significant Accession Details: In use by the Corlett family of Ballaugh in 1850s.

Description: A joiner-made chair with decoratively shaped cross rails and scrolled and shaped arms. The chamber pot was suspended from an under-seat board, and a hinged lid made of boards with a frame and mitred edge covered the pot. The chair is fitted to flat rockers.

Woods: Primary: Pine.

Applied Surface Finish: Painted with black paint.

Dimensions: 60 hh 34 h 36 w 29 d.

Noteworthy Construction Details:
All pegged construction at joints.

Damage/Repairs/Replacement:
Damage to top of left back legs.

Catalogue No: **37.**

Item: Child's commode chair.

Date of Manufacture: 19th century.

Description: A joiner-made child's box commode chair with the base panelled all round, and a leather hinged lid to cover the chamber pot. This chair is made in the manner of Manx joined chairs, without turned parts, and with scrolled and shaped arms.

Woods: *Primary:* Pine.

                        Secondary: Leather hinges.

Applied Surface Finish: Simulated mahogany graining with later coats of black paint or varnish.

Dimensions: 50 hh 30 h 34 w 30.5 d.

Damage/Repairs/Replacement:
Later repairs to leg joints, with screws.

Catalogue No: **38.**

Item: Tall backed chair.

Date of Manufacture: 19th century.

Significant Accession Details: A 'devotional' chair formerly owned by the Gell family, Castletown.

Description: A framed and panelled high backed child's chair. This chair is joiner-made, and apparently unstained, but with a varnished surface. The original accession title is that of a 'devotional' chair, although no explanation for the term is offered.

Woods: *Primary:* Pine.

Applied Surface Finish: Varnish.

Dimensions: 112.5 hh 78.5 h 31 w 24.5 d.

Noteworthy Construction Details:
Glued joints, without pegs.

Catalogue No: **39** A - D.

Item: Four side chairs with Manx emblems.

Date of Manufacture: Circa 1880.

Significant Accession Details: Reputed to have been made for Bridge House, Castletown.

Description: This set of four late - 19th century chairs, made in pine, shows evidence of joiner-made chair frames with specialist turnery work in the front legs and back roundel. The 19th century fashion for chamfering wooden edges in the 'Gothic' manner is apparent. The use of the Manx emblem supports the belief that they are locally made, perhaps for institutional use.

Woods: *Primary:* Pine

Dimensions: A. 96 hh 53 h 46 w 40 d.

B. 97 hh 52.5 h 45 w 40 d.

C. 96 hh 53 h 46 w 40 d.

D. 96 hh 53.5 h 46.5 w 40d.

Catalogue No: **40** A & B.

Item: Two kitchen chairs.

Date of Manufacture: Second half of 19th century.

Significant Accession Details: Abigail Faragher, Earystane, Colby.

Description: Two joiner-made chairs of common Manx form. The backs have four narrow cross slats and probably represent an attempt to interpret design features used in fashionable mahogany chairs from the late - 18th/early - 19th centuries, where a veneered tablet was typically located in the centre as well. There is a single decorative reeding around the back uprights and cross rail, and along the pedestal. These chairs have considerable foot wear on the front stretchers.

Woods: *Primary:* Pine.

Applied Surface Finish: Recent coat of red paint.

Dimensions: A. 88 hh 41.5 h 43 w 37 d.

B. 88 hh 41 h 45.5 w 40 d.

Noteworthy Construction Details: Seat rails mortice through the back uprights. Pegged at joints with oval pegs.

Damage/Repairs/Replacement: Much wear on front leg stretchers. A - replaced seat.

Catalogue No: **41.**

Item: Armchair.

Date of Manufacture: Circa 1850.

Description: The flat, scrolled arms, combined with this chair's overall massiveness and austere form, echo a sense of design from an earlier period. This and some other joiner-made chairs from the Isle of Man seem to be made within a tradition which had retained certain principles of design for perhaps two hundred years. In contrast, the four narrow cross rails in the centre of the back are a reference to a design feature in some fashionable mahogany chairs, *circa* 1820.

Woods: *Primary:* Pine.

Applied Surface Finish: The surface was originally gessoed, and then painted with oak scumble, with a coat of yellow paint over that. The seat is painted black to simulate upholstery.

Dimensions: 107 hh 66 h 59.9 w 41 d.

Noteworthy Construction Details: Pegged construction. Front stretcher morticed into front surface of legs. Arms through-tenoned by the arm supports.

Damage/Repairs/Replacement: The front stretcher may be a replacement using exposed joints.

Catalogue No: **42.**

Item: Armchair.

Date of Manufacture: Second half of 19th century.

Significant Accession Details: From Harry Kelly's cottage, Cregneash. Probably made in the Port St. Mary area.

Description: A square form joiner-made chair with the decorative use of four narrow horizontal cross rails set below the top rail, which is a reference to fashionable mahogany chair designs from *circa* 1820, where a tablet was usually located in the centre. Other chairs which have this design feature are shown in No. 40 & 41. In other respects, this chair exhibits conventional techniques and rectilinear form, which characterise joiner-made chairs from the Island.

Woods: *Primary:* Pine.

Applied Surface Finish: Brown paint.

Dimensions: 93.5 hh 58.5 h 58 w 41 d.

Noteworthy Construction Details:
The cross splats are joined flush with the back uprights. There is no seat support below.

Damage/Repairs/Replacement: The arms are shortened back at the tips, and the leg stretchers are missing. There is an old patch under the seat.

Catalogue No: **43.**

Item: Armchair.

Date of Manufacture: Circa 1850.

Description: A joiner-made chair of a common Manx form. In Manx chairs of this type, the square form is frequently relieved with scrolled arms which echo a design feature from an earlier period. The back has four narrow cross slats and probably represents an attempt to interpret design features used in fashionable mahogany chairs from the late - 18th/early - 19th centuries, where a veneered tablet was typically fitted in the centre. This chair has considerable wear on the front stretcher, and the evidence of an oxidised and weathered surface indicates that it had been left out of doors before its acquisition by the Museum.

Woods: *Primary:* Pine.

Applied Surface Finish: Initial coat of oak scumble, with later black varnish, now oxidised, over this.

Dimensions: 105 hh 59 h 54 w 48.5 d.

Noteworthy Construction Details: Joints pegged.

Catalogue No: **44.**

Item: Armchair.

Date of Manufacture: Circa 1850.

Description: This chair is eclectic in its design influences. Joiner-made, it has the basic square form of many Manx common chairs. However the cross splat decoration in the back is typical of those used in 19th century house joinery, and is indicative of the cross references in design which house joiners can bring to furniture making. The arm shapes are *retardataire* and reflect a much earlier tradition of chair making in the 17th century panelled chairs (No.14). There are no turned parts, reinforcing the impression of joiners' technology.

Woods: *Primary:* Pine.

Secondary: Oak arms.

Applied Surface Finish: Modern black paint.

Dimensions: 110 hh 65 h 62 w 47.5 d.

Noteworthy Construction Details: Pegged and nailed at joints.

Damage/Repairs/Replacement: Top of right arm broken off.

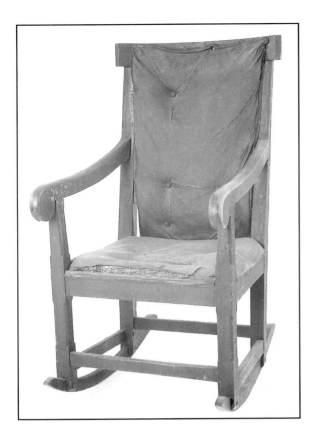

Catalogue No: **45.**

Item: Rocking armchair with padded seat and back cushions.

Date of Manufacture: Second half of 19th century.

Description: This chair combines standard joiners' work in the construction of the pine frame, with the addition of upholstery in the form of padded seat and back cushions. The decorative feature of the chamfered edges to the corners of the front legs is unusual in this tradition, and the massive scroll-shaped arms echo chair design from an earlier period (No. 22). This may illustrate a revival, or the continuity of a historic design feature. The chair is unusual in being purposely made to have a padded cushion for the seat and back. This is evidenced in the accentuated curve of the back rails. The cushions are filled with grasses, possibly meadow hay, and covered with hessian and oil cloth. The buttoning of the back cushion effectively prevents the padding from slipping down, and also offers a fashionable design feature. The seat is padded over a frame which has webbing with a hessian cover, hay padding, and a hessian top cover over this which extends unevenly underneath the seat frame and is nailed. The rockers are original to the chair and are made in a hardwood, ash.

Woods: *Primary:* Pine with ash rockers.

　　　　　Secondary: Seat padded with meadow grasses, with hessian and oilcloth over.

Applied Surface Finish: Painted with red lead and mahogany paint, with later black paint.

Dimensions: 100 hh 64.5 h 56 w 46 d.

Noteworthy Construction Details:
Square-pegged at joints. Cross rails sawn from solid timber.

Damage/Repairs/Replacement:
Seat damaged and some buttons missing in back cushion.

Catalogue No: **46.**

Item: Slat back rocking armchair.

Date of Manufacture: *Circa* 1880.

Significant Accession Details: Said by donor (1955) to have been made by her late husband's grandfather, Mr. Collister of Cross Four Ways, Malew.

Description: A joiner-made chair of massive construction, with three equally spaced cross rails forming the back. The large scroll shaped arms echo earlier chair designs made on the Island (No. 22). This design feature represents a rare conscious act to relieve an otherwise austere and rectilinear chair with a flowing line. The rockers appear original, and were probably supplied as an option to an otherwise standard chair.

Woods: *Primary:* Pine.

Applied Surface Finish: Residues of red mahogany paint, with layers of oxidised black paint over this.

Dimensions: 98 hh 69 h 51 w 44.5 d.

Damage/Repairs/Replacement:
Left arm fractured on back.

Catalogue No: **47.**

Item: Armchair.

Date of Manufacture: Second half of the 19th century.

Significant Accession Details: From the estate of Edward Christian, Northrop, Greeba (1984).

Description: This large joiner-made chair has scrolled arms and an overall massive form, which echoes chair designs from the end of the 17th century, and possibly reflects the continuity which the joiners' sense of chair design maintained on the Isle of Man. The unrelieved austerity of the design echoes the tradition in which it was made, where the essential technology is the joining of timber sections using the most effective and economical methods, and where design aesthetic is largely achieved as the product of the economical use of materials and technology.

Woods: *Primary:* Ash.

   Secondary: Pine seat.

Applied Surface Finish: Mahoganised surface.

Dimensions: 106.5 hh 61 h 53 w 58.5 d.

Noteworthy Construction Details:
Pegged. Middle cross rail pegged at back.

Catalogue No: **48.**

Item: Armchair.

Date of Manufacture: Circa 1850.

Description: A joiner-made armchair with a nailed wooden seat and two cross rails in the back. The swept arms and turned under-arm supports offer decorative additions in an otherwise unremittingly basic form. The wooden seat is nailed to the seat frame, and the front leg stretcher is missing.

Woods: *Primary:* Pine.

Applied Surface Finish: Initial coat of red lead. Later brown paint.

Dimensions: 90 hh 49.5 h 56 w 51 d.

Noteworthy Construction Details:
Pegged joints. Arms morticed into back uprights with visible tenons, but without pegs in this case.

Damage/Repairs/Replacement: Front stretcher missing.

Catalogue No: **49.**

Item: Armchair.

Date of Manufacture: Late-19th century.

Significant Accession Details: From Harry Kelly's cottage, Cregneash. Presumably made in the Port St. Mary area.

Description: A joiner-made armchair with pretensions to the creation of a fashionable swept top back rail, with three simple cross rails below. The swept arms and supports are referred to as 'Windsor Elbows' in the London Price Book of 1802. The square form of the base and the flat nailed seat are typical of those features used in many Manx joiner-made chairs.

Woods: *Primary*: Pine.

Dimensions: 106 hh 63.5 h 60 w 50.5 d.

Noteworthy Construction Details: Cross rails are flush with back posts and only very slightly curved. The under-seat support is fixed front to back.

Damage/Repairs/Replacement:
Left rear/front leg stretcher missing. Front leg stretcher possibly replaced.

Catalogue No: **50.**

Item: Armchair.

Date of Manufacture: Late-19th century.

Description: This armchair epitomises the effects of joinery techniques when employed in furniture manufacture, with uncompromisingly rectilinear lines throughout, and peg-secured mortice and tenon joints. The minimum number of segments are employed consistent with its use, and a square, throne-like quality is emphasised by the absence of decoration. The back has two cross rails, the arms are formed from straight sections of wood, and the wooden seat is nailed to the seat frame.

Woods: *Primary*: Oak.

Secondary: Pine seat (replaced).

Dimensions: 89 hh 57 h 58 w 45.5 d.

Noteworthy Construction Details:
Pegged joint construction.

Damage/Repairs/Replacement:
Replacement pine seat. Front stretcher missing.

Catalogue No: **51.**

Item: Low rocking chair.

Date of Manufacture: 19th century.

Significant Accession Details:
Possibly from the Peel area.

Description: A joiner-made rocking chair. The enclosed base had a side door, now missing. The back design has shaped uprights and a hollowed top rail which passes over the line of the uprights. In using these features, the maker has incorporated fashionable chair features from the 19th century.

Woods: *Primary:* Pine.

Dimensions: 71 hh 37 h 45.5 w 41.5 d.

Noteworthy Construction Details:
All pegged construction. The legs are tenoned through the rockers. The missing door had been pinned at top and bottom rather than hinged.

Damage/Repairs/Replacement:
Door in base, at right side, is missing.

Catalogue No: **52** A - C.

Item: Three side chairs.

Date of Manufacture: Circa 1820.

Description: Three side chairs of closely similar design. These chairs are joiner-made with a basic rectilinear frame design, typical of many made on the Isle of Man (No.31). In these examples, however, they have the additional fashionable design feature of reeded corners to the front legs, shaped and splayed back uprights, a straight top rail which is shaped below, and a central splat. This is fretted in the form of a stylised 'wheatsheaf' motif which is attributable to certain 18th century chair designs, particularly those illustrated by George Hepplewhite in a more elaborate form. The splat in these chairs is asymmetrical, clearly produced without a prepared template, and further illustrates the chair's interpretation by a joiner rather than a specialist maker.

Woods: *Primary:* Oak.

 Secondary: Pine or birch seat.

Applied Surface Finish: Residues of mahogany stain below surface oxidation.

Dimensions: A. 92.5 hh 49.5 h 48 w 38.5 d.

 B. 96 hh 52 h 50 w 36 d.

 C. 94.5 hh 52 h 50.5 w 36 d.

Noteworthy Construction Details: Pegged at joints.

Damage/Repairs/Replacement: A. Seat broken and chair loose at joints. Damage to pedestal which supports splat. Top left corner of splat missing.
B. Back half of seat missing.
C. Lower right front leg broken. Front half of seat missing.

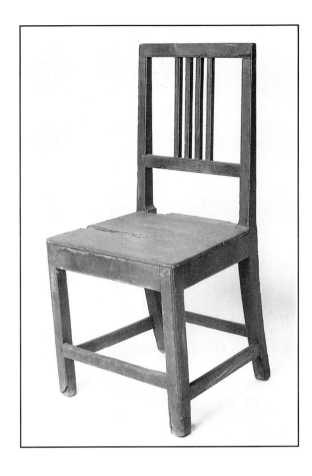

Catalogue No: **53.**

Item: Side chair.

Date of Manufacture: Circa 1800.

Description: This chair represents a vernacular interpretation of a fashionable chair from the late - 18th century, probably from the design book of George Hepplewhite (3rd edition 1798). This is particularly emphasised in the adoption of a curved shaped top rail, and 'wheatsheaf' motif fretting in the back splat. The proportions of the seat, front legs, and stretchers are smaller than is conventional in relation to the proportions of the back. The moulded reed on the outer front corner of the legs is also unconventional in chairs of this type made in England, and it seems probable that that these features signal this as being a Manx-made chair.

Woods: Primary: Oak.

Applied Surface Finish:
Chair has been stripped of surface finish.

Dimensions: 98 hh 54 h 39.5 w 48 d.

Noteworthy Construction Details:
Large square pegs at joints.

Damage/Repairs/Replacement:
Seat replaced. Old repair to top rail. Cracks in upper left front leg.

Catalogue No: **54** A & B.

Item: Two side chairs.

Date of Manufacture: Circa 1790.

Description: Two square form joiner-made chairs in oak. These chairs have counterparts in other British traditions, particularly from East Anglia. See *The English Regional Chair*, B. D. Cotton, 1990. However, the use of oak, a reeded outer edge to the front leg in a standard George III period manner, allied with smaller dimensions for the front legs than was conventional, characterise these as Manx products, influenced by Thomas Sheraton's chair patterns.

Woods: Primary: Oak. Seat wainscot oak.

Applied Surface Finish: Layers of black varnish.

Dimensions: A. 89 hh 46 h 37 w 45.5 d.

  B. 89.5 hh 46 h 46 w 38 d.

Noteworthy Construction Details:
All joints pegged. Seat supported with an oak strip, back to front.

Damage/Repairs/Replacement:
A. Damage to right front leg and seat.

B. Back seat plank replaced with pine plank.

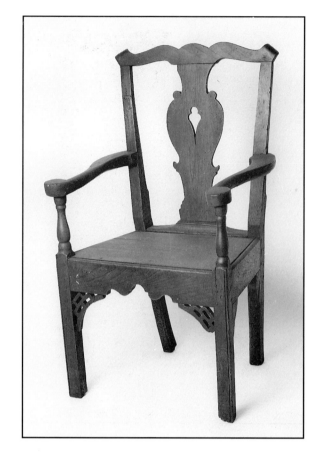

Catalogue No: **55** A & B.

Item: Two side chairs with fretted splats.

Date of Manufacture: Circa 1790.

Significant Accession Details: Originally belonging to the Crellin family of Ballachurry, German.

Description: Two joiner-made chairs dating from the late - 18th century. The fretted splats are asymmetrical, and were made without the use of a template. The front and side stretchers are level with each other, which represents an unconventional constructional device. The front legs are small in section and there is a pronounced taper on the side face of the back legs from the seat from top to bottom, of 4.5 to 3.5 cm. The seat dimensions are small in relation to the back size, and it does not extend under the back pedestal. These features are indicators which may be predictive of this being a Manx-made chair.

Woods: *Primary:* Oak.

Applied Surface Finish:
A. Mahogany stain.
B. Modern varnish over oxidised surface.

Dimensions: A. 95.5 hh 53 h 46.5 w 37 d.

B. 97 hh 52 h 45.5 w 39 d.

Noteworthy Construction Details: Pegged construction.

Damage/Repairs/Replacement:
A. Possibly a replaced seat board.

Catalogue No: **56.**

Item: Armchair with fretted splat.

Date of Manufacture: Circa 1780.

Description: An elm armchair with swept back uprights supporting a shaped top rail, in the manner of chairs by Thomas Chippendale. The back is composed of a wooden splat with an elaborate profile and a central fretted heart motif. The exaggerated and scrolled arms are supported on front legs which terminate in turned under-arm supports, connected by a frieze which is decoratively shaped below and supported by corner brackets. The wooden seat is rebated into the side stretchers, and the legs are not connected by stretchers. This chair has Welsh characteristics, particularly in the use of a lower shaped seat rail and corner brackets.

Woods: *Primary:* Elm.

Secondary: Fruitwood back, seat, stretcher and arms.

Applied Surface Finish: Original brown stain now oxidised.

Dimensions: 98 hh 56 h 58 w 39 d.

Noteworthy Construction Details: Pegged construction of joints, with three pegs to front frieze. The corner brackets nailed to legs. The arms are morticed and tenoned into back uprights, and made from mirrored sections of a round branch.

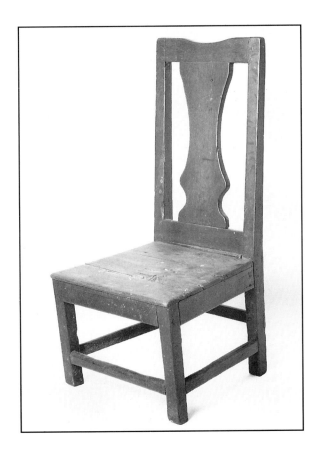 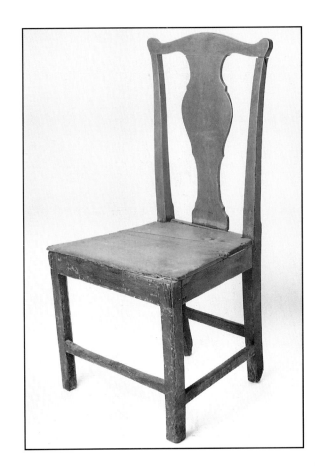

Catalogue No: **57.**

Item: Low side chair with unfretted splat.

Date of Manufacture: Circa 1780.

Significant Accession Details: Believed to be from the Christian family of Balladromma, Maughold.

Description: An oak side chair with a vasiform shaped splat. The straight top rail is fitted between the back uprights in the manner of several 18th century chairs recorded on the Isle of Man. This is a much altered chair which has a lowered seat level, probably to make it into a hearthside or nursing chair.

Woods: *Primary*: Oak.

      Secondary: Pine seat.

Dimensions: 90 hh 58 h 46 w 36 d.

Noteworthy Construction Details: All joints pegged.

Damage/Repairs/Replacement: Old repair with screws to upper back leg. Seat patched and strengthened. Side and front stretchers moved up 6.5 cm, and legs shortened. Back stretcher an addition in wrong position. Front stretcher moved down 2.5 cm, (compared with the chamfer on the front leg).

Catalogue No: **58.**

Item: Side chair with unfretted central splat.

Date of Manufacture: Circa 1800 - 1820.

Significant Accession Details: From Scarlett farmhouse, Castletown.

Description: A joiner-made elm chair with swept back uprights and a curved top rail which is influenced by the published chair designs of Thomas Chippendale. The top rail supports a vasiform shaped splat between itself and the seat rail. The wooden seat is nailed to the seat frame and the left leg stretcher is missing.

Woods: *Primary*: Elm.

      Secondary: Softwood seat, probably pine.

Applied Surface Finish: Mahoganised.

Dimensions: 95 hh 54 h 50 w 41 d.

Damage/Repairs/Replacement: Left lower stretcher missing. Seat rail replaced on left.

Catalogue No: **59.**

Item: Child's commode chair with feeding tray.

Date of Manufacture: Circa 1820.

Description: A child's commode chair with scrolled arms and a later feeding tray. The overall design of this chair shows influence of fashionable English chair designs from the first quarter of the 19th century. The reeding and under-arm carving to the front legs show refinements congruent with the expensive materials used, rosewood and mahogany. The back design has a wide rail which passes over the back uprights, below which two narrow cross rails support a central carved motif.

Woods: *Primary:* Chair frame and seat, rosewood. Mahogany panels and top rail

Applied Surface Finish: Simulated rosewood over mahogany on top rail.

Dimensions: 57 hh 30 h 39.5 w 33 d.

Noteworthy Construction Details:
Pegged construction at joints. No panel at back of commode seat.

Damage/Repairs/Replacement:
The tray is probably a later addition. Restraining bar between the arms is missing.

WINDSOR CHAIRS

CHAPTER 2

WINDSOR CHAIRS

The term Windsor chair is applied, as a definition, to all chairs which have a wooden seat into which legs are morticed from below, with back uprights morticed into it from above. This deceptively simplistic description is applied to a vast array of regionally different chair designs, since the Windsor ranks amongst the most widely interpreted British chair design. Historically, the chairs have included painted garden chairs, made in the early -18th century for wealthy households in London and the Thames Valley, and the term Windsor chair probably derived its name at that time by association with Windsor Castle. Later in the 19th century, the trade extended out from London and became centred on High Wycombe in the Chiltern Hills, where the Windsor trade developed into a major industry which continues to the present day.

The West Country, too, had its own tradition of making painted Windsor chairs, which included some designs which were influenced by London styles. Yet others developed as distinctly West Country designs, some of which were made by coastal coopers. In this tradition the practice of painting Windsors, usually blue, green or red, continued throughout the 19th century, long after the practice had been discontinued in the Thames Valley tradition.

Important centres of Windsor chair making arose in the north - east Midlands as well, particularly in Nottinghamshire and Lincolnshire where Windsor chairs were made, with changing design fashions, for over a century. Later in the 19th century, a highly developed trade also arose in Yorkshire, supplying the North-East region with mass produced, low cost Windsors, causing a decline in the north-east Midlands trade.

Other distinct Windsor chair making traditions developed in the Celtic areas of Britain, including Scotland, Ireland, Wales, Cornwall and the Isle of Man. Here, the craft remained one which both householders and local woodworkers undertook on a local basis. The forms of Windsors made in these regions were generally of a stick back variety, where the sections forming the legs, spindles, and arms were usually cleft from round timber, and shaped using a limited range of tools including a side-axe, draw knife, spokeshave, and augers, rather than a lathe and the tools of a specialised chair maker. Often the arm bow was made from either a single section of naturally shaped branch wood, or from a cleft section of an appropriately shaped branch which was then used as

mirrored arm sections, secured at the rear in a variety of ways. The seats of Windsors of this type were often massive, and either cleft or sawn from a tree trunk. The bottoms of the seats often show the marks of a side-axe having been employed to hew it into shape (No. 63).

Windsors of this stick type usually have arms, but Windsor side chairs were also made, and these take the essential form of a back stool (No. 61). The number of legs used in Windsor chairs was usually four, but examples employing three legs were also made (No. 62).

The hand-shaped legs were not usually connected by stretchers, and were typically shaped round in section with a side-axe and draw knife, although some examples do have octagonally shaped legs which terminate in round tenons (No. 63). Where round legs were used, the tenons which entered the seat were normally tapered, passed up through the seat and cross-grain wedged to hold them in place. This was an extremely efficient way of joining the legs, since the seat was forced down onto the tapered tenon when someone was sitting in the chair. This important constructional device was often used to through-tenon the back spindles to the arms and the seat as well. Not all makers chose to fit legs or back spindles in this way, and blind socket joints were also used where the legs and spindles were glued into place.

Windsor chairs made in these ways are commonly called 'primitive' or 'rustic' chairs, in a derogatory way. However, an alternative view is that they offer highly sculptured items which are formed intuitively, using natural, often hedgerow, materials which are shaped using few tools, to provide comfortable robust seating which observed the needs of the human body in a highly perceptive way.

Although regional traditions of Windsors of this type are now becoming evident in different areas of Britain, the examples recorded on the Isle of Man show a rich diversity of forms rather than a single distinctly regional form. These include the refined and dynamic example shown in No. 63, which has a sculptured seat supported on octagonal shaped legs and a widely spread arm bow made with three sections, dovetailed together at the rear. This is supported with six juxtaposed back spindles, to create a highly sophisticated and aesthetically pleasing chair.

Fig. 2.1; Family group with a Windsor chair, outside Carmodil Cottage, Ballaugh.

This example contrasts strongly with the utilitarian example shown in No. 64, which has an arm made of three sections where the middle section is double scarf jointed to the outer arms, and where the hand-shaped round legs terminate, very unusually, in square tenons which are wedged through the seat. The seat, in turn, is made of two sections which are dowelled together. The techniques and constructional devices used in this chair point to its being made by a house joiner, and it serves to emphasise that the skills of different makers are profoundly reflected in pieces which are essentially from the same generic group.

Within a continuum of Windsor chairs which range from highly refined examples to those which exhibit the minimum of transformation from the basic timber, an example shown outside Carmodil Cottage, Ballaugh, in the late -19th century, is clearly one of the latter (Figure 2.1).

This example is a variation of the three legged form where, unusually, one leg is fitted to the front and two to the rear. This chair has the appearance of having a seat made from a little-altered section of tree trunk, with a back and legs made from branches, to form a truly minimalist design.

Such chairs, apart from providing seating, were occasionally used as a convenient chopping bench, and many chairs show marks on the seat resulting from this activity. Mrs. Goldie of Middle Loughan, Jurby, gave evidence of this in 1954 (FLS/G/141A) to the Folk Life Survey, when the researcher recorded that "She showed me a very fine chair made of some hard golden wood. It was very low, wide, three legged, the legs splaying out. No nails were used, the legs and bars of the back being tightly set into holes made for them. The curved back rest was made in two pieces joined by a third small one, so carefully carved and fastened that it is difficult to see how it is joined. See those marks on the seat? When Grandfather killed the pig he chopped the ribs there. Uncle said the chair was made more than a hundred years ago and that Tom a Vulley made it."

In addition to the locally made chairs many 19th century Windsors on the Island, and in the Manx National Heritage collection, are the products of the large manufacturers in High Wycombe, and also from unidentified centres in the north of England. For example, Windsors often formed part of the school furnishings on the Island, and these include children's Windsors from the Wycombe chair makers (No. 69B) as well as high teachers' chairs, similar to those shown in No. 72A. Other Windsors show influences from High Wycombe chair designs, but with sufficient differences to suggest that they were made elsewhere, perhaps on the Isle of Man, in the late-19th century. These include the lath back Windsors shown in No. 73 and 74.

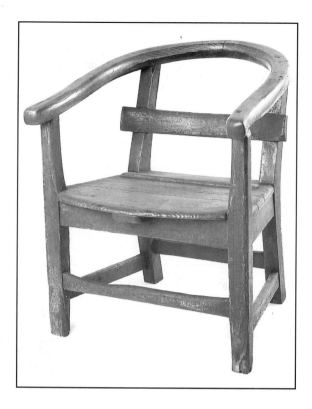

Catalogue No: **60.**

Item: Armchair.

Date of Manufacture: Second half of 19th century..

Description: This remarkable and imaginative chair represents a fusion of two major chair-making concepts in what is possibly a unique interpretation. No other chair of exactly this form has been identified in Britain, but one somewhat similar to it, in essence, is in the collection of the Museum of Southern Decorative Arts, North Carolina, USA. More specifically this chair has two areas of design. The legs, seat, and cross splat are of a conventional joiner-made form of mortice and tenoned square chair design. The arms are made of two mirrored sections of naturally shaped ash, probably a branch which was split into two sections and then sawn to shape, before being finished with a draw knife. These are carefully fitted to the back and front uprights in a way that allows them to sweep down and forward, in the manner of a Bergère chair, the style from which the design impulse for the chair probably arose. Windsor chairs (continuous arm Windsors), using a similar route to their design albeit of a lighter construction, are known in both England and North America. This chair is pegged and nailed at the arms. The seat supporting strut runs front to back, and is tenoned through the back seat rail. The surface was initially stained with mahogany varnish. It has a subsequent coat of oak simulated graining, with later black varnish over this.

Woods: *Primary:* Pine with ash arm.

Applied Surface Finish: Initially mahogany varnished, with later coats of oak simulated painting, and black varnish over this.

Dimensions: 75 hh 42 h 65 w 49 d.

Noteworthy Construction Details: Pegged and nailed at arms. Seat strut runs front to back and is tenoned through the back seat rail. Arm split and sawn to shape with sawing marks showing on right section.

Catalogue No: **61.**

Item: Windsor side chair.

Date of Manufacture: 19th century.

Significant Accession Details: Records relate that this chair was made in August 1885 by Thomas Cormode (who lived in Ballakinnag Road but had a joiner's shop at Lucy's Corner, Smeale) for his sister-in-law, Mrs. J. Callister, to use when bathing her baby.

Description: A 19th century stick form Windsor side chair which is essentially a simple back stool. Made without the use of a lathe, the legs and spindles are carefully shaped with a draw knife and spoke shaved to simulate turned parts. The chair is made in ash and has been varnished. This form of chair appears to be the most logical extension of a stool to a chair, and similar designs were made in Wales, Ireland and Scotland. Other more sophisticated forms of this design were made in the North-Eastern counties. See *The English Regional Chair*, B. D. Cotton, *1990*, Chap III, pp134-136.

Woods: *Primary:* Ash.

Applied Surface Finish: Varnished.

Dimensions: 62.5 hh 34.5 h 40 w 27.5 d.

Noteworthy Construction Details:
Dowel construction throughout.

Catalogue No: **62.**

Item: Windsor chair.

Date of Manufacture: First half of 19th century.

Description: A 19th century Windsor armchair which has three legs only. This is a most stable form of chair when used on uneven floors, and a form made in Wales but not typically elsewhere in Britain. This otherwise most rudimentary chair has an arm bow composed of two different woods, ash and sycamore, which are united at the rear with a simple lap joint. The back spindles are driven through the seat from above. The spindles also pass through the arms and are cross-wedged to hold them in place. The back has four replacement spindles, with the old tenons and wedges left on the upper surface of the arms, and six original spindles in pine. The front of the seat is made of elm, and the rear is ash. It has had cloth nailed over the seat, leaving nail holes. The chair was finished with a coat of red lead paint, which has a later coat of black paint over this.

Woods: Primary: Ash left arm, sycamore right arm. Four replacement and six original pine spindles. Front of seat elm, rear seat ash.

Applied Surface Finish: Initial coat of red lead with black paint over.

Dimensions: 71 hh 32.5 h 62 w 38 d.

Noteworthy Construction Details:
Octagonal legs shaved to round section at seat, tenoned through seat and wedged. Lap jointed arm at rear. Original spindles morticed through sawn arm bow and wedged.

Damage/Repairs/Replacement: Four replacement spindles, (1, 2, 3, & 5) with old tenons and wedges left on surface of arms. Has had cloth nailed on seat, leaving nail holes.

Catalogue No: **63.**

Item: Windsor chair.

Date of Manufacture: First half of 19th century.

Description: An extremely dynamic example of a Windsor chair, made of ash with an oak seat. This example is an unusual interpretation of this type of chair, in that it offers few functioning vertical elements (six back spindles and four legs). The angles of these segments are, however, juxtaposed to create both high stability and rigidity through the reciprocating and opposing angles of the components. The arm bow is made from two parts with a union to the back made with a dovetail joint. Three wooden plugs are evident in the upper arm support which perhaps conceal screws. A curved upper section supports the joint above. The arm is supported with four turned rear spindles only, the outer two of which are larger in diameter. These spindles are angled slightly backwards, and framed outwards. The support which these offer is highlighted by the opposition to them which the two forward inclined under-arm supports give. The four octagonally shaped legs are blind socketed into the seat, and sharply angled outwards, to maximise stability. The seat is unusually thick and sculptured to accommodate the human form. The under-arm supports are formed from thin branches. The chair has an initial coat of red lead with a later coat of dark varnish, now worn, over this.

Woods: Primary: Ash with oak seat.

Applied Surface Finish: Original coat of red lead with later dark varnish, now worn, over this.

Dimensions: 59 hh 29 h 68 w 26.5 d.

Noteworthy Construction Details:
Under-arm supports formed from thin branches. Dovetail joint on back arm bow. Three plugs on upper-arm support, perhaps concealing screws.

Catalogue No: **64.**

Item: Windsor chair.

Date of Manufacture: 19th century.

Significant Accession Details: From Ballaragh, Lonan.

Description: A Windsor armchair with seven back spindles, morticed and wedged through both seat and arm sections. The arm is made from three sawn sections of pine, the outer two arm sections of which are double scarf-jointed (above and below the union) into the curved back support section. This unusual form of jointing suggests a joiner's house roofing technique, and points to the maker training in that trade. This is further indicated in the use of square mortice and tenon leg joints which pass through the seat and are wedged to secure them. The legs and back spindles are made from cleft and hand-shaped sections.

Woods: Primary: Pine arm bow, seat and legs.

Secondary: Ash spindles

Dimensions: 64 hh 36 h 60.5 w 34.5 d.

Noteworthy Construction Details:
Sticks pass through the arm bow and are wedged. A dowel passes through the two seat pieces from front to back as a jointing mechanism. The legs, although round in section, have tenons which are square in section.

Catalogue No: **65.**

Item: Windsor chair.

Date of Manufacture: Late-19th century.

Significant Accession Details: Belonged to family of John Teare, The Rheast, Smeale, Andreas, grandfather of donor.

Description: A Windsor armchair with an ash arm bow, made in three sections, the outer arms sawn to shape and supported at the rear joint with a curved cross piece. The pine seat is made from three sections of wood which are united with two wooden supports nailed below. The hand-shaped pine legs are morticed through the seat, but not wedged. The back spindles are octagonally shaped, and have sharply tapered tenons which pass through both the arm-bow and the seat. There is evidence of blue/green paint residues on the chair, which has been over-painted with coats of red lead, black and brown paints.

Woods: Primary: Pine.

Secondary: Ash arm bow and horizontal back support.

Applied Surface Finish: Blue/green paint over-painted respectively with red lead, black, and brown paint.

Dimensions: 77.5 hh 35 h 61 w 46.5 d.

Noteworthy Construction Details:
Three-plank seat with nailed plank supports below seat. Legs morticed through seat, not wedged. Back spindles are morticed through arm bow and back support and seat.

Catalogue No: **66.**

Item: Windsor chair.

Date of Manufacture: First half of 19th century.

Description: A Windsor armchair made with minimal technology, the original spindles and legs cleft and shaped with an axe and a draw knife. The arm bow, unusually in chairs of this type where naturally occurring arm shapes were preferred, is sawn and bent rather than made from a cleft segment. The legs are tapered and morticed and wedged through the seat. The chair is made predominantly in ash, with a pine seat and three pine legs (the fourth leg is made of ash). There are traces of red lead finish on the chair. All the back spindles are replaced except the middle one. The left back leg is replaced, and a pine right leg may also be an early replacement.

Woods: *Primary:* Ash arms, spindles, and left front leg.

   Secondary: Pine seat and legs.

Applied Surface Finish: Traces of red lead finish.

Dimensions: 71 hh 38 h 64 w 39 d.

Noteworthy Construction Details:
The two seat planks are joined with two internal wooden tenons driven through seat and plugged at ends.

Damage/Repairs/Replacement: All back spindles replaced except middle one. Left back leg replaced. Pine right leg may be an early replacement.

Catalogue No: **67.**

Item: Windsor chair.

Date of Manufacture: 19th century.

Significant Accession Details: Stated by donor to have been made at The Howe, Rushen, for the Watterson family of Ballanane, Rushen.

Description: A Windsor armchair with an arm bow made from two naturally curved sections, 'V' jointed together. The eleven back spindles were fashioned from cleft wood using a side-axe and draw knife and are morticed through the seat. The legs were similarly shaped and are morticed and wedged through the seat. The front right leg is replaced and the front part of the seat is also a later addition. The chair shows evidence of coats of blue/green paint over-painted with red lead, with a coat of black paint over this. This chair has an unusually high arm bow and represents a highly individual interpretation of a Windsor chair.

Woods: *Primary:* Woods painted over, unidentifiable visually.

Applied Surface Finish: Initial coats of blue/green paint, over-painted respectively with red lead and black paint.

Dimensions: 71.5 hh 39 h 52 w 33 d.

Damage/Repairs/Replacement: Front right leg replaced. Front part of seat is an addition.

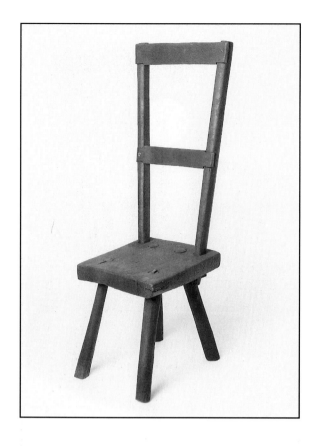

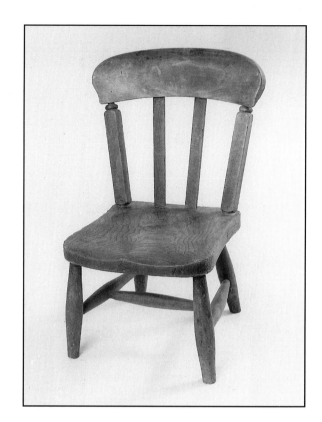

Catalogue No: **68.**

Item: High backed child's chair (back stool).

Date of Manufacture: 19th century.

Description: A back stool made from softwood, with an unusually tall back, morticed through and pegged below the seat. This form of construction probably created greater stability than standard mortice and tenon joints. The base of the chair has the construction of a square topped stool with four round legs, morticed and wedged through the seat.

Woods: *Primary:* Softwood, probably pine.

Applied Surface Finish: Darkened.

Dimensions: 85 hh 55.5 h 32 w top 27 w seat 28.5 d.

Noteworthy Construction Details: Unusual through-morticed and wedged back uprights..

Catalogue No: **69** A & B.

Item: Two children's chairs.

Date of Manufacture: Circa 1900.

Description: Two closely similar children's or kindergarten Windsor chairs, of a style produced in large numbers and sold to education authorities throughout England during the second half of the 19th century and the first half of the 20th. Chairs of this type were made by chair manufacturers in High Wycombe, (see example shown in *School Furniture in the Vernacular Tradition* C. Gilbert, Temple Newsam, 1978, which was used in a Leeds school but probably made in High Wycombe). The legs were tenoned on a 'pencil sharpener' device mounted at the end of a lathe. The back spindles are tenoned and wedged through the seat. The surface of the chairs has been varnished.

Woods: *Primary:* Beech with elm seat.

Applied Surface Finish: Varnished.

Dimensions: 52 hh 23 h 30 w 31 d.

Noteworthy Construction Details: Top of legs turned on a 'pencil sharpener' device at end of lathe.

Catalogue No: **70.**

Item: Child's square backed side chair.

Date of Manufacture: Circa 1840.

Description: A child's 'scroll' or square backed Windsor chair in beech with an elm seat and cross rail, made in the Buckinghamshire / Oxfordshire Windsor chair making tradition. See *The English Regional Chair*, B. D. Cotton, 1990, Chapter II, for further illustrations of this design.

Woods: *Primary:* Beech uprights, legs, and stretchers.
Elm seat.

   Secondary: Elm top and middle cross rails.

Applied Surface Finish: None visible. Light staining and varnishing were usual in this tradition.

Dimensions: 56 hh 34 h 29 w 27 d.

Catalogue No: **71.**

Item: Child's chair with commode seat.

Date of Manufacture: Late-19th century.

Significant Accession Details: Claimed to have been made by a joiner who was a member of the Faragher family, Ballacomish, Arbory.

Description: Despite the donor's claim, this appears to be a mass-produced child's Windsor chair with a commode seat, possibly from a north of England chair manufacturing centre, *circa* 1880. See *The English Regional Chair*, B. D. Cotton, 1990, for examples of closely similar chairs made by W. Brear and Sons of Addingham, near Leeds, Yorkshire. The chair is made in pine or birch, with a pine seat which has a crudely cut circular hole made in it to hold a chamber pot.

Woods: *Primary:* Pine or birch with pine seat.

Applied Surface Finish: Walnut stain with varnish over.

Dimensions: 57.5 hh 35 h 34 w 30 d.

Noteworthy Construction Details: Seat made in three pieces of band sawn timber. 'Sharpened' tenons to spindle ends.

Damage/Repairs/Replacement: Circular chamber pot hole in seat crudely made, later than the chair's production.

Catalogue No: **72** A & B.

Item: Two teacher's chairs..

Date of Manufacture: Circa 1880.

Significant Accession Details: Chair (72A) used in Bride School until *circa* 1948.

Description: A specialised form of Windsor high chair with a foot rest made for a school teacher's use whilst sitting at a high desk. These examples were probably made in one of the High Wycombe chair manufactures, and show the use of beech turned and shaped parts and elm seats which typifies wood use in chairs from this centre. See the catalogue of Hearn Bros, chair manufacturers of High Wycombe, *circa* 1880, Figure 2M which illustrates this form of chair within a range of other domestic chairs. Another version of this form of chair which was also probably made in High Wycombe is illustrated in the exhibition catalogue, *School Furniture in the Vernacular Tradition*, C. Gilbert, Temple Newsam, 1978. These chairs were originally finished with walnut or mahogany stain, then varnished.

Woods: *Primary:* Beech with elm seat.

Applied Surface Finish: Originally walnut or mahogany, stained and varnished.

Dimensions: A. 107 hh 41 h 40.5 w 37.5 d.

                 B. 107 hh 42 h 36.5 w 38 d.

Noteworthy Construction Details: Step front legs wedged through top. Circular saw marks visible under step of B.

Catalogue No: **73.**

Item: Lath back Windsor rocking chair.

Date of Manufacture: Circa 1880.

Significant Accession Details: Used on Marown farm until 1970.

Description: A beech lath back kitchen chair without arms, with the legs fitted to rockers. The legs have a large ball and concave turning motif and vase-shaped turnings to the lower front legs. The rear legs have no vase shaped feet, but are turned directly as a gentle rounded shape, with a turned dowel which locates them into the rockers. This form of lath back kitchen chair was a popular chair design in the second half of the 19th century, and was produced in large numbers by the chair manufacturers of High Wycombe and other nearby chair-making centres in Buckinghamshire. This example, however, although significantly similar to the type produced in the Buckinghamshire centres, shows differences in dimensions and shaping of parts which suggest that it was made elsewhere. The seat shape is reminiscent of kitchen chairs made in the North American tradition of painted kitchen chairs *circa* 1820, particularly those from the New York, Boston, and Hitchcock Connecticut traditions, where relatively thin, rectangular seats, rounded to the front, were common. The tapered joints of the thin slats into the top rail and the seat are reminiscent, too, of the so-called 'arrow-back' design of painted chairs from the North American tradition, where arrow-shaped slats join the top rail and seat with similar tapered round tenons. See *American Painted Furniture*, D. Fayles, chair 416. These features suggest that the chair is an amalgamation of both American and English designs, possibly manufactured on the Isle of Man. A further chair in the collection, which is also mounted on rockers (No. 74) is clearly from the same manufacturing tradition, and like this example has been on the Island since at least the early part of the 20th century.

Woods: *Primary:* Beech.

Applied Surface Finish: Originally mahogany stained, with later black varnish.

Dimensions: 95 hh 61.5 h 38 w 36 d.

Catalogue No: **74.**

Item: Lath back kitchen Windsor rocking armchair.

Date of Manufacture: Circa 1880.

Description: A lath back kitchen chair made of elm and beech, and painted matt black. The legs have a three ring turning motif, and 'H' form stretchers. This form of lath back kitchen chair was a popular design, produced in large numbers by the chair manufacturers in High Wycombe and other nearby centres in Buckinghamshire during the second half of the 19th century, continuing into the 20th. This example, although closely similar to the type produced in the Buckinghamshire centres, shows differences in dimensions and shaping of parts. A specific major design difference between the Buckinghamshire design and this example lies in the thinness of the laths and the round, tapered terminals as they enter the broad top rail. This feature, combined with other interpretations of the design's dimensions, confirm its manufacture elsewhere, possibly on the Isle of Man. The tapered joints of the slats into the top rail are reminiscent, too, of the so-called 'arrow-back' design of painted chairs from the American tradition, where the arrow-shaped slats also join the top rail and seat with tapered round tenons. A further armless chair in the collection, which is also mounted on rockers (No. 73) is clearly from the same manufacturing tradition, and like this example has been on the Island since at least the early part of the 20th century.

Woods: *Primary:* Elm seat arms, back slats and uprights. Beech legs stretchers, under-arm turnings and rockers.

Applied Surface Finish: Black paint.

Dimensions: 101 hh 69 h 63 w 43 d.

Catalogue No: **76.**

Item: Office or low smoking chair.

Date of Manufacture: Circa 1880.

Description: A Windsor armchair with the familiar feature of a three part arm construction which typifies the low smoking or office Windsor, made in a number of regional centres in England, including High Wycombe, Bristol, and Worksop. This chair also has a number of features which suggest a strong American influence in its design, including the use of the rounded front edge to the seat, rounded arm shape, and the simulated rosewood painted decoration with gold lining. These are features of chairs made, for example, by the Hitchcock firm of Connecticut, USA, particularly in chairs known as Boston chairs. However, its woods, beech for the arm sections and turned parts, with a birch or pine seat, suggest that this is a British rather than an American-made chair. It is possible that it is a chair from the design group of which No.77 is an example. This is strongly suggested since it, too, shows evidence of repeater lathe turned parts, and has leg mortice angles in common with this latter type of chair. Given its American appearance, it may have been part of a range of chairs primarily made for export by an English chair manufacturer.

Woods: Primary: Beech with pine or birch seat.

Applied Surface Finish: Simulated rosewood painted surfaces lined in gold.

Dimensions: 79 hh 40 h 61 w 47 d.

Noteworthy Construction Details: Repeater lathe turning marks on side stretchers.

Catalogue No: **75.**

Item: Lath back armchair.

Date of Manufacture: Circa 1850.

Description: A 19th century lath back Windsor armchair which was originally made to fit on rockers. This chair is of a type made by many chair manufacturers in High Wycombe, and is a characteristic product of this chair making centre. It is made typically of beech and elm. The chair was originally painted with red lead paint, and has later varnish over this. The initials, 'J.A.' stamped on the back of the seat are the initials of the chair framer, and reflect the workshop organisation in this tradition. For further detail of this practice, see *The English Regional Chair*, B. D. Cotton, 1990, Chapter II.

Woods: Primary: Beech.

            Secondary: Elm comb rail and seat.

Applied Surface Finish: Originally painted with red lead, with later varnish over this.

Dimensions: 104 hh 42 h 52 w 55 d.

Damage/Repairs/Replacement: Originally fitted to rockers, now missing.

Catalogue No: **77.**

Item: Bentwood office chair.

Date of Manufacture: Circa 1880.

Description: This late-19th century armchair is an example of a very popular form of mass-produced Windsor chair, made during the second half of the 19th century and into the second quarter of the 20th. This type of chair incorporated new manufacturing techniques with more traditional ones, including steaming and bending both solid and laminated ash (in this example solid, sawn sections of ash alone were used) to form the arm bows. The back legs are birch, and the seat is made of plywood which was mechanically cut, drilled, and steam-pressed to shape, representing one of the earliest uses of plywood in furniture making. The back spindles, legs, decorative front stretchers, plain side and back stretchers and curved back legs all have the appearance of being produced on a repeater lathe, designed to produce multiples of similar turnings. Numerous variants of this form of extremely robust and comfortable chair were made in the chair-making centres of High Wycombe, London, Liverpool, and other parts of Britain. They were also made in countries where British influence was felt, including America and Australia, where factories making this type of steam-bent chair produced them in large quantities. See *Chairs in Australia* by Cuffley & Caring, 1974.

Woods: Primary: Ash.

  Secondary: Plywood seat. Back legs birch.

Applied Surface Finish: Varnish.

Dimensions: 76 hh 34 h 55.5 w 45 d.

Noteworthy Construction Details: Parts turned on a repeater lathe.

Catalogue No: **78** A & B.

Item: Two kitchen chairs.

Date of Manufacture: Circa 1900.

Description: Two closely similar kitchen chairs with three ring turned legs, of a design which dates this chair to the second half of the 19th century. See the sequence of Windsor leg designs from *The English Regional Chair*, B. D. Cotton, 1990, Chapter II. The extensive use of alder or birch in this chair probably points to its origins in the north of England, where large manufacturers producing Windsors of the kitchen variety arose during the second half of the 19th century. The design is unconventional in embodying box form stretchers. The design of this chair has some similarity with American Windsor designs made in the first half of the 19th century, and it is possible that the chair gains its design impulse from this source.

Woods: Primary: Birch or alder.

Applied Surface Finish: These chairs were finished with mahogany varnish, which is now largely eroded.

Dimensions: A. 85 hh 43 h 33 w 35 d.

  B. 84.5 hh 43.5 h 33 w 34.5 d.

Noteworthy Construction Details: Chair 78 B back right leg has a different foot turning, but this appears to be original to the chair.

Catalogue No: **79.**

Item: Windsor side chair.

Date of Manufacture: Circa 1840.

Description: A Windsor hoop back side chair made with beech legs, stretchers, and spindles; elm seat; ash hoop, and a replacement splat in oak. This form of chair was made in large numbers at the Buckinghamshire chair-making centre of High Wycombe, and the large single ball motif turned as part of the leg design dates it to *circa* 1840. See *The English Regional Chair*, B. D. Cotton, 1990, Chapter II, for further illustrations of chairs of this type.

Woods: *Primary:* Beech legs, stretchers & spindles. Elm seat. Ash hoop.

         Secondary: Replaced oak splat.

Applied Surface Finish: None visible, although light colour staining and varnishing was usual in this tradition.

Dimensions: 87 hh 47 h 38 w 35.5 d.

Damage/Repairs/Replacement: Splat (oak) replaced.

FASHIONABLE CHAIRS
18th Century & Regency Period

CHAPTER 3

FASHIONABLE CHAIRS
18th Century & Regency Period

The Manx National Heritage collection has a small number of fashionable chairs dating from the 18th and early - 19th centuries. Notable amongst these are a group of three walnut chairs dating from *circa* 1720 (No. 80 A - C). These have the fashionable cabriole legs which epitomise metropolitan-made chairs from that period. The front legs have foliate carvings on their knees, and the backs of the chairs are made with curved splats and back uprights which are shaped to fit the human shape.

A mahogany day bed dating from the 18th century, *circa* 1740, is also present in the collection (No. 85). This was made at the end of the period when such items were fashionable, by a skilled cabinet maker who used elements of contemporary chair design to produce a striking, if *retardataire*, day-bed.

Other chairs in this group include a provincially interpreted mahogany armchair, *circa* 1780 (No. 81) which is influenced by Thomas Chippendale's designs. Two *faux* bamboo chairs from the Regency period are also included in the collection (Nos. 82 and 83), as is a fashionable mahogany side chair (No. 84) with a tablet top rail, probably inspired by the designs of Thomas Hope.

Fig.3.1; A walnut side chair with fasionable cabriole shaped legs.

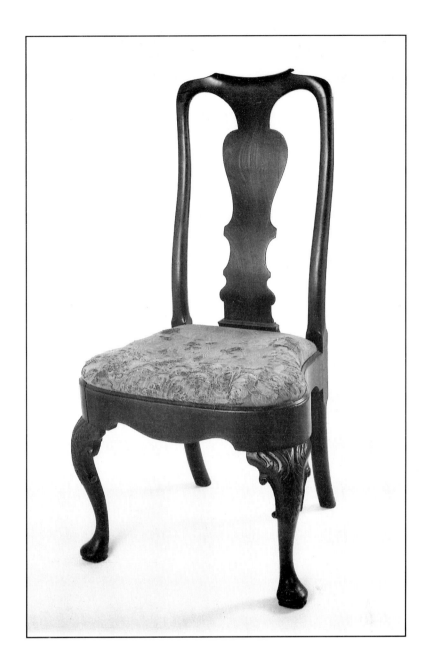

Catalogue No: **80** A - C.

Item: Three walnut side chairs with cabriole legs.

Date of Manufacture: Circa 1720.

Description: Three walnut side chairs, with carved foliate decoration to the front of the cabriole shaped legs. The curved back uprights support shaped top rails and curves. Vasiform-shaped back splats. The drop-in upholstered seats have worn fabric covers, which fit into curvilinear shaped seat frames. These are made of oak and veneered on their outer surfaces with walnut.

Woods: *Primary:* Walnut.

       Secondary: Oak seat frame, veneered in walnut, variously incised III, IV and V, on inner surface.

Dimensions: A. 103 hh 60.5 h 51 w 41 d.   B. 103 hh 61 h 51.5 w 41 d.   C. 103 hh 61 h 54 w 41 d.

Noteworthy Construction Details: All pegged construction.

Damage/Repairs/Replacement:

A. Scroll on top left of crest rail missing. Later hardboard nailed under seat.

B. Broken section on right front foot. Two screw repairs to the right front and left back legs. Pedestal split out to the back.

C. Split in banding of right front leg. Carving on cresting rail broken.

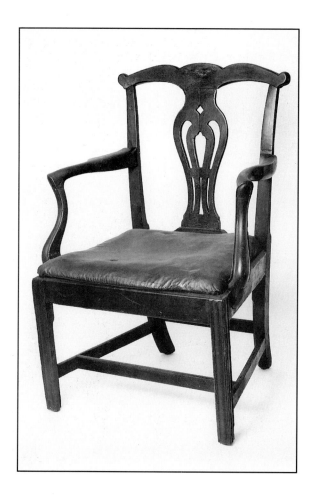

Catalogue No: **82.**

Item: *Faux* bamboo turned armchair on later rockers.

Date of Manufacture: *Circa* 1820.

Significant Accession Details: From house of Fred Cubbon, tailor of Ballabeg, Arbory.

Description: A *faux* bamboo chair of the Regency period, with neo-classical influences derived from ancient Egyptian prototypes. Made with a beech frame, this chair was originally gessoed and japanned. The seat was originally caned, and now has a replacement wooden board seat nailed to the frame. The legs are fitted to later rockers.

Woods: *Primary*: Beech.

Dimensions: 81 hh 41 h 53 w 42 d.

Damage/Repairs/Replacement: Replacement wooden seat. The seat was originally caned. The rockers, in pine, are a later addition.

Catalogue No: **81.**

Item: Armchair.

Date of Manufacture: *Circa* 1780.

Significant Accession Details: Belonged to James Cubbon, master-mariner, of Colby.

Description: A provincially made mahogany armchair with an upholstered drop-in seat. The chair was made by a competent cabinet/chair maker, who had knowledge of fashionable forms. The construction elements support this view, including the use of mitred joints at the junction of the leg cross stretchers: the use of curved cabriole under-arm supports, and 'French elbows' (arms) as well as the moulded decoration on the front legs. This chair is a regional adaptation of a fashionable chair design, dating from the mid-18th century, and particularly embodies influences from Chippendale's chair designs. The chair shows evidence of having been converted to a commode chair at some point after its manufacture, and later returned to its original form.

Woods: *Primary*: Mahogany.

Secondary: Later pine commode surround.

Dimensions: 94 hh 54 h 67 w 47.5 d.

Noteworthy Construction Details: Mitred dovetails connecting 'H' stretcher.

Damage/Repairs/Replacement: This chair was converted to be a commode. Subsequently the lower frieze 'skirt' has been removed. Nail marks on the legs suggest that a cloth frieze was nailed between the legs. Old repairs to upper right leg and left leg.

Catalogue No: **83.**

Item: Faux bamboo armchair.

Date of Manufacture: 1810 - 1820.

Description: An early - 19th century chair, described as a 'fancy' chair by specialist makers of *faux* bamboo turned furniture. This example was probably made in a metropolitan centre where fashionable furniture of this kind was made and sold in Fancy Chair Warehouses. The tablet in the upper back may originally have had a topographical scene or flower motif painted on it. The seat would have been finely rush seated and probably painted.

Woods: *Primary:* Ash.

        Secondary: Pine tablet.

Dimensions: 80.5 hh 41 h 52 w 43 d.

Damage/Repairs/Replacement: Replacement wooden seat - originally rush seated. Front stretcher missing.

Catalogue No: **84.**

Item: Side chair.

Date of Manufacture: Circa 1800.

Description: A fashionable form of side chair made in mahogany with a stuffed over-seat. This style of chair was widely produced in the late - 18th century, and throughout the first quarter of the 19th. It owes its design impulse to the furniture pattern books available to cabinet makers at this time, and particularly designs produced by Thomas Hope (1807). This example was provincially made, and although competent and well observed in its overall proportions, it has details which indicate it to be the product of a cabinet maker 'in ordinary'. See for example the unresolved reeding lines at the bottom of the left hand vertical row of three lines on the tablet-shaped top rail.

Woods: *Primary:* Mahogany.

        Secondary: Not investigated. Seat covered with oil cloth and lined with wadding over natural fibre stuffing.

Dimensions: 83 hh 37.5 h 47 w 39 d.

Noteworthy Construction Details: All glued joints, no pegs used.

Damage/Repairs/Replacement: Damage to left front leg, and lower right hand corner of top rail.

Catalogue No: **85.**

Item: Day-bed with adjustable end.

Date of Manufacture: Circa 1740.

Significant Accession Details: From Bridge House, Castletown.

Description: Day-beds were usually provided as a place to rest in the reception rooms of prosperous households during the 17th century and into the 18th. This example was made in the 18th century, at the end of its period of fashionable use. It was made in a cabinet shop practiced in making fashionable furniture in mahogany, and it is expertly observed in its constructional detail. The reclining end is unusually hinged and supported on two chains.

Woods: *Primary:* Mahogany.

   Secondary: Beech seat frame.

Applied Surface Finish: Probably stained and varnished originally, now oxidised to a dark mahogany colour.

Dimensions: 55 hh 41 h 75 w 186 d.

Noteworthy Construction Details: Pegged construction.

Damage/Repairs/Replacement: Two wooden cross supports below the mattress are missing on base. Five original castors, one oversized one.

CORNER CHAIRS

CHAPTER 4

CORNER CHAIRS

*Fig. 4.1. Mrs. Teare outside her Jurby home in 1897:
a traditional corner chair can clearly be seen behind her.*

Low chairs made with a triangular shaped seat to the front, and commonly called corner chairs, were made in the 18th and 19th centuries. Their name and shape certainly suggest that they were intended to be placed in the corner of a room. However, contemporary illustrations show them as desk chairs, and in use by card players.

A reference to such a chair in the Gillows of Lancaster *Estimate Sketchbook* of 1787, (344/94, p.162) illustrates and costs such a chair in mahogany and oak at 14s 3 ³/₄d.

It is described as a smoking ('smocking') chair. This title offers confirmation that such chairs were indeed intended as an alternative form of a comfortable armchair design.

Manx National Heritage has three examples of this form of chair; Nos. 86 and 87, which are simple carpenter-made examples, and No. 88, which is of a conventional 18th century design in oak and is scratch-dated 1771. This example probably originated in Lancashire.

Catalogue No: **86.**

Item: Corner chair.

Date of Manufacture: Circa 1800.

Significant Accession Details: Donor formerly of Knockaloughan, Santon.

Description: A joiner-made corner or smoking chair of the most simple form, using cleft segments of wood throughout, and made without turned parts. Bark is still in place on some segments. The back corner post is larger than the others.

Woods: *Primary:* Ash uprights, top rail and seat rail.

Secondary: Pine seat and bottom rails.

Applied Surface Finish: Initial coat of red lead paint with later varnish over this.

Dimensions: 86 hh 38.5 h 72 w 66 d.

Noteworthy Construction Details: Lap joint on rear arm corner.

Damage/Repairs/Replacement: Two front stretchers missing. Central plank on seat replaced.

Catalogue No: **87.**

Item: Corner chair.

Date of Manufacture: 20th century.

Description: This 20th century interpretation of a corner or smoking chair is made within the tradition of many Manx chairs which were produced by carpenters and joiners. The simple triangular frame is joined at the top by sawn sections to form two curved arm sections, supported at the rear by two triangular blocks. The arms and supports are screwed to the legs rather than jointed, whereas all the other joints are conventionally morticed and tenoned, and secured by pegs. The seat is nailed to the seat frame, and in design terms, the curved front seat support relieves the otherwise severe triangular shape.

Woods: *Primary:* Pine.

Applied Surface Finish: Overall stained brown.

Dimensions: 71 hh 28 h 73 w 48 d.

Catalogue No: **88.**

Item: Corner or 'smoking' chair.

Date of Manufacture: Inscribed on a false rear pedestal '1721 C' which corresponds with the approximate date of manufacture.

Significant Accession Details: Attributed to Manx manufacture in Port St. Mary/Colby area.

Description: This corner or 'smoking' chair, made in elm with a pine seat, is of conventional 18th century design. The 'spur' shaping of the arms is unusual, and reflects a design motif produced as part of the arm style of a particular chair design from the Billinge area of Lancashire, suggesting that this example may have originated in that region. (See *The English Regional Chair*, B. D. Cotton, 1990. p. 387, NW237).

Woods: *Primary:* Elm.

    Secondary: Pine seat.

Applied Surface Finish:
Initial coat of red lead paint with later varnish over this.

Dimensions: 67 hh 29 h 78 w 60 d.

Damage/Repairs/Replacement:
Right arm support is replaced.
Pine seat may be a replacement.
Metal repairs to legs.

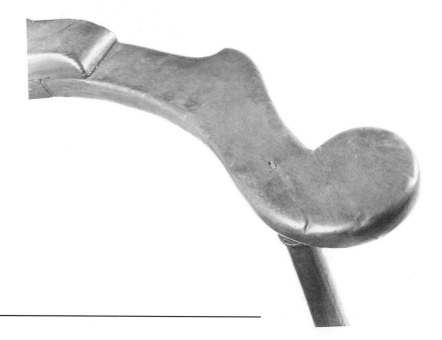

19TH CENTURY CHAIRS

Reproduction & Upholstered Chairs.

CHAPTER 5

19TH CENTURY CHAIRS
Reproduction & Upholstered Chairs.

During the second half of the 19th century, different styles of upholstered and wooden chairs proliferated. Amongst them were chairs which were made as reproductions or influenced in some way by fashionable chairs from the 17th century. These styles often reflected the rise of romanticism in the 19th century, when architecture and furniture looked to historical antecedents in which mediaeval, Elizabethan, and 17th century fashions all provided rich source material.

The Manx National Heritage collection includes a set of six chairs (No. 89 A - F) made with walnut frames, which are influenced by Restoration chairs (*circa* 1670). They show the complex techniques used to turn the curved back legs and the flowing carving of the top rail and front leg stretcher which characterise chairs of this type. The accuracy of the frame interpretation, however, contrasts with the use of upholstery in the back and seat. This is a nineteenth century preference in a chair design in which cane back and seat panels would originally have been more usual.

It is apparent that these chairs were made to a design illustrated by J. C. Loudon in 1833 under the sub-heading of 'Elizabethan Furniture for Villas' (pp 1098 - 1099) His illustration 2027 is closely similar to the chairs held in the Museum collection. Although Loudon's drawing shows a cane-work back and seat, he comments that "Flemish chairs","scrolled chairs" and "turned chairs" are either "stuffed in one upright long panel, or filled in with wickerwork (sic): the seats also being stuffed and covered with costly kinds of materials as varied as their shapes." Loudon describes his chair as a drawing room chair, sent to him by Mr. Shaw. This is probably Henry Shaw who in 1836 published *Specimens of Ancient Furniture*, showing examples from mediaeval to Tudor times based on actual items. It was this text which provided much inspiration for the mediaeval revivalist furniture of the 19th century.

A further arm chair in the collection (No. 90) takes its design from a 17th century upholstered winged arm chair with a barley twist front leg stretcher. The analogue for this chair may have had a fixed back frame: equally the back may have hinged at the seat to form a reclining back which was supported on metal ratchets fixed to the arms.

17th century chairs also included those made entirely in wood, usually oak, where the arm chairs are typically of a throne-like construction with panelled backs and often with vigorous carving or inlay decoration. The

north of England, in particular, was also the home of the wooden side chair. These are usually referred to as 'backstools', and variations in design were legion. Amongst these, a particular style is attributed to Yorkshire and Derbyshire. This has sawn back uprights terminating in crozier carved devices and with two carved and shaped cross splats which often have acorn-shaped pendant turnings along the lower edges. The chair shown in No. 91 is a copy of a chair of this type where the surface has been stripped of its original black staining varnish.

Fashionable chair designs from the 18th century were also reproduced in the 19th century. The Manx National Heritage collection has a further set of six chairs (No. 92 A - F) made in this manner, with four side and two armchairs. These were made in the second half of the 19th century, and take their design impulse from fashionable mid-18th century mahogany ladder-back chairs. These chairs adopted the vernacular form of rush and wood seated ladder-back chairs as their design derivation, and have backs composed of shaped and fretted cross splats and generous hollow upholstered seats.

Other upholstered chairs which were particularly associated with fashionable High Victorian design were made from the second quarter of the 19th century. These were made with or without arms and with rounded back frames, often ornately carved, and cabriole front legs. An example made without arms is shown in No. 93. Although closely associated with Victorian parlour and bedroom furniture, this style is essentially an interpretation of exuberant rococo expression and particularly its influence on 18th century French chair design. This in turn acted as the inspiration in England for the designs published by Thomas Chippendale in *The Gentleman and Cabinet Maker's Directory*, 3rd Ed. 1763, Plates XX, XXII and XIIII which illustrate French chairs. Similar designs were also illustrated by Ince and Mayhew in *The Universal System of Household Furniture*, 1762, Plates LVIII and LIX, and particularly in their designs for back stools (Plate LVI).

Many 19th century manufacturers were influenced by the designs produced by these and other 18th century designers, and this is evidenced in many of the chair designs which they illustrated in catalogues showing their repertoires of fashionable chairs and other furniture. The firm of Henry Lawford, for example published a pattern book in 1855 entitled *The Chair and Sofa Manufacturer's Book of Designs* in which

Fig.5.1; A 19th century side chair, showing design features prevalent in the Restoration period.

the homes of all social classes. Chairs of this type were also bought for use in all kinds of polite social contexts, for example in banks, men's social clubs, council offices and doctors' surgeries, where they formed part of a respectable and prosperous social milieu in which comfort was a secondary issue.

The Manx National Heritage collection has a number of chairs of this type, including a set of three (No. 95 A-C) made with large oak frames and foliate carving of the highest quality between the arms and seat. The backs and seats have a webbing base onto which metal coiled springs are sewn, covered with hessian, padding, and an imitation leather material. Similar chairs to these were offered by many furniture manufacturers. For example the catalogue of Wyman and Sons, 1877, illustrates similar chairs, as does the catalogue produced by C. & R. Light in 1881. A further chair of this general type is illustrated in No. 96, which in addition to an upholstered back and seat has galleries of turned spindles in the upper back and below the arms.

balloon back chairs of the type shown in No. 93 were illustrated.

W. Thoms, a "carver in general", demonstrated in his *36 New Original and Practical Designs for Chairs* that as early as 1840 chairs in the dining and drawing rooms of many households included curved backs, often of balloon shape with carved ornament and buttoned upholstery, turned and carved front legs and curved back legs.

Other forms of upholstered chairs were produced around the middle of the 19th century, and the Museum collection has an example of a turned side chair (No. 94) with an upholstered seat and upper back. The back is partly open and a wooden splat with the Isle of Man logo carved on it is set below the upholstered panel in the back. This chair, although most probably made on the Island, is closely similar to a chair pattern published by the firm of Richard Charles in 1866, which shows a floral logo in the upper back.

Of the multitude of different upholstered chairs produced in the 19th century those with massive square frames and upholstered seats and backs, often embellished with carving or galleries of turned spindles and with turned front legs, were extremely popular in

Catalogue No: **89** A - F.

Item: Six Restoration style side chairs.

Date of Manufacture: Circa 1860.

Description: A set of six 19th century upholstered side chairs, made in the style of 17th century chairs, *circa* 1670. The use of walnut for the frame is historically congruent. However, this particular style would normally have been finished with a cane back and seat. This chair is probably made to a design illustrated by J. C. Loudon in his *Encyclopaedia of Cottage, Farm and Villa Architecture*, 1833, p. 1099, illustration 2027, with the exception that Loudon's drawing shows the chair to be cane backed and seated. Loudon describes this design as a drawing room chair.

Woods: *Primary:* Walnut.

            Secondary: Upholstered in dull red velvet.

Applied Surface Finish: Shellac varnish.

Dimensions: 121 hh 71 h 46 w 36 d.

Noteworthy Construction Details: Not pegged - glued joints.

Damage/Repairs/Replacement:

A. Break on right front leg.   D. Left leg joint into seat is loose.   E. Right joint into seat loose.

Catalogue No: **90.**

Item: Upholstered wing armchair.

Date of Manufacture: 19th century.

Significant Accession Details: Claimed by donor to have been the chair of Bishop Wilson (died 1755).

Description: The visible woodwork of this armchair has the superficial appearance of 17th century design and production techniques, including the turnery devices and hand carved spiral stretcher. Close examination suggests, however, that the chair dates from the 19th century. The chair has had some alteration and at some time has been upholstered between the arm and the seat. The square front uprights were also covered with fabric at this time. The present fabric probably dates from the second quarter of the 20th century, and is of an Arts and Crafts inspired design.

Woods: Primary: Oak.

Applied Surface Finish: Stained black.

Dimensions: 105 hh 65 h 60 w 44.5 d.

Noteworthy Construction Details: Pegged construction. Hand carved spiral front leg stretcher. Marks at joints where metal supports have been removed. Seat upholstered onto frame without the use of springs.

Damage/Repairs/Replacement: Right front leg has a serious fracture.

Catalogue No: **91.**

Item: Back stool or side chair.

Date of Manufacture: 18th or 19th century, made in 17th century style.

Description: This style of chair is associated with Yorkshire and Derbyshire from the 17th century. Typically chairs of this type were stained black. The dehydrated and scrubbed condition of this example now makes it difficult to ascertain its precise age. The replaced back leg made from wood which had a prior beetle infestation indicates that it had sustained damage and was consequently dismantled, and it is also possible that the cross splats were replaced at that time. The chair may be *retardataire*, dating from the 18th/19th centuries rather than the 17th century. The use of round pegs throughout, rather than square pegs, further supports this speculation.

Woods: Primary: Oak.

Applied Surface Finish: Washed (scrubbed) surface.

Dimensions: 96 hh 56.5 h 49 w 41 d.

Noteworthy Construction Details: Round pegged construction.

Damage/Repairs/Replacement: Finials missing from lower edge of splats (five each on upper and lower splats). Back stretcher, back seat plank, and left back leg replaced. Back splats possibly replaced.

Catalogue No: **92** A - F.

Item: Ladder-back chairs (four side and two armchairs).

Date of Manufacture: Second half of the 19th century.

Description: Four side and two armchairs made in a mid-18th century fashionable style. These chairs are made with mahogany frames and with hollow stuffed over-seats which have replaced silk covers. The backs have three cross splats below a shaped top rail, shaped and fretted in the manner of ladder-back chairs. The chairs are imprecisely made with irregular mouldings to the front legs and without pegging to the joints.

Woods: *Primary*: Mahogany.

       Secondary: Oak and birch seat rails. Upholstered seat.

Applied Surface Finish: Mahogany stained and varnished.

Dimensions:

A. 88 hh 63 h 63 w (Arms) 58 w (seat) 47 d.

B. 88 hh 61 h 61 w (Arms) 58 w (seat) 47 d.

C. 97 hh 51 h 58.5 w 45 d.

D. 97.5 hh 51 h 59 w 64 d.

E. 97.5 hh 50.5 h 58 w 46 d.

F. 97.5 hh 50.5 h 58 w 46 d.

Noteworthy Construction Details: Not pegged - glued joints.

Damage/Repairs/Replacement:
A. Break in bottom ladder - replaced end piece.

E. Cross rail joint displaced and poorly repaired.

Catalogue No: **93.**

Item: Upholstered low chair.

Date of Manufacture: Circa 1850.

Description: An upholstered occasional or lady's fireside or bedroom chair, made in a fashionable design preferred by Victorians of prosperous means. The floral fabric cover is enhanced by bead embroidery, reflecting ladies' pastimes of the period, and is probably original to the chair. The chair has castors which allowed it to be moved easily when required for use, a feature which emphasises its mobile use. The flowing lines of the mahogany frame and the cabriole form of the leg represent a 19th century interpretation of the rococo form.

Woods: *Primary:* External frame and legs mahogany.

      Secondary: Not explored.

Applied Surface Finish: Stained and highly polished.

Dimensions: 82 hh 49 h 48 w 39 d.

Damage/Repairs/Replacement: Beading on front edge is loose. Moth larvae damage to fabric. Seat springs now dislodged.

Catalogue No: **94.**

Item: Upholstered side chair.

Date of Manufacture: 1887.

Description: A turned and upholstered side chair made in oak with an upholstered seat and upper panel to the back, below which is a carved splat with the Manx Three Legs emblem carved on it. The back is made separately from the lower back legs and is screwed to the rear of the seat. A similar design was illustrated by Richard Charles in 1866, in his catalogue of fashionable furniture.

Woods: *Primary:* Oak.

Applied Surface Finish: Japanned.

Dimensions: 99 hh 53 h 46.5 w 38 d.

Noteworthy Construction Details:
Back is made separately from the base, and joined at seat level.

Damage/Repairs/Replacement: Replacement on back of top. Badly broken on top of left front leg.

Catalogue No: **95** A - C.

Item: Three upholstered armchairs.

Date of Manufacture: Circa 1890.

Significant Accession Details: Abigail Faragher, Earystane, Colby.

Description: Three fashionable upholstered chairs of a style which was widely interpreted by furniture manufacturers during the last quarter of the 19th century and into the first decade of the 20th century. The rectilinear frames of the chairs are substantially made of oak. The under-arm areas have carved decoration of highly skilled execution. The upholstery is composed of a system of metal springs sewn between webbing frameworks, and covered with hessian and padding with imitation leather covers. See Wyman and Sons' Catalogue, 1877, which shows a similar chair with other styles in their range.

Woods: *Primary:* Oak in visible frame and turned parts.

        Secondary: Imitation leather top cover.

Applied Surface Finish: Varnished.

Dimensions:
A. 121.5 hh 80.5 h 62.5 w 61 d.

B. 121 hh 79.5 h 63 w 61 d.

C. 121 hh 79 h 63.5 w 61 d.

Noteworthy Construction Details: Robust construction with skilled carving.

Damage/Repairs/Replacement: A. Webbing and springing collapsed. B. Left front castor missing. Synthetic covering torn at the back. C. Webbing and springs collapsed underneath.

Catalogue No: **96.**

Item: Upholstered armchair.

Date of Manufacture: Circa 1890.

Significant Accession Details: Abigail Faragher, Earystane, Colby.

Description: A fashionable upholstered arm chair of a type which was popular during the closing years of the 19th century and in the first decade of the 20th. The chair frame is rectilinear in design, with a gallery of spindles below an arched top rail which has simple foliate carving and with galleries of spindles below the arms. The upholstered back has a small central splat below it. This example is made with mahogany for the visible frame and turned parts. It is sprung with metal springs over webbing supports and covered with a synthetic imitation leather product. See the catalogue of C. & R. Light, *circa* 1881, which shows other chairs made in a similar stylistic range.

Woods: *Primary:* Visible framing and turned parts mahogany.

        Secondary: Internal metal springs and castors.

Applied Surface Finish: Stained and varnished with mahogany finish to visible wooden parts.

Dimensions: 101.5 hh 69 h 65 w 58 d.

Damage/Repairs/Replacement: Damage to hessian below seat.

HALL CHAIRS

CHAPTER 6

HALL CHAIRS

During the 18th and 19th centuries, a particular style of decorative wooden side chair was made to stand in the entrance hallways of prosperous households. In the 18th century, such chairs often had the coats of arms of the owner carved or painted on them. They were intended partly as formal decoration in the porch or entrance hall, and also for waiting servants to sit on. This form of chair continued to be made during the 19th century, often decorated with spurious heraldic devices. J. C. Loudon (1833) commented that "This style of chair may be made either of mahogany or oak or deal (pine) painted and grained in imitation of the latter wood. In the backs are tablets or panels, for heraldic shields or crests which were generally painted but which have a more architectural effect when carved out of the solid wood, or when cast in composition, glued on and painted afterwards." The fact that in London, in 1833, they cost thirty five to fifty shillings each, naturally restricted their use to wealthy households. However, as the 19th century proceeded, chairs of this type were made at all levels of cost, and became pretentious parts of the furnishings of many bourgeois households. The Manx National Heritage collection includes an example of a hall chair of this style, amde in oak *circa* 1890, (No. 97), which is well made and decorated with fashionable motifs of its period.

Catalogue No: **97.**

Item: Hall seat.

Date of Manufacture: Circa 1890.

Significant Accession Details: Possibly made by Kelly Bros, Kirk Michael. In Rushen parish church until 1920.

Description: An oak hall chair made with turned front legs and a nailed seat which, in common with the back uprights, has chamfers on the edges. The back legs are swept backwards and terminate at seat level. The back, which is made with a central panel below a gallery of five spindles and with a decoratively carved pediment above, is fixed to the seat with steel screws.

Woods: *Primary*: Oak.

Applied Surface Finish: Stained with oak stain and varnished. Black painted carved line decoration and spindles.

Dimensions: 192 hh   49 h   45.5 w 36 d.

Noteworthy Construction Details: The back is made separately from the back legs, and screwed to the seat frame.

20TH CENTURY CHAIRS

CHAPTER 7

20TH CENTURY CHAIRS

The Manx National Heritage collection includes a number of 20th century chairs. Of these, a group of Lloyd Loom chairs illustrates a major innovation in furniture making which developed from the hand craft of traditional wicker-work furniture. The invention which made this possible was made in the early years of the 20th century by Marshall Burns Lloyd, who developed machinery for making simulated wicker-work with twisted paper. This was woven into panels which were nailed onto simplified chair frames with woven strips then nailed around the edges.

This revolutionary invention provided a method by which it was possible to mass-produce wicker-work style furniture with greater rapidity and at lower cost than producing it in traditional materials. Lloyd patented his technique in 1917, and his factory at Menominee in Minnesota expanded and found a receptive market for its products throughout America.

The right to produce Lloyd Loom furniture in Britain was obtained by the firm of William Lusty, who produced chairs, stool, desks, tea trolleys, bedroom furniture and children's furniture. Their products were popular, and their success continued until 1940 when the factory was destroyed in a bombing raid. After 1945 the firm began producing wicker furniture again, but never with the same vigour as before.

Lusty labelled and dated his products with different labels during the period of production from 1920 until they ceased trading in 1968. These labels allow for reasonably precise dating of items, and the chronology is shown in the publication *Lloyd Loom*, Lee J. Curtis, Salamander Books, 1991, pp 132 - 133. An example in the Manx collection of a chair having a Lusty's cardboard label is No. 101. William Lusty had his imitators in the 1950s, making cheaper products with plastic simulated wicker. The Manx National Heritage collection has a number of these, including Nos. 98 & 99, which carry a label with the trade name 'Sirrom' on them.

Two other easy armchairs dating from the 1950s are included in the Museum collection. These are typical of the mass-produced fireside chairs of the time and have seats and backs supported on plastic covered springs which are stretched across the frames to support synthetic foam filled upholstery (Nos. 100 & 101).

Four other chairs in the collection represent a further departure into design innovation. These chairs are made of flowing bentwood parts which are screwed together, with either drilled and pressed plywood seats or cane seats. They are made in the manner of designs by Michael Thonet an Austrian furniture designer (1796 - 1871) who produced techniques for making sturdy, inexpensive furniture by steaming and bending wooden rods into curvilinear shapes. These were exported widely to other countries in parts and then screwed together. Thonet's chair designs were made from the mid-19th century and continue in production to the present day (1992). The examples shown in Nos. 106 and 107 are typical of Thonet's designs, with round bent backs. Two further chairs are also included with round bent parts and turned spindles, forming a less conventional square back design (Nos. 108 and 109).

Other chairs in the collection also illustrate the impulse of 20th century furniture designers to work with bent wood. The first of these is an invalid chair, where the principal frame of s-shaped supports is made from bent sections of ash which are mounted on wheels (No. 110) A more recent chair in the collection, again made of bent laminated ash (No. 111) was made as part of a large group for the Manx Millenium celebrations in 1979, and represented a truly modern approach to wood technology when it was made.

The final chair listed in this section (No. 112) is an oak armchair, *circa* 1930, with classic decorative features associated with the Art Nouveau period. This chair is based on Art Nouveau motifs, and was made by the Kilkenny Woodworkers' Co-operative in the Republic of Ireland.

Catalogue No: **98.**

Item: Lloyd Loom style armchair.

Date of Manufacture: Circa 1950.

Significant Accession Details: Abigail Faragher, Earystane, Colby.

Description: A Lloyd Loom style chair. This chair is made using a plasticised material to imitate the spun fibre (paper) product used in Lloyd Loom chairs. This material is nailed over the frame and has a braided plastic edging strip nailed around the edges of the arm and back. The seat edge of the chair has a plain plastic strip edge. The frame is made in a similar way to the Lusty chairs, with a steamed and bent beech frame, but with the legs joined by a bent tubular metal frame which is screwed to them. The seat of this chair has been modified to become a commode chair. The seat is upholstered over a solid plywood seat. This chair is closely similar to chair No. 99, and was probably made by the same firm, Sirrom.

Woods: *Primary:* Ash. Under seat framing in beech.
             Secondary: Metal leg stretchers. Plastic material
             nailed over frame. Upholstered seat.

Applied Surface Finish: Simulated cane sprayed yellow.

Dimensions: 77.5 hh 38 h 63.5 w 41 d.

Noteworthy Construction Details: Metal stretchers screwed to the legs.

Damage/Repair/Replacement: Commode attachment an addition.

Catalogue No: **99.**

Item: Lloyd Loom style armchair.

Date of Manufacture: Circa 1950.

Significant Accession Details: Abigail Faragher, Earystane, Colby.

Description: A Lloyd Loom style chair. This chair is made using a plasticised material to imitate the spun fibre (paper) product used on Lloyd Loom chairs which was intended to simulate wicker furniture. This material is nailed over the frame and has a braided plastic edging strip nailed around the edges of the arm and back. The seat edge of the chair has a plain plastic striping edge. The frame is made in a similar way to the Lusty chairs, utilising a steamed and bent beech frame, but it has legs joined by a bent tubular metal frame which is screwed to them and painted in the same colour as the wooden frame. The seat is made of synthetic foam material mounted onto a fixed base board of plywood. The foam seat is covered in a brown velvet-like material, as is the upholstered cushion. The seat frame is painted gold. A black metal trade label bearing the name Sirrom in silver is attached to the back of the chair seat frame.

Woods: *Primary:* Ash. Under seat framing in beech
             Secondary: Metal leg stretchers. Upholstered
             cushion front. Plasticised material
             covering on back and sides.

Applied Surface Finish: Simulated cane sprayed yellow.

Dimensions: 77 hh 42 h 62 w 41 d.

Noteworthy Construction Details: Metal stretchers screwed to the legs.

Damage/Repair/Replacement: Velvet cover probably a replacement.

Catalogue No: **100.**

Item: Lloyd Loom style armchair.

Date of Manufacture: Circa 1950.

Significant Accession Details: Abigail Faragher, Earystane, Colby.

Description: A Lloyd Loom style chair, made using a plasticised material to imitate the spun fibre (paper) product used on Lloyd Loom chairs. This material is nailed over the frame and has a braided plastic edging strip nailed around the edges of the arms and back. The seat edge of the chair has a plain plastic strip edge. The frame is made in a similar way to the Lusty chairs with a steamed and bentwood beech frame but with the legs joined by a bent tubular metal frame which is painted in the same colour as the wooden frame. The seat is made of synthetic foam material mounted onto a base board of plywood. The foam is covered with a brown velvet-like material, as is the front seat board. The seat frame is painted gold. This chair is closely similar to chair No. 99, and was probably made by the same firm, Sirrom.

Woods: *Primary:* Ash. Under seat framing in beech.
        Secondary: Metal leg stretchers. Upholstered cushion and front. Plasticised material covering on back and sides.

Applied Surface Finish: Simulated cane sprayed yellow.

Dimensions: 77.5 hh   42 h   61 w 41.5 d.

Noteworthy Construction Details:
Metal stretchers screwed to the legs.

Damage/Repairs/Replacement:
Velvet cover probably a replacement.

Catalogue No: **101.**

Item: Lloyd Loom Lusty chair.

Date of Manufacture: Circa 1950.

Significant Accession Details: Abigail Faragher, Earystane, Colby.

Description: A Lloyd Loom style chair, made by William Lusty & Sons of Bromley-by-Bow, London. This chair is made with an ash steamed and bent wood frame covered with Lloyd Loom patented spun fibre (paper) simulated wicker cover on the back and sides. The exterior is painted with gold paint over the whole surface. The seat is upholstered with flock material over a plywood base board and covered with a leaf-patterned damask type material. This continues over the front board, and is nailed underneath and edged with a decorative braid. The rear of the seat frame has a bracket which was screwed to the underneath of the seat board to prevent it from falling forwards when being moved. The rear of the front seat board has a card label, fixed with two tacks, which states "Lloyd Loom Trade Mark. A Lusty Product."

Woods: Primary: Ash.
       Secondary: Beech front seat support. Plywood seat.

Applied Surface Finish: Painted gold.

Dimensions: 68 hh   40 h   54 w 46 d.

Damage/Repairs/Replacement:
Damage to seat cover.

Catalogue No: **102.**

Item: Lloyd Loom Lusty chair.

Date of Manufacture: Circa 1950.

Significant Accession Details: Abigail Faragher, Earystane, Colby.

Description: A Lloyd Loom style chair, made by William Lusty & Sons of Bromley-by-Bow, London. This chair is made with a beech steamed and bent wood frame covered with the Lloyd Loom patented spun fibre (paper) simulated wicker. The exterior is painted with pink/red paint over the whole surface and overpainted with gold paint inside the back and sides. The seat (now missing) was probably similar to that in chair No. 101, which is upholstered with flock material over a plywood base board. The rear of the seat frame shows a bracket outline with three screw holes. This was probably screwed to the underneath of the seat board to prevent it from falling forwards when being moved. The rear of the front seat board shows outline evidence of a card label being fixed with two tacks. The date 'MAR 54' is indented, and this is probably the chair's date of manufacture.

Woods: *Primary:* Beech legs and stretchers.
           Secondary: Ash front strip.

Applied Surface Finish: Painted gold and pink.

Dimensions: 69.5 hh 36.5 h 52 w 40 d.

Damage/Repairs/Replacement:
Seat with cushion attached is missing.

Catalogue No: **103.**

Item: Lloyd Loom Lusty chair.

Date of Manufacture: Circa 1950.

Significant Accession Details: Maker's label - Sirrom. Chair used in the Hydro Hotel, Port Erin.

Description: A Lloyd Loom style chair, made using plasticised material to imitate the spun fibre (paper) product used in Lloyd Loom chairs which was intended to simulate wicker furniture. The material is nailed over the frame and has a plain plastic edging strip nailed around its base, and a woven edge strip around the back edge. The frame is made in a similar way to Lusty's chairs, utilising a steamed and bent beech frame, but the legs are united by a bent tubular metal frame which is screwed to them. The seat is made with a solid plywood base board which is fixed to the seat frame and upholstered with flock, covered with a patterned silk damask-type material. This extends over and down the front of the chair, and is nailed to the frame. The chair is painted with bronze-gold paint. A maker's tin label is nailed to the rear rim of the seat showing the trade name Sirrom.

Woods: *Primary:* Beech.
           Secondary: Pine seat front. Metal leg stretchers. Plastic material nailed over frame. Upholstered seat.

Applied Surface Finish: Bronze-gold painted surface.

Dimensions: 75 hh 35.5 h 44 w 43.5 d.

Damage/Repairs/Replacement:
Upholstery fabric is worn, revealing flock stuffing.

Catalogue No: **104.**

Item: Upholstered Bergère style chair (tub chair).

Date of Manufacture: Circa 1950.

Significant Accession Details: Abigail Faragher,
Earystane, Colby.

Description: An upholstered chair made with a beech frame
which is sprayed with a dark brown synthetic spray sealer.
The shape of the curved arm is inspired by a Bergère style
chair. The seat cushion has springs internally and is also
supported on seven plastic-covered springs which are held
back-to-front across the seat frame. The sides and back are
filled with synthetic foam which is covered by a fabric cover
which is decorated with a woven Lion, Unicorn, Rose, and
Thistle, in a repeated linear pattern. This pattern may
indicate that the chair design coincides with the Festival of
Britain (1950), which had these motifs as festival symbols.
This chair bears no maker identification, but was probably
made by a manufacturer from the furniture-making centre of
High Wycombe, Bucks.

Woods: Primary: Beech.

Applied Surface Finish: Spray-on sealant and varnish.

Dimensions: 73 hh 38 h 61 w 46 d.

Catalogue No: **105.**

Item: Cintique armchair.

Date of Manufacture: Circa 1950.

Significant Accession Details: Abigail Faragher,
Earystane, Colby.

Description: An upholstered armchair with a beech frame.
The synthetic foam filled back and seat cushions are
removable from the frame and are supported on a network of
plastic-covered springs which are stretched across the back
and seat frameworks. A label sewn to the underside of the
seat cushion states that 'This is a Cintique Chair.' The arms
are padded and upholstered, and the visible wooden frame is
sprayed with a dark brown synthetic spray sealer.

Woods: Primary: Beech.

Applied Surface Finish: Synthetic spray sealer finish.

Dimensions: 98 hh 62.5 h 61 w 52 d.

Noteworthy Construction Details: Upholstered seat and
back cushions filled with synthetic foam over plastic-covered
metal springing.

Damage/Repairs/Replacement: Original upholstery fabric
covered with a later floral cotton tie-on cover.

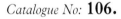

Catalogue No: **106.**

Item: Child's bentwood high chair with tray.

Date of Manufacture: Circa 1920.

Description: This child's table or high chair is from the bentwood range of chairs which was popular in England and on the Continent from the mid-19th and continues into the 20th century. Bending turned parts to create seating forms was a particularly innovative technique originally developed by Michael Thonet, an Austrian furniture designer in the mid-19th century.

Woods: Primary: Beech.

Applied Surface Finish: Japanned.

Dimensions: 97.5 hh 39.5 h 37 w 35 d.

Damage/Repairs/Replacement: Cane seat and back panel damaged. Footboard missing.

Catalogue No: **107.**

Item: High bentwood side chair.

Date of Manufacture: Circa 1920.

Significant Accession Details: A chair used by customers of Moore's Milliners, Strand Street, Douglas.

Description: A high bentwood chair made of steamed and bent beech parts, with a later plywood seat. It is made to a pattern developed by Michael Thonet, an Austrian furniture designer who in the 19th century pioneered a method of steaming and bending wooden rods which could be assembled to form chairs of different designs.

Woods: *Primary:* Beech.
              Secondary: Replaced plywood seat.

Applied Surface Finish: Black painted finish.

Dimensions: 91 hh 31 h 33 diam.

Noteworthy Construction Details: Bentwood chair made of steamed and bent parts which are screwed together.

Damage/Repairs/Replacement: Original cane seat replaced with plywood.

Catalogue No: **108.**

Item: Bentwood rocking chair.

Date of Manufacture: Circa 1920.

Description: A fashionable mass-produced chair from the bentwood range of chairs, designed by Michael Thonet, which were popular in England and on the Continent from the mid-19th and into the 20th century. Chairs of this type used innovative techniques of mechanically steaming and bending turned parts and in this case incorporating these with turned backs and steamed and pressed plywood seats.

Woods: *Primary:* Beech.
          Secondary: Plywood seat.

Applied Surface Finish: Dark varnish.

Dimensions: 92 hh 59.9 h 45 w 43 d.

Damage/Repairs/Replacement: Seat is a replacement.

Catalogue No: **109.**

Item: Bentwood armchair.

Date of Manufacture: Circa 1920.

Description: A bentwood armchair. The turned parts are in beech, with a bent seat support and leg stretchers in beech or birch. The arms are made in elm. The seat is made of plywood steamed, drilled and mechanically pressed to shape.

Woods: *Primary:* Birch or beech.
          Secondary: Elm arms. Plywood seat.

Applied Surface Finish: Originally mahogany stained, but now painted brown with varnish over this.

Dimensions: 98 hh 56.5 h 59 w 48 d.

Noteworthy Construction Details: Back legs bolted into seat support. Seat support steamed and bent.

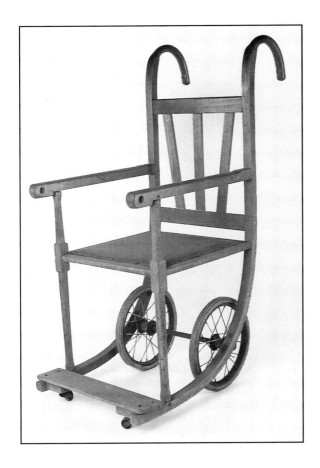

Catalogue No: **110.**

Item: Invalid chair.

Date of Manufacture: Circa 1920.

Significant Accession Details: Used in original Noble's Hospital in Douglas, the building which now houses the Manx Museum.

Description: An invalid wheel chair made from two steamed and bent continuous shaped back uprights made of ash. The back is composed of two cross rails supporting three flat uprights. The seat frame is tenoned to the bent uprights to the rear, and to two turned front legs which have simple Art Nouveau forms. The straight arms end in holes through which a restraining bar could be passed, or perhaps a folding tray table fitted. The seat is unusually deep front to back, presumably to allow cushions to be placed behind the invalid, and has a thin layer of padding with an imitation leather cover. The chair has a foot rest above two small front wheels (one broken). The two rear wheels are of a simple spoke type made for perambulators, and have solid rubber tyres. A round maker's plastic identification badge is set into the rear of the seat rail, and is imprinted 'British made. EEDEE'.

Woods: Primary: Ash back legs, horizontal rails and seat surround. Beech splats, front legs, arms and foot rest.

Dimensions: 114 hh 66 h 49 w 48 d.

Noteworthy Construction Details: Arms morticed and dowelled into back legs.

Damage/Repairs/Replacement: Restraining bar or tray-table missing. Right front castor missing.

Catalogue No: **111.**

Item: Ceremonial chair.

Date of Manufacture: 1979.

Significant Accession Details: Made by Remploy, Cardiff, for the Isle of Man Millenium of Tynwald celebrations.

Description: An armchair made from laminated ash, with a synthetic foam-filled upholstered seat. The back has a Viking ship emblazoned on it.

Woods: Primary: Ash laminate.

Applied Surface Finish: Varnished over natural wood.

Dimensions: 94 hh 51.5 h 66.5 w 48.5 d.

Noteworthy Construction Details:
Steamed and bent construction.

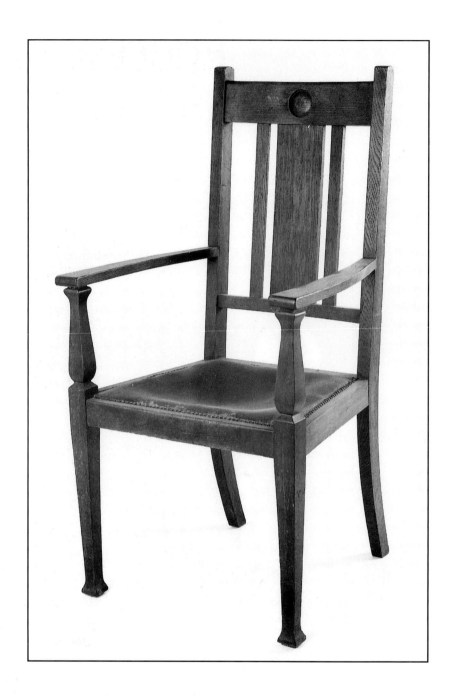

Catalogue No: **112.**

Item: Armchair.

Date of Manufacture: Circa 1930.

Significant Accession Details: Abigail Faragher, Earystane, Colby.

Description: An oak armchair of fashionable design from the Art Nouveau period, made by the Kilkenny Woodworkers' Co-operative in the Republic of Ireland (Design No. 094). The frame is made entirely of oak and the seat, now covered with a fabric and nailed around the edges, shows evidence of originally having had a drop-in seat. The design of the chair exhibits the stylised and simplified, often organic, forms which characterise this school of design.

Woods: Primary: Oak.

Applied Surface Finish: Sealed with varnish.

Dimensions: 112 hh 68 h 60 w 48 d.

Noteworthy Construction Details: All glued joints, no pegging.

Damage/Repairs/Replacement: Original drop-in seat replaced.

ECCLESIASTICAL 'GLASTONBURY' CHAIRS

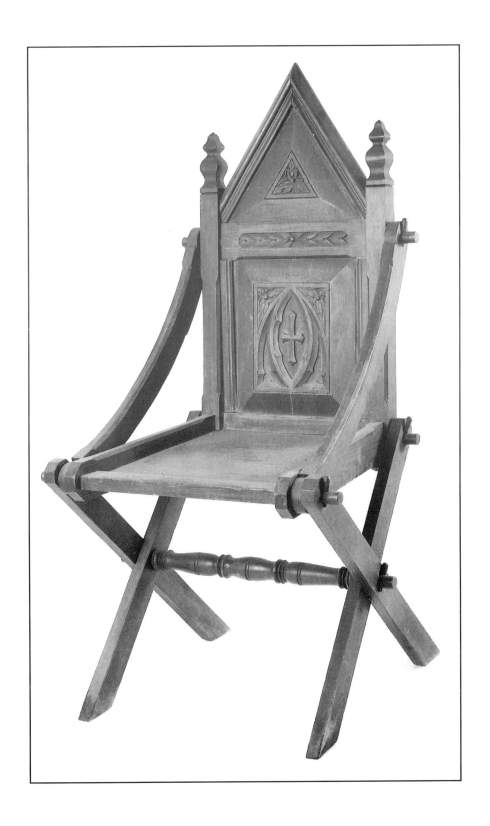

CHAPTER 8

Ecclesiastical 'Glastonbury' Chairs

Fig.8.1; St. Peter's Church, Peel. Two chairs, one presumably No.113, can be seen to either side of the altar.

Arm chairs form part of a long tradition of church furnishings in Britain, and chairs variously dating over the past four hundred years, often provided for visiting Bishops to parish churches, abound. Of these, a particular ecclesiastical style known as the 'Glastonbury' chair is probably the most common. Chairs of this type have 'X' framed bases, wooden seats and backs and flat shaped arms. These are jointed so that a chair can be folded or dismantled by virtue of a system of round tenons which protrude through the sides and are pegged through their ends to hold them in place. This form of tenoning and pegging enabled the chairs to be knocked apart: the presumption being that the chair could be transported to provide a seat for an important person, a Bishop in particular.

Chairs of this type are known from the end of the 16th century, and were probably derived from an Italian prototype. However, the term 'Glastonbury' chair derives from Henry Shaw's *Specimens of Ancient*

Furniture (1836), in which he described a folding chair of this type as 'The Abbott's Chair, Glastonbury', on the assumption that the words 'Monachus Glastonie' carved on the top rail of a chair was linked to that plundered Abbey. The original chair to which Shaw refers is exhibited at the Bishop's Palace, Wells Cathedral, and there is also a chair of this type which carries the carved legend in the Glastonbury parish church.

The Manx National Heritage collection contains two interpretations of 'Glastonbury' chairs (Nos. 113 & 114). The first, made of oak in Gothic form, was used in St. Peter's Church, Peel. The second example is made in pine, of standard sized joiners' timbers. The chair has exaggerated shaped arms which are permanently fixed to the frame, and in the same way as the first example it is designed merely to create the illusion that it could be taken to pieces or folded.

Catalogue No: **113.**

Item: Ecclesiastical 'Glastonbury' chair.

Date of Manufacture: Second half of 19th century.

Significant Accession Details:
From St. Peter's Church, Peel.

Description: This ecclesiastical 'Glastonbury' chair is made of Scots pine, a wood which was widely used in the 19th century for church furniture, including pews, as well as for the internal architectural fittings. This chair has a cruciform motif carved on the back panel, a feature which confirms its ecclesiastical purpose. The Gothic form of the back design corresponds to a decorative mode commonly adopted in the period.

Woods: *Primary*: Scots pine.

Applied Surface Finish: Varnish.

Dimensions: 120 hh 74 h 66 w 43.5 d.

Noteworthy Construction Details:
Round tenon and pegged joints fixed in place, giving the illusion that the chair can be dismantled.

Catalogue No: **114.**

Item: Ecclesiastical 'Glastonbury' chair on rockers.

Date of Manufacture: Circa 1880

Significant Accession Details: Said by donor to come from an Andreas farmhouse.

Description: This late - 19th century ecclesiastical 'Glastonbury' chair is unusual in its massive form, and was probably made by a joiner using standard timber sizes cut and shaped to form the frame, and with a raised fielded panel to form the back. The top rail is shaped and the foliar fretted decoration is simply formed by turning a large bit through the rail. The dowel joints may be hand shaped. The rockers are original to the chair.

Woods: Primary: Pine.

Applied Surface Finish: Originally mahogany-stained, with later coats of paint.

Dimensions: 101 hh 68 h 68 w 41.5 d.

Noteworthy Construction Details:
Round tenon and peg construction, fixed in place, creating the illusion that the chair can be dismantled.

STOOLS & BENCHES

CHAPTER 9

STOOLS & BENCHES

Benches or forms of a simple type, made with a plank top, often with an underfrieze each side, and with upright plank ends, were used as basic kitchen seating on the Isle of Man, and were a part of many households' furnishings. Often they were used in conjunction with a long table. Mr. Kinrade of Lezayre (FLS/K/21), speaking in 1968 about life on the Island around the turn of the 20th century, described the use of benches in farmhouses thus; "Benches and forms were used, as in the farmhouse would be big days like the Mill Day when there would be a lot seated for meals".

The common plank-made bench, made on the Island (Nos. 115 - 117) illustrates a particular interpretation of this furniture item, one which was commonly made in Scotland as well as in some other parts of Britain. The other common form, made with a plank or cleft log top and with round stick legs morticed into it, appears to have been a less popular type on the Island.

In addition to benches or forms, both three and four-legged stools abound on the Island, and were used as seating for children and others to sit near the fire. In the same manner as Scottish stools, they were often called 'creepy' stools. Describing traditional life on the Island in the late - 19th century, Miss Alice Watterson reported to the Folk Life Survey in 1954 (FLS/NA/G11) that "A creepy is the name given to the four-legged stools which mothers with children used to sit on in front of the fire to bathe and feed their babies. A hole in the centre enabled it to be carried easily to any part of the room. The hole was shaped so the hand could pick it up comfortably." Examples of four-legged stools and other forms of hand-made stools are shown in Nos. 118, 119, 120 and 121.

Further evidence given to the Folk Life Survey by Mr. John Kneen of Ballaugh Curraghs in 1950, (FLS/K-J-A), also supports the idea that stools provided the common seating for children. He said, "Wooden settles took the place of sofas in the houses, and the children sat on wooden stools instead of chairs."

In addition to four-legged stools, many were made with three legs, often with a crotch-shaped top of ash or Scots pine, which were naturally forked and joined across the fork with a thin section of oak to complete the seat. Stools of this kind, (Nos. 122, 123, 124 and 125) were often provided with legs made of gorse stems. Mrs. Annie Clague of Dalby, giving evidence to the Folk Life Survey in 1949 (FLS/C/33-A)

supported this, in saying that she had no memory of three-legged chairs, "But there were three-legged stools galore - they were made of sections of tree trunk and gorse legs."

The construction of some of these stools shows evidence of mechanical sawing and finishing, and it may be that some of them were produced in one workshop which produced them as a specialised product. The use of naturally shaped sections of wood in stools and chairs was also traditionally used in Scottish Highland seating, where similar sections were used in Windsor chairs as well as stools. This particular constructional device is virtually unknown elsewhere in Britain.

In addition, stools were occasionally produced from naturally shaped pieces of wood which could be directly utilised as a seat. An example of such a stool is shown in No. 126. These, often sculptured shapes, epitomise the use of locally-grown materials which formed much of the impulse in vernacular furniture making.

Catalogue No: **115.**

Item: Bench.

Date of Manufacture:
Mid-19th century.

Description: A long bench
with plank top and vertical
ends which have sections
fitted across them to form feet.
The end supports are also
morticed through the top with
square tenons, and are
connected to the top with two
diagonal stretchers. Seating of
this type was common in Isle
of Man cottages, where they
were often used for sitting at
tables.

Woods: *Primary:*
Pine. Top made
with through and
through sawn plank.

Applied Surface Finish: Residual coat of blue paint covered by light brown paint.

Dimensions: 45 h 215 w 19 d Top 5cm thick.

Noteworthy Construction Details:
Solid end support morticed through top and feet with two square tenons.

Damage/Repairs/Replacement: One replaced foot.

Catalogue No: **116.**

Item: Bench.

Date of Manufacture:
Circa mid-19th century.

*Significant Accession
Details:*
From Ballafesson House,
Surby, Rushen.

Description:
A joiner-made bench with a
top made of a single plank,
solid vertical supports
morticed through the top,
and cross sections morticed
to form feet. The bench is
made of Scots pine.

Woods: *Primary:*
Scots pine.

Dimensions:
44 h 112 w 20.5 d.

Noteworthy Construction Details: End supports morticed through seat and feet with square tenons.

Damage/Repairs/Replacement: One foot replaced, and loose.

Catalogue No: **117.**

Item: Bench.

Date of Manufacture:
Second half of 19th century.

Description:
A bench made of pine with
plank ends, painted and
grained to simulate oak. The
original flat topped bench has a
later, additional, unpainted
seat nailed to it, which slopes
down towards the front and
was evidently added at a later
date to raise the seating height.

Woods: *Primary:* Pine.

Applied Surface Finish:
Bottom bench scumbled and
simulated as oak.

Dimensions: 42 h (originally) 50 - 52 h now 183 w 27 d.

Damage/Repairs/Replacement: One under-seat brace is missing.

Catalogue No: **118.**

Item: Stool.

Date of Manufacture:
19th century.

*Significant Accession
Details:*
Said to have been made by
William Collister of Ballanass,
Lower Foxdale, Patrick.

Description:
A pine, plank-ended stool with
two 'V' cuts fretted to create
the feet. The ends are
morticed and wedged through
the slab top, which has a heart
fretted in it. This is a
commonly used motif in Irish
and Welsh furniture. The
cross wedges securing the
tenons in the plank ends have
been noted in stools from
Cornwall. The top is possibly
made of a reclaimed piece of
wood, since the heart is not
centrally placed.

Woods: *Primary:* Pine.

Dimensions: 25 h 50 w 18d.

Catalogue No: **119.**

Item: Stool.

Date of Manufacture:
19th century.

Description:
A pine rectangular topped stool with
four octagonal shaped legs, which are
rounded at their tops and morticed
through the stool top.

Woods: *Primary:* Pine.

Dimensions: 28 h 38 w 18d.

Noteworthy Construction Details:
Legs morticed through the top.

Catalogue No: **120.**

Item: Stool.

Date of Manufacture:
19th century.

Significant Accession Details:
Said to have been used in Kerrookeeill
chapel by Tom Taggart, cellist.

Description:
A rectangular shaped stool with
rounded edges. There is a fine frieze
below the top which mortices into four
chamfered legs, which are made of
pine.

Woods: *Primary:*
Pine.

 Secondary:
Top probably birch.

Dimensions: 44 h 45 w 28 d.

Damage/Repairs/Replacement:
Repairs to top underneath.

Catalogue No: **121.**

Item: Stool.

Date of Manufacture: 19th or 20th century.

Significant Accession Details: Owned by William Corlett, tailor of Sulby, Lezayre, *fl.* 1882.

Description: A pine plank topped stool with two cross supporting blocks nailed below, into which four hand-shaped legs are morticed. A number of stool types are recorded on the Isle of Man, and the use of blocks to provide mortice points for the legs is an alternative form to the through-morticing found in other types. See No. 119 for example. The evidence of the use of a band saw on the blocks, and a circular saw on top, suggests its manufacture from mechanised joiners' shop timber.

Woods: Primary: Pine.

Dimensions: 28 h 42 w 19 d.

Damage/Repairs/Replacement: Metal bolt repair to right hand block. Legs firmed with rag washers.

Catalogue No: **122.**

Item: 'U' shaped stool.

Date of Manufacture: Late - 19th or early - 20th century.

Significant Accession Details: From Port St. Mary district.

Description: A stool with a Scots pine, crotch shaped top and a thin oak support nailed across the fork to complete the seat. Bent sections of Scots pine branches and one of gorse (replacement) are morticed through the top to provide the legs. This stool, and others of this type recorded on the Isle of Man, appear to have the precision of mechanised production, and they may have been part of a self-conscious manufacture of nostalgic 'cottage' furniture.

Woods: *Primary;* Scots pine.

      Secondary: Oak cross piece.

Dimensions: 36 h 35.5 w 37.5 d.

Noteworthy Construction Details: Top made from the crotch of a tree.

Damage/Repairs/Replacement: Left front leg replaced, in gorse.

Catalogue No: **123.**

Item: 'U' shaped stool.

Date of Manufacture:
Late - 19th or early - 20th century.

Description: A stool with an ash
crotch-shaped top, still bearing bark,
and with an oak support nailed across
the fork to complete the seat. The three
round pine legs are socketed into the
seat, and bear facet marks which
indicate that they were hand-shaped
with a draw knife or spoke-shave. The
edges of the top also indicate that they
were finished with a draw knife. The
surface of this stool was varnished.

Woods: Primary:
Ash.

Secondary:
Oak cross-support.
Pine legs.

Applied Surface Finish: Varnished.

Dimensions: 34 h 40 w 40 d.

Noteworthy Construction Details:
Top made from crotch of tree.
No wedges in legs.

Catalogue No: **124.**

Item: 'U' shaped stool.

Date of Manufacture:
Late - 19th century.

Significant Accession Details:
From Bay View, Castletown, prior to
1900.

Description: A stool with an ash
crotch-shaped top, still bearing bark,
and with a thin oak support nailed
across the fork to complete the seat.
Bent sections of gorse stems are
socketed into the top to provide the legs.
This stool, and other stools of this type
recorded on the Isle of Man, appear to
have the precision of mechanised
production, and they may have been
part of a self-conscious manufacture of
nostalgic 'cottage' furniture.

Woods: Primary:
Ash.

Secondary:
Oak cross-support.
Gorse legs.

Applied Surface Finish:
This stool has been dark stained and varnished.

Dimensions: 35 h 38 w 45.5 d.

Noteworthy Construction Details: Top made from the crotch of a tree.

Catalogue No: **125.**

Item: 'U' shaped stool.

Date of Manufacture:
19th century.

Description: A hand-made stool,
utilising a crotch-shaped section of pine,
and with three hand-shaped round legs
morticed, but not wedged, through the
top. The use of natural wood shapes in
furniture construction has a long history
in vernacular forms, where adaption of
available materials was important. The
use of a tree fork, as in this stool type, is
echoed in chairs and stools in many
dispersed communities including, for
example, Scotland and Newfoundland.

Woods: *Primary:* Pine.

Applied Surface Finish:
Initial coat of red lead.

Dimensions: 18 h 33 w 41 d.

Noteworthy Construction Details:
Round legs morticed through seat, not wedged.

Catalogue No: **126.**

Item:
Free-form wall-supported stool.

Date of Manufacture:
19th century.

Description: An example of minimalist
seating furniture in the form of a stool
produced from a naturally shaped and
eroded piece of wood. This stool has
two natural projections forming two
front legs, and the rear of the seat is
probably levelled to fit onto a fixed
support, perhaps the stone edge of an
internal house wall.

Woods: *Primary:* Unclear.
Weathered prior to use.

Applied Surface Finish:
Blackened, possibly painted.

Dimensions: 34 h 52 w 35 d.

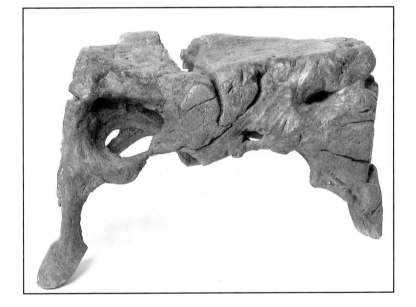

Catalogue No: **127.**

Item: Stool frame.

Date of Manufacture:
Circa 1770.

Description: The frame of a mahogany stool, *circa* 1770, which would have originally held a drop-in upholstered seat. This base has suffered much use and abuse, and shows signs of cracking and dislocation at the corner joints. The corner supports are later replacements.

Woods: *Primary:*
　　　　　Mahogany.

　　　　　Secondary:
　　　　　Brass castors.

Applied Surface Finish:
Stained and polished.

Dimensions: 43 h 53 w 39.5 d.

Noteworthy Construction Details:
Central stretcher is mitre-jointed into the side rails and morticed through them.

Damage/Repairs/Replacement:
Cracks and misalignment in all corner joints. Two castors worn, one missing.

Catalogue No: **128.**

Item: 'U' shaped stool.

Date of Manufacture:
Late - 19th century.

Significant Accession Details:
From Harry Kelly's cottage, Cregneash.

Description: A three-legged stool made from a natural crotch-shaped section of ash for the top, and with a thin oak cross-piece nailed across the fork. This stool shows signs of being made in a mechanised workshop, with precise saw cutting of the natural crotch-shaped timber which forms the top. The use of a thin oak support has been documented on a number of other stools of this type on the Isle of Man, and perhaps suggests the product of one workshop. The pine legs are shaped with a draw knife, and blind-socketed into the top.

Woods: *Primary:* Ash.
　　　　　Secondary: Pine legs.
　　　　　Oak supporting strip.

Dimensions:
31 h 42 w Slab 3.5 thick.

Noteworthy Construction Details:
Legs not morticed through the top. Legs shaped with a draw knife.

Catalogue No: **129.**

Item: Square footstool.

Date of Manufacture:
19th century.

Description: A turned stool with a birch top and with three turned legs made of beech, and a fourth in oak. Stools of this type were common in the north of England. The firm of William Brear of Addingham, near Leeds, produced large numbers of white (unstained) stools of this kind. *The English Regional Chair*, B. D. Cotton, 1990, p.208 for details.

Woods: *Primary:*
Top probably birch.

Secondary:
Legs: 1 oak, 3 beech.

Dimensions: 19 h 22 w 15.5 d.

Noteworthy Construction Details:
Circular saw marks below top.

Catalogue No: **130.**

Item:
Round stool with three turned legs.

Date of Manufacture:
19th century.

Description: An ash turned topped stool with an ambiguous central hold. Three turned legs, one of which is a replacement in pine, and one is very eroded. One leg only wedged across the tenon.

Woods: *Primary:*
Ash.

Secondary:
One pine leg.

Dimensions: 36 h 28 diam.

Damage/Repairs/Replacement:
One replacement leg. A further one is very eroded.

Catalogue No: **131.**

Item: Luggage stand.

Date of Manufacture: Circa 1950.

Significant Accession Details: From the hall of the Belvedere Hotel, Loch Promenade, Douglas.

Description: A hotel luggage stand on which guests typically unpacked their luggage in hotel bedrooms. This example was probably made by Berry's of Chipping, Lancashire, a firm which specialises in producing turned chairs, stools, and other hotel orientated seating. The top of the stand is made of mahogany, and the turned base parts are made of beech, over-painted (crudely) to appear, superficially, as mahogany.

Woods: *Primary:*
Mahogany top. Beech legs.

Applied Surface Finish: Top varnished. Base mahoganised over red lead.

Dimensions: 45 h 75 w 52.5 d.

SETTLES & SOFAS

CHAPTER 10

Settles & Sofas

Fig. 10.1: New Court Farm, Sheepwash, Devon, circa 1920
The 'S' shaped arm rests to the settle can be clearly seen.

(Beaford Centre, Devon)

Settles are wooden seats made to provide communal seating for two or more people. The most common forms have high backs as a protection from draughts, and were placed close to the fireside. Settles of this type were made in a number of English regions, including the West Country and Yorkshire. An example of this high backed type with sweeping 'S' shaped arm rests and vertical backboards is shown in Figure 10.1 as part of the furnishings of a Devon farmhouse. Other examples of a similar type made in the Isle of Man are shown in Nos. 132 & 133. Similar settles, but with lower backs in which the backboards were nailed horizontally, were also made on the Island. Figure 10.2 shows a settle of this type in a cottage at Niarbyl, south of Glen Maye, *circa* 1890. Other examples are shown in Nos. 134 & 135.

Evidence given to the Folk Life Survey suggests that other types of settles were made on the Isle of Man. These were probably closely similar to the low backed

settles which were common in Scotland during the 19th century, made with slats or turned spindles in their backs. For example, in 1966, Mr. and Mrs. Corlett of Andreas were reported to have "two long settles in their kitchen, made by a John Killip, relative of the Corletts, who was a joiner in Sulby. Both settles are well over six foot long, though one has been shortened. The seat is a solid plank, and the back of one has regularly placed slats, the other has them in fours." (FLS/C/193).

A further example of a settle of this type was described by Mrs. Mary Kewin of Andreas in 1975 (FLS/K/28-G). "A very old settle [is] in the house - made long ago by a joiner named Harrison. It is about five feet long with upright bars in the back and slightly sloping arms on either side. The wood is yellow, possibly pitch pine."

Fig. 10.2: The interior of a Niarbyl cottage at the end of the 19th century, with the settle close up to the range.

No settles of exactly this type have so far been recorded on the Island, but one which was used in Staward Farm, Sulby, now in the Museum collection (No. 136) incorporates the work of both a joiner and turner, with sawn uprights and cross stretchers to form the frame, and with a wooden seat nailed to the seat frame. The front legs, arms and back are composed of decoratively turned elements, including sixteen decoratively turned parts compared with eleven sawn sections and a nailed seat. The use of turned arms, a feature usually reserved for children's chairs in Britain, is unusual too, and further emphasises the central role of the turner in manufacturing this settle. The form of

the settle closely follows the design of examples made in Scotland, where they were commonly used in farmhouses and bothies. In a similar way to Scottish settles, the depth of the seat, front to back, is sufficient to allow a person to lie down on it as well as sit. In cultures where settles of this type were a common part of the house furniture, they often reflected the kind of periodic work which the men did, attending fish traps for example, and allowed them to rest lying down for short periods between spells of work.

Though now apparently rare, it may be that this type of settle was perhaps common on the Island during the 19th century. Certainly Mr. John Kneen, reporting to the Folk Life Survey in 1950 when he was in his 97th year, said that "they, [turners] chiefly worked with wood, and one of the chief things done was spinning wheels and repairing them. Also they did such things as legs of tables, legs of settles, chairs, and arms of settles and chairs, anything which needed turning, and thus in this way they assisted the joiner in his work".(FLS/K-J-A).

In identifying two distinct forms of settles on the Island, it is worth noting that designs were made in different regions of Britain which have not been recorded in the Isle of Man. For example, settles with cupboards in the back made to hold bacon flitches were made in the West Country. Other low backed settles were made with an enclosed lidded seat to hold household items, including logs for the fire. These were common throughout Wales in the 19th century.

In Ireland, low backed settles were made with a box form seat which would fold down to make a bed. These were found in many areas of Ireland after 1850, when they provided a convenient form of bed which could be folded away during the day time.

In the north west of England, where industrialisation produced relatively higher levels of affluence, settles were typically made in an elegant mode, in oak with raised, fielded panels in the back, often cross-banded with mahogany, and with rope seats to support a padded cushion.

In addition to wooden settles, the upholstered settee or couch became increasingly popular during the mid-19th century. The design of these owed much to the styles produced by many of the classical furniture makers in the 18th century. For example, Ince and Mayhew produced a variety of neo-classical designs for couches with double scroll ends, in their publication, *The Universal System of Household Furniture*, 1762.

The double ended settee was the common form until the 19th century when couches or sofas, as they came to be called, were made in many forms, often with one scrolled end. These included Grecian and Roman designs, as well as French rococo style, Gothic and Jacobean seats (see the variety of these forms from the sketch book of T. King, 1835, and Bridgen's catalogue of 1838.) The example shown in No. 137 of a French Empire/Romanesque-influenced design is a naive and unsophisticated interpretation which represents the unease which vernacular versions of fashionable furniture often display, in direct contrast with the competence and surety of design which the same makers usually show when working within their own local traditions.

Catalogue No: **132.**

Item: Settle.

Date of Manufacture: Circa 1850.

Description: A 19th century pine settle of small proportions, made with backboards tongue-and-grooved together, and with nailed construction throughout. The end uprights are shaped in a conventional sweeping 'S' form, a typical feature of fireside settles made in several regions of England, including the West Country and Yorkshire, where they were commonly used as inn and farmhouse fireside seating. See Figure 10.1 which shows a similar settle in a West Country farmhouse.

Woods: Primary: Pine throughout.

Applied Surface Finish:
A coat of 20th century brown paint.

Dimensions: 95 hh 52 h 61.5 w 30.5 d.

Noteworthy Construction Details: Nailed construction. Tongue-and-groove boarding used for the back.

Damage/Repairs/Replacement: One lower back plank missing. Old repair to left side.

Catalogue No: **133.**

Item: Settle.

Date of Manufacture: 19th century.

Description: A pine settle made with
vertical backboards which are butted
together and moulded to simulate
tongue-and-groove boarding. The end
uprights are shaped in a sweeping 'S',
which was the convention for providing
arm rests in settles from several regions
of England, including the West
Country and Yorkshire, where they
were commonly used as inn and
farmhouse fireside seating. See Figure
10.1 which shows a similar settle in use
in a West Country farmhouse.

Woods: Primary: Pine.

Applied Surface Finish:
Painted with 20th century black gloss
paint, worn on the seat and arms.

Dimensions: 95 hh 52 h 61.5 w
30.5 d.

Noteworthy Construction Details:
Backboards butted, but with a moulding on one side to simulate tongue-and-groove boarding.

Damage/Repairs/Replacement: Rear reinforcement of vertical backboards.

Catalogue No: **134.**

Item: Settle.

Date of Manufacture: 19th century.

Significant Accession Details: From Ned
Beg's cottage, Cregneash.

Description: A settle made of pine, painted
with traces of red lead paint and grained over
this to simulate oak. Settles of this type,
adopting two vertical end uprights with
sweeping 'S' shaped arm rests, were common
in many parts of England in the 18th and
19th centuries, including the West Country
and Yorkshire where they were usually made
with high backs to act as screens from
draughts, and were located by the fireside.
See Figure 10.1 showing a settle of this type
in use in a West Country farmhouse. This
settle is an unusual interpretation of the type,
being made with a low back of horizontal
boards (see settles Nos. 132 and 135 for
other Manx examples adopting this form of
construction).

Woods: Primary: Pine.

Applied Surface Finish:
Red lead paint with oak graining over this on the front and sides only.

Dimensions: 89 hh 45 h 186 w 40 d.

Noteworthy Construction Details: Nailed construction. False tongue-and-groove boarding on back.

Damage/Repairs/Replacement: Left support missing from foot.

Catalogue No: **135.**

Item: Settle.

Date of Manufacture: 19th century.

Description: A settle made of pine, with traces of red lead paint, and grained over this to simulate oak. This settle is carpenter made with plank construction in the back, lap-jointed and moulded to simulate tongue-and-groove jointing, and nailed to the seat and end uprights. Settles of this type, adopting two vertical end uprights with sweeping 'S' shaped arm rests, were common in many parts of England in the 18th and 19th centuries, including the West Country and Yorkshire where they were usually made with high backs to act as screens from draughts, and located by the fireside. See Figure 10.1 showing a settle of this type in use in a West Country farmhouse. This settle is an unusual interpretation of the type in being made with a back of horizontal boards, the top board having an upward curve on its top edge (see settles Nos. 132 and 134 for other Manx examples adopting this form of construction).

Woods: *Primary:* Pine.

Applied Surface Finish: Traces of initial red lead, over-painted later to simulate oak grain.

Dimensions: 133 hh 66 h 188 w 43 d.

Noteworthy Construction Details: Backboards lap jointed together and moulded to represent tongue-and-groove jointing. Nailed construction throughout.

Damage/Repairs/Replacement: Reinforcement inside legs. Seat and arm disjointed on right side.

Catalogue No: **136.**

Item: Settle.

Date of Manufacture: Circa 1850.

Significant Accession Details: Used until Museum acquisition in 1991 in kitchen of Staward Farm, Sulby.

Description: A 19th century settle made in pine, with residues of mahogany stain. This settle is made with a combination of turners' and joiners' work. The basic frame is made with common joiners' form of chair construction from the Isle of Man, which includes a wooden nailed seat, sawn uprights and cross supports, with decoratively turned front legs and arms, and with four groups of three turned spindles composing the back. This example is similar to many 19th century settles made in Scotland, where design variations included backs with low panels, vertical splats, and spindles.

Woods: Primary: Pine.

Applied Surface Finish: Residues of original mahogany finish.

Dimensions: 98 hh 49 h 199 w 51 d Spindles 23 h.

Noteworthy Construction Details: Square pegged at joints. Two planks forming the seat.

Catalogue No: **137.**

Item: Sofa.

Date of Manufacture: Circa 1880.

Significant Accession Details: Abigail Faragher, Earystane, Colby.

Description: An upholstered sofa, *circa* 1880, made with birch turned feet and a pine frame. The upholstery has metal springs stitched to webbing supports, with hessian linings over this, covered with patent imitation leather. The inexact construction of this item indicates that it was made by a non-specialist furniture maker. For example, the decorative scrolls to the front of the arms show an unskilled use of gouges. The back shows replacements and strengthening of parts with modern (1980s) timbers and steel screws. The turned feet were probably bought from a specialist sundries supplier and fitted to the frame.

Woods: Primary: Pine, possibly reclaimed timber.
 Secondary: Birch legs. Synthetic imitation leather upholstery.

Applied Surface Finish: Dark staining varnish on woodwork.

Dimensions: 102 hh 59 h 191 w 54.5 d.

Damage/Repair/Replacement: Right back leg replaced with square timber.
Backboards replaced, and tenons firmed with extra wedges.

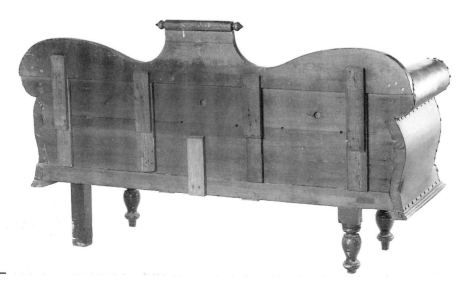

TABLES

CHAPTER 11

TABLES

Tables made for cottages and farmhouses on the Isle of Man were of both the rectangular and round topped varieties. The largest tables, made for farming families, which had to seat both family members as well as farm workers, were of the type shown in No. 138. This example, made of pine, has a sturdy joined frame with four square legs, united by stretchers which show considerable wear caused by the boots of those sitting around it. The top, which is reversible, was used on the scrubbed side to prepare and eat food, and was turned over when not in use for these purposes. Numerous references to Manx tables being used in this way were given to the Folk Life Surveyors, and Miss Annie Radcliffe of Ramsey (in October 1949) described the furnishings of Manx farmhouses thus; "There was a large table, a long form and a few chairs in the kitchen - a settle and a corner cupboard. The table was scrubbed each day after dinner. I have heard of one with a loose top which was turned each day after scrubbing" (FLS/R/3-A). The use of a reversible table top was not usual in the British Isles generally, but it was a feature of cottage life in Cornwall, and has also been recorded in other parts of the West Country.

Other smaller types of rectangular topped tables were made with a base composed of square legs joined by 'H' form stretchers, and usually with a fixed top. Drawers were often fitted into the frieze to hold kitchen utensils. Tables of this type would have stood under a window to provide a work surface to prepare food on, and would also have been drawn into the centre of the room for people to eat at, usually with benches or simple joined chairs to sit on (see No. 139 for an example of this kind of table). Rectangular tables with turned legs and two flaps which could be folded down when not in use were also used on the Island, and an example of this type is shown in No. 140.

This form of table was universally used in Britain during the 19th century, and was made by local carpenters and joiners as well as by large furniture making firms. See, for example, *Cottage and Farmhouse Furniture in East Anglia*, B. D. Cotton, p 50, for an almost identical example made by a furniture maker in North Walsham, Norfolk.

In addition to rectangular topped tables, those with round tops were also common in cottage homes. Two styles of these have been recorded on the Island. The first type was widespread, usually made in pine with a round top supported on a base of three rhomboid, triangular, or occasionally hexagonal, shaped legs, and sometimes with a lower shelf supported between the legs (No. 141). Tables of this design usually date from the late - 18th century or the first half of the 19th.

This style of table, which was made by joiners on the Island, is closely similar to those made in other parts of the British Isles. However, no 17th or 18th century examples have been recorded on the Island to date (1992). This is surprising, since round topped tables with three legs were made elsewhere in Britain from the 17th century, and continued to be made into the 20th century, as a common part of home furnishings. They were also used in alehouses, where they provided a highly stable table on uneven floors. The common contemporary term for tables of this type is a 'cricket' table, but this is a misnomer, and historically inaccurate. An authentic term from the early - 19th century is provided by *The Preston Cabinet and Chair Maker's Book* of 1802, which lists a round drinking table (p. 128) under a general heading of deal (pine) work. The pricing list shows that such tables were made with a triangular frame, with or without lower rails, or with the option of a shelf on lower rails (see *Common Furniture*, C. Gilbert, Yale 1991, figure 35). At that time the basic table, with lower rails and a shelf, cost 4s. 3d.

We may assume that the legs of the tables listed in the Preston book of prices were rhomboid in section, in order that the under top framing, or lower stretchers, could mortice directly into the legs. This is an unusual shape for the legs of furniture, and is used in tables of this type alone.

During the second half of the 19th century and into the 20th, a second style of this table was made which had three heavily turned legs (No. 142). In this case no lower shelf was provided, although occasionally these were added later.

Round tables of these two kinds, with straight and turned legs, were probably the main tables on which meals were eaten in the Isle of Man. Mrs. Corkish of Bride (1991) recalls that in the first quarter of this century her family's round table with turned legs was used by her grandmother for eating indoors, and also it was used outside for both food preparation and to eat at when the weather was fine.

Fashionable forms of occasional round topped tables have been recorded on the Island too. These have turned columns supported on three cabriole shaped feet, and a round top which would pivot into a vertical position in order that the table could be stood against a wall when not in use (No. 150). Such tables were known as 'snap' tables or sometimes 'screen' tables in the 18th century. Often these tables date from the 18th century, and they were widely used in homes during this period.

Other tables used in fashionable houses and made in mahogany or walnut also have a place in the Manx National Heritage collection. These include a folding tea table (No. 151) and an oval Loo table (No. 152) dating from the 19th century. Tables of these kinds offer us a glimpse of the types of furnishings which may have been brought to the Isle of Man as part of the property of the constant stream of incomers who found the Island a convenient alternative to living on the British mainland.

It is often not clear whether such furniture was necessarily brought to the Island; however, since cabinet makers are recorded in Douglas during the first half of the 19th century, it may be assumed that these makers' products were made in the manner of items from the British mainland.

Fig.11.1; A round topped pine table. The 3 legs are rhomboid in section, an unusual shape for furniture legs.

Catalogue No: **138.**

Item: Farm table.

Date of Manufacture:
19th century.

Description: A large pine framed and pegged farmhouse table, with connecting stretchers between the legs. The top is reversible. Pronounced foot-wear on all the stretchers indicates that this was a farmhouse dining table, seating a number of people at one time. The table base is framed with half tenons. The table end-cleats are step-tenoned at the table top ends. The four legs are cleft quarters of probably the same round 'billet' or trunk of wood. The table was painted with red lead paint with traces of later light brown paint over this.

Woods: Primary: Pine. Legs (9·5cm x 7.5cm) made from quartered sections of pine trunk.

Dimensions: 73.5 h 192 w 79 d.

Damage/Repair/Replacement: Excessive foot-wear on leg-connecting stretchers.

Catalogue No: **139.**

Item: Table with two drawers.

Date of Manufacture:
19th century.

Significant Accession Details: Part of furnishings of Harry Kelly's cottage in Cregneash in 1938. Probably made in the Port St. Mary area.

Description: A pine joiner-made food preparation table. The top is nailed to the base, which is made with four square legs connected by 'H' form stretchers. Two deep drawers are fitted into one frieze, to hold kitchen utensils. The base is painted with red lead paint with a later coat of brown paint over this. Tables of this kind were

usually placed by a window to prepare food on, and they could be lifted out into the room at mealtimes.

Woods: Primary: Pine.

Applied Surface Finish: The base has an initial coat of red lead.

Dimensions: 74 h 61.5 floor to drawer base 159 w 69 d.

Noteworthy Construction Details: Cleats nailed with iron nails. Centre stretcher morticed through ends. The top is tongue-and-grooved and fixed to the base with iron nails. Drawers entirely nailed construction. Thumb moulding round drawers' edges. Drawers measure 56 x 14, with L/R bottom boards.

Damage/Repair/Replacement: Turned handles missing.

Catalogue No: **140.**

Item: Kitchen table.

Date of Manufacture: Circa 1880.

Description: A kitchen table with turned beech legs which are painted and mahoganised, and which support a rectangular top with a central fixed section and two equally sized flaps. These may be either folded down or raised independently and held horizontal with the support of two central square section bars, pivoted in the top of the side stretchers. The top is made of alder or hornbeam, which is an unusual selection of wood for this use, pine being more commonly used for this purpose. Tables of this kind, used as an all-purpose kitchen table, were universally popular in Britain throughout the 19th century and were cheaply made by many furniture-making firms, who offered them as standard kitchen items.

Woods: *Primary:* Top and frame, hornbeam/alder.
          Secondary: Beech turned legs.

Applied Surface Finish: Base mahoganised. Top scrubbed.

Dimensions: 77 h   123 w   49 d folded   101 d extended.

Noteworthy Construction Details: Three hinges for each leaf. Unusual leaf support.

Damage/Repair/Replacement: Drawer missing. One swivel support not functioning because of warped top.

Catalogue No: **141.**

Item: Round kitchen table with three legs.

Date of Manufacture: Circa 1845.

Description: A round topped pine table. The top is composed of six sections butted and glued together, with one supporting strut screwed across below. The top is supported on a base of three rhomboid legs which are united near the base by stretchers and a triangular shelf. The base of the table shows evidence of oak scumble paint, particularly around the edge of the top. The base has several layers of brown paint over this. There are two ambiguous holes in the lower shelf, suggesting that reclaimed timber was used in the production of this table. The date, 1845, is carved under the lower tray, approximately equating with its date of manufacture.

Woods: Primary: Pine.

Applied Surface Finish: Oak scumble around edge of top. Several layers of brown paint on base.

Dimensions: 78 h 78 diam.

Noteworthy Construction Details: Pegged joints on base. Base shelf sections butted and nailed, as are those composing the top. Two ambiguous peg-filled holes in the lower shelf, suggesting that this part of the table was made from re-cycled wood.

Damage/Repair/Replacement: Has had cover on top under which furniture beetle larvae have tunnelled, leaving exposed lateral channels. Table top has been removed at some stage and replaced with one support strip missing. Evidence of use of small vice having been attached around the edge of the table.

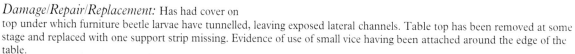

Catalogue No: **142.**

Item: Round topped table with turned legs.

Date of Manufacture: Circa 1840.

Description: A round topped table with three turned legs. The top is formed from five sections of timber which are butt jointed and glued together, with one supporting strut screwed below. The top rests on a base composed of three turned legs, which have narrow ring turnings below the frieze, and modal simulated bamboo turnings above the feet. The legs are connected by stretchers below the top, which have ogee-shaped decoration to their lower edges. The table is of a weathered appearance, and had probably been left out of doors for some time before its acquisition by the Museum.

Woods: Primary: Pine.

Applied Surface Finish: Top unstained. Base has residues of red lead based paint.

Dimensions: 72 h 78 diam.

Noteworthy Construction Details: All glued construction.

Catalogue No: **143.**

Item: Small round table with shelf.

Date of Manufacture: First half of 19th century.

Significant Accession Details: From Ned Beg's cottage, Cregneash.

Description: A round topped pine table. The top comprises three sections butted together, with one supporting strut screwed below. The top is supported on a base with stretchers and a triangular shelf. The original stretchers uniting the legs at the top have broken tenons, and have been reinforced with three boards nailed over them. The base of the table shows evidence of grain filling, with a coat of oak scumble over this.

Woods: *Primary:* Pine.

Applied Surface Finish: Base has residues of oak scumble.

Dimensions: 73 h 55 diam.

Noteworthy Construction Details: One supporting strut under top. Top planks butted and glue-jointed.

Damage/Repairs/Replacement: Repairs to under top frieze.

Catalogue No: **144.**

Item: Round topped table.

Date of Manufacture: First half of 19th century.

Significant Accession Details: From Ned Beg's cottage, Cregneash.

Description: A pine round topped table. The top is made from four sections which are butted and glue-jointed together. There is one supporting stretcher below the top and a further supporting block also present. The top is nailed to the base of three legs which are unusual in having six facets, in section, contrasting with the more usual rhomboid shape. The legs are joined at the top with plain stretchers. The top of the table is unstained, in the conventional manner, and the base is mahoganised.

Woods: *Primary:* Pine.
   Secondary: Cleft oak supporting blocks.

Applied Surface Finish: Top unstained. Base mahoganised with lead based paint, with a coat of brown paint over this.

Dimensions: 76.5 h 67 diam.

Noteworthy Construction Details: Base glued, not pegged. Top butt-jointed. Six facets on legs, rather than four.

Damage/Repairs/Replacement: Top possibly a replacement. Marks of a clamp which has been tightened onto the top. Two supporting blocks missing.

Catalogue No: **145.**

Item: Round kitchen table with three legs.

Date of Manufacture: Circa 1840.

Description: A round topped pine table. The top comprises five sections butted and glued together, with one long supporting strut screwed below, and three other later struts fixed as added support. The top is supported on a base of three triangular shaped legs which are united near the base with stretchers and a triangular shaped shelf. The base of the table shows evidence of being painted with red lead paint over which coats of brown and black paint have been added.

Woods: Primary: Pine.

Applied Surface Finish: Originally painted with red lead, followed by brown, then black paint on base. The top appears always to have been unpainted, and would have been washed off to clean it.

Dimensions: 76.5 h 77 diam.

Noteworthy Construction Details: Five planks to the top, butted together. Base through-pegged under top support (skirt). The tray is glue-jointed.

Damage/Repairs/Replacement: Three later struts support the table top.

Catalogue No: **146.**

Item: Round topped three-legged table.

Date of Manufacture: Circa 1850.

Significant Accession Details: From Harry Kelly's cottage, Cregneash.

Description: A round topped pine table, the top showing evidence of decay and unevenness. The top comprises five sections butted and glued together, with one supporting strut screwed below. It is supported on a base of three rhomboid legs, which are united near the base with stretchers and a triangular shelf. This has butted boards moulded to simulate tongue-and-groove joints. The base of the table shows evidence of having been painted with red lead, with coats of blue and brown paint.

Woods: Primary: Pine.

Applied Surface Finish: Initial red lead, over-painted with blue paint, and later brown paint.

Dimensions: 65 h 79.5 diam.

Noteworthy Construction Details: The base is pegged at joints. The top and shelf are nailed. One cross support screwed under the top. The tray and top are made of butt-jointed planks and the trayboards are moulded to simulate tongue-and-groove boarding. Legs rhomboid in section.

Damage/Repairs/Replacement: The table is not level. One support stretcher replaced. Top has been removed and relocated at a slightly different position.

Catalogue No: **147.**

Item: Round topped table with turned legs.

Date of Manufacture: Circa 1880.

Description: A 19th century round topped table made of
pine. The top has four sections which are butted and glue-
jointed together, supported by a cross stretcher screwed
below. The top rests on a base of three turned legs which are
decorated with a large ball and concave turning motif. The
legs are connected by stretchers below the top, each of which
is made in two pieces, with ogee curves fretted along the
lower edges.

Woods: *Primary:* Pine.

Applied Surface Finish: Top unstained. Base mahogany
stained.

Dimensions: 71 h 88.5 diam.

Noteworthy Construction Details: All nailed
construction to the base. Four-piece top with one central
supporting strut. Frieze sides made in two pieces.

Catalogue No: **148.**

Item: Round topped table.

Date of Manufacture: Circa 1880.

Significant Accession Details: From Ned Beg's cottage,
Cregneash.

Description: A 19th century pine round topped table which
has a top comprised of three sections butt-jointed and glued
together, supported by a cross-stretcher screwed below. The
three turned legs have inverted cup and incised line
decoration. The legs are united by stretchers decorated with
an ogee curve to the lower frieze edges, and are now also
joined by a lower shelf, which is a later addition. The top is
unstained, and the base was stained mahogany. One of the
shelf boards is stencilled underneath 'W.S. Gibb, Port Erin.
MAN.'

Woods: *Primary:* Pine.

Applied Surface Finish: Base has been mahogany stained.

Dimensions: 72 h 83 diam.

Noteworthy Construction Details: All glued
construction. One strut supporting top. Top comprised of
three planks.

Damage/Repairs/Replacement: The shelf which is
rebated into the legs is an addition. One corner support
block missing.

Catalogue No: **149.**

Item: Round topped table.

Date of Manufacture: Circa 1880.

Description: A pine round topped table. This table is probably made with a top which came from another table, composed of three sections with a thin edging strip nailed around its edge. The top is now nailed to a framework of three legs triangular in section, which are crudely united below the top with three stretchers nailed to the outside of the legs. The legs are decoratively faceted with chamfers.

Woods: *Primary:* Pine.

Applied Surface Finish: The surface was originally gessoed, with coats of white paint, and a recent coat of black paint.

Dimensions: 61 h 46 diam.

Noteworthy Construction Details: Nailed construction, including frieze boards. One strut supporting top.

Damage/Repairs/Replacement: Broken at bottom of one leg.

Catalogue No: **150.**

Item: Pedestal table with a tilt top.

Date of Manufacture: Circa 1770.

Description: This example is of a classical generic style which was perhaps the most widely made and convenient form of occasional table made during the 18th and early - 19th centuries. The top could be folded vertically in order that the table could be stood against a wall when not in use. Such tables were made in varying degrees of embellishment, craftsmanship and woods, and were to be found in homes across all social classes in the 18th and 19th centuries. Made from mahogany, this restrained piece exhibits the craftmanship of a thoroughly trained cabinet maker and turner, with precise shaping, turning and carving techniques. The feet are dovetailed into the base in the manner conventional for this form of table. The top has been removed at some time and realigned, and the pivoting mechanism has been replaced in birch.

Woods: *Primary:* Mahogany.
Secondary: Birch (replacement pivots).

Applied Surface Finish: Originally varnished.

Dimensions: 70 h 69.5 diam.

Noteworthy Construction Details: Brass 'Y' support underneath pedestal to support the swept feet. The top pivots on two wooden pegs. Foot pads integral with legs, but marked with an indent to simulate a pad.

Damage/Repairs/Replacement: Top has been realigned. One foot has been broken and restored. Birch pivots are replacements.

Catalogue No: **151.**

Item: Tea table.

Date of Manufacture: Circa 1820.

Description: A Regency period mahogany folding tea table. The top is mahogany, with a broad band of rosewood cross-banding around the edges of the top, and a frieze of mahogany veneered onto birch or pine. The base has a turned pillar supported on four curved feet, made in the French neo-classical manner, and leaf carving on the knee of each leg. Cast brass animal paw castors are fitted to each foot. The table top swivels and folds open to form a square table on which tea could be served, as opposed to similar tables which had green baize attached to the inner surfaces of the top, on which cards were played. A well is formed between the top and the floor attached to the frieze, which could be used to hold small items or perhaps a table cloth. Tables of this type became fashionable during the first half of the 19th century and continued to be made, with increasing flamboyance, throughout the second half of the century when they formed a popular part of the furnishings of fashionable homes.

Woods: *Primary:* Mahogany (both solid and veneered).
           Secondary: Frieze veneered onto softwood, probably birch or pine. Rosewood cross-banding. Brass castors.

Applied Surface Finish: Highly polished.

Dimensions: 72.5 h 91 w 45.5 d (folded) 91 d (extended).

Damage/Repairs/Replacement: Some cross-banding missing on top. Veneers missing on back frieze.

Catalogue No: **152.**

Item: Pedestal table.

Date of Manufacture:
Circa 1860.

Description: A separate top and base of a large folding oval-topped dining table, with a central column and four branched feet. Made with both veneered and solid walnut, this form of table was made by furniture manufacturers in many parts of Britain throughout much of the 19th century, beginning about 1840. They were made in various sizes as fashionable items for many Victorian homes, and with different qualities of workmanship and materials for purchasers of differing socio-economic status. The top, separated from the base, has been crudely stripped of its veneers, which were probably walnut, and now shows the damaged oak substrate. The original walnut edging strip is intact. The blocked skirt below the top was also originally veneered, and this, too, has been stripped off. The cross framing below the top is elm. The ornate base is made in a 19th century interpretation of the rococo style, with extravagant mouldings to the extended feet, terminating in

French conch-style carved mouldings, which have castors fitted below. The 'bed' on which the top fits is made of elm, and parts of the base are veneered in flamboyantly grained walnut.

Tables of this kind were made by many makers of fashionable furniture during the 19th century. Some of them produced catalogues showing their range of designs. Amongst these, the firm of William Smee and Sons of London produced designs for similar tables, with various shapes of tops on bases closely similar to the example catalogued here.

Woods: *Primary:* Walnut base (solid and veneer). Oak top.
            Secondary: Pine 'skirt'. Elm under-frame. Pine and elm tilt mechanism.

Applied Surface Finish: Originally French polished.

Dimensions: 71 h 101 w Top 103 x 142.

Damage/Repairs/Replacement: Much veneer missing.
One piece of carving missing on foot.

Catalogue No: **153.**

Item: Tilt-top snap-top table.

Date of Manufacture: Circa 1770.

Description: This table is made with a combination of unrelated parts. The tripod base, made in elm or ash, is of a conventional 18th century pattern which would originally have held a round top. This would have tilted on a square platform held on top of the central upright or stem. The under-sized top now fitted is a replacement in pine, fixed to the original platform. The three feet have been raised above their normal height by the addition of thick under-pads.

Woods: *Primary:* Elm or ash base.
          Secondary: Pine replacement top.

Applied Surface Finish: Painted brown.

Dimensions: 73 h 52 diam.

Damage/Repairs/Replacement: Top has been replaced. Feet raised.

Catalogue No: **154.**

Item: Writing table.

Date of Manufacture: Circa 1850.

Description: A library or writing table made in oak, stained black, with pine as the secondary wood. The top is covered with two panels of simulated leather. The two frieze drawers are missing. This table is made in the mannerist Renaissance style as part of the mediaeval revival movement in furniture and architectural design during the second quarter of the 19th century, a style which continued in various forms until the end of the century. This example has carved and turned end supports in 17th century Italianate manner, and classical foliate carving along each vertical face, of a type commonly used by 17th century English oak furniture makers. Furniture of this type was widely made during the 19th century, incorporating many motifs from furniture dating from the mediaeval period to the 17th century - see Richard Bridges, who produced a prominent book in 1838 entitled *Furniture and Candelabra and Interior Decoration* which included items in the Gothic, Grecian, and Elizabethan styles, and was influential in disseminating furniture designs and mannerist decorative motifs to furniture makers.

Woods: *Primary:* Oak.
   Secondary: Pine in-fills in panels in top.

Applied Surface Finish: Oak, stained black.

Dimensions: 77 h 130 w 49 d.

Damage/Repairs/Replacement: Two drawers missing.

Catalogue No: **155.**

Item: Occasional table.

Date of Manufacture: Circa 1910.

Significant Accession Details: Abigail Faragher, Earystane, Colby.

Description: A small occasional table made entirely of mahogany. The top has a thumb moulded edge on all sides, and is fixed to the base with steel screws, screwed from below. The absence of a drawer in the frieze and the moulded edge present on all sides suggests that this table was originally made to stand in the centre of a room. The slender tapered legs are supported by later pine stretchers nailed to the outside of the legs.

Woods: *Primary:* Mahogany.
            Secondary: Pine stretchers (additions).

Applied Surface Finish: Black paint.

Dimensions: 77 h 66.5 w 45 d.

Noteworthy Construction Details: Screwed and glued construction.

Damage/Repairs/Replacement: Extra stretchers attached to the legs.

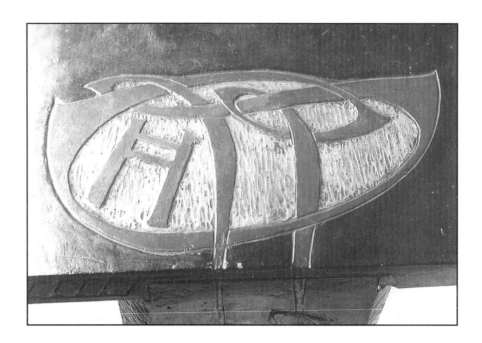

Catalogue No: **156.**

Item: Hall table.

Date of Manufacture: Circa 1920.

Significant Accession Details: Made by P. E. Humphrys.

Description: A hall table made by P. E. Humphrys in the manner of Archibald Knox. This table is made of beech and painted over-all with black matt paint. The Celtic entwined motifs at each end of the top include the initials L and H, and are highlighted in red and gold paint. The end supports are gouge carved on their edges to simulate timber from which the bark has been peeled. The outside faces have a cascading motif which is continuous with the motifs on the top. The motifs have a cut-away ground which also shows similar gouge carving as a decorative background. The end supports are morticed into cross feet, and connected between the uprights with two square stretchers onto which a lidded box is also highlighted in red with a gold background. The design of this table illustrates many of the radical stylistic structures associated with the Arts and Crafts movement, combined with strong themes from traditional sources - in this case a table with a box fixed to the stretchers to hold small items (perhaps gloves or scarves). The Celtic motifs are directly traceable to the influence of Archibald Knox (1864 - 1933) a significant designer born in the Isle of Man who produced designs for silver and other metalwork for Liberty & Co. of London, as well as textiles.

These had complicated Celtic ornamentation and, in the case of metalwork, were adorned with blue or turquoise enamel. His furniture designs typically have tapering outlines and large elaborate metal hinges and handles. This table is technically an inferior piece in the sense that it was made from unseasoned timber which has consequently warped in most planes. The jointing techniques are, perhaps deliberately, of a simplistic and inexact form, and the end joints which unite to the top show pronounced gaps.

Woods: *Primary*:
    Beech with pine glove box.

Applied Surface Finish:
Matt black paint.

Dimensions: 77 h 113 w 44 d
 Glove box: 15 h 44.5 w 30 d.

Noteworthy Construction Details:
Circular saw marks underneath top. Plane marks on top. Glove box dovetailed.

Damage/Repairs/Replacement: Top warped.
Loose tenon of left upright into top.

DRESSERS

CHAPTER 12

DRESSERS

Throughout Britain in the 18th and 19th centuries, the dresser held a highly significant and symbolic place in family life, and in design terms was widely and often imaginatively interpreted from region to region. The dresser was the centre for the storage of items used to prepare the table for meals. J. C. Loudon (1833) suggested that it was the custom for an array of domestic items to be kept in the dresser, including "clean table cloths, towels, dusters, and cutlery, the cupboards for wines, biscuits, groceries, tea cups and glasses." In addition to the purpose of storage, the dresser was, supremely, the place to display the prosperity and taste of the household in the form of pottery or pewter ware, as well as gifts and items bought for their decorative qualities. This latter function tended to grow in importance, and 19th century photographs of household interiors show dressers with their shelves crowded with all kinds of pottery and glassware, with extra hooks often added to the sides of the shelves to allow more objects to be displayed.

The general appeal of the dresser in Britain was such that householders of widely differing economic status owned them, from cottagers at the lowest income levels to prosperous farmers and the owners of manor houses. Indeed, in affluent households two dressers were frequently present, with a lesser quality example, often made of pine, in the kitchen for everyday use, and another, usually made of a hardwood, kept for display purposes in the parlour. Other uses for dressers were possible too, and the grandest forms of dressers were made for manor houses. Examples of large, imposing dressers have been recorded in the ownership of wealthy families from Yorkshire, in particular, where they were placed on an upstairs landing. They were used to display dessert services on the upper shelves, with early morning tea services kept in the cupboards in the base and linen in the drawers.

This distribution of ownership through different socio-economic groups meant that dressers varied greatly in the types of woods used, and in the quality of their manufacture. Although no hard and fast regional rules can be laid down, it may be said that simple dressers made of pine, often painted to simulate other more costly woods, or to produce decorative surfaces, were the least costly, and that these tended to be made in the economically poorest regions, including the south west counties of Devon and Cornwall, East Anglia, and the Isle of Man, as well as Scotland and Ireland.

Other more affluent regions of England, although producing dressers made of pine as less costly versions, typically produced dressers made of hardwoods. This particularly applied to the diverse system of Welsh dressers, where oak was the predominant wood used. A preference for elm as the common wood for dressers also appears in certain regions, and particularly in the Welsh border country dresser styles associated with Herefordshire. Dressers made in the West Midlands and the North-West are predominantly made of oak, and in this region elegant, elaborate dressers with cabriole legs were made, as well as simpler forms of dresser with four straight tapered legs, and a shelf structure above which often included a small cupboard each side of the rack.

The dressers made in the North-West region are typically made of oak, and are characterised by mahogany cross-banding round the drawer edges, often on the top surface edges of the base, and on the edges of the shelves and rack cupboards as well. Such decorative devices place the Midlands and North-West regional dressers in direct contrast with the simpler forms of painted pine dressers from other parts of Britain, and were the product of a generally more industrialised and prosperous way of life.

Isle of Man dressers dating from the 19th century were commonly found in Manx homes of all types, from cottages to large country houses, until recent times. A survey of furniture on the Island made in 1991, however, showed traditional dressers to be scarce in Manx homes, although evidence from the Folk Life Survey gives evidence of dressers as a significant furnishing of cottage and farmhouse homes. Of these, two major forms were described by participants in the Folk Life Survey, and these have subsequently been confirmed in the dressers recorded on the Island. The first type was described in 1971 (FLS/G/55) as part of a general description of a farmhouse at Ballachrink, Jurby, which was of traditional form. "A large farmhouse, but the back left uncompleted - there being no dairy - the shelves under the stairs used instead. In one of the front rooms of the house, the *chiollagh* can still be partially seen - though there is a kitchen range, the recesses of the open hearth have been left open - the opening here must have been very wide - the recesses are now used as shelves, there was a goose wing ready for use in one of them. This room has the ceiling joists left exposed, the rest of the house has been ceiled in. The datestone above the porch is 1838. In the back kitchen there in the rounded arched open fireplace, which formerly must have had a fire on the

Fig. 12.1. Dresser and rack made in oak for a farmhouse near Rhayader, Wales, in 1829.
It is of large proportions, being 2.53m long. The rack can be removed from the dresser base. This dresser shows similar design
elements to the Isle of Man example No. 157. (Private Collection).

hearth - the *swee* or crane is still there on which the pots and kettles hung. The recess is now fitted with shelves. A large open dresser stands against the back wall in the front kitchen. It is very high, fitting up under the joists. The upper shelves are open and have no back, there are three drawers, and below closed cupboards. It is painted light green."

This form of dresser is of the type shown in No. 157, which is reputed to have been part of the furnishings of Harry Kelly's cottage at Cregneash. A further very similar dresser has also been recorded in a cottage at nearby Port Erin. This type of dresser closely resembles dressers made in some regions of England and Wales, with the exception that in the form made elsewhere in Britain, dressers typically have vertical boards filling the back behind the shelves (Figure 12.1 shows a similar cupboard dresser from Rhayader, mid-Wales).

Such dressers had similar uses to those on the British mainland, and Mr. F. A. Comaish of Glen Wyllin in 1949 described the dressing of a dresser (*coamreyder*) thus: "There was a grand display of old jugs, willow

pattern plates, rosy basins, gilt teapots, etc. The dresser was the pride of the cottage. It had three drawers in which were stored the spoons, knives and forks etc. Some of the spoons were made of lead, a few of horn. The greater number were metal. Under the drawers there was a cupboard with two doors which was used to store linen in, etc." (FLS/C.F.A.).

Not all Manx dressers were of this type, with cupboards in the base. Mr. Cooper of Castletown (FLS/C.J.H.) whilst describing cottage furniture to a Folk Life surveyor in 1952 when he was in his 82nd year, stated that cottages had a "locally made dresser, shelves for crockery on top and [a] row of drawers under [the] top, open underneath usually, but sometimes with doors." The first form of dresser which he describes, without doors below, probably refers to the second type of dresser on the Island which is based on a common design from Ireland which has continuous sides for the base and rack. The example shown in No. 158 is of this type, and has a rack which has open shelves without backboards, and three

Fig. 12.2.
Irish Pine dresser with continuous sides, circa 1850, from County Galway; with shell carving in the top corners of the rack, and a fretted vasiform splat in the base. This dresser shows similar design elements to the Isle of Man example, No. 158.
(Private Collection).

Fig. 12.3. The interior of Miss Abigail Faragher's cottage at Earystane, with its glass-fronted dresser.

drawers above an open base with a vasiform shaped splat in the centre, and also fan carved corner brackets (Figure 12.2 on the preceding page, is an example from Ireland which illustrates a similar design to the Manx example).

In common with other parts of Britain, a further form of dresser came into use in the Isle of Man towards the end of the 19th century. This type had drawers and cupboards below, and was either partially or fully fitted with glazed doors which enclosed the shelved areas above. Miss Janie Griffiths of Ballaglonney, Fleshwick, Rushen (FLS/G/44, 1967) in describing the contents of this farmhouse, recorded that still in the house was a "glass dresser - a dresser with a small covered-in cupboard below and three drawers above this, and the top section has glass fronted doors instead of open shelves - this was better than the open dresser." Dressers of this type, which included glazed doors, reflected changes in domestic hygiene rules and were intended to keep pottery free from dust. Other uses included keeping fragile objects free from damage, and protecting bone china tea services which were used only occasionally for socially important occasions. An example of this form of dresser was used in Abigail Faragher's cottage at Earystane, and a photograph of this in use is shown in Figure 12.3. The glazed top of this dresser was not originally made for the base, although the base shows evidence of having had a similar top fitted to it. An illustration of the base with a more detailed description is shown in No. 159.

Catalogue No: **157.**

Item: Dresser.

Date of Manufacture: 19th century.

Significant Accession Details:
From Harry Kelly's cottage, Cregneash.

Description: A carpenter-made dresser of 19th century design, with removable open shelves above a base of three drawers and two double doored cupboards, which are intersected by a central panel. This form of dresser is similar to designs made in both England and Wales, and is clearly related to this extended generic group (Figure 12.1). Some features of this dresser are, however, local interpretations in their specific design. For example, the cornice of the rack may be a unique Manx example, since it extends beyond the ends of the rack sides and finishes with square ends. The rack sides slope down at the top to fit under the eaves of a roof, and the extended cornice may have been intended visually to conceal this feature. The case is made completely without dovetail or mortice and tenon joints, and sections are joined by rabbet or lap joints, and nailed throughout, confirming the carpentry techniques used in its manufacture. The shelves are supported at their ends as they join the rack sides, with strips nailed below them. This is an unusual way of fixing shelves, which are normally simply nailed or morticed into the sides. A further dresser (No. 158) also has its shelves fixed in this way, and this too may reflect a Manx constructional device.

Woods: *Primary*: Pine.

Applied Surface Finish:
Painted to simulate oak grain.

Dimensions:
227 hh base 87 h 191 w base 39.5 d rack 19 d.

Noteworthy Construction Details:
No dovetails in drawer construction.

Damage/Repairs/Replacement: Central shelf supports a later addition.

Catalogue No: **158.**

Item: Dresser.

Date of Manufacture: Second half of 19th century.

Significant Accession Details:
From Baroose, Lonan.

Description: A painted pine dresser with shelves above, three drawers below, and an open base with a central vasiform splat and fan shaped corner brackets. The form of this dresser is reminiscent of some dressers made in Ireland (Figure 12.2) including the use of continuous rack and base sides, although in this case the sides of the shelves have been sawn through at base level to make the rack detachable. The shaped central vasiform splat is also typical of particular Irish regional dresser types, as is the use of decorative fan shaped corner brackets. The use of the sawn and nailed form of construction throughout indicates this is a carpenter-made dresser, made by someone working with experience of the Irish dresser tradition.

Woods:　*Primary:* Pine.

Applied Surface Finish:
Later matt red paint over original coat of red lead paint.

Dimensions: 200 hh base 83 h 165 w base 83 d.

Noteworthy Construction Details:
Nailed construction throughout.

Damage/Repairs/Replacement: The rack has been lowered approximately 10cm at top. The two outer drawer handles are replaced. Strengthening sections are missing from top back of rack. The sides of the rack have been cut just below the base top to make the shelves detachable.

Catalogue No: **159.**

Item: A low dresser with an additional glass cupboard above.

Date of Manufacture: Second half of 19th century.

Significant Accession Details:
From the kitchen of Abigail Faragher's, Earystane, Colby.

Description: A low dresser with a later glazed top placed above. The dresser base is made of good quality softwood throughout, and shows evidence of having been stained with mahogany stain, with layers of dark varnish over this. The top of the base also shows evidence of brown paint. This dresser is unusually well designed and commodious for an item which was often of the most utilitarian kind. For example, the two banks of outer drawers are graduated in their depth, to provide different kinds of storage, and the central cupboard, which has one internal shelf, is stylishly recessed with a shaped frieze above and a further narrow drawer above this. The glass handles are replacements; turned knob handles would probably have been originally fitted. The turned feet are original to the piece, and help to date the item to the second half of the 19th century. The piece was made by a competent cabinet maker who used dovetail joints throughout in the drawer construction, and who included complete dustboards between the drawers. The top of the dresser shows evidence of there having been a cupboard which was probably similar to the one used on it. The glazed cupboard which stood on the top of the base in Miss Faragher's cottage was probably added in the 20th century to provide a china cabinet with drawers below, and it was used in the kitchen as such. (Figure 12.3)

Woods: *Primary:* Pine.

Applied Surface Finish:
Was mahoganised, with later dark varnish over this. Top has later brown paint.

Dimensions: 211 hh base 92 h 152 w 51 d.
                        top 119 h 132 w 36 d.

Noteworthy Construction Details:
Drawers dovetailed. Full dustboards. Vertical back boards.

Damage/Repairs/Replacement: Handles are replacements. Some evidence in paint markings suggests that another top was fitted on the base previously.

CHAPTER 13

CUPBOARDS

Free-standing cupboards formed a relatively insignificant part of the storage furniture in Manx homes, with lidded chests for storing clothes and linen, and dressers for food and domestic pottery being preferred. The exception to this was the use of small cupboards located either side of the fireplace. Mr. Fred Costain, born *circa* 1885, speaking to the Folk Life Survey, described cupboards of this type. "By the side of the fireplace, not by the early open *chiollagh*, but beside the latter range type of grate, there would be one or more cupboards, one above the other. Alternatively, there was sometimes only one with a space or recess above or below, according to whether the cupboard was set at ground level or half way up the wall." (FLS/C171/B).

A further respondent to the Folk Life Survey, Mr. William Stowell of Glen Roy (FLS/KM-J) also referred to the use of small cupboards in a farmhouse at Ballaheaney, which was built in 1832, saying, "There were small cupboards in the walls, perhaps eighteen inches high and a foot deep - a candle could be placed in these, or they could be used for storing things."

Of the few free standing cupboards which the Manx National Heritage collection has, two are firmly entwined with Manx history. The first is a framed and panelled oak cupboard with two doors, made during the 17th century and used originally to hold official Manx documents at Castle Rushen, and later at the Rolls Office in Douglas (No. 160). This cupboard is made of cleft quartered oak, and cleaving marks can be seen on the reverse of many parts. The doors are each composed of eight panels, framed with chamfered and edge-moulded stiles, which are joined with mason's mitres. The corner uprights are similarly moulded at their inner edges, externally. Each door is hung with decorative iron strap hinges which are nailed in position, and the left hand door has a simple iron lock. The sides are constructed with four vertical rectangular panels framed in a similar way to the door panels.

The back of the cupboard has many layers of whitewash, and is made of massive vertical cleft oak boards, nailed to the frame, and with each board showing evidence of the side-axe marks which shaped them. The backboards are narrowed down their right hand edge to fit into a grooved mortice in the adjacent board. These form a system of interlocked boards, which are more commonly associated with archaic wall cladding used in some yeoman housing in Europe, from the mediaeval period. The cornice is a later addition, and it is probable that no cornice was fitted originally.

The internal construction of the cupboard confirms its use as a storage piece, since the upper and lower shelves appear contemporary with the rest of the cupboard. The shelves have rows of eroded iron nails at intervals, front to back across the shelves, indicating that four vertical divisions existed originally, creating five compartments to each shelf, which could have formed document storage compartments. The present middle shelf is a later replacement, as are the present vertical uprights, and there is no evidence that a middle shelf existed originally.

That the cupboard has been on the Isle of Man for many years is clear. However, it is closely similar to cupboards made in Scotland, and it may be that it was originally made on the Scottish mainland and brought to the Island. The historic Scottish term for such a storage item was aumry, aumbrey or aumbry, which referred widely to wooden storage furniture, including cupboards and dressers. A very similar example to the Rolls Cupboard is in the Highland Folk Museum collection, Kingussie (Accession No. KNE 2).

A further cupboard in the Manx collection, (No. 161), rectangular in shape and with two doors, was also made to hold official documents at the Rolls Office in Douglas. This cupboard, dating from the late - 18th or early - 19th centuries, was of all-nailed construction, from unseasoned oak. The cupboard is without feet, and was probably made to rest on a table. It has an internal flap which, when folded up, stopped the contents falling out when the doors were opened.

Other cupboards in the Manx National Heritage collection include two glazed cupboards dating from the 18th century, to hold small items (No. 162). A further fashionable style is exemplified by a wall hanging corner cupboard, made of well chosen mahogany by a competent cabinet maker. This example dates from the second half of the 18th century, and is an example of a very popular form of storage item in English and Welsh homes particularly. J. C. Loudon (1833) remarked that corner cupboards were most desirable since "in small rooms, these cupboards are very convenient, as they occupy very little space, and, for a modest sum, supply a handsome article of furniture" (p. 298). Corner cupboards originally served much the same function as a cupboard dresser, and were commonly used to house cups and saucers, glasses, tea caddy, biscuits, salt, spirits or wine, and other tableware. However, corner cupboards appear to have been scarce in Manx homes, and the example described above may have been imported from the British mainland.

Catalogue No: **160.**

Item: Cupboard.

Date of Manufacture: 17th century.

Significant Accession Details:
Formerly in Castle Rushen Rolls Office, and later in the Rolls Office, Douglas.

Description: A framed and panelled oak cupboard, with two doors and partitions and shelves internally. Cupboards of this generic type are usually fitted with pegs along the inside top back horizontal stile for hanging clothes on. This example is not fitted in this way, and the function which tradition suggests for it, to hold the Government Rolls of Mann, seems totally supported by the cupboard's internal construction. The upper and lower shelves seem original to the cupboard (the central shelf and vertical divisions being later additions,) and have rows of eroded iron nails which probably held wooden divisions, creating pigeon holes for the storage of documents. The cupboard is made in the manner of some Scottish aumbries, and probably originated in Scotland.

Woods: *Primary*: Oak.

Applied Surface Finish: Back has several coats of whitewash.

Dimensions: 197.5 h 144 w 51 d.

Noteworthy Construction Details: Vertical backboards morticed into eachother. Roof boards laid front-to-back. Entirely made from cleft wood.

Damage/Repairs/Replacement: Cornice and middle shelf are replacements.

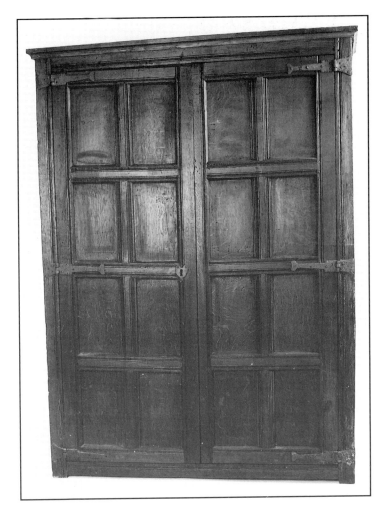

Catalogue No: **161.**

Item: Oak cupboard.

Date of Manufacture: Late - 18th/early - 19th century.

Significant Accession Details:
Used in the Rolls Office, Douglas.

Description: An oak cupboard with a pine back, made or adapted to hold documents. The cupboard is constructed from unseasoned oak, now warped, with carpentry techniques including butted and nailed joints throughout, doors made of boards, and borders nailed and mitred around the edges to simulate framed and panelled doors. Internally, a folding flap creates a well to hold documents and prevent them from spilling out when the doors are opened.

Woods: *Primary*: Oak.

   Secondary: Pine back.

Dimensions: 43 h 77.5 w 41 d.

Noteworthy Construction Details: Mitred borders create the illusion of framed and panelled doors. Three vertical boards on the back, and two on top.

Damage/Repairs/Replacement: Doors warped.

Catalogue No: **162.**

Item: Two hanging glass fronted cabinets.

Date of Manufacture: Circa 1720.

Description: Two small glazed cabinets made in pine, walnut and oak, with veneers around the edges of the two doors, and walnut glazing bars. The glass shows imperfections congruent with that made in the 18th century. The two cabinets are similar to each other in design, but with small differences in dimensions between them. These differences are combined with similar borders of vertical blind fretting on the left side of one, and the right side of the other cabinet, which, in combination with otherwise plain exteriors, indicate that these cabinets were architectural structures, probably being built into a wall as two fitments and separated by an unknown interval. It is likely that they protruded to reveal the border of blind fretting. Their purpose is therefore open to speculation, but they were probably intended to hold fragile objects such as glasses or porcelain.

Woods: *Primary:* Walnut veneered onto pine. Fretted side is solid walnut.

       Secondary: Shelf and base of pine.

Applied Surface Finish: Inside stained a rose colour.

Dimensions: Right 43.5 h 65 w 21d.

       Left 44 h 60 w 21 d.

Noteworthy Construction Details:
Fixing holes on unfretted sides. Fretting carved on the solid walnut sides. Dovetailed construction.

Damage/Repairs/Replacement: Each cupboard has been deepened by 4cm. all round, apparently at the point of manufacture, possibly as an afterthought.

Catalogue No: **163.**

Item: Glass fronted bookcase.

Date of Manufacture: Original glazed cupboard, *circa* 1880, with alterations in the 20th century.

Description: A pine cupboard, made from the upper part of a two-part storage piece which now sits independently on four later turned feet. A shaped pediment and the cornice are later additions. The cupboard is over-painted to simulate mahogany graining, and the internal shelves are adjustable.

Woods: *Primary:* Pine.

Applied Surface Finish: Over-painted to simulate mahogany grain.

Dimensions: 112 h 101 w 25.5 d.

Noteworthy Construction Details:
Adjustable shelves.

Damage/Repairs/Replacement: Feet, cornice and pediment are all later additions. Glass broken.

Catalogue No. **164.**

Item: Corner cabinet.

Date of Manufacture: Circa 1920.

Significant Accession Details: Made by P. E. Humphreys to a design initiated by Archibald Knox.

Description: The cabinet is made with plywood sides, top, bottom and back, and has plywood shelves. The structure framing and the door are in beech, and the shelf supports are oak. The top of the cabinet has two slot-in border sections missing. The cabinet is painted black and has a raised zoomorphic motif showing a lizard with an entwined tail on the door, and painted foliar motifs on the two side panels. The decorative metal hinges are typical of those favoured by Knox for his furniture designs. Pieces of furniture with flat fronts and canted sides were fashionable from the late - 19th century until the 1920s and Heals (London) catalogue of 1884 shows two corner cabinets of this generic type. Other designers working within the style of the Art Nouveau period utilised this geometric form in producing dressing tables, exotic alcove seats and wash stands. See, for example, *Quaint Furniture for the Bedroom*, by H. Pringuer, *circa* 1880.

Woods: *Primary:* Beech frame and door. Plywood panels and shelves.

          Secondary: Shelf supports oak.

Applied Surface Finish: Black paint to create *faux* japanning.

Dimensions: 107 hh 79 w 56 d.

Damage/Repairs/Replacement: Two slot-in border sections on top missing.

Catalogue Number: **165.**

Item: Corner cupboard.

Date of Manufacture: Circa 1780.

Description: A hanging corner cupboard made primarily in mahogany, with cross-banding to the door panel also in mahogany, and fluted pilasters each side of the door. The backboards, top, and base are replacements in pine. The shelves, painted green and shaped to the front edges, are also made in pine, and are probably original to the cupboard. The shelves have a beading nailed towards the rear to hold plates upright, probably indicating the display function which this cupboard had. This cupboard is typical of the high quality cabinet making skills associated with English 18th century cabinet making traditions. This is supported by the careful choice of the mahogany used, particularly in the solid section of crotch-cut mahogany used in the door panel, which exhibits a vivid leaf-like grain. Corner cupboards of this kind, or alternatively with upper and lower sections, were made as free-standing pieces as well as being built in without backboards.

Woods: *Primary:* Mahogany, with mahogany cross-banding.

   Secondary: Pine back boards and top (replacements). Original pine shelves.

Applied Surface Finish: Inside painted green - apparently original to the cupboard.

Dimensions: 115 h 84 w 43 d.

Noteworthy Construction Details:
High quality cabinet skills used in manufacture.

Damage/Repairs/Replacement: Top, bottom, and backboards are replacements.

CHAPTER 14

CHESTS OF DRAWERS

The development of chests with drawers had occurred in England by the 16th century. They took their form and decoration from examples made in the Low Countries, and had two doors to the front which concealed plain fronted drawers inside. Commonly, a single drawer was fitted above the doors, and following continental fashion the door fronts and stiles were often inlaid with exotic woods, including ebony and cedar, as well as bone, ivory, mother of pearl, and occasionally soft metals such as pewter and silver. Split baluster mouldings were often included as part of the applied decoration, as were geometric and cushion mouldings.

Chests of this kind often stood on turned feet, and represented the height of fashion in an item of furniture which offered advances on the chest or coffer with a hinged lid, in which clothing and linen were stored without the advantage of the discreet compartments provided by drawers.

During the 17th century chests of drawers developed as the front doors were rejected in favour of exposed drawers individually decorated with inlays and mouldings. Typically, these drawers were suspended on narrow side runners, nailed to the interior sides of the chest, and fitting into a square rebate which was cut longitudinally in the drawer sides. Gradually, this method of running the drawers in and out was replaced during the second half of the 17th century in favour of the drawer bottom sliding directly along drawer runners which were nailed each side, level with the drawer intervals.

The earliest chest of drawers held in the Manx National Heritage collection (No. 166) is made of oak and has decorative inlays and constructional features which date it to the 17th century. In this example, however, the drawers run on their bottoms rather than on side runners, and it is this feature which designates it as a traditional chest of drawers, made *circa* 1680, but containing decorative and other design features from the mid-17th century.

The extensive geometric decoration to the front (Figure 14.1) suggests that this chest was London made, either by an immigrant craftsman from the Low Countries, or by an English craftsman who had learned the use of black and white inlay forms from immigrant craftsmen. This particular style of decoration was popular purely as a geometric form, or as a reference to paintings using perspectival images, produced in

Fig. 14.1.
A detail of the decoration on the front of chest of drawers No.166, utilising inlays of ivory contrasted with black stained bog oak.

Fig. 14.2 A chest of drawers, made by Hugh Kaighin of Kerrowglass.

Holland, as well as in intarsia work. These in turn reflected decoration from Renaissance Italy.

The geometric ornamentation on the facade of this chest is achieved using inlays of ivory, contrasted with black stained bog oak. In other areas of the chest strips of stained oak are juxtaposed with walnut inlays.

The specific inlay forms adopted in this chest illustrate the variety of which 17th century furniture decoration was capable, and included inlays of black and white chevrons; white diamonds on a black ground; white diamonds on a black ground bordered by a strip of obliquely inlaid black and white sections; inlays of alternate black and white squares; central panels of ivory, cross-hatched with black stained oak and bordered with walnut, and alternate chevron inlays of walnut and black stained oak. The inlays used to decorate this chest are unusually varied, although the basic geometric impulse is part of a well-documented London tradition. See a further example in *Oak Furniture, The British Tradition*, V. Chinnery, 1979. This form of inlay was also transmitted to America in the 17th century.

Chests of drawers, usually of a plainer form, were made more widely in the 18th century to fill the need for clothes and linen storage for a wider population than had been the case in the 17th century. The use of indigenous hardwoods including solid oak and elm were common in vernacular styles, and walnut and mahogany were widely used in fashionable examples. Other exotic woods were introduced as veneers in the second half of the 18th century.

The 19th century brought the mass production of chests of drawers, often made in softwoods painted and simulated to represent more prestigious woods, or painted and decorated in fashionable colour schemes with stencilled borders. Chests of this type were made by firms who manufactured inexpensive household furniture, not necessarily using mechanised methods, but by the employment of many skilled cabinet makers. See, for example, the furniture catalogues produced by various furniture manufacturers in the 19th century, including W. Smee & Sons, *circa* 1850, J. Shoolbred & Co. 1876, and G. Maddox, 1882, which illustrate common types of chests of drawers with two short drawers at the top and two or three long drawers below. These were fitted with stained turned wooden handles, or more costly ones of white porcelain or glass, and supported on turned feet.

The Manx National Heritage collection has three chests of this type, all of which came from the home of Abigail Faragher at Earystane, Colby. A fourth example which is virtually identical to these is believed to have been made by Hugh Kaighin of Kerrowglass, a joiner who made furniture, and is shown in Figure 14.2.

Of the chests of drawers which belonged to Miss Faragher, two are made of pine, one being painted to simulate either rosewood or mahogany (No. 167) and the other stained to simulate mahogany (No. 168). Both these chests were probably made on the Island, using the poorest quality woods. See the detailed photograph of the drawer linings shown with No. 167, which shows the use of timber which has many knots and splits, although the jointing of the drawers and the general construction shows evidence of highly competent cabinet making skills. Other aspects of these chests' construction, however, indicate economies in their manufacture, with drawer runners nailed rather than jointed to the sides, and with half rather than full dustboards between the drawers being used.

A third chest of drawers from the same source was possibly made by a relative of Miss Faragher, and although of the same style as those described above is made from elm with pine backboards, and, unusually, with sycamore drawer linings and dustboards (No. 169). The use of sycamore is uncommon in case furniture, and indicates a locally available timber. The elm handles were turned from freshly felled green timber which have ovalled on drying. The brown hand painted diamond shaped escutcheons on the drawer fronts, rather than the more conventional stained bone inlays, also point to a chest of local construction, made by a joiner who had limited resources. The technical qualities of this chest are, however, higher than the two pine examples, with drawer runners rebated into the sides and with full dustboards being fitted. Figure 18.2 shows this chest in the small bedroom of Miss Faragher's home at Earystane.

The origin of the chests of drawers from the Faragher household, and others mentioned in the diary of the joiner, Hugh Kaighin, (p. 30, February 10th, 1896) suggest that chests of drawers may have been generally found in more prosperous households on the Isle of Man, the homes of the middle classes and farming families, rather than in poorer cottages. This impression is further reinforced by the description which Mr. Robert Cretney of Ballacallin, Marown (FLS/C/164) gave to the Folk Life Survey, of a farmhouse of his acquaintance: "Their present house is also an old one. It has a lean-to back kitchen added. The kitchen is flagged and has an iron range, the flagged floor continues on one level into the back kitchen and dairy, all the flags visible, no covering used except hearth rugs. They also have a quantity of Manx-made furniture. A very large dresser in the back kitchen, closed in underneath with drawers and cupboards, it covers an entire wall in length and height. In another corner is a joiner-made chest of drawers of plain design, but well made."

The relative lack of references to chests of drawers on the Island in the Folk Life Survey contrasts markedly with numerous references made to kists or lidded chests being used for storage, and it seems that these items of furniture were significantly more popular for the purpose, probably because they represented a cheaper and more traditional solution to clothes storage than chests of drawers. See pp 147-166 for a fuller description of chests.

Catalogue No: **166.**

Item: Inlaid chest of drawers.

Date of Manufacture: Circa 1670.

Description: An inlaid oak chest of drawers in two parts. This highly decorated chest has conventional construction throughout, with the exception that the drawers run on their bottom boards, on flat runners, rather than having side grooves along which they can run on a runner nailed to the chest side. The chest splits into two equal parts, a common option for chests of this period, enabling them to be carried more easily when families moved between houses. The sections were also more easily carried up narrow stairways. This chest now has turned feet on the front, but originally the corner stiles extended to form feet, in the manner of the back stiles. The drawer configuration includes a shallow drawer at the top, a deep drawer below, and two equal sized drawers below this. The lower three drawers have steel locks, and the upper narrow drawer has a wooden spring lock (now broken) below the drawer bottom. The lower three drawers are cushioned (raised) in design, and the top drawer front is flat. The centre of each drawer has an armorial inlay of a brown wood, possibly lightly stained holly, sycamore, or poplar which has two oblique hatchments inlaid in walnut across the shield, with a black bird inlaid in the top right and lower left. The significance of this

armorial is untraced, but it must be a later addition to the original chest since it is laid over the original handle hole. Initially, a brass single drop handle would have been fitted with two brass strips, passing through the hole in the chest front, which were nailed to either side of the hole. The hole and the nail holes either side which were used with these strips can be seen on the reverse of the drawer fronts, behind the armorial inlays. (see Figure 14.1, p. 138, for detail photograph).

Woods: *Primary:* Oak.

   Secondary: Stained oak, walnut, ivory inlay.

Dimensions: 107 hh bottom part 60 h 112 w 36d.

Noteworthy Construction Details:
Halves held together on wooden splines. Cleft wood used in back, and backboards nailed. Dovetailed drawers at front, nailed at back.

Damage/Repairs/Replacement: One replaced handle. One plank loose on back. Feet replaced on back and additional turned feet on front. Waist moulding missing on sides. Metal bracket reinforcing top right corner. Some replacement timber in the frame of the bottom half of chest.

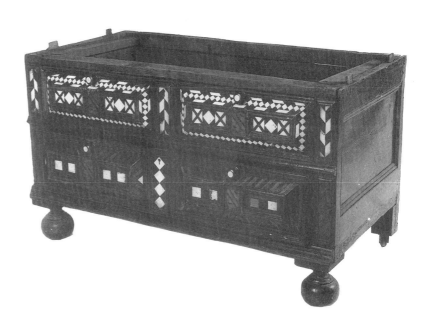

Catalogue No: **167.**

Item: Chest of drawers.

Date of Manufacture: 19th century.

Significant Accession Details: Abigail Faragher, Earystane, Colby.

Description: A chest of drawers with two short drawers and three long drawers, and turned feet. This chest is made in the manner of an English design, of a type made in large numbers for use in cottages, farmhouses and urban artisan housing during the 19th century. The example reviewed here shows many competent cabinet making features produced in the most economical ways, including the use of half dovetailed interval rails between the drawers uniting the drawer intervals to the sides; the use of nailed side runners; the use of half rather than full dustboards between the drawers, and the use of small dovetails uniting the drawer corners. These reduced technical aspects are combined with the use of poor quality timber (see detail of drawer jointing for an illustration of the knotty split timber used in the drawers). The drawer fronts are made of birch and the drawers lined with pine. Each drawer has a steel lock, and the white china handles are probably original. The exterior of the chest is painted and grained with a mahogany based paint and dark annual ring patterning which creates a vivid simulation of perhaps mahogany or rosewood.

Woods: *Primary*: Birch front.

   Secondary: Pine.

Applied Surface Finish: Simulated as mahogany or rosewood.

Dimensions: 113 h 107 w 50 d.

Noteworthy Construction Details:
Dovetailed drawers. Half dustboards. Drawer runners nailed to the case. Top overhangs the back.
Drawers numbered 21 to 25.

Catalogue No: **168.**

Item: Chest of drawers.

Date of Manufacture: 19th century.

Significant Accession Details: Abigail Faragher, Earystane, Colby.

Description: A chest of drawers with two short drawers and three long drawers, and turned feet. This chest is made in the manner of an English design, of a type made in large numbers for use in cottages, farmhouses and urban artisan housing during the 19th century. The example reviewed here shows evidence of cabinet making skills used in the most economical ways, including the use of half dovetailed intervals between the drawers, and the drawer runners being rebated into the chest sides, as opposed to being nailed. This chest has the unusual feature that the bottom drawer is contiguous with the bottom plinth, being part of the drawer front. The black stained drawer knobs are glued and wedged with wood to secure them and each drawer has a lock. The top has a mitred corner edging strip, and the chest is painted and simulated as mahogany.

Woods: *Primary*: Pine.

Applied Surface Finish: Mahoganised.

Dimensions: 117 h 114 w 52 d.

Noteworthy Construction Details:
All drawers dovetailed.

Catalogue No: **169.**

Item: Chest of drawers.

Date of Manufacture: 19th century.

Significant Accession Details: Abigail Faragher, Earystane, Colby.

Description: An elm chest of drawers with two short drawers and three long drawers, and turned feet. This chest is made in the manner of an English design, of a type made in large numbers for use in cottages, farmhouses and urban artisan housing during the 19th century. Although this chest of drawers has many of the features of those made by the large manufacturers, it is unlikely to have originated from this source since it is made from hardwoods which craftsmen had access to, but which were not those typically used by large manufacturers. The top, sides and drawer fronts are made of elm, the backboards are pine, and the dustboards are sycamore. Very unusually, the drawer linings are also made of sycamore (see footnote). The maker's high cabinet making competence is reinforced in the drawer construction, which shows the skilled use of dovetails front and back. The drawer bottoms run left to right and are rebated into the drawer sides. They each have a lock and a brown diamond shaped escutcheon painted over each key hole. This is an unusual simulated decoration. The drawer knobs are made of turned unseasoned elm, and on drying have ovalled in section. The knobs have a blacksmith made screw and nut driven into them to attach them to the drawer fronts. The turned feet are painted black and are also in elm. The latter details probably indicate that the maker was also a turner who made all the wooden parts for this chest, an unusual range of skills in a trade where cabinet makers typically bought turned parts from a specialist.

FOOTNOTE: Sycamore is an unusual wood in case furniture and is largely restricted to dairy items: tables, bowls, cheese stands, spoons, butter moulds and pats, where its non-aromatic qualities were favoured since it did not contaminate food. The wood also offers a clean fresh surface when washed with water.

Woods: *Primary:* Elm.

       Secondary: Pine back. Sycamore drawer linings and dustboards.

Applied Surface Finish: Escutcheons painted. Varnished.

Dimensions: 109 h 107.5 w 44 d.

Damage/Repairs/Replacement: Right back foot loose.

Catalogue No: **170.**

Item: Glazed top on chest of drawers.

Date of Manufacture: Circa 1890.

Significant Accession Details: Abigail Faragher, Earystane, Colby.

Description: A mahogany stained pine chest of drawers with an unrelated glazed pine cupboard placed on top. The base is a standard mass-produced chest of drawers of a type which was made in large numbers by furniture makers in many metropolitan centres (see the catalogue of the London furniture-making firm of Maddox in 1882, which shows this form of chest with two small drawers and two long drawers, turned handles and turned feet). The glazed cupboard may have been made especially to fit the chest of drawers or it could have been salvaged from an existing chest. It too, is made of mahogany stained pine, painted white inside. It was used in Abigail Faragher's home as a china cabinet.

Woods: *Primary:* Pine.

Dimensions: 182 hh 101 w 39 d Chest 86 h.

        Top 95 h 93 w 37.5 d.

Noteworthy Construction Details:
The chest has full dustboards and dovetailed drawers. It has a small raised ledge at the back. No lock on small right hand drawer.

Damage/Repairs/Replacement: Glazed top is an addition.

Catalogue No: **171.**

Item: Base of a press cupboard.

Date of Manufacture: Circa 1790.

Significant Accession Details: Abigail Faragher, Earystane, Colby.

Description: This piece is the base of an oak press cupboard of a conventional type, which originally stood on bracket feet and probably supported a cupboard with two doors above. The use of mahogany cross-banding on the three long drawers indicates that the press was made in the North-West of England cabinet making tradition. The turned handles are a later addition and replace original brass bale handles.

Woods: *Primary:* Oak.

  Secondary: Mahogany cross-banding. Pine vertical backboards. Birch handles.

Applied Surface Finish: Stained and polished.

Dimensions: 71.5 h 133 w 59 d.

Noteworthy Construction Details:
All drawers dovetailed. Full dustboards.

Damage/Repairs/Replacement: Top section and bracket feet now missing.

CHESTS & STORAGE BOXES

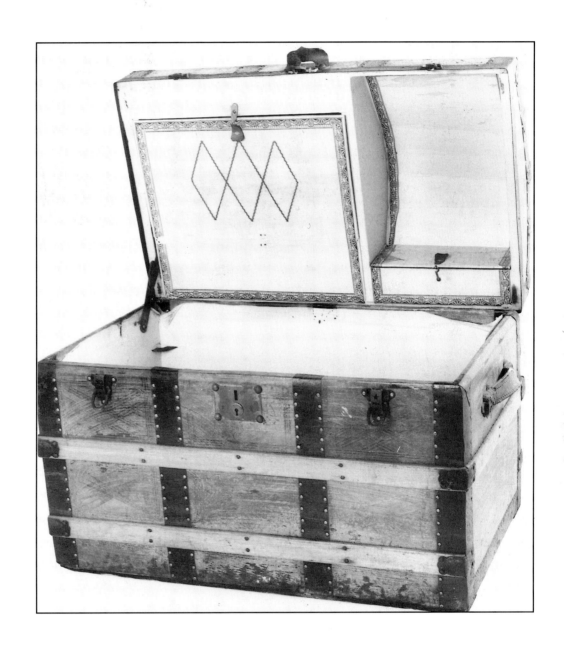

CHAPTER 15

CHESTS & STORAGE BOXES

Chests made to hold linen and other possessions were the most widely used forms of storage furniture in Europe before chests of drawers became fashionable in the mid-17th century. Even after this time, chests continued to be made in slowly evolving forms until the present day.

The term chest is derived from the Latin *cista*, and a corruption of this word to kist, chist, or chissis is still used on the Isle of Man, and occasionally elsewhere in Britain. These terms all refer to a box with a flat hinged lid, which is raised from the floor on four legs.

A box, which was also used for storage, is distinguished from a chest in that it rests on its bottom boards, without legs or feet. Yet other storage pieces of similar form, resting on bottom boards but with curved lids, are properly termed coffers, and in the 17th century and for several centuries before were the domain of specialist makers called cofferers. Another form of the curved top coffer was made as a travelling box, and was termed a trunk.

The Manx National Heritage collection contains examples of all these forms of storage items, except for coffers, dating variously from the 17th to the 20th centuries. The earliest example in the collection is a small chest (No. 172). It is probable that this item was made originally for church use, as it has the pierced

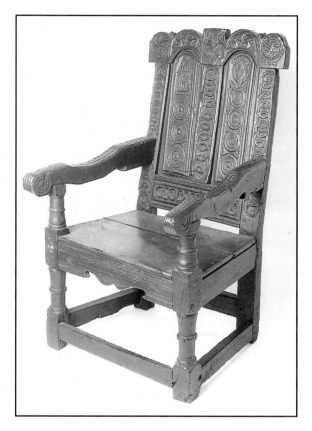

Fig. 15.1.
A joined, carved chair. Scottish, dated 1690. Collection: National Museum of Scotland. Acc. No. KNB 19.

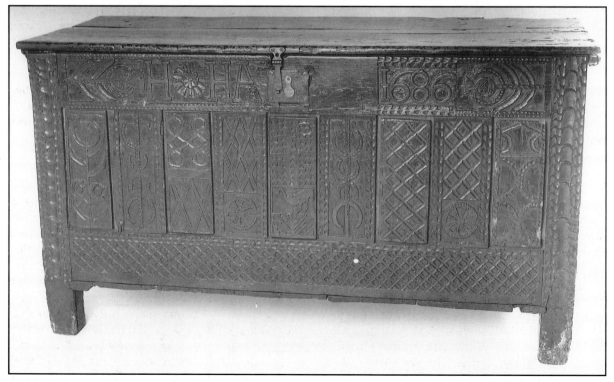

Fig. 15.2. Chest No. 173, showing clear design similarities to the Scottish chair in Fig. 15.1.

Fig. 15.3.

Oak chest, No. 174. Scottish, 17th century, showing internal till and hasp with a spigot which fits into a metal plate in the rear board.

arcaded carved motifs associated with ecclesiastical carvings and particularly the designs of 15th and 16th century rood screens, pew ends, and door decoration. The chest ends have four square sections cut from the solid wood to simulate frame and panel construction, and this form of *faux* panelling was a common form adopted in chests during the medieval period [1]. Unusually for a chest made in the late Middle Ages, this example is made in pine. Oak was common in the British tradition, with walnut and cedar being the woods most often used in Europe.

The Museum collection also contains a number of chests which date from the 17th century. Amongst these is a chest made with free-style carvings on its multi-panelled front and stiles (No. 173). This chest is Scottish in origin, and other carved 17th century furniture from Scotland echoes similarly intuitive decoration, including the national thistle emblem combined with lines of repeated gouge carving. The constructional similarity with Scottish traditions is clear, too, in the use of narrow panels with square edges to their raised central sections. A 17th century Scottish joined chair is shown in Figure 15.1, which reflects many of the forms and devices shown in the chest (Figure 15.2). This complex and highly decorative chest contrasts with a further 17th century chest in the collection (No. 174) which is also probably Scottish in origin. This chest is made from six massive planks nailed together, and has a lid which has metal strap hinges and a hasp which passes to the rear and joints into a hole in the backboard (Figure 15.3). The use of large single dovetail joints at the corners of the chest is an unusual way of joining sections. It is a device recorded in some Scottish furniture particularly, for example, in the jointing of head boards to the rear rocker. This is found in some Scottish cradles dating from the late - 18th and early-19th centuries.

Chests of this massive type were often made for ecclesiastical or other institutional use, where guarding the contents safely was more important than mobility. The secure nature of this chest indicates that it was made to hold documents or other objects of some importance. Its accession into the Museum collection from Castle Rushen, at the same time as the Rolls Cupboard (No. 160) which also probably originates in Scotland, suggests that this chest may have had a similar official role.

In addition to the two chests of Scottish origin, the Manx National Heritage collection includes chests of English design which also date from the 17th century. These include Nos 175 - 177. The first (No. 175) is a plain oak panelled chest with three flat panels on the front, top and rear. The smaller chest (No. 176) has two panels on the top, rear and front, and on the front panels carved lozenge decorations with swirls at their points, a characteristic motif on fixed woodwork from Yorkshire. The third panelled chest (No. 177) has elaborate carving along its front stiles, and the front panels are richly carved with a central arch and lozenge and flower carving each side. This chest has a replaced carved frieze to hold it off the floor.

These three examples were probably made in England. However given the widespread use of chests of this type in England and Scotland, it is possible that similar chests were also made on the Island during the 17th century. A report given to the Folk Life Survey in 1971, describing the large farmhouse at Ballachrink, Jurby, indicates that chests of this type were in use into the 20th century. It was noted that "There are two old chests in the house, used for storing clothes. One has an upper tray at one side in which family documents are kept. The chest standing on the landing is panelled, and was Mr. G's mother's chest . . . she was a member of the Quayle family from the hills in Sulby . . . has ring hinges, they appear to be screwed into the wood, two in the lid and two in the rim of the chest, the rings fitting like links . . ." (FLS/G/55). The description of ring hinges to fix the lid in one of the chests is interesting and virtually confirms the date of that chest to the 17th or early - 18th century, at which time this hinging device went out of fashion.

Panelled chests of this type, together with simple boarded chests made of six planks, were the most common form of domestic storage in England prior to the end of the 17th century. Most houses had at least one, and probably several. Wealthy households had many chests in differing sizes, some elaborately carved and others plain. Inventories show that some chambers had up to six such chests for the storage of linen, clothes, weapons, books, glass and plate. Internally, a till or lidded compartment to hold small items was also a common feature.

The materials stored in these chests were piled one on the other, and in the 18th century chests were often made with drawers at the bottom in order that items could be separated. A chest of this type in the collection (No. 178) dates from the first quarter of the 18th century but is now much altered. In addition to chests, coffers and trunks are also frequently referred to in pre-18th century inventories. The distinction between the two is not easy to make today, although clearly contemporary inventory makers had no such difficulty. Both items have curved lids which sometimes slope downwards at either end. Coffers were certainly made in the 17th century and before by specialist makers, who made these storage chests with thin boards which were then covered with leather or cloth and bound with iron bands or fixed with nails.

By the 18th century, however, the trade of coffer makers had largely adopted the new name of trunkmaker. Craftsmen working in this trade produced an ever-expanding repertoire of travelling trunks which could be used on coaches and ships, and in the 19th century on railways. The Manx National Heritage collection has one trunk (No. 179) dating from the late - 19th century which is covered in patterned leather and has wooden strips and thin metal edge brackets to protect it. A leather carrying handle is fixed at each end and the front has a secure brass lock. The inside is lined with paper which has motifs from the

Indian sub-continent - probably the origin of this trunk.

Travelling boxes with flat lids were also popular in the 18th and 19th centuries, and examples were made with metal, often brass, corner and edge brackets. They were fitted with carrying handles which were hinged and recessed so that they did not protrude from the box sides, thus allowing for closer storage. The Manx National Heritage collection includes one box of this type (No. 181) dated *circa* 1840, which has a walnut outer case and an inner lining of cedar. Cedar is a pleasantly aromatic wood and was used to scent the clothes and linen stored in boxes. The corners and edges of this box have brass edge brackets, and there are carrying handles at the sides.

During the 19th century the most common form of storage box, however, was of a simple and robust rectangular shape with a flat lid, usually called a 'lodging box'. Boxes of this type, usually made of pine, were simply painted or simulated as a more prestigious wood. Scottish examples often have wildly imaginative decorative painted surfaces.

These boxes were frequently made for boys and girls leaving home to enter farm or domestic service, and served as sturdy containers for clothing and other personal items. They could also be used as seating, or as a desk to write on, and generally provided a multi-purpose, functional item. In coastal or island regions from which men and boys went to sea, boxes of this simple type were also used as seamen's chests.

Another box of this type in the Manx National Heritage collection is carpenter-made from tongue-and-groove boards, which are nailed to four upright internal corner stiles. It is painted with mahogany varnish, and is said to have been used as a sea chest by a Manx fisherman in the 19th century (No. 183).

Although common lodging boxes were used on board ship, other forms of seamen's chests were also made specifically for use at sea. These sometimes had sloping sides, giving greater stability to the chest. Leather or wooden blocks were used on the ends, through which plaited leather or rope handles could be passed, and these sometimes had carved and painted motifs such as hearts and diamonds on them. During the 19th century a tradition arose for painting landscapes or sailing ships inside the lid of such chests, and the Manx National Heritage collection holds a remarkable example dating from the 19th century (No. 184).

This chest is made from thin sections of walnut, dovetailed at the corners, and with thin brass corner brackets. The sides have tooled leather covered handle blocks and plaited rope handles, made in the manner of decorative leather work from the Iberian peninsula whence the box probably originated.

Inside the lid is a most striking series of three paintings

Fig. 15.4.
The inside of the lid of No.184, showing the painted scenes.

(Figure 15.4). The two outer paintings are of waterfalls and dramatic scenery; one is untraced, and the other depicts a scene in the Lake District. The central painting is of a sailing ship. The Manx Three Legs emblem is painted in the upper corners of this central panel, and the British rose, thistle and shamrock are painted below the sailing ship. On the outside of the simulated grained box, below the escutcheon plate, are painted the initials of the owner.

Perhaps the most widely made form of domestic storage chest on the Island was called a kist, chist, or chissis, and Mr. John Kneen of Ballaugh Curraghs, reporting to the Folk Life Survey in 1950, said: "In every house these wooden chests would be found. They were used for storing things in, and the family's clothes were kept in them - they served the same purpose as the wardrobe does today. Old people called them *chissis*, and no house would be considered furnished without one of these or a few of them. They were made by the joiner and painted different colours. When closed, they also acted as a seat. In latter years some of these old chests were prepared inside with ordinary wallpaper to make them look more attractive." (FLS/K-J-B).

Chests of this type were carpenter or joiner made, with horizontal boards nailed to the corner stiles which extended below the bottom of the chest and provided supports for bracket feet. Internally, such chests often had a till with two small drawers below, in the manner of Scottish chests.

These pieces were usually painted with fanciful patterns, or to simulate oak or mahogany graining. A chest made by Hugh Kaighin, joiner of Kerrowglass, Michael (Figure 15.5) illustrates the use of an exuberant painting technique to decorate an otherwise plain chest. In it, he has written "This box cost 6s 11^{1}/2d besides lock and labour" (Figure 15.6).

Occasionally, chests were made with one or two drawers in the base, reflecting 18th century styles. See for example No. 186 which came from the home of Miss Abigail Faragher at Earystane, Colby. This is a rather superior example of its kind, well made, painted red, and with white porcelain knob handles on the drawers.

The Manx National Heritage collection holds two further chests which are raised from the floor on feet, but are otherwise simple lodging boxes. The first (No. 187) is a precisely constructed and finished small chest, which is reported to have belonged to a ship's captain who died in 1893, and to have been used for the storage of ship's papers. However its lack of carrying handles and the addition of bracket feet would suggest that it was not used on board ship.

The final chest, (No. 188), now much dilapidated, forms part of the furnishings of Harry Kelly's cottage at Cregneash. This box has deep supports nailed around the lower frieze, and it was probably made in this way simply to keep it high off the damp cottage floor.

Fig. 15.5 (above).
Hugh Kaighin's chest, enlivened by the paint finish. (Private Collection).

Fig. 15.6.
Detail of the interior and Hugh Kaighin's note about the cost of the chest.

Reference: (1) *Ancient Church, Chests and Chairs,* Roe, F., 1929, Figure 77, p.99.

Catalogue No: **172.**

Item: Carved chest.

Date of Manufacture: Late-15th / early-16th century.

Significant Accession Details: Said by donors (1939) to have possibly come from Jurby Church.

Description: The Gothic tracery on the front of this chest is entirely congruent with carving from the 15th and early-16th centuries, and probably dates the chest's manufacture to this period. The accession details suggest an ecclesiastical association for the chest before it entered private hands, and it is probable that it was made for church use. This assertion is supported in that much decorative church carving during the 14th to the early-16th centuries adopted different interpretations of Gothic motifs. Such vivid carving traditions were expertly produced by groups of specialist tradesmen, who travelled from place to place to create carved fixed woodwork items including pulpits, pew ends, door decoration, and roodscreens.
For examples see *English Church Furniture*, F. R. Crossley, 1917.

Such craftsmen may have been responsible for carving movable furniture items too. Gothic motifs, and indeed the style of furniture and other fixed woodwork during this period, owed much to continental and particularly Iberian influences which were transmitted to England during the mediaeval period. In this way chests of this type could equally be part of continental furniture traditions in stylistic terms. See for example Plate IV, from *History of Oak Furniture*, F. Roe, 1920, which shows a similar 15th century chest from Northern France.

It should be noted that the majority of continental and Iberian chests of this type are made in walnut, whereas the majority of English examples are in oak, with pine being only occasionally used.

This chest is carpenter-made, with lap and wooden pegged joints at the corners. The simple plank top has a thumb-nail moulded edge to the front and sides, and now turns over a bevel on the top edge of the rear plank of the box on replaced hinges. The hasp to the front is a later fitting. The lid has the remains of earlier iron butterfly hinges nailed to it. The present iron hinges probably date from the 17th century.

This chest may be earlier in date, but it includes a particular way of producing the ends of chests which continued until the 16th century. The lower simulated cross rails are missing on the left end. It has one iron carrying handle which may be original. The handle on the right side is missing. The right hand side panel is thicker than the left hand one, and has a recess which originally had a cover to conceal a secret compartment. The front plank of the chest is tapered left to right, suggesting that it was produced from a cleft quartered section of timber. The sides of the chest were originally higher, and provided feet which raised it from the floor. This view is reinforced since considerable erosion can be seen on the bottom of the chest ends. This suggests that the box at one time stood on a damp floor which encouraged decay.

Woods: *Primary:* Pine.

        Secondary: Oak base.

Dimensions: 35.5 h   78 w   35 d.

Damage/Repairs/Replacement:
Original lock missing. Now covered with later oak plate.

Catalogue No: **173**

Item: Joined, carved and dated oak chest.

Date of Manufacture: Circa 1690.

Significant Accession Details: Descended in the Kewley family, having been given to an ancestor by Bishop Claudius Crigan (1784 - 1813.)

Description: An oak joined, panelled chest dated 1686 to the right of the front top frieze, and initialled H. and H. A. intersected with a flower motif. Such juxtaposition was common as a marriage statement during the 17th century, where the left, single, initial referred to the woman's Christian name, and the two letters represented the man's Christian and surnames.

The chest has a flat lid which now pivots on later end braces and metal spigots and brass hinges. Originally, metal strap hinges were fitted. The back and front of the chest have five narrow panels jointed into the four intersecting stiles which are of the same dimensions as the panels. The panels are also jointed into the outer framing. The five panels to the front are level with the stiles and are variously carved with different patterns and motifs so that, excluding the outer frame, nine carved vertical sections are decorated with a vivid array of devices.

From left to right, the panels have motifs as follows:
1. Stylised Scottish thistle motif with three thistle heads.
2. Horseshoe devices with two small and two larger shoes shown in pairs, facing upwards and downwards, and with small gouge carvings which simulate nail holes.
3. Celtic knot and geometric patterns.
4. Geometric lattice pattern above an eight spoke wheel.
5. Upper section with simple chip or gouge carving above an ibis-like bird standing on a carved foliate base.
6. Repeat of the horseshoe pattern shown in 2. In this example the lower shoe lacks simulated nail holes.
7. The complete panel is decorated with a geometric lattice pattern.
8. This panel essentially repeats the decoration on panel 4, with the exception that the lattice pattern is in a more complex form.
9. A pattern composed of four decorated semi-circles, perhaps stylised horseshoes, below a shaped pediment.

The lower frieze is carved with complex lattice carving along its whole length. The outer vertical stiles are gouge carved with large carvings in the centre and borders of smaller carvings (details above). The upper frieze has initials and the date, and also stylised thistle carvings. The central lock and hasp are later additions. The floorboards run front to back and are not concealed to the front. The outer ones are later replacements in pine.

Although this chest has some generic features which approximate to those found in English chests of the period, including its conventional overall dimensions, it also has others which suggest that it is not of English manufacture. Amongst them are the multi-panelled front and back construction, and the rounded internal corner braces. These features, combined with the particular arrangement of carved devices and particularly the repetition of stylised thistles, suggest that the chest is probably of Scottish manufacture and may have been imported to the Isle of Man.

Woods: *Primary:* Oak.

      Secondary: Two pine replacement floorboards.

Applied Surface Finish: This chest was probably originally stained with a black varnish stain, which forms the present overall colour.

Dimensions: 69.5 h   130 w   55 d.

Noteworthy Construction Details: All joined construction. Originally had strap hinges, but now pivots on brass hinges and metal spigots. Five panels on back and two on each side. Rounded corner stiles on inside corners of chest.

Damage/Repairs/Replacement: Parts of floor replaced in pine.

Catalogue No: **174.**

Item: Chest.

Date of Manufacture: 17th century.

Significant Accession Details:
Treasury chest from Castle Rushen Rolls Office, and later the Rolls Office in Douglas.

Description: An oak carpenter-made chest of archaic form but probably dating from the 17th century, made from six substantial planks of oak measuring 3cm. thick. The front and backboards are, unusually, secured to the sides by large single dovetail joints at each corner. These were originally secured with square wooden pegs. Later hand-made nails have also been driven through the

dovetails into the ends. The end planks extend below the bottom of the chest to raise it above the floor, and these fit flat to the floor. The bottom, made from two planks of oak, is fitted flush to the edges of the front and back, and secured in place with square wooden pegs. The lid, like the other sections, is made of a single plank of oak and hinged with heavy hand-forged hinges which are fitted internally with nails (see Figure 15.3, p. 149, for interior view). The back shows signs of other hinges being secured externally and extending down the back. The lid is secured with a strong internal metal cross strap which to the rear fits into a metal plate screwed to the back with a round crank-shaped tenon. The front of the strap is a hinged hasp which fits into a steel lock of some antiquity (17th century). A later steel hasp and lock (18th century) are fitted to the right hand end of the chest internally, and has wooden pintles on which the lid swivels.

Woods: *Primary:* Oak.

Dimensions: 49.5 h 127 w 42 d.

Noteworthy Construction Details: One large dovetail at corners. Planks 3cm. thick. Bottom boards are flush with front and back and are pegged through to secure them.

Damage/Repairs/Replacement: Beading missing along the front of lid, and possibly along the sides of lid.

Catalogue No: **175.**

Item: Chest.

Date of Manufacture: 17th century.

Description: An oak panelled chest dating from the late - 17th century. This conventional form of chest has three flat panels comprising the lid, front and back. These are framed, morticed and pegged into the surrounding stiles using mason's mitres. See *Oak Furniture, The British Tradition*, V. Chinnery, 1979, p. 114, for a detailed diagram of this form of jointing. The floor is replaced and the internal corner blocks are additions. The interior has a lidded till to the left hand side, and its lid swivels on integral pintles. The lid is hinged on iron butterfly hinges which are nailed in place.

Woods: *Primary:* Oak.

Applied Surface Finish: Black stained and polished.

Dimensions: 53 h 122.5 w 58 d.

Noteworthy Construction Details:
Pegged and framed construction.

Damage/Repairs/Replacement: The floor is a replacement, and the corner blocks are additions.

Catalogue No: **176.**

Item: Joined panelled chest.

Date of Manufacture: Circa 1650.

Description: An oak joined, panelled chest of typical 17th century English design and construction. The chest has two panels to the back, top, and front, and single panels at each end. The bottom boards run front to back. The interior has no till. The upper frieze is decoratively carved with nulling (gouge carving). The two front panels have lozenge carving in their centres. The lozenges have carved central decorative swirls and gouge carved stylised fleur-de-lys at their points, in the manner of many examples of this carving device emanating from Yorkshire. See Fig. 3:376A, p 367, from, *Oak Furniture, the British Tradition,* V. Chinnery, 1979. See also a somewhat similar chest, *ibid,* 3:371, p. 361, and also p.360 for more information on boarded and joined chests.

Woods: *Primary:* Oak.

Applied Surface Finish: Stained with black varnish.

Dimensions: 57.5 h 90 w 44.5 d.

Noteworthy Construction Details:
Additional internal blocks to strengthen corners. Three-plank bottom with pit saw marks on central bottom plank. Originally had long metal hinges located onto the back stiles.

Damage/Repairs/Replacement: Lid has been re-positioned, probably when it was re-hinged. Two pegs are a later repair to front stile.

Catalogue No: **177.**

Item: Carved chest.

Date of Manufacture: Circa 1640.

Description: An oak joined chest of typically English form, with four panels in both the back and top, three panels to the front, and one panel at each end. The three panels at the front of this chest are carved, the outer two with central decoratively carved lozenges and stylised flowers in the corners of the panels and the centres of the lozenges. The centre panel is arcaded, with a central recessed panel above, on which the carved initials DK are followed by 1641 and IMB, almost certainly referring to a marriage at that date. The upper frieze has a row of interlocked curvilinear and stylised fleur-de-lys carvings. The four vertical stiles have simple foliate carving extending their whole length. The feet or extended stiles have been removed, and the scalloped base plinth and feet are later fitments which have been sympathetically carved to articulate with the original carving. The base boards of the chest are replacements in pine, and there is an applied section of wood on top of the bottom back stile to support it.

Many of the individual segments of this chest are made from cleft rather than sawn oak, which is unusual in the English tradition where quarter-sawn oak is preferred. The internal till is a later replacement, although its lid may be original.

Woods: *Primary*: Oak. Many sections from cleft timber.

Dimensions: 63 h 121.5 w 52 d.

Noteworthy Construction Details:
All joined construction.

Damage/Repairs/Replacement:
Lower stiles removed and replacement frieze and feet added. Replacement pine floor.
Additional strengthening support to back stiles.

Catalogue No: **178.**

Item: Carved chest.

Date of Manufacture: First quarter of 18th century.

Description: An oak chest dating from the 18th century, now with substantially replaced parts in its lower area. This chest is of a conventional form associated particularly with Welsh origins. The front has three raised and fielded panels below a carved frieze which incorporates the initials W and S E and the date 1716. The top, made of thin planks and supported by (replaced) end cleats nailed under the edges, is locked. Its original staple hinges have now been replaced with later strap hinges. The back is replaced with plywood, and the two bottom drawers are replacements, as are the central vertical and lower horizontal stiles. The section below the lower side stiles is also replaced. The carved initials W and S E probably refer to a marriage where the W refers to the Christian name of the bride and the S E to the Christian and surname of the bridegroom. The date 1716 approximates to the date of production of this chest.

Woods: *Primary:* Oak.

Dimensions: 74.5 h 133 w 52.5 d.

Noteworthy Construction Details:
All pegged construction. One panel at each side, and an upper row of three panels with two below on the back.

Damage/Repairs/Replacement:
The form of the chest is conventional, but it has replaced drawers, bottom, back and lid cleat supports. The hinges are replaced. Infill to floor is an addition.

Catalogue No: **179.**

Item: Trunk.

Date of Manufacture: Circa 1880.

Significant Accession Details: Associated with Gorrey's Drapers.

Description: A curved-topped travelling trunk, fitted inside the lid to hold small items and lined throughout with paper. The trunk is constructed with an unidentified wood which has been covered with leather and tooled with geometric patterns. The leather cover is held in place with bands of tin nailed over it at intervals. Wood strips are nailed to the front and sides, and held with thin metal corner brackets. The trunk has leather carrying handles at each end, a central brass lock and two metal clasps either side of the lock to hold the lid closed. The lid can be held upright with an internal folding metal support. The lining paper inside the lid has a stylised border which probably refers this trunk's place of origin to the Indian sub-continent. The surface of the trunk has been painted blue, but this was probably not its original paint. Cleaning on the front has revealed a tooled geometric decoration on the leather covering.

Woods: *Primary:* Unknown.

Applied Surface Finish:
Traces of blue paint on lid.

Dimensions: 56 h 81.5 w 47 d.

Catalogue No: **180.**

Item: Panelled chest.

Date of Manufacture: Reconstructed in the 20th century from 19th century panelling.

Description: A theatrical item of furniture made from sections of walnut panelling, fitted together to form the sides of a chest. The sloping back suggests that it was made for a particular (unknown) use or location. The indications of prefabrication from existing woodwork include the base moulding and feet, which although an apparently integral part of the chest, are in fact a separate oak base on which the walnut panelled chest sits. The end panels, which have metal handles, have sections filling in a gap where the heights of the panelled side sections did not correspond with the front height. The top is later in date than the panelling, and made of oak with a thumb moulded edge.

Woods: *Primary:* Walnut panels, stiles and front. Oak top, base moulding and stiles.

　　　　Secondary: Pine bottom boards. Metal carrying handles.

Applied Surface Finish: Varnished.

Dimensions: 40 h 116 w 50 d.

Noteworthy Construction Details:
Panels had been pegged. Chest now of nailed construction.

Catalogue No: **181.**

Item: Travelling box.

Date of Manufacture: Circa 1840.

Description: A travelling box made with a walnut outer case and floor, and an inner lining of cedar wood. Walnut and cedar were costly, and their use indicates that this was intended as a superior trunk which utilised the prestigious grain of walnut on the exterior and the aromatic qualities of cedar internally. The latter was especially used in chests and boxes to scent fabrics stored in them, and to deter the clothes' moth. The high technical qualities of construction used in this piece are evidenced in the mitred and dovetailed jointing at the corners, which produces a strong union. The box is also protected on its corners (vertical edges and base) with brass brackets, which in combination with the flush fitting brass ring-pull and brass carrying handles identify it as a travelling trunk intended to be stacked with other boxes. It would have needed to withstand the exigencies of travel on a coach or ship. The base has thin flat corner brackets to raise the box off the floor. The brass lock and key escutcheon are English-made and have three crowns and the word 'Patent' struck on the top of the lock.

Woods: *Primary:* Walnut with cedar lining.

            Secondary: Brass fittings.

Dimensions: 40 h 91 w 46 d.

Noteworthy Construction Details:
Walnut exterior mitred and glued. Cedar interior mitred and dovetailed. Two extra struts underneath.

Damage/Repairs/Replacement: Chain to stop the lid falling backwards is missing.

Catalogue No: **182.**

Item: Box.

Date of Manufacture: Circa 1810.

Description: A box with brass carrying handles. This box is jammed, and internal examination is therefore not possible at this time. However, the deep frieze below the caddy top is usual in boxes where internal fitments are provided to hold bottles, or otherwise fitted to hold fragile objects. The wood in which it is made is a dense, exotic hardwood of unidentified species.

Woods: *Primary:* Unidentified exotic hardwood.

Dimensions: 46 h 61 w 50 d.

Noteworthy Construction Details: The corners are rabbeted. The base has two strips nailed to the bottom to raise the box off the floor.

Damage/Repairs/Replacement: The thumb moulding to edge of lid is broken. There is a screwed repair to the front.

Catalogue No: **183.**

Item: Lodging box.

Date of Manufacture: Circa 1880.

Significant Accession Details: Used by donor's grandfather as a sea chest.

Description: A pine lodging box or sea chest painted with mahogany varnish. It has metal carrying handles at the ends and two nailed strips on the bottom to raise it above the floor. This box is carpenter-made from tongue-and-groove joined boards, and has nailed joints throughout. The two plank sides back and front are nailed to four upright corner stiles.

These are not common features of lodging box construction elsewhere in Britain, but are found on the Isle of Man as an integral part of the construction of kists or chests which stand on extended corner stiles. This box is made without a till to hold small items. The lid and base have a moulding nailed around the side and front edges, and the top is mitred at the corners. The steel lock and hasp appear original to the box. Such items of furniture were common throughout the British Isles.

Woods: *Primary:* Pine.

Applied Surface Finish: Mahogany varnish.

Dimensions: 44.5 h 83 w 52 d.

Noteworthy Construction Details:
Stiles morticed through base boards. Two planks on all faces, apart from base which has $3^{1/2}$ cm. planks laid front to back. Applied edge moulding on lid and box.

Damage/Repairs/Replacement: Lid broken off at hinges.

Catalogue No: **184.**

Item: Sea chest.

Date of Manufacture: 19th century.

Significant Accession Details:
Owned by Philip H. Cain of Sulby.

Description: A seaman's chest in walnut, with three painted panels inside the lid. This chest is made from flimsy sections of timber, dovetailed at the corners and fitted with a deep lid which hinges at the rear. The corners are strengthened with thin brass brackets. Two strips nailed to the bottom raise the box above the floor. The interior has an unlidded till. At the ends the tooled leather brackets, with star decoration and woven rope carrying handles, are a prominent feature of the chest and point to its probable origins in the Iberian peninsula. This chest has oval painted scenes of the waterfalls so much loved by Victorian artists. The left hand scene is entitled 'Waterfall at Lowbok' (sic); and the one to the right has the caption 'Lower Fall at Rydal'. The central scene shows a clipper in full sail in a round frame, entitled 'Homeward Bound'. Logos of the Three Legs of Man are painted below with a rose to the left, thistle to the right and shamrock leaves in the centre (see Figure 15.4, p. 151, for view of painted interior of lid). The lid has a steel lock and hasp to secure it, and below the escutcheon plate are scripted the initials P.H.C.

Woods: *Primary:* Walnut.

   Secondary: Leather-covered blocks with rope handles.

Applied Surface Finish: Grained on outside and inside. Scenes painted inside lid.

Dimensions: 49 h 109 w 49 d.

Noteworthy Construction Details:
Corners mitred. Bottom is composed of one board with a skid at front and back.

Catalogue No: **185.**

Item: Kist (chest).

Date of Manufacture: Late - 19th century.

Significant Accession Details:
Abigail Faragher, Earystane, Colby.

Description: A pine storage chest, without
drawers below. This chest is carpenter-made
with three horizontal boards on each side and on
the ends of the chest, which are butted and nail
jointed throughout. Internal corner stiles extend
below the bottom of the chest, to which the
bracket feet were nailed (now missing). The base
moulding which supported the bracket feet, and
covered the edges of the front-to-back bottom
boards, is also missing. Internally, an unlidded
till is fitted with two small drawers below, which
have tacks nailed into the fronts to act as knobs.
The chest was originally painted all over with
brown paint and the visible surfaces are later
over-painted in red. Kists of this type provided
substantial and inexpensive storage, particularly for clothing and linen.

Woods: *Primary:* Pine.

Applied Surface Finish: Initially painted brown externally, visible surfaces now painted red.

Dimensions: 67.5 h 104.5 w 61 d.

Noteworthy Construction Details: All nailed construction. Three planks on all sides. Four planks on top and six planks in
bottom. Stiles chamfered on top corners and continued through the base.

Damage/Repairs/Replacement: Brackets on front legs and back left leg missing.

Catalogue No: **186.**

Item: Large kist (chest).

Date of Manufacture: Second half of 19th
century.

Significant Accession Details: Abigail
Faragher, Earystane, Colby.

Description: A pine storage chest with two
drawers below, raised on large bracket feet and
with a hinged lid. The exterior surfaces are
painted with red paint, except on the back and
bottom, and the porcelain knob drawer
handles are probably original. The chest is
carpenter-made, with butted and nailed
construction and with integral corner stiles
which extend below the chest and support the
bracket feet. The top is made of thin planks
held in place with edging mouldings to the
sides and front, which extend over the lips of
the chest to keep it in place. The drawers are
cock-beaded to the edges of the openings, and a decorative moulding is nailed around the bottom edge of the chest to support
the bracket feet. A number of chests or kists of this design have been recorded on the Island, where they provided commodious
storage for clothing, linen and other small items.

Woods: *Primary:* Pine.

Applied Surface Finish: Painted red externally, apart from the back and bottom.

Dimensions: 89.5 h 129 w 64 d.

Noteworthy Construction Details: Nailed construction. Three planks used on ends, sides and top.

Damage/Repairs/Replacement: Parts of bracket feet dislodged.

Catalogue No: **187.**

Item: Chest.

Date of Manufacture: First half of 19th century.

Significant Accession Details: Owned by donor's grandfather, Capt. John Keggin, Port Erin, master of the schooner *Jilt* (died aged 50 in 1893). It is reported that the ship's papers were kept in this chest.

Description: This small chest is carpenter or joiner-made, with lap joint and nail construction, and braces internally to support the corners. The nails, hasp and hinges are blacksmith-made, and the lock is made of steel. The chest has a flat lid and half round beading around the edge to locate it onto the base. The bracket feet and deep bottom frieze are glued and nailed to the chest lower edge and corner stiles. The interior contains a till which has a sliding partition to conceal a hidden drawer. The exterior is painted and simulated as rosewood over a gessoed surface. This chest has been maintained in a clean and undamaged condition.

Woods: *Primary:* Pine.

Applied Surface Finish: Gessoed and simulated as rosewood.

Dimensions: 37 h 53 w 32.5 d.

Noteworthy Construction Details: All nailed construction with corner strengthening braces.

Damage/Repairs/Replacement: Top warped.

Catalogue No: **188.**

Item: Lodging box on raised feet.

Date of Manufacture: 19th century.

Description: This basic form of box was universally used throughout the British Isles, and commonly called a lodging box. Its function was largely to provide boys and girls with a sturdy clothing and effects box when they left home for domestic service, farm or other employment. On the Isle of Man such boxes were also used by seamen to keep their possessions in on board ship. This example is unusual in having its corner stiles protruding below the floor with a moulded plinth around the base. The height has been further extended with added side pieces and front brackets. It has iron strap hinges. The till had no lid originally.

Woods: *Primary:* Pine.

Applied Surface Finish: Oxidised black paint.

Dimensions: 74 h 90 w 54.5 d.

Noteworthy Construction Details: Nailed plank construction. Raised on feet with later side panels.

Damage/Repairs/Replacement: Right bracket foot missing. Left edging strip around top missing.

LONG CASE CLOCKS

CHAPTER 16

LONG CASE CLOCKS

Clock and watch making on the Isle of Man can be traced to the late - 18th century, when at least four watch and clockmakers are recorded as working on the Island. These were J. Smith, 1793 [1], John Atkinson of Douglas, 1785 [2], who in addition to making clocks and watches held a seven year lease of salmon fishing in all the bays of the Island, granted for £22.00 in 1785; John Crawford, who was from Belfast, and took a shop in Peel in 1794, where he declared that he "intends carrying on the business in its full extent. He makes and repairs all sorts of clocks, likewise plain, horizontal, and repeating watches" [3], and J. Graham, who is reported to have taken a shop in Ramsey in 1794 [4].

No clocks produced by these makers have yet been recorded, and it is probable that other clockmakers worked on the Island at earlier times in the 18th century, for whom no records have yet been established. The earliest clock in the Manx National Heritage collection, dating from the late - 17th century, was made in London (No. 189). The maker, John Longland, was admitted to the Clockmakers' Company in 1677, and was described as a "clockmaker of repute". This clock is of the highest London quality, with an oak case decorated in walnut oyster veneers and cross-banding, and with central panels of floral marquetry. It is brass faced, and has an eight day plate frame movement.

The greatest evidence of long case clocks made or assembled on the Island, however, dates from the 19th century, and the majority of examples held in the Manx National Heritage collection originate from the period 1820 to 1850.

Ownership of time pieces in Manx cottage homes was limited, particularly in the 18th and early - 19th centuries, and many poor people relied on public clocks and chimes to tell the time by. Mr. Cooper of Castletown reported to the Folk Life Survey in 1952, in his eighty second year, that "There were grandfather [long case] clocks, wall clocks, alarms in my time. A lot of people who had no clocks went by the Castle clock and Brewery bell which rang about seven o'clock in the morning, twelve noon, and six in the evening. Also people about Balladoole House went by the bell that rang there at twelve noon and six p.m. to warn the men working in the fields, and later when the trains ran, the men in the fields went by them." (FLS/C.J.H./A.)

That long case clocks were probably quite rare in poor cottage homes is suggested by Mr. J. Kneen of Ballaugh Curraghs, who reported to the Folk Life Survey in 1950, when he was in his ninety seventh year, that "The only clocks were hung on the walls. These were round faced and sometimes square faced. From the face hung two chains to which two heavy weights were hung: they lifted one weight and pulled the chain down . . . All the works in these old clocks were without any covering." (FLS/K-J-A).

Mrs. Corkish of Ramsey, describing her family home in Sulby Glen in 1960, said, "On the other wall there was a great big clock with no frame on it, and a great big pendulum going back wards and forwards all the time. They were calling that kind of clock the sheep's liver and lights." (FLS/C. 104).

The use of mounted wall clocks which have hanging weights and a pendulum, in the manner of movements in long case clocks, has a history dating back to the 17th century. They continued in production into the early - 19th century, in various forms. Sometimes the movements of this type sat on wooden wall brackets, or alternatively were hung from the rear on a peg on the wall. An Austrian-made movement of this type, made to hang on the wall, belonged to Miss Abigail Faragher of Earystane, Colby, but in this case a long pine case was made in the 20th century to hold it, and it now appears as a conventional long case clock, No. 190 (see also Figure 16.1).

In the second quarter of the 19th century mass produced wall clocks were imported into Britain in large quantities from America and Europe. Clocks of this type were rectangular in shape, and could either be hung on a wall, or stood on a mantelpiece. They provided the first reliable inexpensive clocks for working people, although the cheapest of them came from America, and had wooden movements which sometimes suffered from the damp conditions on board ship. The advent of competitively priced clocks of this type led to changes in the clockmaking trade, with local clockmakers also finding less expensive ways of providing the native long case clocks. As clocks became cheaper to buy, the number of clockmakers grew. Some forty eight clock and watch makers and repairers, working variously in Douglas, Peel, Ramsey and Castletown in the first half of the 19th century, were noted in a survey conducted by Margaret Stevenson for the Manx Museum in 1938 [5].

The clockmakers maintained their traditional role as specialist craftsmen who made and repaired clocks and watches, but in addition to responding to the demand for cheap imported clocks they also purchased cheap mass produced long case clock movement parts from

Fig: 16.1.
An Austrian made movement originally designed to hang on a wall, but subsequently hung inside a later long pine case.
(No. 190)

manufacturers, in Birmingham particularly, and acted merely as assemblers who had their names painted on the white faced dials before the clocks were sold.

The cases into which the movements were fitted were also usually purchased from specialist mass produced case makers, who made a variety of designs to accommodate different shapes and types of movements. However, the skills of clockmakers cannot be judged by their involvement with cheap imported clocks, and it is clear that the importation of timepieces was resisted by some makers. For example it appears that at least one 19th century Manx clockmaker, William Muncaster (I), (1776 - 1851), who worked in Ramsey and Douglas, made his own movements. A newspaper advertisement dated June 9th, 1829, declares "Wm Muncaster, watch and clock manufacturer, announces his removal from Ramsey to Factory Street, Douglas", and recommends, "the advantages of clocks made by him over those imported in a finished state" [6].

There can be little doubt, either, that many members of the clockmaking trade on the Island were skilled makers of watches, chronometers, and probably other scientific instruments as well as clocks. When the death of John Garret in 1842 was reported, for example, his career was described in glowing terms with reference to "J. Garret's death on 25th. Sept. at Peel, a self taught

watchmaker, and one of the greatest mechanical geniuses that the Island could boast" [7].

A public announcement about another Island clockmaker, Thomas Goldsmith, provides further evidence of the versatility of men in this trade. Goldsmith was referred to several times in the press between 1848 and 1865, including; "T. G. can accurately repair Chronometers & Duplex watches as well as Horizontal, Geneva, Lever and Verge Watches. T. G. is about forming a clock & watch club that working men may obtain a good watch or clock by small payments" [8].

However, it is evident that in the first half of the 19th century, clockmakers also imported both movements and cases. This practice was widespread elsewhere in Britain, and accounts for the apparent ambiguity, for example, of clocks with case design features of those made in the north of England appearing in Welsh households which are otherwise furnished with Welsh furniture. It is probable that all the 19th century long case clocks and cases in the Manx National Heritage collection were similarly imported, and sold under different clockmaker's names, rather than being made by them. The source of the imported parts differed, however, and the Museum collection includes clock case examples from south-east Scotland, (Nos. 192 - 195) and a second group of five clocks with cases

Fig: 16.2.
The interior of Harry Kelly's cottage, Cregneash, showing the dresser and clock, both 'display items'.

made in the north of England, probably in west Yorkshire. These latter clocks all have mass produced white dials and eight day movements made by Birmingham movement makers (Nos 196 - 200).

The 'Scottish' group includes an unnamed clock (No. 194) which has a high quality mahogany case with an oval patera of figured mahogany below the door, in the manner of a clock illustrated by Loomes [9], which shows a similar case designed by John Paterson of Leith, *circa* 1815.

Three of the clocks, made with oak cases, also have features of clock cases from south-east Scotland. Motifs on the cases include reeded quadrant columns on either side of the door, and rectangular applied panels below the door. See Loomes [10] for an example of a clock from south-east Scotland, *circa* 1825, which is similar to the clock case designs discussed below.

The first of these, No. 195, has John Cottier's name painted on the dial. This maker had experience of the Liverpool clock trade before setting up in business in Ramsey in 1830. From there he moved to Douglas in 1838. The second clock of this type, No. 193, has John Kneale's name and the date 1825 painted on the dial. This maker was born about 1795, and his obituary in 1837 reported that he had lived in Malew Street,

Castletown and was found drowned in the harbour near the stone bridge. "Mr. Kneale will be long remembered for his scientific knowledge. He was probably the best watchmaker on the Island, and has made many very curious pieces of mechanism" [11]. The third clock, showing Scottish features, No. 192, *circa* 1825, has 'Muncaster, Isle of Man' painted on the dial. This name refers to William Muncaster (I) (1776 - 1851) who probably imported this case through the port of Whitehaven. His advertisement when he moved his business from Whitehaven in 1810 suggests that importation was not without its difficulties. "Wm., Muncaster, Clock and Watchmaker, Whitehaven, gives notice that owing to the damage and inconvenience of bringing goods from Whitehaven he has fitted up a shop at the house of Mr. Dan McDonald, Duke Street, for the making and repairing of Clocks, and he has appointed Peter Stock to direct the business" [12].

Within the second group of clocks, the cases show features of those from the north of England, and particularly west Yorkshire. Loomes [13] illustrates a clock by Richard Snow of Pateley Bridge, *circa* 1840, which shows generic features of clock cases from that region. These include a broad case with a short door, and in this example spirally turned columns each side of the door.

Clock cases of this type are slightly later in date, *circa* 1845, than the Scottish influenced clocks mentioned above. They include examples sold by Thomas Goldsmith of Douglas, (fl. 1848 - 1860); Basil Mylrea of Market Street, Peel (fl. 1861); William Clucas of North Quay, Douglas (fl. 1844 - 1862): and by a further William Muncaster (II), who was born in Lancaster in 1815, and was working as a clockmaker in Castletown by 1836, and in Douglas by 1855. The clock with this Muncaster name on it forms part of the furnishings of Harry Kelly's cottage at Cregneash, and has a case which is closely similar to the Snow clock from west Yorkshire.

References:

(1) *Manx Mercury*, November 5, 1793.

(2) Comm. Report, App. A. No. 34, 1785.

(3) *Manx Mercury*, December 20, 1794.

(4) *Manx Mercury*, February 8, 1794.

(5) Stevenson, M., 'Clock and Watchmakers of the Isle of Man 1750 - 1850, *Journal of the Manx Museum*, Vol. IV. No.63, 1938-40, pp 211-214.

(6) *Manx Sun*, June 9, 1829.

(7) 'Clock & Watchmakers', p. 212.

(8) *Manx Sun*, January 28, 1860.

(9) *Grandfather Clocks and their Makers*, Loomes, B., 1985, p 278, Plate 360.

(10) Ibid, p. 279, Plate 361.

(11) *Manx Sun*, March 8, 1837.

(12) *Manx Advertiser*, September 8, 1810.

(13) *Grandfather Clocks and their Makers*, Loomes, B., 1985, p.258, Plate 328.

Catalogue No: **189.**

Item: Marquetry long case clock. Signed John Longland, London.

Date of Manufacture: Circa 1690.

Significant Accession Details: Restored *circa* 1935 by E. Kneen, cabinet maker and E. Mekin, watchmaker.

Description: The case of this long case clock is typical of those made in London in the second half of the 17th century. The clock is decorated with walnut oyster veneers and walnut cross sides, with corner panels of inlay to the door and base, and central panels of inlay. The floral motifs are of combined inlays of holly and walnut with green stained holly leaf forms set within a ground of black stained oak. The door has an oval glass graticule, and a brass lock and escutcheon plate. The hood is oyster veneered and cross-banded in walnut. The barley twist hood pillars are in stained black oak, as are the black base mouldings and upper hood mouldings. The blind fretted frieze above is now cleaned but was originally green stained holly or sycamore. The scrolled pediment is now in bare oak but may have been gilded originally; a gilt central ornament is now missing.

The movement is an eight day plate frame, anchor escapement movement, with pillar profiles typical of the 17th century. The brass face has spandrels of the early London cherub head (small) variety, dated 1670 - 1690. The chapter ring has a narrow outer minute ring with modern numbers each five minutes, and an inner ring with black engraved Roman numerals. The inner circle is tool marked brass with a date chapter and second hand and ring. The two winding holes are present in the inner circle, as are the decorative minute and hour hands.

The maker's inscription "John Longland Londini Fecit" is engraved along the lower edge of the square face. G. H. Baillie, *Clock and Watch Makers of the World*, Vol I, records: Francis Longland, Clockmaker London 1671, John Longland, Clockmaker of repute London 1677 - 95. *Old Clocks and Watches and their Makers*, F. J. Britton, p. 471, records: Francis Longland apprenticed 1671 to Bert Powell, John Longland admitted to Clockmakers Company 1677, Thomas Longland 1725.

Woods: *Primary:* Oak.

       Secondary: Stained oak. Holly. Walnut. Sycamore inlays.

Applied Surface Finish: Old surface has been cleaned off on the sides.

Dimensions: 219 hh Plinth 36 w 19 d Middle 28 w 16 d Door 105 x 33 Dial 24 diam.

Damage/Repairs/Replacement: Finial missing. Cresting is a replacement. "A carved dolphin pediment was removed and replaced with the present less elaborate one" (accession notes, 1950). Repairs carried out *circa* 1935. Corner missing from hood. Bell cracked. Uprights at back of hood are additions.

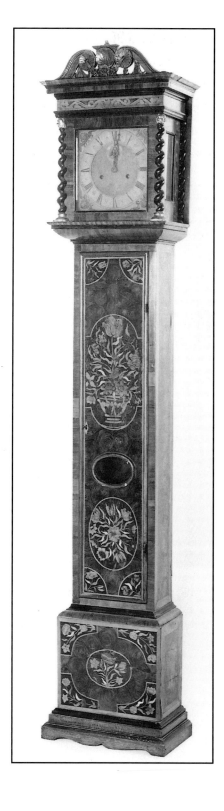

Catalogue No: **190.**

Item: Long case clock.

Date of Manufacture: Movement *circa* 1830. Case *circa* 1920.

Significant Accession Details: Abigail Faragher, Earystane, Colby.

Description: A long case clock made in amber stained pine, and fitted with an Austrian or German thirty hour painted dial movement. The movement and the case come from different cultural contexts, and have been conjoined to appear as a conventional English clock dating from *circa* 1830. The thirty hour movement is of a type associated with Austrian clock design, and was intended to hang on the wall or sit on a plinth, without a case, so that the weights hung in an exposed position. The arched and painted face of the clock is made of *papier maché*, slightly raised in the centre. The movement is boxed in with pine (one side now missing) to protect it from dust, and two inscriptions are pencilled on the rear. The top one reads "Freiburg", and the one at the back of the movement reads "Johanes Rombach 92. Goller Freiburg Buffrin". The wooden rear plate of the clock movement has a hole on which it now hangs on a wooden peg inside the case. Two further, lower, pegs are attached to the back of the movement to hold it level in the vertical plane. The movement has an hour strike mechanism, and the bell can be seen above the boxed movement. The case is competently made in a simplified manner, in the style of an English case made *circa* 1820 - 30, but it was probably made in the first quarter of the 20th century.

Woods: *Primary*: Pine.

Applied Surface Finish: Mahoganised.

Dimensions: 207 hh 51 w (hood) 24.5 d (plinth) Door 67 x 20.

Damage/Repairs/Replacement: Glass cracked.

Catalogue No: **191.**

Item: Clock case.

Date of Manufacture: circa 1730.

Significant Accession Details: Case said to have been made from timber grown on Ballayonaigue, Bride. Accession notes state that a clock movement by Wm. Taylor of Whitehaven was in this case in 1951.

Description: A long case clock case, made in pine and painted with coats of black varnish, now oxidised. The base of the case is covered with a leather-like fabric, and the base plinth is missing. Two columns set either side of the hood door are loose. The case has plain quarter columns each side. The movement of this clock is missing, but it is probable that it would originally have had a thirty hour movement with a brass face and a single hand. It would, therefore, have had two internal weights which were hand raised in the winding movement.

Woods: *Primary:* Pine.

Applied Surface Finish: Dark varnish, now oxidised.

Dimensions: 197 hh Bottom 25 d 64 w Middle 20 d 36 w Door 92 x 22.

Damage/Repairs/Replacement: Movement and plinth missing. Hood broken.

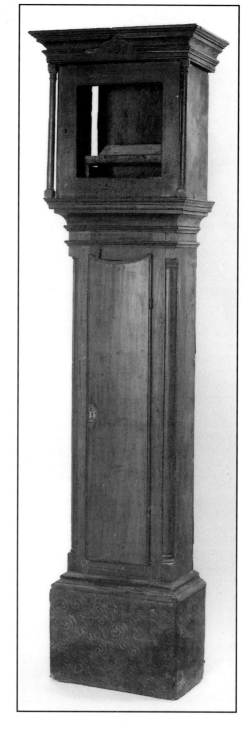

Catalogue No: **192.**

Item: Long case clock.

Date of Manufacture: Circa 1820 - 1830.

Description: A long case clock with an eight day movement and arched painted dial inscribed "Muncaster, Isle of Man". The case is made of oak with quarter round reeded columns to the case corners, and has a frieze of mahogany veneer below the hood. The door has a flowing curved top and a brass escutcheon plate. An oak rectangular tablet which has broad mahogany cross-banding is applied to the case below the door. The door, which also has a border of thick mahogany cross-banding, shows the beginnings of a shortening process which continued until short, wide doors of the kind seen in No 194 became fashionable in the second quarter of the 19th century. This feature allows the clock to be dated *circa* 1820 - 1830. The base of the case has a border of mahogany cross-banding, and flat canted corners. A flat plinth has been added to replace the original moulding and feet. The hood has delicate turned columns, and a scrolled pediment with a central plinth which would originally have supported a brass ornament. The white painted dial has an arched painted calendar movement, and the face has Biblical characters painted in the corners. There are also two second hands and dials in the centre of the face. The clock has similar characteristics to those made in the south-east of Scotland *circa* 1820 - 1830, and it appears that William Muncaster imported the case and movement into the Isle of Man and assembled and sold it under his own name. Two other clocks in the Manx National Heritage collection have similar cases, Nos. 193 & 195.

Woods: *Primary*: Oak.

              Secondary: Thick mahogany cross-banding. Pine back.

Applied Surface Finish: Stained and polished.

Dimensions: 217.5 hh Case 41 w 18 d Plinth 51 w 24 d Door 56 x 28.5 Dial 31 diam.

Damage/Repairs/Replacement: Replaced plinth.

Catalogue No: **193.**

Item: Long case clock.

Date of Manufacture: Circa 1825.

Description: A long case clock dated 1825 on the dial. This clock also has the maker's (assembler's) name "John Kneale Ballachrink" painted on the dial. It has an oak case with square reeded corners, and a rectangular mahogany tablet applied to the case below the door. The door shows the beginning of a shortening process which continued until short wide doors of the kind shown in No. 194 became fashionable in the second quarter of the 19th century. This clock has its original turned feet. The base has canted corners. The hood has an arched pediment and turned columns. There was probably a brass ornament held on the central plinth of the scroll pediment which is now missing. The frieze below it has a wide band of mahogany veneer. The movement has a white faced dial painted in the arch with a hunting scene and with floral motifs in the corners. The centre of the dial has a second hand and dial, two winding holes and a small calendar.

The clock has similar characteristics to those made in the south-east of Scotland, *circa* 1820 - 1830, and it seems likely that Kneale imported the case and movement into the Isle of Man and assembled the movement and sold the clock under his own name. Two other clocks in the Museum collection have similar cases Nos. 192 & 195.

Woods: *Primary*: Oak with mahogany veneer on frieze under hood.

        Secondary: Mahogany tablet and pine back.

Applied Surface Finish: Polished.

Dimensions: 214 hh Case 41 w 18 d Base 52 w 24 d Door 55 x 26 Dial 31 diam.

Damage/Repairs/Replacement: Back feet damaged. Veneer raised.

Catalogue No: **194.**

Item: Long case clock.

Date of Manufacture: Circa 1830.

Description: A long case clock with an arched painted dial *circa* 1820 - 30. This clock has no maker's name on the dial, but the stylistic characteristics of the case indicate that it was made in Scotland. It has an eight day painted dial movement, with an arched dial which has an integral calendar showing the phases of the moon. The corners of the face are also painted with scenes. The clock has high quality solid cut mahogany sides and door, and a pine back. The case has finely cut mahogany veneers on the front and an oval patera of highly figured mahogany below the door, which is cross-banded around the edge with walnut. The stringing used elsewhere on the case is also in walnut.

Woods: *Primary:* Solid mahogany and mahogany veneers elsewhere.

Secondary: Pine back and walnut cross-banding and stringing.

Applied Surface Finish: Varnished.

Dimensions: 241 hh Case 48 w 19 d Base 59 w 24 d Door 53 x 25 Dial 33 diam.

Damage/Repairs/Replacement: Back feet missing. Front feet damaged. Some lower backboards missing.

Catalogue No: **195.**

Item: Long case clock.

Date of Manufacture: Circa 1820 - 30.

Significant Accession Details: The maker John Cottier married in 1830 and moved to Douglas in June 1838.

Description: A long case clock with an eight day movement and arched painted dial signed "John Cottier, Ramsey". The case is made of oak with black stained oak stringing and black painted square reeded columns. The door has a flowing curved top and bone escutcheon plate and an oak rectangular tablet is applied to the case below it. The door shows the beginnings of the shortening process which continued until short, wide doors of the kind shown in No. 194 became fashionable in the second quarter of the 19th century, allowing the clock to be dated *circa* 1820 - 1830. The base of the case has flat, canted corners and a moulded plinth added to replace the original moulding and feet. The hood has delicate turned columns, and a scrolled pediment with a central plinth which would originally have supported a brass ornament. The white painted dial has an arched painted calendar movement, and the face has floral devices painted in the corners. There is a second hand and dial in the centre of the face, with a calendar below. The clock has similar characteristics to those made in the south-east of Scotland *circa* 1820 - 1830. It is probable that Cottier imported the case and movement into the Isle of Man and assembled and sold it under his own name. Two other clocks in the collection have similar cases Nos.192 & 193.

Woods: *Primary*: Oak.

        Secondary: Pine strengthening struts on back of door.

Applied Surface Finish:
Stained and polished.

Dimensions:
228 hh Case 41 w 17 d Plinth 54 w 24 d Door 59 x 28 Dial 34 diam.

Damage/Repairs/Replacement: Replaced plinth.

Catalogue No: **196.**

Item: Long case clock.

Date of Manufacture: Circa 1850.

Description: A long case clock, made in pine and painted and grained to simulate mahogany. The name of the clock assembler painted on the dial is "W. Clucas Castletown". The painted dial movement is a mass produced eight day type, and the dial has a painted scene and calender in the arch. The case is of the most basic type, being made in pine and painted to simulate mahogany and rosewood, with later coats of dark varnish applied over this. The clock case is largely intact, with the exception that the bracket feet and a corner section of the base are missing.

Woods: *Primary:* Pine.

Applied Surface Finish:
Simulated rosewood and mahogany. Later coats of dark varnish.

Dimensions: 216 hh Base 62 w 25 d Case 50 w 17d Door 36 x 53 Dial 21 diam.

Damage/Repairs/Replacement: Plinth and bracket feet missing.

Catalogue No: **197.**

Item: Long case clock.

Date of Manufacture: Circa 1830-1840.

Description: A long case clock with an eight day movement and a painted arched dial with a rocking ship movement in the arch. This style of clock, with a broad case and short door, was a preferred style in the north of England, particularly Yorkshire, during the period 1820 - 1840. They were often made in extravagantly veneered and decorated designs. The case of this clock, however, is of the most basic type, being made in pine and stained to simulate mahogany. It was evidently united with a face and movement which was probably bought from a specialist manufacturer in Birmingham. The assembler, Clucas of Douglas, had his name put on the face before offering it for sale.

Woods: *Primary:* Pine.

Applied Surface Finish: Mahoganised with painted black stringing.

Dimensions: 211 hh Middle 42 w 20 d Bottom 53 w 25 d Door 50 x 29 Dial 32 diam.

Damage/Repairs/Replacement: The surface is heavily oxidised.

Catalogue No: **198.**

Item: Long case clock.

Date of Manufacture: Circa 1850.

Significant Accession Details: Harry Kelly's cottage, Cregneash.

Description: A long case clock, with an eight day movement, which has an arched, painted dial and a 'rocking ship' in the arch. The case was probably imported from the north of England, most likely from west Yorkshire, and united with a mass produced movement from Birmingham. The name of the assembler, Muncaster of Castletown, would have been painted on the face before sale. The carved hood and case columns have a rope twist motif, with tulip shaped turnings above and below. The base of the case may be a replacement.

Woods: *Primary*: Pine. Front originally mahogany veneered over pine, with a solid mahogany door and columns.

Applied Surface Finish:
Pine simulated as mahogany on the case sides, and including the mahogany door.

Dimensions: 207 hh 58 w 28 d.

Noteworthy Construction Details:
The back is detachable, and held in place with two wooden pins.

Damage/Repairs/Replacement:
Mahogany veneers missing on front. Base may be replaced. Replaced hood glass. Brass finial on pediment missing.

Catalogue No: **199.**

Item: Long case clock.

Date of Manufacture: Circa 1840.

Description: A mahogany long case clock with an eight day movement and an arched painted dial with a 'rocking ship' in the arch. This clock has a case design typical of those made in the north of England, particularly Yorkshire, and it was probably imported to the Island from that region and fitted with a Birmingham made movement. The assembler's name, Basil Mylrea of Peel, would have been added to the face before sale. The case is well made in the manner of much North Country cabinet work, with a solid mahogany door and carved and turned pillars. It has well chosen mahogany veneers over a pine ground elsewhere, and is cross-banded in distinctive brown oak. The face of the movement is painted with rural scenes in the corners and in the semi-circles above the face. A sailing ship is painted in the arch and this rocks to and fro with the movement of the pendulum. The face has two winding holes in the centre and a second hand above. The brass finial on top of the hood seems original to the clock.

Woods: *Primary:* Solid mahogany and mahogany veneers on pine.

        Secondary: Cross-banded in brown oak.

Applied Surface Finish:
Varnished. Dial painted (not local scenes).

Dimensions:
233 hh Plinth 23 d Case 18 d 47 w Door 53 x 26 Face 31 diam.

Noteworthy Construction Details:
Pillars are laminated sections of mahogany.

Damage/Repairs/Replacement:
Small area of veneer missing near the lower right hand hinge of the door.

Catalogue No: **200.**

Item: Long case clock.

Date of Manufacture: Circa 1850.

Significant Accession Details: Said by donor to have come from Ballacowin, Lonan, where the earth floor of the cottage was dug out to accommodate the clock.

Description: A long case clock made in pine and painted and grained to simulate mahogany. The assembler of the clock is named on the dial as Thomas Goldsmith, who was listed in the 1861 Census as a clockmaker, aged 38, living at 7 Great Nelson Street, Douglas. The wide case of this clock is typical of clock cases made in the north of England, particularly in Yorkshire and the North-East. The case has had some alterations and additions, including the plinth to replace bracket feet and a replaced carved scrolled pediment. The movement is probably an inexpensive mechanism imported from a Birmingham manufacturer, with the assembler's name and place painted on the dial. The dial movement is of an eight day type, and the clock has an arched dial with a calendar, and architectural scenes painted in the corners.

Woods: *Primary*: Pine.

Applied Surface Finish: Simulated mahogany.

Dimensions:
213 hh Case 50 w 18 d Pediment 62 w 24 d Door 51 x 36
Dial 36 diam.

Damage/Repairs/Replacement:
Cornice and pediment probably replacements. Lower plinth replaced.

WRITING FURNITURE

CHAPTER 17

WRITING FURNITURE

In the 17th century, furniture intended for writing on or storing papers in was made for use by the relatively small number of literate people in society, including land owners and their families, military officers, clergy, merchants and their clerks, and some yeoman farmers. During the first half of the century writing materials were commonly kept in oak boxes with sloping lids. These were often elaborately carved and dated, and could be free-standing and used on table tops or, less often, rested on a separate turned stand. Boxes of this type were ubiquitous, and continued to be made throughout the 17th and into the 18th centuries.

Fig. 17.1; No 201. Oak desk, dated 1715, but of a style common in the 17th century. The stand is later.

More substantial sloping front desks which had integral stands were also made, and from the mid-17th century onwards *bureaux*, or desks with drawers below a sloping front which concealed interiors fitted with small drawers and pigeon holes, became fashionable. These were sometimes made with separate upper and

lower sections, and had carrying handles to enable the two parts to be easily transported. The tradition of making furniture in oak continued throughout the 17th century and into the 18th, often following the fashions of many years before. During the second half of the 18th century a parallel system of furniture evolved, following the Restoration of Charles II in 1660, when fashionable furniture designs from Europe became part of the decor in England. Writing furniture, influenced by continental designs, was usually veneered in walnut, and in the more elaborate items inlaid with marquetry and other decoration. These items included desks with sloping lids which enclosed an interior of pigeon holes, and which could be supported on a turned base with legs which swung outwards to support the writing slope in the horizontal position.

Larger pieces of writing furniture called *escritoires* were also made. In veneered walnut, these had a base with long drawers below an upper cabinet which was fitted internally with small drawers, and a small central door behind which small 'secret' drawers were usually fitted. The drawers were concealed behind a vertical door which folded down for writing.

Other small, flat topped desks with drawers and central recesses became popular towards the end of the 17th century. They were known as "Buroe Tables", and now as knee-hole desks.

Small sloping front desks were also made in walnut, without stands, and were intended to provide a small bureau for use on the lap.

The Manx National Heritage collection has an example of an oak sloping front desk which is made in a 17th century free-standing style (No. 201). It is carved and dated 1715, which is a later date than might have been anticipated considering the style of the desk (Figure 17.1). This may, however, be the correct date of manufacture, and illustrates that styles continued to be made in provincial areas after they had declined in fashion in metropolitan centres. This is evidenced by a closely similar example which is illustrated in *Oak Furniture, The British Tradition*, V. Chinnery, 1979 (p.377, Fig. 3, 426A), which is dated some sixty five years earlier. The example held in the Manx National Heritage collection is now supported on a later turned stand, probably 19th century but of 17th century design. A further plain sloping front desk dating from *circa* 1800 is also included in the Museum collection, and this, too, rests on a later stand.

Fig. 17.2; No.205. The sloping front drops to form a writing surface with numerous drawers for storage behind.

The 18th century brought great diversity in the design and production of desks and writing tables. The largest of these were flat topped desks, which were usually called library tables, or in modern parlance, pedestal desks. These free standing desks often had drawers or cupboards on both sides. Other desks were made which had drawers each side of a central recess, and were made to stand against a wall.

During the mid-18th century a further item of writing furniture was made. It was originally described as a writing or reading table, and is now often, but erroneously, described as an architect's table. The Manx National Heritage's example of such a table, No. 203, is made in mahogany, and is closely similar to two examples illustrated by Ince and Mayhew in their *Universal System of Household Furniture*, published between 1759 and 1762, (Plate XXIV). This style of table was described by Ince and Mayhew as having a "double rising top", where "the slider comes against part of the front, which falls down for conveniency of leaving papers etc. on the slider when shut." As this description suggests, the top rises or slopes upwards away from the user and can be adjusted on a folding rear stand. The front of the table draws forward to stand on half front legs, and in doing so draws forward a fitted interior which reveals small drawers and a flat writing surface.

18th century tables of this kind were considered amusing conceits which demonstrated a growing tendency in cabinet makers to provide technically complex items. Often such items were ingenious in their capacity to reveal versatile purposes for furniture, a trend which reached its height during the second half of the 18th century when many designs of desks and writing tables had roll tops or tambours. These were made with jointed sections which could be raised and lowered to cover the writing areas. Both George Hepplewhite and Thomas Sheraton published designs for these desks, which included solid curved, as well as segmented, covers for writing desks. Similarly, the firm of Gillows of Lancaster also produced designs for desks which has these design features.

The Manx National Heritage collection includes a bureau-bookcase whose design is taken from Thomas Sheraton's *Cabinet Maker's and Upholsterer's Drawing Book* of 1793, part 1, pp. 40 - 47. However, the Museum example was made some fifty years after Sheraton's original drawing. The style of veneering, using broad geometric bands of mahogany crossbanding, and the ivory escutcheons suggest that this piece is a product of one of the major cabinet making centres in the North-West region of England, probably Liverpool or Manchester. It has a curved solid cover to the desk area, a style which Thomas Sheraton described as a cylinder desk (No. 204). There is also a decoratively glazed bookcase above, which has glazing bars in an identical pattern to that shown in Sheraton's drawing.

Further items of writing furniture, in the form of small travelling desks or boxes with folding lids and interior drawers for stationery and writing materials, were made towards the end of the 18th century, and such items were popular throughout the 19th century. Boxes of this type were often carried on their owner's travels, and were usually made in mahogany or rosewood, sometimes with brass bindings and corner brackets to protect them.

Bureaux with drawers below and a sloping front which could be lowered to write on were perhaps the most popular vernacular form of writing furniture made in the 18th century. They usually utilised indigenous timbers, often in solid form, although fashionable versions in veneered walnut and mahogany and other exotic veneers were also made from the end of the 17th century onwards.

The Manx National Heritage collection has two examples of bureaux dating from the late - 18th or early - 19th centuries (Nos. 205 and 206). Both of these have sloping fronts enclosing interiors which have small drawers and a small central door (Figure 17.2). These bureaux are of substantial proportions and were clearly made to hold much paperwork, perhaps related to a farm or other business concern. The bureau shown in No. 205 is veneered in mahogany and inlaid with light and dark wood stringing, in the manner of furniture which emanates from the North-West and West Midlands regions of England.

The second example, No. 206, is made of oak with secondary woods of poplar or birch and pine. Its large proportions again suggest that it was made to hold the papers of an estate or other business concern, and its regional origin is probably the north of England.

Sloping front desks on high stands, or less commonly with drawers below, made for trade purposes and for institutions, proliferated from the second half of the 18th century onwards. Clerks employed by corn chandlers, auctioneers, factories, banks, railway offices, prisons or barracks, and in many places of work, could all be expected to keep records, either standing or sitting on high stools or chairs to work. Teachers' desks were also made in a similar way.

Essentially, desks of this kind were of a similar form, with a sloping lid enclosing a shallow interior which sometimes had a bank of small drawers or pigeon holes. On the top, to the rear, there is often a turned gallery or a low board with a narrow shelf, which afforded some separation between clerks and their clients. The unusual height of a clerk's desk was also probably designed to afford a degree of privacy to his work, and in the case of school desks, to enable the teacher to supervise pupils more easily. The desk was usually made with an integral base with long turned or straight legs, although some examples were made as separate desks resting on a base (see, for example, the

prison ration desk No. 273, which was used in the Isle of Man prison in Douglas at the end of the 19th century).

The Manx National Heritage collection has an example of a desk with an integral base, made in pine for use as a teacher's desk. This example is of a common design made by suppliers of school furniture throughout Britain, including the North of England School Furnishings Company Ltd., who illustrate a similar desk in their 19th century catalogue. See also *School Furniture in the Vernacular Tradition*, C. Gilbert, Temple Newsam, 1978, which illustrates a desk made by this firm, closely similar to the one held in the Museum collection. Specially made high chairs with a foot rest were made for use with desks of this type, and two examples are included in the Museum collection (No. 72 A & B).

Catalogue No: 201.

Item: Desk on stand.

Date of Manufacture:
Desk 18th century. Base 20th century.

Description: A sloping front oak desk on a turned stand. The desk is of a type commonly made by box makers in the 16th and 17th centuries. The initials A. W. and the date 1715 which are carved on the front frieze are a little late in date for this type of free-standing desk, but may coincide with its date of manufacture. Towards the end of the 17th century desks of this type were usually intended to rest on a table or shelf and were less often made to rest on turned stands. However, this stand is of 20th century origin, and the desk was probably of a free-standing type. The desk was used to write on and to keep personal papers in. Its interior is fitted with two drawers which would have held smaller items, and the original iron lock, hasp, and front plate are intact. A further example, similar to the one described here, is shown in *Oak Furniture, The British Tradition*, by V. Chinnery, 1979, p. 377, Fig 3:426A, which although similar, is dated some sixty-five years earlier.

Woods: *Primary:* Oak.

Applied Surface Finish:
Finished with dark staining varnish.

Dimensions: 116 hh 71 w 42 d. Stand 85 h.

Noteworthy Construction Details: Desk nail jointed. Horizontal boards on back of desk.

Damage/Repairs/Replacement: Desk now fitted to later stand. Replacement edge to drawer support.

Catalogue No: 202.

Item: Desk on stand.

Date of Manufacture: Circa 1800.

Significant Accession Details: Abigail Faragher, Earystane, Colby.

Description: A clerk's desk, made in pine, which has residues of blue/green paint with a later coat of red lead. Desks of this type were widely used in trade circumstances for a clerk to stand and work at, or to sit at on a high stool. Corn chandlers, agricultural auctioneers, estate and farm offices and industrial offices were all places of work where desks of this type were commonly used. This example has a separate detachable sloping front desk, which could originally be locked. It is dovetail jointed at its corners, indicating that it was made by a furniture maker with good technical skills. Conversely the base is made with through mortice and tenons joining the top stretchers to the legs, and the drawer is made with butted and nailed joints. The top of the stand has reclaimed timber nailed across it on which the desk rests. These constructional features indicate that the base and top were not made by the same hand, and that they have been brought together to create a high desk at a later time. The base has later stretchers nailed around the legs to support the weakened corner joints.

Woods: *Primary:* Pine.

Applied Surface Finish: Originally painted with blue/green paint. Later over-painted with red lead based paint.

Dimensions: 81 h (back) 91.5 h (front) 62 w 47 d.

Noteworthy Construction Details: Desk dovetail jointed. The base is through-morticed. Nail construction in drawer. Made of reclaimed timber.

Damage/Repairs/Replacement: The desk has a replacement board in the bottom. Top of base has later boards. Supporting struts around legs are a later addition.

Catalogue No: **203.**

Item: Writing or reading table.

Date of Manufacture: Circa 1765.

Description: A mahogany writing and reading table. Tables of
this type are commonly called architect's tables, but they were
more probably made for use in gentlemen's libraries. This
example was evidently influenced by the design published by the
cabinet makers John Mayhew and William Ince of London who
produced a closely similar table in their influential publication of
1762 entitled *The Universal System of Household Furniture*, which
was intended to rival Chippendale's *Directory*. The example
reviewed here is closely similar in terms of its mechanical form,
with a folding top held on a ratchet to hold large books or sheets
of paper. The interior is fitted in a similar way to the left hand
drawing shown by Ince and Mayhew, and a small ink and quill
pen drawer in the right hand frieze is also included. The interior
contains various partitions to create storage spaces for writing
materials, and also includes secret drawers to the interior of the
left hand side. A slide is included to draw over the interior to
create a flat writing surface, and the front of the desk draws

forward on a slide system to create a convenient way to sit at the flat surface. The legs are made from triangular sections which
have decorative features on their inner edges. In the case of the table reviewed here, the frieze has a plain mahogany veneered
surface with Gothic edge decoration and originally Gothic corner brackets would have been fitted. These are now missing.
Some of the legs have vertical turned columns internally. Two of these are missing from the right hand side. The single rococo
style brass handle on the front frieze appears original to the piece. The table is made in deeply coloured mahogany
throughout but abuse has resulted in much damage occurring to both the surface and to the structure of the piece.

Woods: *Primary:* Solid mahogany, and mahogany veneer on a mahogany ground.

       Secondary: Oak slide.

Applied Surface Finish: Highly polished.

Dimensions: 76 h 91 w 60 d.

Noteworthy Construction Details:
Competent metropolitan workmanship. Secret drawers under the writing slide.

Damage/Repairs/Replacement: Corner brackets and two columns missing. Rest for main top a replacement.

Catalogue No: **204.**

Item: Cylinder front desk with bookcase.

Date of Manufacture: Circa 1840.

Description: A mahogany cylinder desk with glazed bookcase above. Made in the manner of Thomas Sheraton's (1793) original design, this bureau-bookcase is made with the highest metropolitan cabinet making skills, and stylistic references suggest that it was made in one of the northern cities, probably Liverpool or Manchester. This style of bookcase was drawn and described in perspective terms by Thomas Sheraton in his *Cabinet Maker's and Upholsterer's Drawing Book* of 1793, Part I, pp.40 - 47.

Although not absolutely identical to Sheraton's original drawing, this bookcase clearly takes its inspiration from it and adopts the central design element of a cylinder shaped fall to the desk front. This slides back into the case to reveal pigeon holes and drawers internally. Sheraton does not specify how these should be made but in this case they are meticulously made, with cedar linings and mahogany fronts which are veneered in satinwood. Below the drawers is fitted a writing slide: this is also shown in Sheraton's drawing. This bookcase has a further writing feature, a hinged, leather lined writing slope which is fitted internally and can be held adjusted to write on. This feature does not appear in Sheraton's drawing.

The base of Sheraton's bookcase shows flat fronted doors with shelves internally. The bookcase reviewed here is different in this respect, and has two graduated drawers to the left and right of a central recessed cupboard which has two small doors, and a single drawer above. Both the lower side drawers are fitted as baize lined cellarettes. The black turned knob handles are original to the piece and help to place its manufacture after *circa* 1820, as do the broad cross-banded veneers on the cylinder front and the lower drawers and doors. The ivory or bone inlaid diamond shaped escutcheons are also features of furniture made *post* 1820, and were widely used in mahogany furniture made in the North-West region of England. The turned feet were also fashionable *post* 1820, and in contrast, have replaced the graceful bracket feet shown in Sheraton's drawing. The glazing of the bookcase is an exact copy of Sheraton's example, and the cornice design is closely similar too, but the scrolled fretted pediment is absent. The shelves in the bookcase are adjustable by virtue of notches in the bookcase sides.

Woods: *Primary:* Mahogany with mahogany and satinwood veneers.

   Secondary: Drawer fronts veneered onto pine. Cedar linings. Ebony stringing. Pine panelled backboards.

Dimensions: 234 hh. Base 115 h 107 w 61 d.

Noteworthy Construction Details: Impeccable cabinet making techniques throughout. See fine dovetailing in internal drawers for example.

Damage/Repairs/Replacement: Damage around lock of cylinder fall.

Catalogue No: **205.**

Item: Bureau with inlays.

Date of Manufacture: Circa 1780.

Significant Accession Details: Donor formerly of Knockaloughan, Santon.

Description: A bureau made with an oak carcase veneered with mahogany. It is cross-banded around the edge of the fall and the drawers with mahogany, and divided from the central veneers with stringing of holly or sycamore and ebony. The drawer fronts have matched pairs of veneers. The fall has a large central star inlay of holly or sycamore and dark stained wood, to create a three dimensional effect. The brass handles and escutcheons appear to be original to the bureau (one handle is missing). The interior writing section of the bureau shows a series of oak drawers both sides of a central aperture. Five of the small drawers are now missing, and it seems probable that there was originally a central door. The fall is rebated to hold a baize or leather writing surface (now missing) and it is probable that this was an additional feature not made at its date of production. This is a very substantial bureau, made with an oak carcase which is extended to include the dustboards and drawer linings. The use of fine dovetails, including mitred dovetails at the back of the drawers, indicates a high level of skill in its manufacture. The drawer size configuration is unconventional, and suggests that it was made to a special order. The particular use of stringing and the star inlay suggest that its region of origin is the North-West of England or the West Midlands.

Woods: *Primary:* Oak with mahogany veneers.

   Secondary: Holly or sycamore and ebony stringing.

Applied Surface Finish: Polished.

Dimensions: 101 h 99 w 59 d.

Noteworthy Construction Details: All dovetailed construction. Mitred dovetails at back of drawer linings. Full oak dustboards. Horizontal backboards.

Damage/Repairs/Replacement: Much damage to feet and plinth. Five small drawers missing. Stringing and cross-banding damaged.

Catalogue No: **206.**

Item: Bureau.

Date of Manufacture: Circa 1800.

Significant Accession Details: Said by donor (1960) to have been made by one of the Quarrie family of St. Judes.

Description: A substantial bureau, principally made in oak with pine linings to the base drawers. The drawers have cock beading around the edges and the elaborate brass handles and escutcheons appear contemporary with the piece. The varnished surface of the bureau is damaged by erosion and the low gallery on the top of the bureau is a later addition, as is the lower plinth which replaced the bracket feet which would probably have been fitted to this piece. The writing interior is elaborately fitted with upper pigeon holes and two lower rows of small drawers. The inner bank of drawers is elegantly curved and fitted either side of a central recess which also has small internal drawers. A door was fitted over this recess originally, and is now missing. Two shallow frieze drawers above the pigeon holes were intended as secret drawers. The fall, which has its original brass lock, has a later internal baize cover for writing.

Woods: *Primary:* Oak, with oak interior drawers.

       Secondary: Poplar or birch bottoms and pine linings to main drawers. Pine back.

Applied Surface Finish:
Was varnished, surface now badly oxidised.

Dimensions: 106 h 95 w 54 d.

Noteworthy Construction Details:
All dovetailed construction.

Damage/Repairs/Replacement:
Replacement plinth and upper gallery.
Cock beading to drawers.
Central door missing in top.

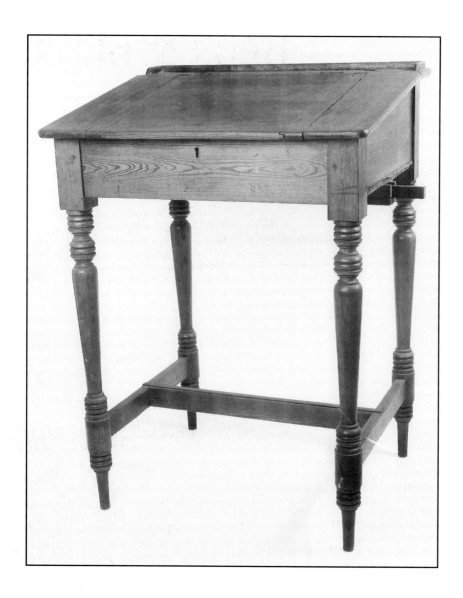

Catalogue No: **207.**

Item: Teacher's desk.

Date of Manufacture: Circa 1910.

Significant Accession Details: Donor formerly of Knockaloughan. Santon.

Description: A teacher's high desk made in Scots pine. This form of desk was produced by many furniture suppliers. Similar desks were made, for example, by the North of England School Furnishing Co. Ltd., Darlington, and illustrated in their catalogue of 1909. See Exhibit 17 in *School Furniture in the Vernacular Tradition,* C. Gilbert, Temple Newsam, 1978, which shows a desk with two side leaves to hold paper and books. The example reviewed here has the sliding lopers which originally supported side leaves, but these are now missing. The centre stretcher uniting the leg stretchers has a metal strap screwed to it to protect it from foot wear. A high chair, usually with a foot rest, was made to accompany desks of this kind.

Woods: *Primary:* Scots pine.

       Secondary: Varnished.

Dimensions: 112 h 83 w 87 d.

Noteworthy Construction Details: Stretcher is morticed through the side rails.

Damage/Repairs/Replacement: Side leaves missing.

BEDS & BEDROOMS

CHAPTER 18

BEDS & BEDROOMS

Accommodating beds and sleeping areas into the limited space offered by traditional single storey housing was a problem which required much ingenuity to resolve, since beds needed at night-time became an encumbrance during the day. Various solutions were adopted in different areas of the British Isles. For example, in Ireland many adaptable beds were made, including box settles where the base folded down to make a bed, and could be folded up again to form a seat during the day. The architecture of the house in Ireland, particularly, could also be made to accommodate a wooden bed placed in an alcove which protruded out from the main wall of the house (a bed outshot). Yet other solutions were reached by making false wardrobes which contained bed frames which folded down to form the base of a double bed and could also be folded away during the day.

In other cases, box beds were used. This type of bed took the form of a three-sided panelled bed which had either curtains or wooden shutters across the front. Box beds were widely used in Scotland and Ireland, and to some extent in Wales. In England, however, their use was confined to the North-East, and Northumberland and Durham are the only English regions known to have had beds of this type. A limited use of box beds was also found on the Isle of Man.

In traditional single storey housing on the Island, the provision of beds and sleeping areas was an issue which was also closely reflected in the design and layout of the home. Mr. F. A. Comaish of Glen Wyllin told the Folk Life Survey (FLS/C.F.A., 1949) that "Most of the crofters and working people had thatched cottages . . . On your left as you entered by the front door was the door leading to the bedroom. There were usually two beds in this room which were used by the parents and the female children. There was a loft over this room in which the male children slept. It was commonly called the cockloft, and was reached by a step-ladder going up out of the kitchen."

The use of a sleeping area or cockloft for children under the roof of single storey houses was also found in other regions of Britain where single storey houses were built. However, it seems that in some instances on the Island the adults also slept in this space, preferring to keep the two downstairs rooms for cooking and living in. Mrs. Corkish of Ramsey recalled in 1960 that "The house at Creg Mooar was not a very big one: there was the kitchen and the parlour, and then there was a cockloft going up and you could see a bed up there" (FLS/C/104).

The beds used in such houses were probably of the stump bed design, made entirely from wood with four corner posts which extended above the mattress level some two to three feet, joined at mattress height by rectangular rails. There was perhaps a head or foot board made from a single plank of wood, with a rope network to support the mattress woven through holes made in the bed rails. No beds of this type have been recorded on the Island and it is probable that in common with other areas of Britain the mass production of iron and brass bedsteads in the 1820s quickly led to the simple wooden beds being disposed of in favour of the more fashionable styles.

Other types of beds are mentioned by respondents to the Folk Life Survey, although it may be that these were unusual and thereby merited comment. For example Mrs. Craine of Glen Maye (FLS/C/37A) commented in 1951, when she was ninety-two years of age, that "Old Aunt Betsy Paie lived out at Glen Rushen in a tiny tholtan, and she had great pride in her camp bed - a wooden bed with four posters and a canopy, and the canopy was covered with blue check gingham, and so were the curtains of blue check material and they pulled right around the bed. She was shut in like a box". Beds of this type, called tent beds, were illustrated by J. C. Loudon in 1833, p. 334, figure 697. This bed has a curved rail each side connecting the head and foot posts, creating a flowing shape when covered in material. It may be, however, that the ones of this type noted on the Island had a simple framework of flat rails connecting the bed posts at the top, which represented another common method of construction.

The use of blue and white check or plaid may have been more generally popular on the Island for bed and window curtains. Miss Radcliffe, reporting to the Folk Life Survey in 1949 (FLS/R/3-A) gave a description of Manx bedclothes. "Our beds were Manx blankets and quilts. There was a quillade made of cloth patches and lined with an old blanket. This was very heavy. They had woven linen and wool sheets, too, in the old days. The curtains on the windows and beds were made of home-spun linen, usually in a broken plaid of blue and white."

Fig. 18.1; A four poster bed in the main bedroom of the Grove Rural Life Museum, Ramsey.

Fig. 18.2; The small bedroom at Abigail Faragher's home, Earystane, Colby.

Other four poster beds are mentioned in the Folk Life Survey and these were probably of the type described by Mrs. Craine. For example, Mr J. Kneen of Ballaugh Curraghs mentioned in 1950, that "The posts were sometimes six feet high around which the curtains were put, and they just looked for all the world like old coaches" (FLS/K-J-A). Such beds were probably not of the full tester type dating from the 17th century, which had a wooden canopy over the bed and a carved and panelled head board of full height. However, a now mutilated bed in Harry Kelly's cottage at Cregneash may have been of the full tester type, although its posts have now been cut off.

Prosperous households on the Island did have both full tester and half tester beds made of mahogany, dating from the 19th century. An example of a full tester bed of this type can be seen at The Grove, a small country house which Manx National Heritage has open to the public. This has turned posts at the bottom of the bed, an ornate footboard between them, and a cornice around the top of the bed connecting the turned posts with the rectangular ones at the head (Figure. 18.1). The tester is created with fabric stretched across the top framework.

Other forms of beds reported in use on the Island were probably of a press bed type, where the bed frame folded away when not needed. This may have appeared as a smaller item of furniture; a false bureau or chest of drawers, for example, or a specially constructed low cupboard with two doors. Mrs. Craine reported in 1951 that "There were pull-down beds in Dubois house. They lived in three rooms under the schoolroom. One was the parlour, and there were box beds that let down" (FLS/C/37.A). Beds which folded away in this manner were made by commercial

furniture manufacturers as well as local craftsmen throughout the 19th century, but like stump beds they have often been discarded in favour of modern divans or bed settees.

Where box beds were used in the various regions of Britain they were built into both two and single storey houses. When they were fitted into single storey dwellings they often formed a central division between rooms, and were built in pairs. In the Isle of Man there is no evidence that box beds formed part of single storey houses, but an example is reported as part of a two storey house where it was built upstairs. An account given to the Folk Life Survey in 1975 (FLS/E/6) records that at Ellan Rhennee, a small farm in the Ballaugh Curraghs, "The house is small, stone built, two storeyed, with a brick porch . . . A window in the west side has the name scratched W. Corlett 1838. Upstairs in the house there seems to have been a kind of box bed. The whole thing is encased in wood, and slats of wood are laid across, and an upright bar of wood at the foot. The door opening just allows room to get into the bed, and when closed forms parts of the side of the bed. There is an opening at the top . . . to give some ventilation".

The provision of beds in 19th century cottage homes was usually accompanied by other furniture related to aspects of personal hygiene and clothes storage; commodes, dressing and washing tables, as well as chests for clothes, and perhaps a tin bath which could be brought into the house when needed. Such items probably did not form a significant part of Manx cottage furniture. Mrs. Radcliffe commented that "There were no baths - a tub was used, the wash tub, where folk had a sponge bath in the kitchen when the rest of the family had retired" (FLS/R/3A, 1949).

196

However, in more prosperous homes on the Island, where greater space and affluence allowed, other furniture was provided for these purposes. This is illustrated in the bedroom furnishings held in the Manx National Heritage collection which were bequeathed by Miss Abigail Faragher.

A descendant of a farming family of long standing in the south of the Island, Miss Faragher lived in a small two storey dwelling at Earystane, Colby, until her death in 1988. The furnishings of her house are highly significant in that they illustrate the complete furnishings of a family which included craftsmen, blacksmiths and woodworkers, as well as farmers. Their prosperity was such that they accumulated many items of furniture which were variously handed down in the family or acquired as utilitarian but fashionable mass produced items of the kind which could be purchased from furniture stores or ordered from mail order catalogues. Other items of furniture were made locally, perhaps by her father or other relatives. Miss Faragher's bed is wooden and of a mass produced type which was usually offered in birch, mahogany or walnut (No. 208). Although made of parts from at least two beds, Miss Faragher's bed had decorative solid head and foot boards, connected by side rails which support cross slats on which the mattress rests. Such beds were made in Britain and other parts of Europe as popular alternatives to iron and brass bedsteads.

Furniture connected with personal washing was also present in Miss Faragher's home, namely wash stands, used to provide washing facilities in bedrooms where there was no running water in the house, except perhaps in the kitchen. A glazed pottery jug filled with water stood in a bowl or basin on top of the stand and the water was poured into the bowl for washing. The rear of the stand had a splash board. Other wash stand designs had a hole cut in the top into which the pottery bowl was fitted, and often a shelf attached to the back splash board on which to place toiletries. Some wash stands had a shelf fitted just above floor level and occasionally they were made with a cupboard in the base.

Of the four wash stands from Miss Faragher's house, one is a locally made example in pine with delicately turned legs, a flat top and a shaped splash board to the rear. The base is painted to simulate mahogany and the top to represent blue veined marble (No. 209). Simply made items of bedroom furniture of this kind were sometimes made by householders or local joiners or carpenters, who bought the turned front legs from a turner or sundries merchant and then built the piece using standard sized boards and timbers.

A further example of a wash stand from the same source, but with a shelf connecting the legs below, is No. 210. This stand was probably locally made to a pattern which was widely known elsewhere in Britain during the 19th century, and which continued to be

Fig. 18.3;
No. 219. A pot-cupboard masquerading as a small chest of drawers.

made until at least the 1930s by firms such as Scott & Son Ltd. of Kings Lynn. They advertised very similar items in their catalogue of 1931, in which they offered two finishes in "light or mahogany-colour at 14s 11d" (75p).

Two other wash stands were owned by Miss Faragher, both of which have Sicilian marble tops and variously a marble or ceramic splash board to the rear. The first of these stands, No. 211, epitomises the pretensions of much 19th century mass produced furniture. It is made in the style of an 18th century console or pier table which might have stood in the hallway of a fashionable house. The design of this wash stand was produced by a number of metropolitan furniture makers who were working in the 19th century, and a closely similar example appears in the catalogue of C. & R. Light (1881). This example shows a marble soap dish attached to the splash board.

The second stand, No. 212, is the most elaborate of the four wash stands. It has a ceramic splash board and a cupboard fixed on a lower shelf below the frieze.

Wash stands of this kind were fashionable towards the end of the 19th century, and the catalogue of Clozenberg & Co., London, *circa* 1905, illustrates a similar example in an advertisement as part of a bedroom suite valued at £10. A further illustration in the catalogue of R. Downey & Sons of Belfast also shows a virtually identical stand.

Towel rails were also a common feature in bedrooms, where they could be used in conjunction with wash stands. They were made in a variety of forms, including simulated bamboo and Gothic interpretations. The towel rail shown in No. 213 is closely similar to examples offered for sale by George Maddox (1882). His catalogues specialised in bedroom furniture and an early issue in about 1865, entitled *The Illustrated Catalogue of Bedroom Furniture and the New Exhibition Chamber Furniture* was based on furniture exhibited at the International Exhibition in 1862.

In addition to wash stands, a dressing table made of stained and varnished birch was amongst bedroom furnishings in Miss Faragher's home (No. 214). Dressing tables of this utility design were made in large quantities in the late-19th and early-20th centuries. Typically, they formed part of a bedroom suite composed of a bed, wardrobe, dressing table, wash stand, and often a night commode, a cane-seated chair and a turned towel rail. Bevelled mirrors of the kind used on this dressing table were fashionable and were also used in wardrobe doors. The aluminium handles used on this example are probably original, and help to date this table to *circa* 1910. An advertisement produced by R. Downey & Sons of Belfast, *circa* 1900, shows a virtually identical dressing table within its compatible group of bedroom furniture items.

Free-standing toilet mirrors which swivelled between two uprights were a common item of bedroom furniture. Their design altered with changes in furniture fashion and never more so than in the 19th century, when numerous designs were offered for sale by furniture makers in London and other major cities. The design of the mirror No. 215 is closely similar, for example, to those found in the catalogues of Wyman, 1877, and G. Maddox, 1882.

Wardrobes, too, formed a fashionable part of mass produced bedroom furniture towards the end of the 19th century. Miss Faragher's house contained three examples dating variously from around 1900 - 1920. Two of these were made in the Art Nouveau style, with mirrored doors and carved stylised floral motifs on the outer panels. Wardrobes of this type were made in large quantities in the late-19th and early-20th centuries, typically as part of a bedroom suite. The catalogue of R. Downey & Sons of Belfast, *circa* 1900,

shows a glass-doored wardrobe of the type shown in No. 216. This is illustrated with a tiled wash stand and a dressing table. The second example shown in No. 217 is closely similar to one illustrated in the catalogue of C. & R. Light, 1881.

The third example from Miss Faragher's home is made of highly grained elm veneered plywood, and dates from around 1920 (No. 218). This example coincides with the introduction of plywood which was cheap and easy to cut. This, combined with the spread of electrification in manufacturing, allowed the press shaping of parts and resulted in the production of mass produced inexpensive furniture by many furniture manufacturers in the East End of London and in other centres. In the 1920s and '30s these included the firms of Lebus, Bluestone & Elvin, B. & I. Nathan, and Beautility. These firms moved out of the East End to the Lea Valley in the '20s and '30s and by increasing their machinery-based production techniques manufactured massive quantities of furniture of the type illustrated here.

A pot-cupboard in the Manx National Heritage collection, No. 219, illustrates a form of commode which masquerades as a chest of drawers (Figure 18.3) Commodes of this type were fashionable in prosperous households during the first half of the 19th century, and were often made in veneered mahogany and other exotic woods, as well as in painted pine. The firm of William Smee of 6 Finsbury Pavement, London, produced a 374 page catalogue of designs in 1850-55 entitled *Designs for Furniture* in which they showed two similar commode designs to No. 129.

Catalogue No: **208.**

Item: Bed.

Date of Manufacture: Mid-19th century.

Significant Accession Details: Abigail Faragher, Earystane, Colby.

Description: A wooden bed frame whose parts are of mixed origins. The wooden head and base boards are composed of two outer turned uprights joined by shaped decorative solid boards. The head and base boards can be connected by two outer supports which are rebated down their length to hold wooden cross slats on which the mattress rests. Inexplicably, the two side supports fit to the top and bottom boards very inexactly, and it may be that these are not the correct supports for the bed. The head board is made of stained birch, with mahogany columns, whilst the base board is from a different bed and is made of walnut with a decorative ribbon moulding applied in an oval.

Woods: *Primary:* Head board stained birch with mahogany columns. Base board in walnut. Bed slats pine.

Applied Surface Finish: Varnished.

Dimensions: Internal 122 w 183 d.

Damage/Repairs/Replacement: Side struts do not appear to fit head and foot boards properly.

Catalogue No: **209.**

Item: Wash stand.

Date of Manufacture:
Late-19th or early-20th century.

Significant Accession Details: Abigail Faragher,
Earystane, Colby.

Description: A pine wash stand or dressing table of the
most simple design with two delicately turned front legs and
rear legs made of standard joinery. The plain top has a
decoratively shaped backboard and is without side boards.
The base is mahogany stained and varnished and the top is
naively simulated as blue veined marble over the bare wood,
which was not prepared with grain filler before painting.

Woods: Primary: Pine.

Applied Surface Finish:
Wood not filled. Simulated blue marble finish on top. Base
simulated as mahogany.

Dimensions: 75.5 h 75.5 w 44 d. Splash board 11 h.

Noteworthy Construction Details: All nailed
construction. Top boards butt-jointed. Side under-top
stretchers morticed through legs.

Catalogue No: **210.**

Item: Wash stand.

Date of Manufacture:
Late-19th or early-20th century.

Significant Accession Details: Abigail Faragher,
Earystane, Colby.

Description: A pine wash stand painted brown and with
decorative wood grain simulation to the front frieze. The top
has a curved rear splash board and shaped sides. A lower
shelf with a shaped front edge connects the turned legs
below.

Woods: Primary: Pine.

Applied Surface Finish:
Brown paint and wood simulation on front frieze.

Dimensions: 76 h 86.5 w 43 d. Splash board 22 h.

Noteworthy Construction Details:
Glued construction. Splash board dovetailed at corners.
Timber in back legs placed to show wide profile to front
view.

Catalogue No: **211.**

Item: Wash stand.

Date of Manufacture: Circa 1880.

Significant Accession Details: Abigail Faragher, Earystane, Colby.

Description: A wash stand with a Sicilian marble top, on a base with solid mahogany cabriole shaped front legs and with mahogany veneered onto a birch substrate elsewhere.

Woods: *Primary:* Solid mahogany legs. Mahogany veneered onto birch.
Sicilian marble top.

Dimensions: 70 h 121.5 w 50 d. Splash board 20 h.

Damage/Repairs/Replacement: Some bits missing on base of back supports: Veneer raised on frieze. Marble chipped on corner.

Catalogue No: **212.**

Item: Wash stand.

Date of Manufacture: Circa 1900.

Significant Accession Details: Abigail Faragher, Earystane, Colby.

Description: A pine wash stand, stained to simulate mahogany and varnished over. The prominent rear splash board has a central panel of twelve glazed and patterned ceramic tiles, held in a wooden frame and surmounted by a decorative pediment. The base has a top of Sicilian marble and the wooden frieze below this has a central drawer and turned towel rail fixed to the right hand side of the frieze. The turned legs terminate in brown porcelain castors and are joined by a lower shelf on which a central cupboard is fixed.

Woods: *Primary:* Pine.

Applied Surface Finish:
Mahogany, stained and varnished.

Dimensions: 78 h 118 w 46 d. Splash board 58 h.

Noteworthy Construction Details: All joints morticed and tenoned and blocked inside.

Catalogue No: **213.**

Item: Towel rail.

Date of Manufacture: Circa 1880.

Significant Accession Details: Abigail Faragher,
Earystane, Colby.

Description: A turned towel rail made of pine and painted
yellow, with graining effects on the square bases of the
uprights to simulate decorative painted black lines.

Woods: *Primary:* Pine.

Applied Surface Finish: Gessoed and simulated as
satinwood with black line decoration.

Dimensions: 79 h 61 w 22 d.

Catalogue No: **214.**

Item: Dressing table.

Date of Manufacture: Circa 1900.

Significant Accession Details: Abigail Faragher,
Earystane, Colby.

Description: A dressing table made of stained and
varnished birch, with a large adjustable mirror with small
drawers each side and two long drawers below. The
aluminium Art Nouveau handles on the drawers are original
to the piece.

Woods: *Primary:* Birch.

Applied Surface Finish: Varnished.

Dimensions: 163 hh. Base 65.5 h 107.5 w 43.5 d.

Catalogue No: **215.**

Item: Toilet mirror.

Date of Manufacture: Circa 1880.

Significant Accession Details: Abigail Faragher, Earystane, Colby.

Description: A toilet mirror with solid mahogany uprights, knobs and feet and veneered mahogany surface onto pine elsewhere. The rectangular mirror can swivel between the uprights.

Woods: *Primary*: Solid mahogany uprights and feet and veneers.

          Secondary: Pine base wood and pine back to mirror.

Dimensions: 49.5 h 42.5 w 20 d.

Noteworthy Construction Details: Glued and morticed and tenoned throughout.

Damage/Repairs/Replacement: Back right foot missing. Some veneer missing on curved front edge.

Catalogue No: **216.**

Item: Wardrobe.

Date of Manufacture: Circa 1900.

Significant Accession Details: Abigail Faragher, Earystane, Colby.

Description: A wardrobe made in the Art Nouveau style, with a mirrored central door and two raised fielded panels each side. These have Art Nouveau floral mortifs carved into the upper panels. The single drawer below has Art Nouveau brass handles and the carved cornice is detachable. This wardrobe is made in mahogany-stained and varnished birch. Typically manufacturers of this form of mass produced furniture also offered American walnut, ash and fumed mahogany.

Woods: *Primary*: Birch.

Applied Surface Finish: Mahoganised.

Dimensions: 211 h 104.5 w 40 d.

Noteworthy Construction Details:
Vertical backboards. Drawer dovetailed.

Damage/Repairs/Replacement: Odd handles on drawer.

Catalogue No: **217.**

Item: Wardrobe.

Date of Manufacture: Circa 1900.

Significant Accession Details: Abigail Faragher, Earystane, Colby.

Description: A wardrobe made in two parts. It is made of stained birch and American black walnut, with an oak panelled back and top and oak linings to the drawer. The door has a full length mirror. The cornice is now missing. The wardrobe is made in the Art Nouveau style with decorative vertical panels each side of the door, decorated with carved stylised foliar designs.

Woods: *Primary:* Birch and American black walnut, with oak panels and top and oak lined drawers.

          Secondary: Pine base board.

Applied Surface Finish: Varnished.

Dimensions: 184 h 106 w 42 d.

Noteworthy Construction Details: Top part panelled. Lower part tongue-and-groove boarding. Machine cut dovetails in drawer.

Damage/Repairs/Replacement: Cornice missing.

Catalogue No: **218.**

Item: Wardrobe.

Date of Manufacture: Circa 1920.

Significant Accession Details: Abigail Faragher, Earystane, Colby.

Description: A narrow wardrobe with a single door. It is made with vividly grained elm plywood veneers and mahogany beading on the edges.

Woods:　*Primary*: Elm-faced plywood.

　　　　Secondary: Mahogany beading.

Applied Surface Finish: Highly varnished.

Dimensions: 184 h　75 w　55 d.

Damage/Repairs/Replacement: Some damage to the top and bottom edges.

Catalogue No: **219.**

Item: Pot-cupboard.

Date of Manufacture: Circa 1820.

Description: A pot-cupboard or commode, simulated to appear as a small chest of drawers. The commode is made in pine and was gessoed and over-painted in red lead, with a later coat of blue/green paint over this. The interior is painted green, which was probably original to the piece. The exterior is now painted with a later coat of yellow/cream paint with decorative black lining to the edges of the drawer fronts. The gilt and brass handles on the *faux* drawer fronts seem original to the piece. The upper front and top hinge to the rear to reveal a fitted toilet seat and pottery chamber pot, which is suspended in the base below a seat frame. Narrow arms are fitted around the inside upper edge of the sides.

Woods: Primary: Pine.

Applied Surface Finish: First sealing coat of gesso, followed by red lead and a top coat of blue/green paint. Visible parts then painted yellow/cream and lined out in black.

Dimensions: 71 h 59.5 w 46 d.

Noteworthy Construction Details: Nailed construction.

Damage/Repairs/Replacement: Back of top has been repaired and a replacement strip fitted, presumably where hinges have split out. Three replaced brackets on feet. All corner bracket feet are replacements.

WOODEN CRADLES

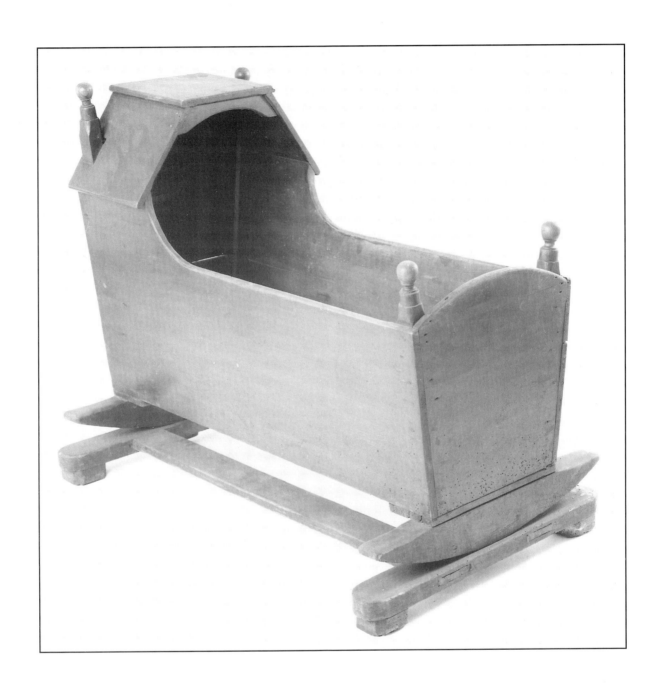

CHAPTER 19

Wooden Cradles

Wooden cradles are beds for infant children, typically made in the form of an oblong box with either sloping or upright sides and ends, and often, but not always, with a wooden hood at one end. The box is mounted on two rockers fixed to the base, which allow the cradle to be rocked by foot or hand to soothe the sleeping infant. They formed an essential part of domestic life in many countries, over many centuries. Cradles continued to be made in many areas into the 20th century, although there was a general tendency in most parts of Britain for wooden cradles to be superseded by wicker cradles (bassinettes) and cots after about 1840.

with the same material, dry straw and the peelings of briars" (FLS/K-J-A).

The purpose of providing infants with cradles was based on sound reasoning when cottage homes were typically draughty and damp. The hooded end probably also protected the child from pieces of the under-thatch falling into its face. Infant mortality was extremely high, and parents made efforts to protect their infants from the poor environmental conditions. Loudon wrote in 1833, of wicker cradles particularly, that there was a need to keep out draughts and to provide the baby with a "hair mattress stuffed very soft

Fig. 19.1; No. 229. The cradle rests on a low frame, raised from the floor on corner blocks.

In addition to wicker cradles, others were made of coils of straw joined to each other by lengths of split bramble, a craft known as lip-work. Craftsmen who worked at this trade made beehive baskets and 'hoppers' from which corn was sown. Mr. J. Kneen of the Ballaugh Curraghs, recorded as part of the Folk Life Survey in 1950 that "In olden times there were certain men went around the countryside making . . . cradles for babies and baskets to hold eggs . . . made

and a small down pillow." Such well endowed bedding was unusual, however, and for the most part babies lay on small flock filled mattresses with folded blankets below and above them, often with a knitted cover over this. In Scotland, mothers traditionally went further and knitted tapes which they crossed back and forth over the sleeping baby and around turned knobs fitted to the sides of the cradle.

Fig. 19.2; A wedge attached to the cradle's rockers slots into the frame, enabling the cradle to rock on its stand.

Manx customs and superstitions relating to birth, marriage and death, provide special and cautionary tales in relation to babies left unattended in cradles, since it was a widespread belief that babies were considered to be vulnerable to abduction by fairies, or to being changed for other babies. This was especially likely to happen, according to Manx mythology, before the baby was baptised, after which they were beyond the grasp of fairies. Writing in *The Folklore of the Isle of Man* (Chap. VIII, p. 157) A. W. Moore notes that at this vulnerable time, a person was invariably appointed for the baby's special protection; if the child had to be left alone in the cradle, the fire tongs, which must be made of iron, would be placed on the cradle until the protector's return. Other recorded fairy stories tell of the dire effects on children of not being protected in this way (see *Manx Fairy Tales*, Sophia Morrison, 1929, pp 89-90).

The twelve wooden cradles held by Manx National Heritage represent an unusually large and rich collection, from the earliest example which has a date 1770 carved on the side rail, to others which date to the last half of the 19th century. The great majority of cradles in the collection were made by joiners or carpenters, with the use of square corner posts in some examples. Those with decoratively turned finials probably involved the work of a skilled turner. Cradles, perhaps above all other items of furniture, were handed down in families, and it is not surprising that in certain cases a great deal of information is known about their history. Even the makers' names are occasionally known (see, for example, Nos. 225, 230 & 231).

The box parts of the cradles are made to a common pattern, and have sloping sides which are either butted and nailed at the corners or, more rarely, are dovetailed and sometimes mitred together. Some examples have corner posts which protrude through and above the hood and backboard and terminate in either turned finials or faceted geometric shapes. The main distinguishing feature between the cradles is in the variety of forms of the hood. These include simple geometric shaped hoods made of three sections of wood, as well as various interpretations of domed and curved profiles. In these terms, the Manx cradles

closely resemble examples made in Ireland, Wales and England (but not in Scotland, where a distinctive form was made which more closely resembles those from the Scandinavian countries.)

However, a number of cradles from the Island have a feature which appears to be unique to the Isle of Man. This is the use of a low frame made in rectangular form raised from the ground on small corner blocks. In these examples, the rockers are fitted with a central wedge which slots into an over-sized mortice cut into the frame on which they rest, thus allowing the cradle to rock on the stand (Figure 19.2). The purpose of the stand is not entirely clear, except that being raised from the floor in this way meant that the baby was kept on an even base, and further away from the damp of earthen floors and low draughts.

Although stands for cradles were known in some other cultures, for instance in the Mennonite culture of Canada, and in some Scandinavian examples, these were later than those made on the Isle of Man.

The bottoms of the Manx cradles are all made with solid boards running the whole length. In other regions, however, although solid boards were also used, slatted boards were used as an alternative, and in yet other examples small holes were drilled in the base board to allow for urine drainage.

All but one of the cradles are made completely of pine and were variously painted on the outside with different coloured paints, amongst which blue/green, red lead paint or mahogany staining varnish were common. Others were painted and grained to simulate oak or mahogany. In some cases, brown paint was applied over these finishes in the late-19th and 20th centuries. Interestingly, some cradles were painted light blue inside, which probably simulated an earlier tradition of lining cradles with blue paper. Others were painted in pale milk based paint (No. 224). In one case the interior is painted in mahogany to match the exterior, but it shows evidence of having been painted down to the level of the baby's bedding only (No. 229).

In only one example are woods in addition to pine used. This is in No. 231, which is made in Scots pine with alder rockers and edging strips of elm. The hood is decoratively inlaid with motifs in ebony and holly or sycamore.

Cots were made to accommodate children as they grew, and these were typically made as larger beds supported on four legs, with slides to stop the child from falling. The Museum collection has one cot of this factory-made type dating from the 20th century which has a metal frame and base with decorated and varnished birch panels (No. 232).

Catalogue No: **220.**

Item: Panelled cradle.

Date of Manufacture: Circa 1650 - 1780.

Description: This cradle was made within the joiners' tradition of the 17th and 18th centuries, with a framed construction which holds a series of raised fielded panels. The hood is made of framed and panelled sides which slope to the back. Across these a flat section of timber is nailed. The stiles which frame the sides tenon into the corner posts, which extend down to fit around and support the rockers. Complex layers of painted decoration have been added, probably in the 19th century over an earlier treatment of gesso and mahogany stain. However, micro analysis is needed to determine the precise typology and sequence of the painted layers (for an observational account, see Applied Surface Finish entry below). The cradle has the date 1770 incised on the top side stile, with the initials W. K. branded on each side of the date. This may represent a birth commemoration rather than the date of manufacture of the cradle (see detail photograph below).

Woods: *Primary:* Pine.

Applied Surface Finish: *Hood* - Originally painted with at least two coats of red/brown paint. *Carcase* - Some parts mahoganised, but later green and yellow/gold over this, possibly not all in the 19th century. Partial decoration on inscribed side. *Rockers* - Mahoganised coat with later coats of light green and dark green paint. *Inside* - Yellow over earlier red mahogany paint.

Dimensions: 72.5 hh 52 h 47.5 w 97 d.

Noteworthy Construction Details:
Foot end incorporates cleft timber. Hood includes some reclaimed timber. Knobs are turned.

Damage/Repairs/Replabement:
Replacement foot on right head corner.

Catalogue No: **221.**

Item: Cradle on stand.

Date of Manufacture: 19th century.

Description: A carpenter/joiner-made cradle of unusual form with a rectangular base on which the cradle rocks: the rockers have two flat tenons morticed into them which fit into two slots in the base ends. The cradle includes an unusual refinement in that the shaped hood was sawn from the solid wood to create flowing shapes for the sides, rather than being made from flat sections. The hood also has a geometric tablet nailed to the top in a manner typical of house joinery decoration detail (see detail photograph below). This cradle is of all nailed construction, with narrow boards forming the sides and ends. These are nailed to corner posts which terminate in turned finials.

Woods: *Primary:* Pine.

Applied Surface Finish: Unstained. Varnished over.

Dimensions: 64 hh 42 h 35 w 87.5 d.

Noteworthy Construction Details:
Nailed construction.

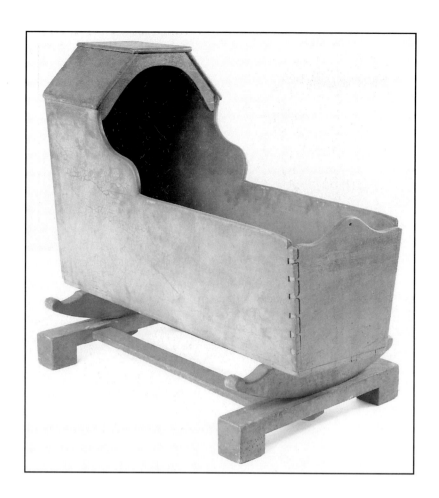

Catalogue No: **222.**

Item: Cradle on stand.

Date of Manufacture: Circa 1840.

Description: A pine cradle on a stand, which is, unusually, dovetailed at its corners, rather than nailed, and has the refinement of rounded edges to the top of the box and soft flowing lines to the base and head boards. The surface of the cradle is painted with an initial coat of mahogany stain, and has a later coat of simulated oak graining over this. The hood is geometrically shaped, being made of three flat sections of wood nailed together and supported with a shaped front frieze. The rockers are decoratively shaped at the ends, and are fitted to the stand with two tenons which slot into rectangular mortices in the base.

Woods: *Primary:* Pine.

Applied Surface Finish: Initial coat of mahogany stain with later coat of simulated oak graining and varnish over this.

Dimensions: 70.5 hh 39 h 36 w 91 d.

Noteworthy Construction Details: Dovetailed at head and base of box. Boards in base are tongue-and-grooved.

Catalogue No: **223.**

Item: Cradle.

Date of Manufacture: Circa 1840.

Description: A cradle made with nailed construction throughout. This cradle was made with an unusual degree of design consciousness and refinement. The rectangular form of the box is relieved with a foot board which is curved at the top, and is mitred to the corners of the side boards. All top surface edges are rounded and the two short end supports have decoratively faceted terminals. The hood sides are, unusually, made from the same wide board as the side boards, and are shaped with a flowing line which is contiguous with the sides of the hood. These are of a complex flowing design, and were made by being sawn from a solid block of wood. The separate top section of the hood complements this line in being slightly domed, and is supported at the front with a decoratively shaped frieze. The internal back corners of the cradle were also supported by two square uprights which project below the floor of the cradle and support the rear rocker. The exterior of the cradle was stained a mahogany colour and this was continued only a little way into the interior, with the majority of the internal surfaces of the cradle left unstained. The rockers have two tenons projecting below, indicating that the cradle once stood on a stand.

Woods: *Primary*: Pine.

Applied Surface Finish: Mahogany stained exterior: inside only partially stained. Corner supports not stained.

Dimensions: 73 hh 37 h 37.5 w 90.5 d.

Noteworthy Construction Details: All nailed construction. Corners mitred at foot only. Curved hood sections cut from solid wood, not steam-bent.

Damage/Repairs/Replacement: Stand missing. Rocker at head of cradle loose.

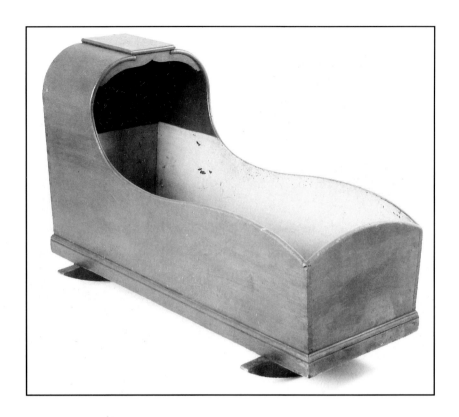

Catalogue No: **224.**

Item: Cradle.

Date of Manufacture: Circa 1840.

Description: A cradle of dovetailed construction at its corners. This example has an unusual design refinement: the flowing lines of the top edge of the rectangular box articulate with the shape of the hood to create a softness of line which contrasts with the formal linear shape of many cradles recorded on the Isle of Man. The flat surmounting section of the hood, the backboards and the shaped front support are nailed together to provide a secure fixing for the hood sections. The bottom edge of the cradle has a moulded plinth which is mitred at the corners. The rockers appear to be original, and may have been fitted to a stand originally. The exterior of the cradle is mahoganised and the interior is painted with a pale milk paint.

Woods: *Primary*: Pine.

Applied Surface Finish: Mahoganised on outside, with pale milk paint on inside.

Dimensions: 57 hh 35 h 36 w 95 d.

Noteworthy Construction Details: Dovetailed joints securing sides to hood and foot board.
Curves in hood cut from solid timber.

Damage/Repairs/Replacement: Possibly had a stand originally.

Catalogue No: **225.**

Item: Cradle with pyramidal finials.

Date of Manufacture: Circa 1840.

Significant Accession Details: Said by donor (in 1962) to have been in her family (Brew family of Ballaugh) for more than 150 years. Last used by the Hazelwood family of Ballaugh.

Description: A carpenter/joiner-made cradle of nailed construction. The rectangular box has a less accentuated slope to the sides than many cradles recorded on the Isle of Man. It is simply formed with curved hood sides, onto which a geometrically shaped top formed from three flat sections is nailed, without the benefit of a curved support at the front. The edges of the cradle box and the exterior of the end panel are finished with thin edging strips which are nailed and mitred at their corners. The short end posts which support the end panel and the sides terminate in pyramidal shaped finials. The rockers are original, and appear not to have fitted onto a stand, in the manner of many cradles recorded on the Isle of Man. The cradle had two pegs (one now missing) on the outer top edge which would have served to secure a tape or ribbon to restrain the baby in the cradle.

Woods: *Primary*: Pine.

Applied Surface Finish: Originally pale blue/green painted all over. Later coats of red/brown paint with blue borders on outside.

Dimensions: 63 hh 38 h 36 w 85 d.

Noteworthy Construction Details: All nailed construction. Edging strips around the top edge of the cradle and around the foot board are mitred at the corners.

Damage/Repairs/Replacement: Tie knob on left side missing.

Catalogue No: **226.**

Item: Cradle.

Date of Manufacture: Second half of the 19th century.

Description: A carpenter/joiner-made cradle of the most simple geometric form. This is a generic design which could have been made in many parts of the British Isles. It is of nailed construction throughout and is made without corner posts. The hood is of the least complex form, being made of three flat sections of timber supported with three frontal sections of wood nailed to them.

Woods: *Primary:* Pine.

Applied Surface Finish: Red lead with later brown.

Dimensions: 62 hh 30 h 35.5 w 89 d.

Noteworthy Construction Details: Nailed construction.

Damage/Repairs/Replacement: Unexplained mortices on rockers suggest the use of recycled timber.

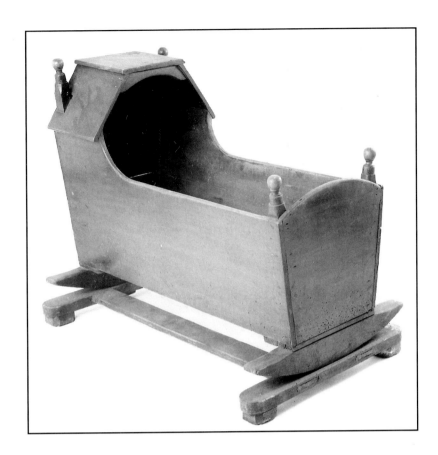

Catalogue No: **227.**

Item: Cradle on stand.

Date of Manufacture: Second half of the19th century.

Significant Accession Details: Said by donor to have been made in Peel in 1896.

Description: A joiner/carpenter-made cradle of nailed construction. This example has unusually high sides which sharply taper towards the floor. The corners of the cradle are supported by square uprights which terminate in decoratively turned finials. The hood is made from three flat sections of wood nailed together, the outer sloping sections being morticed to fit around the extended corner uprights. The foot board is curved on the top edge. The base boards are missing and the cradle sits on two wooden sections nailed across its ends, which in turn are nailed to the rockers. These have tenons which fit into mortices on the base and allow the cradle to rock on the frame. The exterior of this cradle is stained to simulate mahogany and this is continued on the inside down to the level of the bedding only.

Woods: *Primary:* Pine.

Applied Surface Finish: Mahogany stain, to level of bedding only on inside.

Dimensions: 71 hh 41 h 39 w 92 d.

Noteworthy Construction Details: Nailed construction.

Damage/Repairs/Replacement: The cradle base boards are missing.

Catalogue No: **228.**

Item: Cradle.

Date of Manufacture: 19th century.

Description: A carpenter/joiner-made cradle of nailed construction. This example was decoratively painted blue in the interior and finished in simulated oak grain on the outside. The paintwork was evidently produced by a craftsman practised in this skill; the tangential or heartwood graining on the side panels requires a technique of some sophistication to produce and indicates that the maker probably had the additional skills of painter and decorator. This cradle has the refinement of flowing and rounded lines to the top edges of the cradle box which continue upwards and around the edge of the hood. The hood is composed of three nailed sections, with the outer two sawn from the solid wood in a curved shape to articulate with the shaped lines of the sides. This example may have originally stood on a stand.

Woods:　*Primary:* Pine.

Applied Surface Finish: Simulated oak grain on outside. Coats of blue paint on inside.

Dimensions: 63 hh 35 h 46 w 91 d.

Noteworthy Construction Details: Nailed construction throughout.

Damage/Repairs/Replacement: Possibly had a stand originally.

Catalogue No: **229.**

Item: Cradle on stand with domed hood.

Date of Manufacture: Second half of the 19th century.

Significant Accession Details: Said by donor (1957) to have been made by a Mr. Harrison, joiner of Regaby, and used regularly at St. Olave's Church, Ramsey, for nativity plays etc. Bottom boards not original and showing woodworm infestation were destroyed on Museum acquisition, 1957.

Description: A carpenter/joiner-made cradle on a stand. The use of a separate cradle stand appears to have been common on the Isle of Man, a feature which is not known elsewhere in Britain. This example is made with nailed board construction. The domed top is made separately from the box from sections of wood, tongue-and-grooved together, and nailed to the curved, sawn, supporting sections. The corner posts at the foot have rounded domed finials. A mahoganising stain was applied over the whole of the exterior of the cradle, as well as inside the hood for a short way down the sides, but not lower than the level of the bedding. The cradle is fixed to rockers which move on a raised stand by virtue of two shaped tenons screwed to the cradle base and fit into two mortices in the stand (see detail photograph, Figure 19.2, p. 209).

Woods: *Primary*: Pine.

Applied Surface Finish: Mahoganised surface on exterior surfaces and interior down to level of the bedding.

Dimensions: 72 hh 35.5 h 37.5 w 91 d.

Noteworthy Construction Details: Nailed construction. Hood is tongue-and-grooved jointed with curved side sections sawn from solid wood. Hood is made separately.

Damage/Repairs/Replacement: Removeable floor boards now missing (see accession notes above)

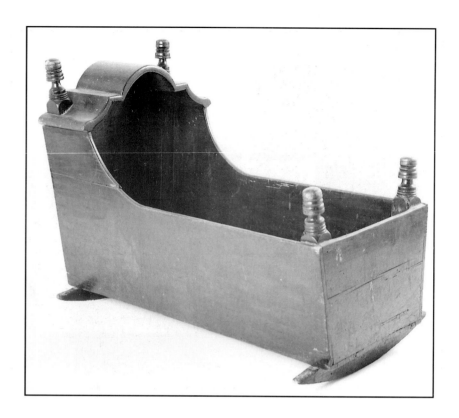

Catalogue No: **230.**

Item: Cradle.

Date of Manufacture: Last quarter of the 19th century.

Significant Accession Details: Said by the donor to have been made for his (Barron) family at Bishopscourt by James Cannell, joiner and crofter of Glebe Farm, Michael, who died in 1924, aged 70. The 1871 Census lists a James Cannell, joiner, aged 18, at Ballarhenny.

Description: A joiner/carpenter-made cradle of nailed construction. This cradle has an unusually detailed attribution to both maker and user, and in this is one of the most highly provenanced items of Manx furniture. The design of the cradle follows the conventional wedge-shaped form of many cradles recorded on the Island, nailed at its corners and mounted on two rockers. Various unexplained holes and mortices suggest that it was made from reclaimed timber. The exterior of the cradle is stained with mahogany stain. The hood is unusually elaborate and is made from three sawn sections, nailed together in the shape of a classical ogee curve. The corners of this cradle are supported by square uprights which terminate in elaborately turned finials suggesting that a specialist turner may have been employed in producing it.

Woods: *Primary:* Pine.

Applied Surface Finish: Mahoganised.

Dimensions: 67 hh 34.5 h 41 w 91 d.

Noteworthy Construction Details: Nailed construction. Hood curves cut from solid timber. Evidence of having been made from reclaimed timber.

Catalogue No: **231.**

Item: Cradle with decorative hood.

Date of Manufacture: 1875.

Significant Accession Details: Said to have been made by George Gelling (1845 - 1931), a joiner of Ballasalla, for his first child, James, born 1875, and used for his fourteen other children. It was last used for his grandson in 1916. The donor is one of George Gelling's children.

Description: A joiner/carpenter-made cradle of nailed construction. This example has detailed information about its production and family use, and is one of a small number of Manx Cradles which is highly provenanced (see No. 230 for a further example). The body of the cradle is made with nailed sections with a hood surmounted on it which is made in a flowing shape from short nailed sections (see detail photograph below). The foot board is supported in the corners with two square uprights which terminate in inlaid and decoratively sawn shaped terminals. The base of the cradle has a simple plinth made of elm. The cradle, unusually, is not stained or painted, and evidently uses the highly defined grain which Scots pine has as a form of decoration. Decoration of the cradle is also achieved with diamond shaped inlays of ebony around the outer edge of the hood front. This is contrasted with square flat sections of ebony which are applied to the lower front edges of the hood, and centrally inlaid with a diamond of light coloured wood, probably holly, sycamore or box. The front supporting frieze of the hood is decoratively fretted with a rose spray motif.

Woods: *Primary:* Scots pine.

Secondary: Elm edge beading. Ebony and box, holly or sycamore inlays. Alder rockers. Hood lined with newspaper.

Dimensions: 71 hh 40 h 92 w 41 d.

Noteworthy Construction Details: Nailed construction. Applied edging strip around sides and end. Right side of cradle box made from cleft wood.

Damage/Repairs/Replacement: This cradle possibly had a stand originally. End edging strip replaced in oak. Old metal repair inside hood.

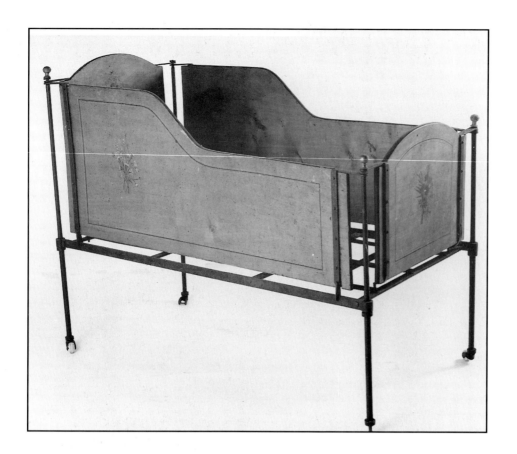

Catalogue No: **232**

Item: Child's cot with metal frame.

Date of Manufacture: Circa 1920.

Description: A child's cot made with a black painted metal frame. It is mounted on castors, and has brass knobs on the corner posts. The horizontal base has metal cross straps to hold the mattress and metal brackets are attached to the outer edge of the base frame and the corner uprights, to which four shaped panels of varnished birch are screwed to form the ends and sides of the boards which follow the curve of the panels. A spray of flowers is painted on each board. The use of cots for children of intermediate years, between leaving the cradle and sleeping in a bed, have been specifically recorded from at least the 16th century. However, they have typically been the prerogative of affluent households and were virtually unknown in working class homes until the 19th century

Woods: *Primary*: Birch.

　　　　　Secondary: Metal frame. Brass knobs.

Applied Surface Finish: Varnished wood and black-painted metal frame.

Dimensions: 81.5 hh 66.5 h 54.5 w 116.5 d.

Damage/Repairs/Replacement: One castor broken and one missing. One missing brass finial.

SPINNING WHEELS & WINDERS

CHAPTER 20

SPINNING WHEELS & WINDERS

The tasks of collecting, carding, spinning, and hanking wool were an important part of a Manx woman's work; one which apart from providing wool for knitted garments, could also provide a saleable product to contribute to the household income. Mrs. Mylecraine of Ballaugh, speaking in 1949 of this aspect of household life, said that in the first part of the 20th century spinning was very much a winter activity . . . "In winter, the spinning wheel was in use, and there was always a basket of wool in the corner which had been washed once: this had to be gone through and bits of grass, twigs . . . removed before sending to Southward's Mill to be made up into suitings, or flannel, or blankets, whichever was most needed" (FLS/WRC-4). Spinning was probably more a winter's activity simply because the long dark nights were a time when other tasks could not easily be done. Margaret Killip says in *Folklore of the Isle of Man* that there was a saying "Te foddy ny share ve snieu tra ta ny kirree cadley" (It is far better to be spinning when the sheep are asleep).

Flax was also processed and spun in cottage homes on the same wheels as wool. Bed linen, checked shirt and curtain material, and fabric for working smocks were all made from the woven linen of differing weights and qualities. Linsey-woolsey, a particularly hard-wearing fabric with a linen warp and wool weft, was extensively used and valued on the Island.

Many late - 19th century photographs of Island life show that spinning was indeed widespread, and perhaps particularly the domain of elderly women whose skill and dexterity could be utilised in this productive task whilst they remained in the home (Figure 20.1).

Manx National Heritage has an extensive collection of spinning wheels as well as different forms of skein or hank winders, some of which measured the length of the wool in the skein. The forms of wheels used were of two main types: the great wheel and the treadle operated bobbin-flyer wheel. The great (or walking) wheels of which the Museum collection has three examples (Nos. 233 - 235) are made in the general pattern of great wheels from Europe and North America. Regardless of the style or origin of the great wheel, however, certain parts are common to all.

There is a drive wheel, usually with a flat rim of varying widths and constructed of wood. The wheel drives the spinning mechanism by means of a drive belt or cord of tightly twisted cotton or linen, and is mounted on a post rising from a table or 'saddle'.

Early manuscripts depicting the European great wheel show that the table was supported on either two or four legs. Three legged wheels like the English ones are similar in style to, but smaller than, those commonly found in North America.

Rising from the table at the opposite end from the wheel is a post on which the spindle mechanism is mounted. Surviving wheels throughout the British Isles commonly have a flat board, as do those in the Manx collection, and the board or post on which the spindle is mounted has leather straw ties in which the spindle rotates. A slot is cut into the post to allow room for the movement of the pulley.

Operating the great wheel was less convenient than the foot treadle wheel, since the spinner had to walk in order to perform her task. Starting close to the spindle, she placed her right hand on the wheel and took the carded wool in her left. As she turned the wheel she stepped back, drawing the wool out, and allowing the twist from the spindle to bind the fibres together. When she had walked back as far as she could, the wheel was backed off (reversed), and the length of spun yarn was wound onto a spindle. See *Spinning and Spinning Wheels*, Eliza Leadbeater, 1979.

The second and evidently much more popular form of wheel on the Isle of Man, at least during the 19th and into the 20th century, was the smaller treadle operated wheel which allowed the spinner to sit down whilst operating the wheel with hands and foot (Figure 20.2). Within the Museum collection, the great majority of wheels (eighteen) have a sloped table supported on three legs, on which the wheel and the spinning apparatus is held. One other wheel in the collection is made in another conventional form, with a vertically supported wheel above which the spinning mechanism is set (No. 258).

Although it is probable that the majority of spinning wheels in the Manx collection were made on the Island, at least two are made to a Scottish pattern and probably originate from there (Nos. 239 & 251). A further wheel originates from Scandinavia (No. 236).

However, regardless of their method of construction or origins there are certain parts in common. The 'U'-flyer and bobbin mechanism are mounted in leather bushes between two posts called maidens. One of these maidens is moveable, or constructed so that the bobbin-flyer can be removed. When the bobbin is full of spun wool it can then be replaced with an empty one. The maidens usually fit into a cross-bar called the

Fig. 20.1; *Etty Quilliam of Ballagawne, Rushen, spinning outside her home in 1880.*

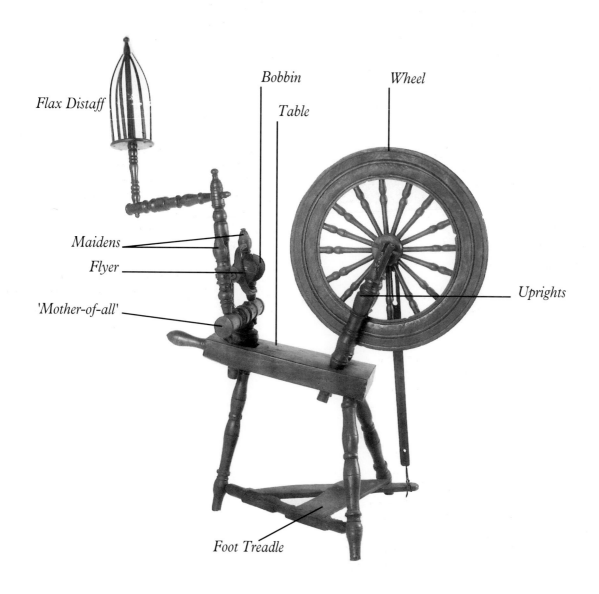

Flax Distaff

Bobbin

Wheel

Table

Maidens

Flyer

'Mother-of-all'

Uprights

Foot Treadle

Fig. 20.2; A treadle operated spinning wheel.

mother-of-all, which is mounted on the wheel in a variety of ways.

The wheel itself is mounted in slots, in two uprights which often have stays for extra support (see *Spinning and Spinning Wheels*, Eliza Leadbeater, 1979).

Many wheels were fitted with a distaff which provided a place for fibres of flax to be presented in a manner ready for spinning. However, only one of the Manx National Heritage collection of wheels has a complete distaff for flax spinning, No. 255, although some others have parts of a distaff present, and yet others have a hole drilled in the table to hold one. Other wheels were made not to hold a distaff at all.

Accounts given by Islanders to the Folk Life Survey indicate that spinning wheel making and repairing was a widespread craft on the Isle of Man, with some

makers specialising in the work. For example, a detailed account of spinning wheel making was noted as part of the Folk Life Survey in 1960 by Mr. J. C. Callister of the Lhen Bridge, West Craig, Andreas, who gave unusual insights into the craft. His great-grandfather, Thomas Callister, and his grandfather and father, both named John, were a family of spinning wheel makers. They worked in this trade until the end of the 19th century, when a repair to a spoke cost two pence or threepence, "A new wheel cost eighteen shillings, and he sold the last to Mrs. Sayle, Keeilltushtagh, for that price in about 1890" (FLS/C/59/E).

The account given by John Callister provides a rare and possibly unique insight into the craft techniques used by turners to make treadle wheels. He explained, for example, that "The Callister wheels were all done in the same way and you could recognise the style of the turning. Doing the spokes was the hardest part. Each had to be done separately, and yet all alike. The holes in the hub of the wheel were done with a brace and bit. The shaft that goes through the hub of the wheel is made of charcoal iron and that was turned with a hard steel chisel. The wheels were left after they were finished; they were never sand-papered or touched up in any way, just rubbed with linseed oil. Some of the wheels were varnished" (FLS/C/59/E).

Mr. Callister's detailed knowledge of other aspects of making the wheels provides information which might otherwise only be guessed at. For example, the difficult task of turning the rim or flat outer edge of the wheel is described in great detail. "A spinning wheel rim was made in four or five sections, and the pieces were joined together with wooden dowels. The wood used for the rim pieces was bigger than was usually put on the lathe, and so the face plate had to be used. It was screwed onto the lathe, and was fitted to the shaft of the pulley, and then the wood was fastened to it with small clamps while it was being worked" (*ibid*).

The making of such a large turned part required a high powered lathe, and John Callister recorded that the family's lathe "was worked by a big pit wheel four feet in diameter, and with a six inch crank, and it was pedalled with the foot" (*ibid*).

The wheels in the Museum collection certainly illustrate that many different turnery devices were used to produce the turned parts. These include the legs, wheels, spindles, distaff and distaff holders, the mother-of-all and the maidens (uprights) - see Figure 20.2. Each of these turned parts tended to have a different profile within individual wheels and it is probable that each maker had his own set of turnery signatures which identified his work. Further research may show that these were united by particular rules of combination which probably form particular codes of turnery styles.

Other devices were made for use in combination with spinning wheels. These included the wool winders which were made with one or more spools onto which wool could be directly wound from the 'U'-flyer, and from which multiple ply yarn could be produced. The Museum collection has one example of this device which originally held four spools (No. 259).

Once spun, the yarn was traditionally removed from the bobbin, and the reel was used to skein and measure the spun yarn. Hand held skein winders were generally replaced by hand operated rotary winders which had from four to six arms and could either be in a vertical or horizontal axis.

In their most sophisticated form the vertical models, of which the collection has four examples, had a gearing system in the central column which counted the skein lengths and registered them, either by a clock-like hand

and dial, or by the spinner counting a click made by a thin pliable wooden strip set in the counting cog. Many rotary winders of this kind had one of the arms made to adjust in length, in order that both proper tension and release of the skein could be achieved. See Nos. 260 & 281 for examples which have extending arms and clock style counting mechanisms.

Other forms of rotary winder were made simply by pivoting a cross arm device on a central spigot of wood or metal held on a short wooden stand. This form of rotary winder was turned directly by hand, and the length and tension of the skein was achieved by moving pegs into holes bored along the arms (see Nos. 263 & 265 for examples of this type of winder). Other versions of this form of horizontal rotary winder have four crossed arms of a box-like construction (No. 266).

The skein wound in this way was then ready to be washed and dyed. When dry it could be placed back on the winder to be wound into balls ready for use.

Catalogue No: **233.**

Item: Great wheel.

Date of Manufacture: 19th century.

Description: A great wheel with large flat wheel rim made of cleft ash with hand shaped oak spokes. The table of the wheel is made of cleft oak, and the four pine legs are probably replacements. This wheel is made in the general pattern of English great wheels where the wheel pivots on a rectangular upright which is morticed obliquely into the horizontal table. It is connected by a cord to the spool, which in turn is held on a flat upright morticed into the opposite end of the table. This example is of a simple design, made without a tensioning screw which could adjust the spool upright to tension the drive cord.

Woods: *Primary:* Oak table and spokes. Ash rim
                    to wheel.

            Secondary: Pine legs (probably replacements).

Dimensions: 119.5 h 103 w.

Noteworthy Construction Details:
Spokes are hand-shaped.

Damage/Repairs/Replacement: Various nailed repairs and replacement sections. Pine upright and legs are replacements.

Catalogue No: **234.**

Item: Great wheel.

Date of Manufacture: 19th or early - 20th century.

Description: A great wheel with its flat wheel now missing. This form of spinning wheel is made in an archaic form which follows a general British design. A sloping upright originally held a large, flat drive wheel which rotated on a metal spigot. The rectangular upright is roughly shaped at the bottom to form a round tenon, which mortices through the table of the wheel and is pegged below to hold it in place. At the other end of the table a sloping plank end holds the spool onto which the wool is spun. The end is adjustable by virtue of a large wooden screw which passes through its base and is held in a box built on the table. This could also be used for storage. The table is supported on three chamfered legs which mortice through it with round tenons.

Woods: *Primary:* Pine base.

            Secondary: Oak legs
                    & uprights.

Dimensions: 89 h 85 w.

Catalogue No: **243.**

Item: Spinning wheel.

Date of Manufacture: 19th century.

Significant Accession Details: In use until 1907 by donor's grandmother at Solomon's Corner, Ballamodha, Malew.

Description: Parts of a treadle operated bobbin-flyer spinning wheel. The remaining parts of this wheel suggest that it was made as a conventional type, predominantly from ash with oak spindles and outer wheel, and with birch as a minor secondary wood. The surface of the wheel has several coats of dark varnish. The tensioning screw, mother-of-all and its accompanying parts including the 'U'-flyer and bobbin, the distaff and the distaff holder, are all missing. The treadle is disconnected from the legs and footman.

Woods: *Primary:* Oak spindles and wheel. Ash legs, table and wheel supports.

   Secondary: Ash and birch treadle. Ash treadle support.

Applied Surface Finish: Thick coats of dark varnish.

Dimensions: 92 h 75 w.

Damage/Repairs/Replacement:
Many missing parts (see description). Pine footman may be a replacement.

Catalogue No: **244.**

Item: Spinning wheel.

Date of Manufacture: 19th century.

Description: A treadle operated bobbin-flyer spinning wheel. This wheel is made in a conventional form, with oak used for the mother-of-all, table wheel and spindles. Two legs are replaced in oak, and one is original in oak. Other turned parts are in ash. The wheel is substantially intact, except that the footman, distaff and distaff holder are missing. The 'U'-flyer is broken, and the overall surface of the wheel shows signs of erosion. The table has a split at the opposite end to the tensioning screw. The top of the table has a heart shaped recess cut into it, using three wood bit incisions joined by a chisel, which was probably used to hold water to dampen the flax.

Woods: *Primary:* Oak wheel, spindles, table, legs, and mother-of-all. Other turned parts ash.

   Secondary: Some pine parts in treadle.

Dimensions: 91.5 h 80.5 w.

Damage/Repairs/Replacement:
'U'-flyer broken. Distaff and footman missing.

Catalogue No: **245.**

Item: Spinning wheel.

Date of Manufacture: 19th century.

Significant Accession Details: From Crebbin's House, Cregneash.

Description: A treadle operated bobbin-flyer spinning wheel of a conventional pattern, made predominantly in ash with the wheel and spindles in oak. The table has dentil notching on the two ends. The wheel is substantially intact, apart from the distaff and distaff holder which are missing, and some parts of the 'U'-flyer which have been broken off.

Woods: *Primary*: Oak wheel and spindles. Ash table and turned parts.

   Secondary: Treadle and footman in pine.

Dimensions: 95 h 87 w.

Damage/Repairs/Replacement:
Treadle mechanism unattached. 'U'-flyer broken. Distaff and one wheel spoke missing.

Catalogue No: **246.**

Item: Spinning wheel.

Date of Manufacture: 19th century.

Description: A treadle operated bobbin-flyer wheel for spinning wool and flax. This wheel is made in a conventional design with an oak wheel, spindles and a cleft section of birch for the bed. The treadle is made from pine and ash. The end of the footman is broken. One leg is made in oak and the other two, possibly replacements, are in ash. The uprights are supported by two extra spindles which are screwed to them and the table. The distaff holder upright is present, but the distaff arm and distaff are missing. The table has a heart-shaped recess in its centre, formed from three large wood-bit turnings joined with a chisel, and probably intended to hold water to moisten the flax.

Woods: *Primary*: Oak wheel and spindles. Birch table. Ash for turned parts. Pine front bar and treadle.

   Secondary: One oak leg and two (replacements) in ash.

Dimensions: 87 h 89 w.

Noteworthy Construction Details: Extra turned spindles support mother-of-all.

Damage/Repairs/Replacement:
Treadle assembly disconnected. Replacement tensioning screw in oak.

Catalogue No: **247.**

Item: Spinning wheel.

Date of Manufacture: 19th century.

Significant Accession Details: Purchased in Kirk Michael, 1910.

Description: A treadle operated bobbin-flyer spinning wheel of a conventional pattern, with coats of dark varnish over the surface. Ash is used for the table and for the mother-of-all and its associated apparatus, including the turned supports and the tensioning screw. The wheel and spindles are made of oak, as is the treadle which also has some pine sections. The wheel is substantially intact except that the distaff and distaff holder are missing. The turnery devices used throughout this wheel exhibit an unusual boldness in their profiles.

Woods: *Primary:* Ash table, mother-of-all, tensioning screw, wheel supports and legs. Oak wheel and spindles. Oak and pine treadle.

Dimensions: 83 h 78.5 w.

Damage/Repairs/Replacement:
'U'-flyer broken. Distaff missing.

Catalogue No: **248.**

Item: Spinning wheel.

Date of Manufacture: 19th century.

Description: A treadle operated bobbin-flyer spinning wheel of a conventional pattern, intended to spin both wool and flax. The wheel is coated with dark varnish which obscures some of the woods from which it is made. However, where woods are visible, the legs and tensioning handle are shown to be of ash and the table beech. The wheel and spindles are probably in oak, and other turned parts appear to be in ash. The wheel is substantially intact, with the exception that the treadle, footman, distaff and distaff holder are missing. The two uprights are supported by two extra turned spindles which are screwed to the uprights and the table. There is a decorative diamond shaped recess cut into the centre of the table, probably to hold water to moisten the yarn.

Woods: *Primary:* Ash legs & tensioning handle. Beech table. Ash turned parts. The wheel & spokes are probably oak.

Applied Surface Finish: Coats of dark varnish or black paint.

Dimensions: 92 h 90 w.

Noteworthy Construction Details:
Two extra turned supports.

Damage/Repairs/Replacement:
Treadle, footman, distaff and distaff holder missing.

Catalogue No: **249.**

Item: Spinning wheel.

Date of Manufacture: 19th century.

Description: A treadle operated bobbin-flyer spinning wheel. The wheel is made in a conventional form, with an oak wheel, spindles, footman, table and legs. The tensioning screw is in elm, and there is an addition to the treadle in pine. The wheel is substantially intact with the exception of the distaff and distaff holder which are missing. The sections of the wheel are slightly separated, showing the pegs which unite them. The surface of the wheel has been stripped and is dehydrated.

Woods: Primary: Oak.

Secondary: Elm screw. Pine replacement piece on treadle.

Applied Surface Finish: Has been stripped.

Dimensions: 96 h 86 w.

Noteworthy Construction Details: Two extra turned supports.

Damage/Repairs/Replacement:
Treadle, footman, distaff and distaff holder missing.

Catalogue No: **250.**

Item: Spinning wheel.

Date of Manufacture: 19th century.

Significant Accession Details: Owned by donor's great-grandmother Crellin, and mother (1832 - 1928), born in Arbory.

Description: A treadle operated bobbin-flyer spinning wheel. This wheel is made in a conventional form with an oak wheel, spindles, treadle and footman and a beech table. Other turned parts are in ash. The wheel is substantially intact except that the distaff and distaff holder are missing. Two sections of the wheel are slightly separated, revealing the pegs which unite them.

Woods: Primary: Oak wheel, spindles and treadle. Ash turned parts. Beech table.

Secondary: Pine section in treadle.

Dimensions: 92 h 82 w.

Damage/Repairs/Replacement:
Distaff missing.

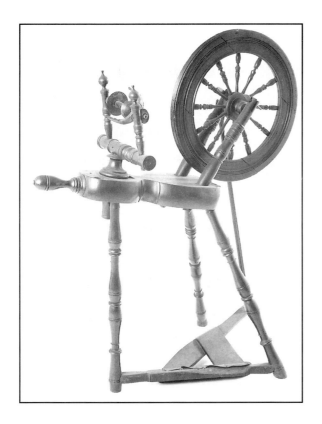

Catalogue No: **251.**

Item: Spinning wheel.

Date of Manufacture: Late - 19th century.

Significant Accession Details: Said by donor to have been "bought new" by her father from the Halsall family of Peel in 1904.

Description: A treadle operated bobbin-flyer spinning wheel, made of mahogany with a beech footman. This wheel is of a conventional pattern, but has a turned and centrally waisted table which is typical of some wheels made in Scotland, where it probably originated. It is unusual in having the addition of an inlaid patera and stringing around the edge of the wheel as decoration. This wheel is largely intact, except that no distaff is present. The wheel is unusually sophisticated in being made principally in mahogany, with decorative stringing around its circumference. The footman is attached to the stretcher with a canvas string.

Woods: *Primary:* Mahogany.

Dimensions: 89 h 80 w.

Damage/Repairs/Replacement: Distaff missing.

Catalogue No: **252.**

Item: Spinning wheel.

Date of Manufacture: 19th century.

Description: A treadle operated bobbin-flyer spinning wheel of conventional design, made with an elm table, oak wheel, spindles, crank and treadle, and with other turned parts in birch. This example was made to spin wool only, without a hole into which the distaff could be fitted. In this it is unusual since the majority of recorded Manx wheels were made to accommodate a distaff to spin flax.

Woods: *Primary:* Oak wheel, spindles, treadle and crank.

Secondary: Elm table. Birch turned parts.

Dimensions: 97 h 87 w.

Catalogue No: **253.**

Item: Spinning wheel.

Date of Manufacture: 19th century.

Description: A treadle operated bobbin-flyer spinning wheel made in conventional form with an oak wheel and spindles, footman and table. The tensioning screw is in ash and although obscured by overall dark varnish, the mother-of-all and its attendant apparatus are also probably made in ash. The wheel is substantially intact, with the exception that the distaff and distaff holder are missing. One leg has been replaced with a plain round leg. The sections of the wheel are slightly separated showing the pegs which unite them.

Woods: *Primary:* Oak wheel with ash spindles and
                        tensioning handle. Oak table.

            Secondary: One leg has a leather washer to
                        hold it firmly in its joint.

Applied Surface Finish: Layers of black stain.

Dimensions: 94 h 84 w.

Noteworthy Construction Details:
Spindles pegged into wheel. One leg firmed with leather washer.

Damage/Repairs/Replacement: Distaff missing. One leg a replacement.

Catalogue No: **254.**

Item: Spinning wheel.

Date of Manufacture: 19th century.

Description: A treadle operated bobbin-flyer spinning wheel of conventional design. Its surface has a red lead based paint which was intended to mahoganise it. Below this, the visible areas of wood indicate that ash is the principal wood used in the legs, tensioning screw and uprights. This wheel is substantially intact except that the treadle, footman, distaff and distaff holder are missing. The table has gouge carved decoration at the corners.

Woods: *Primary:* Too heavily oxidised to
                        distinguish woods other than ash
                        in the legs, tensioning screw and
                        uprights.

Applied Surface Finish: Red lead paint underneath a mahogany stain.

Dimensions: 94 h 88 w.

Damage/Repairs/Replacement: Distaff and treadle missing.

Catalogue No: **255.**

Item: Spinning wheel and distaff.

Date of Manufacture: 19th century.

Significant Accession Details: Abigail Faragher, Earystane, Colby.

Description: An intact treadle operated bobbin-flyer wheel for spinning wool and flax. This wheel is made in a conventional form with an oak wheel, spindles, footman, and table. The treadle is in pine and the turned parts ash. The distaff is made of birch. The wheel is intact, with a complete distaff holder and lantern distaff present. The turned tenons of the uprights pass through the table and are secured by pegs. The ends of the turned parts clearly show lathe stock marks, and may offer a way of comparing other wheels with the same marks (see detail photograph below).

Woods: *Primary*: Oak wheel, spindles and table. Ash turned parts.

    Secondary: Birch distaff. Pine treadle.

Applied Surface Finish: Heavy coats of dark varnish applied.

Dimensions: 96 h (with distaff 122 h) 83 w.

Noteworthy Construction Details: Uprights pegged under the wheel table.

Underneath of table showing through-morticed and pegged tenons.

Catalogue No: **256.**

Item: Spinning wheel.

Date of Manufacture: Original 19th century parts with later 20th century additions.

Description: A treadle operated bobbin-flyer spinning wheel. This wheel is of a conventional design, but shows evidence of being produced by an unsophisticated maker, principally using some parts from a more professionally produced wheel, perhaps the tensioning screw, table, uprights, and mother-of-all. The wheel rim and hand-shaped spindles are clearly of unskilled manufacture. The maidens holding the 'U'-flyer are unsympathetic additions. Two of the three simple legs are turned to an unconventional design, and the third is hand-shaped.

Woods: *Primary:* Not possible to distinguish visually.

       Secondary: Birch tension screw.

Applied Surface Finish: Red paint lines on wheel.

Dimensions: 87 h 74 w.

Noteworthy Construction Details: Hand produced wheel. Round parts hand shaved rather than turned

Damage/Repairs/Replacement: Uprights to 'U'-flyer are later additions.

Catalogue No: **257.**

Item: Spinning wheel.

Date of Manufacture: 19th century.

Significant Accession Details:
Belonged to donor's grandmother (1930).

Description: A treadle operated bobbin-flyer spinning wheel. This wheel is of a conventional pattern, with all visible parts made in oak, but with a beech tensioning screw. The surface is painted with later coats of black varnish. The wheel is substantially intact with the exception of the distaff, which is missing.

Woods: *Primary:* All visible parts oak.

       Secondary: Beech tensioning handle.

Applied Surface Finish: Later coats of black varnish.

Dimensions:
91 h 90 w.

Catalogue No: **258.**

Item: Spinning wheel.

Date of Manufacture: 19th century.

Significant Accession Details:
A vertical wheel owned and used by donor's mother (a vicar's widow) in Douglas.

Description: A vertical (upright) treadle operated bobbin-flyer spining wheel, principally made from birch with ash legs and a walnut treadle. This unusually sophisticated wheel is supported on three turned legs which have simulated bamboo turnings. The spining wheel is of conventional basic design, but with the addition of three spools located between two short turned uprights which are morticed into the base and one of the two main uprights. One turned upright is longer than the other, and has two metal spindles with turned wooden handles which are used to hold the spools in place and can be removed to take out the full spools. The second turned upright has only one spool mechanism. The purpose of the spools is to receive spun wool directly from the 'U' flyer without the need to change the spool, thus increasing convenience of production. The woollen thread was transferred from the 'U'-flyer bobbin by passing upwards from the spool, through a hole in a turned peg which is held in a turned cross bar connecting the maiden and the main upright. From the peg, the strand then passed down to one of the spools and was kept on the right track by being passed around a peg which was held in the shorter upright at the point at which the wheel axle entered it.

Woods: *Primary:* Probably birch. Ash legs.

       Secondary: Walnut treadle.

Dimensions: 85 h 49w.

Catalogue No: **259.**

Item: Wool winder.

Date of Manufacture:
19th century.

Description: A wool winder made in oak and pine. The main vertical upright of this device is morticed into a base, which in turn is supported on four short legs. The upright is hollow down part of its length; a retractable, thinner stem fits into this and allows the top section to be raised or lowered. Into the top upright a flat arm is morticed, with holes irregularly bored along its length and a turned upright support at its end which may have held pegs to guide the winding of yarn onto the spool. Passing between the turned upright and a loosely held section of wood, now tied to the upright, is an oak spindle on which two spools made of oak and pine rotate. Below this device, a further arm extends out from the upright and appears to offer support for the upper spools. Further down, another arm extends, which also has a turned end supporting a horizontal oak spindle on which space for two spools is provided. One spool only is present.

This unusual form of winder is a device onto which wool could be wound onto the four wooden spools directly from the spool held in the 'U'-flyer (see vertical wheel No. 258 which has a similar arrangement of spools, in this case mounted directly onto the bed of the wheel).

Woods: *Primary:* Pine. Two oak arms and vertical turning.

Secondary: Oak ends to spools.

Dimensions: 92.5 h 50 w.

Catalogue No: **260.**

Item: Skein or hank winder.

Date of Manufacture:
19th century.

Description: A rotary hank or skein winder with six arms, one of which has a short turning handle to aid winding the yarn. This example has a clock-style mechanism held in the main vertical stem or box, to record the number of revolutions which the skein turns onto the wheel, and then to record the yarn's length. The winder is made from a number of different woods (see below) and has not been stained or painted. The vertical central pillar, which holds the clock mechanism, is morticed into a flat base supported on four hand-shaped legs.

Woods: *Primary:* Ash arms and base.

        Secondary: Pine or birch box, birch end bobbins. Pine legs, possibly replacements.

Dimensions: 97 h 75 w.

Damage/Repairs/Replacement: Legs possibly replaced.

Catalogue No: 261.

Item: Skein or hank winder.

Date of Manufacture: 19th century.

Significant Accession Details: From Ballavarry, Andreas.

Description: A rotary hank or skein winder with six arms, one of which has an extending section to tension and release the skein. The winder has a clock-style counting mechanism which records the number of complete revolutions of the wheel and thus the length of the skein. This winder is made of a number of different woods and is stained or painted with a rose coloured stain, now faded.

Woods: *Primary:* Ash spokes, oak legs, pine box sides. Birch front and base and probably the central hub holding the arms.

Applied Surface Finish: Body and base stained with rose stain.

Dimensions: 98.5 h 79 w 26 d.

Catalogue No: 262.

Item: Skein or hank winder.

Date of Manufacture: 19th century.

Significant Accession Details: From Ballavarry, Andreas.

Description: A rotary hank or skein winder with five of its original six arms now missing. This example had a clock-style mechanism to count the revolutions of the skein as it was wound onto the arms. The hand of the clock mechanism is now missing, as is the top of the central pillar. The four legs are different from each other. The winder appears not to have been painted or stained.

Woods: *Primary:* Ash.

   Secondary: One oak leg.

Dimensions: 75.5 h 36.5 w (bed only) 29 d.

Damage/Repairs/Replacement: Five arms and top of central pillar missing. Hand to 'clock' mechanism missing. The four legs are different from each other, which suggests they are replacements.

Catalogue No: **263.**

Item: Skein or hank winder.

Date of Manufacture: 19th century.

Significant Accession Details: From Port Soderick, Santon.

Description: A horizontal rotary skein or hank winder which has cross shaped rotary arms with holes drilled into them to hold pegs, around which the skein was wound. The cross shaped winder pivots on a round wooden peg set into a block which, in turn, is fixed to the bed of the base. The bed is supported on four canted square section legs, and is made in the manner of a joiner's or carpenter's saw bench. This form of winder required the user to count the number of revolutions of the arms without the benefit of a click or a clock-style mechanism to aid the counting, which vertical winders usually had.

Woods: *Primary:* Pine legs. Ash block.

        Secondary: Arms probably mahogany.

Dimensions: 66 h 76 x 76.

Catalogue No: **264.**

Item: Skein or hank winder.

Date of Manufacture: 19th or early - 20th century.

Description: A vertical rotary hank or skein winder, with cross shaped rotary arms which have holes drilled through them to hold pegs, and around which the skein was wound. One long tapered peg remains *in situ*. The arms are united at the cross point with a wooden bracket, through which a long metal spigot protrudes, and on which the arms rotate. The spigot is fixed into a branch which has three branchlets cut to make a naturally formed three legged base.

Woods: *Primary:* Base unidentified hardwood, now water eroded.

        Secondary: Oak winding arms.

Dimensions: 53.5 h 98 x 98.

Noteworthy Construction Details: Use of a natural branch form to create a functional furniture item.

Catalogue No: **265.**

Item: Skein or hank winder.

Date of Manufacture: 19th or early - 20th century.

Significant Accession Details:
From Ballahimmin, German (1938).

Description: A horizontal hank or skein winder with cross shaped rotary arms, with five holes drilled through each arm to hold pegs, and around which the skein could be wound. One short peg remains *in situ.* A wooden bracket supports the arms at the cross point, and is attached to the round base upright with a metal bolt around which the arms rotate. The base is made with a turned round section supported on three short rectangular shaped legs, jointed and screwed to the base. A hand-shaped, roughly round upright mortices into the top of the round base and supports the cross arms.

Woods: *Primary:* Pine throughout.

Dimensions: 81 h 91.5 x 91.5.

Catalogue No: **266.**

Item: Skein or hank winder.

Date of Manufacture: Late - 19th or early - 20th century.

Significant Accession Details:
From the loom shed of A. Hudson, weaver of Ballafesson, Rushen. Taken into Manx Museum collection 1939.

Description: A horizontal rotary skein or hank winder. This example has a cross arm mechanism made in box form and supported at its ends with short pieces of wood. The arms rotate around a metal spigot which is attached to a rectangular shaped upright with a leather washer located between the cross arms and the top of the upright. The upright is morticed into the base cross-board which in turn is fitted with housing joints to two thinner cross supports.

Woods: *Primary:* Pine.

        Secondary: Metal spigot.

Dimensions: 67.5 h 54 x 54.

Noteworthy Construction Details:
Made from standard size lathes and other joinery woods.

ORGANS & HARMONIUMS

CHAPTER 21

247

ORGANS & HARMONIUMS

Manx National Heritage has within its furniture collections a group of keyboard instruments which were closely allied with the religious life in churches and chapels on the Island. These include a mechanical barrel organ made by Wrenshall of Liverpool, dating from the late - 18th century and reported to be from Santon church (No. 267), a small late - 19th century five octave organ made of walnut (No. 268) and two mahogany harmoniums, dating from the late - 19th century (Nos. 269 & 270). In addition, the collection holds a pianola roll cabinet, complete with rolls which were used with an American organ (No. 271).

Music in the Island's churches and chapels was an important part of worship, although the general introduction of instruments was not achieved until the second half of the 19th century when gradually, by private donation, organs and harmoniums were purchased from suppliers in other parts of Britain. Before this time, it was common for hymn singing to be led by a regular church member who was considered to be a good singer, and who would 'raise' the hymns. Mr. John Kneen, in reporting to the Folk Life Survey (FLS/K-J-A) in 1950 gave a graphic and amusing account of the transition from song-led music to the purchase of the first organ at a local chapel. . .

"There were no organs in the chapels in those olden days, instead there would be an old gentleman . . . it was his job to lead the singing as the preacher announced each hymn. For many years one old man performed his duties faithfully and well. As time went on and the chapel underwent improvements, a house-to-house collection was made and money raised to purchase an organ. There was great excitement and a full house when the new insturment was to be played for the first time. In his place as usual was the old hymn raiser. To everyone's astonishment, no-one turned up to play the organ. Everybody waited for a while, the preacher began to be uneasy, and at last he asked the old man to raise the tune. The organ was there in the room covered with a cloth and, as the preacher asked him if he would lead the singing once more, the old chap indignantly and with great disgust pointed to the organ and said, 'Let that black monkey in the corner raise the tune! Take the cloak off that black monkey in the corner, and he'll raise the tunes for you'."

The paucity of people able to play organs and harmoniums may have been a further factor which retarded the general introduction of instruments into churches. In some cases American organs, which play when the instrument is pedalled, by mechanical means using toothed metal rollers, were introduced to overcome this since an unskilled person could play them. The Folk Life Survey recorded in 1968 that at Regaby Methodist Church, "There is an American organ with foot worked pedals and stops, and it is at present played by a child of ten" (FLS/R/16).

The cost of installing organs was also a very great inhibitor for poor communities, and this above all must have acted as a bar to the introduction of instruments for a long time. Mr. Kinrade reported to the Folk Life Survey, for example, that as late as 1895 he remembered meeting the organ-builder at the Lhen who put an organ in the Lhen Chapel at that time. Mr. Kinrade said that the Andreas Church organ was put in for £250 (FLS/K/21-H).

It seems that despite organs being installed at great cost, not all of them functioned perfectly after installation, and a report to the Folk Life Survey in 1967, (FLS/M/32-A) from the Primitive Methodist Minute Book, Minorca, Laxey, records: "The organ seems to have needed constant repair (in one entry dated 1870 £1-10-0 was paid to Jas Nicholson for painting and ornamenting organ). It was sold in 1883 - the timber fetched 1/-. A new organ was bought from the Chaplain & Wardens of St. Paul's Ramsey, for £45-0-0. Mr. Hewitt charged £36 for putting it in. The organist at this time was paid."

For reasons of lower cost as well as mobility, harmoniums were often purchased for chapels. They had the extra advantage that they could be carried from the place of worship to accompany singing at open-air meetings, or they could be transported to places of worship where there were no instruments. Sometimes they were played to accompany other instruments. In the late - 19th century Thomas Kinrade, who had boats on the Mooragh at that time,"used to be good at playing the fiddle, and he used it to play in the Bethel Chapel, accompanying the hymns, and the harmonium would be played as well" (FLS/C/210).

The use of organs and harmoniums in places of worship continues as a tradition on the Isle of Man, as it does elsewhere, and many examples remain in the Island's churches and chapels.

Catalogue No: **267.**

Item: Mechanical barrel organ by Wrenshall of Liverpool.

Date of Manufacture: Late - 18th century.

Significant Accession Details: Said to have been Santon Church Organ.

Description: A mahogany mechanical barrel organ with an engraved oval plaque on the front which reads "Wrenshall. Organ Builder. Liverpool." This mechanical organ has the general apperance of a chamber organ, and its exterior design is possibly taken from Thomas Malton's design for a large chamber organ, 1775, or from the many interpretations of chamber organs from this or other designers. See a further chamber organ by Richard Bridge, 1775, which shows the general use of pipes above a case below and an illustration by George Pyke of London (1740 - 77) which shows a barrel organ with a glazed case above.

The example reviewed here was evidently made by Joseph Wrenshall, who was a cabinet maker in Lancaster and Liverpool, 1738 - 1790, and who traded at 7 Liver Street, Liverpool, in 1790. It was probably made as part of a larger repertoire of furniture, and the case shows the particular regional features of broad bands of mahogany veneer laid below the cornice. The stringing to the outer middle section, probably in box, terminates in three stylised berries. The case front has two pairs of false doors, with applied mouldings and imitation ivory or bone escutcheons. The case is made, variously, of solid mahogany and mahogany veneer over pine. The metal pipes are painted to appear as tin. The left side panel is missing, revealing the internal mechanical

apparatus, including bellows which produce the sound from a pre-programmed roll which could be fitted into the base. Stops for altering the tone protrude from the front of the case. No cranking handle, needed to power the piece, is apparent.

Woods: *Primary:* Mahogany, and mahogany veneers over pine.

        Secondary: Bone escutcheons.

Applied Surface Finish: Varnished.

Dimensions: 186 hh Base 57 h 109 w 59 d.

Noteworthy Construction Details: Cabinet made with North-West regional decorative features.

Damage/Repairs/Replacement: Side door missing. Mechanism not functioning.

Catalogue No: **268.**

Item: Organ.

Date of Manufacture: Circa 1900.

Description: A small five octave organ made of walnut and with ebonised internal surrounds. This compact organ is played by pressing the foot pedals alternately to force air into the internal bellows, which then allow air to pass through internal pipes when the keyboard is played. A system of stops and a knee-operated swell allows the tone and volume of the sound to be controlled. This form of organ was used widely in homes and chapels to accompany communal singing in the 19th century and into the 20th. They were musically more versatile, and produced a greater volume of sound, than the harmonium, although they were considerably heavier and less portable. Many organs of this kind are still in regular use in places of worship.

Woods: *Primary:* Walnut.

Applied Surface Finish: Polished and ebonised inside.

Dimensions: Base 95 h 107 w 95 d.

Damage/Repairs/Replacement: An upper structure, possibly a decorative gallery, is missing from the top.

Catalogue No: **269.**

Item: Harmonium.

Date of Manufacture: Circa 1880.

Description: This instrument is played by using a foot treadle mechanism which operates a bellows which, in turn, passes air through a system of notation ducts. The instrument has a five octave keyboard, and a knee operated 'swell' mechanism which is used to alter the volume of the sound. Harmoniums of this type were portable, and could be carried using the two end handles, to provide music at religious meetings, often in non-conformist chapels or private houses, or in the open air.

Woods: *Primary:* Mahogany.

       Secondary: Fabric-covered back, and leather covers nailed to the panels.

Applied Surface Finish: Varnished.

Dimensions: 86 h 101 w 37 d.

Catalogue No: **270.**

Item: Harmonium.

Date of Manufacture: Circa 1900.

Description: A portable mahogany harmonium made by
John W. Reed of Hanover Street, London. The rather self-
important appearance of this harmonium was no doubt
intended to portray it as a more complex instrument, the
organ. However, the absence of the comprehensive pipe
system indicates that it is a harmonium played by using a
foot treadle mechanism which operates a bellows which, in
turn, passes air through a system of notation ducts. The
instrument has a five octave keyboard, and has a knee
operated 'swell' mechanism used to alter the volume of the
sound. Harmoniums of this type were portable, and could be
carried using two end handles, to provide music at religious
meetings, often in non-conformist chapels or private houses,
or in the open air.

Woods: *Primary:* Mahogany.

Secondary: Red fabric behind fret.

Applied Surface Finish: Stained and polished.

Dimensions: 97 h (+ 41 h) 105.5 w 39.5 d.

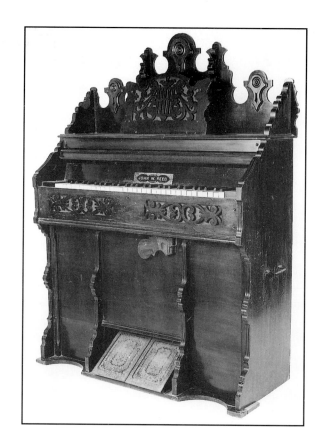

Catalogue No: **271.**

Item: Pianola roll cabinet.

Date of Manufacture: Circa 1900.

Significant Accession Details: Said by donor to have been locally
made, for use with an American organ.

Description: A wall-attached pianola roll cabinet, made in unpainted Scots pine, and with traditional chip-carved compass motifs on
the upper back. The two doors are glazed in different patterns of frosted decorated glass. The edges of the sides and cross boards are
deeply chamfered. The interior has pigeon-holes for thirty five rolls, of which thirty are occupied. These include tunes which were
popular at the end of the 19th and the early - 20th centuries. Of the many music hall and religious songs included, 'Nearer my God to
Thee' and 'The Blue Bells of Scotland' seem to have been the most used. The rolls were rotated in a hand-wound pianola which
reproduced the tunes as if played on a piano.

Woods: *Primary:* Scots pine.

Applied Surface Finish: Varnished

Dimensions: 71 h 44 w 20 d.

PRISON FURNITURE

CHAPTER 22

PRISON FURNITURE

During the 18th century, prisons functioned as private business concerns, operated by gaolers whose main task was to stop prisoners escaping. In such a milieu, conditions were often insanitary and prisoners poorly provided for, except for those who could afford the fees for virtually any facilities beyond the most meagre. This might, for example, vary from accommodation in an over-crowded cell for the poor, to renting a well-furnished room in the gaoler's own house for those prisoners who could afford it.

This *laissez-faire* manner of imprisonment meant that no standard system of furnishings was provided. However, during the 19th century, the British Parliament passed permissive legislation in an attempt to regularise prisons and bring them within a reformed public penal system. From this new sense of prison life, based on a regular routine of measured basic food, hard labour, and religious worship, an increasing sense of conformity arose in the routine and provision of material life. This included the types of furniture provided for prison cells. Christopher Gilbert, writing about prison furniture in *English Vernacular Furniture 1750-1900*, 1991, notes that "Cell furniture must have been supplied under contract to the Surveyor - General of Prisons, but it is not known who made it or supplied it. At Millbank, built in 1812 for prisoners awaiting transportation to Australia, the cells were provided with a square table of plain wood, a stool, and either a hammock or a bed board resting on stone supports."

Such a bleak mode of furnishing and the corresponding regulations which epitomised prison life are also reflected in the two surviving items of Manx prison furniture, which show rare glimpses of prison life into the 20th century. The first item is a bed, No. 272, which was reputedly used for persons undergoing extra punishment. This is a bed of the most fundamental type, and would merely have provided a low platform, perhaps with a thin mattress on it, and a raised pillow section at one end. This bed seems unchanged from the one described in use at Millbank in 1812, and pencilled graffiti underneath it confirms that the bed was being used until at least 1914, when it was used in the Knockaloe internment camp, near Peel.

The second item of prison furniture, a stained pine ration desk, No. 273, is perhaps a unique survival. It has a sloping desk lid on each side, and an internal bank of small drawers in one side only. In the centre of the desk, on top, is a centre board which accommodates a brass scales and weights. The desk was reputedly used to weigh prisoners' rations, perhaps tea, sugar and salt, although neither the small internal drawers nor the open interiors of the desk show evidence of having held food. However, its presence does confirm the careful rationing of food and concern for a balanced diet which had become more general in prisons since the first half of the 19th century.

Catalogue No: **272.**

Item: Prison bed.

Date of Manufacture: Circa 1870.

Significant Accession Details: Donated by the Governor of HM Prison, Victoria Road, Douglas. Originally used at Castle Rushen when this building was the Island's prison.

Description: A low prison bed with an integral raised wooden pillow. The cross supports of the bed base are graduated in height from 9 cm. at the base to 14 cm. at the head, presumably to provide a more comfortable reclining position. The wooden 'pillow' rises 9 cm. above the base. This bed is reputed to have been used by prisoners undergoing extra punishment, and has pencilled graffiti underneath the boards, including "Poor Corky. Christmas 1914 out 31 Dec" and "Knockaloe Camp" - Knockaloe was a First World War internment camp, near Peel."

Woods: *Primary:* Pine.

Dimensions:
9 h base 14 h top +9 h 'pillow' 184 w 67 d.

Noteworthy Construction Details: Chamfer on edges of cross supports. Pillow is dovetailed to the sides.

Catalogue No: **273.**

Item: Prison ration desk on stand with weights and scales.

Date of Manufacture: Circa 1870.

Significant Accession Details: Donated by the Governor of HM Prison, Victoria Road, Douglas, where it had been used. Prior to this, it was used at Castle Rushen.

Description: A prison ration desk with brass scales and weights which were used to dole out rations, perhaps sugar, salt and tea. The desk has a double slope with hinged lids, and is fitted internally with six small drawers with stained turned handles, on one side only. The middle section on top has an oval stand with a brass upright to hold the brass balance and its accompanying set of brass weights. The base of the desk is made of pine which is stained with mahogany stain. The four square legs are joined with a morticed frame at the top, on which the desk rests. The desk top is also made of pine, with a mahogany stained surround, and imitation leather covering the desk lids. The desk was made by a cabinet maker who expertly used dovetail joints at the corners of the desk top.

Woods: *Primary:* Pine with stained pine or birch knob handles.

 Secondary: Birch drawer linings. Black imitation leather on desk tops.

Applied Surface Finish: Mahogany stain on top. Base has red lead stain. Knob handles stained black.

Dimensions: 83 hh 80 h 53.5 w 99 d.

Noteworthy Construction Details: Dovetail construction at corners of desk.

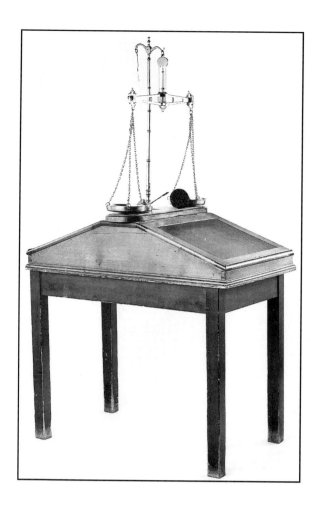

MISCELLANEOUS

CHAPTER 23

Catalogue No: **274.**

Item: Cabinet on stand.

Date of Manufacture: Cabinet *circa* 1650. Stand *circa* 1720.

Significant Accession Details: Said to have belonged to Bishop Thomas Wilson (1663 - 1755).

Description: A cabinet on a stand, the upper part made in Antwerp *circa* 1650, and the lower part a later replacement, probably made in England *circa* 1720. The cabinet has a case of oak and the drawers are finely lined in the same wood. The drawer fronts are probably birch, and have rippled front edge mouldings in an unidentified black stained wood. They have raised central oval panels and borders of red and black tortoiseshell veneers, with ebony and ivory stringing and fretted and moulded silver mounts and inlays. The chest has a classical style pediment of black stained wood, with corner frets and turned galleries of ivory spindles on each side of a central area. This has a (later) silver medallion inserted into its centre. The pediment supports a delicately carved figure of the Madonna, and the side cornices have turned urn shaped knops in ivory at the corners. The front of the pediment had three ivory seals inlaid into it. Two of these have been removed, and the third has been damaged.

The central doors open to show a perspectival vista which has a chequered black and white inlaid floor of ivory and ebony pieces. The walls and back are mirrored, and have gilded carved figures attached to the walls. Each of the doors and drawers has locks. The drawers are lined with pages taken from the *Weekly Miscellany* dated 1738. There is a silver armorial device inlaid above the central doors. The sides of the cabinet are marquetry, inlaid with sections of ebony divided by ivory stringing. Brass carrying handles are attached to each side. Originally, a slide at the base of the cabinet opened to provide a shelf surface. This is now prevented from opening by the edge of the stand which covers the lower edge of the slide.

The stand is finely made in pine and mahogany with cabriole legs to the front, which have acanthus leaf carving at the knees and ball and claw feet. The rear has square sectioned legs and the shaped frieze is made from carved sections of moulding glued to a pine frame. The exterior surface is japanned to co-ordinate with the ebony of the upper cabinet. This stand was presumably made especially to hold the cabinet, in accordance with the fashionable cabriole furniture designs of the 1720s. The original stand to the cabinet would probably have been ornate and made in Baroque style. Alternatively it may have had a relatively plain stand which would have adopted ebonised barley twist legs both at the front and rear, joined by stretchers near the base.

Woods: *Primary:* Birch dustboards and inner carcase. Drawers oak lined. Stand has pine frame. Solid mahogany legs.

   Secondary: Ebony, ivory, tortoiseshell and silver inlays.

Applied Surface Finish: Interior painted in black.

Dimensions: 202 hh Cabinet 118 h 101 w 41 d. Stand 83 h 111 w 47 d.

Damage/Repair/Replacement: The stand is a later replacement. Medallions missing. Veneers raised on the left side.

Catalogue No: **275.**

Item: Carved and turned seat of romantic and fanciful form.

Date of Manufacture: 19th or 20th century.

Significant Accession Details: Known as the 'Abbot's Chair' - erroneously claimed to have been formerly at Rushen Abbey.

Description: This seat is a decorative amalgam of shaped wooden sections joined to form solid arms and outer seat areas. These articulate with a continuous central seat and flat inclined back. The fronts of the arms are carved with an incurved stylised leaf motif of archaic form used commonly in 17th century carving. The back has a vertical flowing plant carving. The upper seat and back are supported on three heavy 'barley twist' turned legs.

Woods: *Primary:* Oak.

Applied Surface Finish: Stained and varnished.

Dimensions: 104 hh 59 h 54 w 34 d.

Noteworthy Construction Details: Idiosyncratic constructional form.

Catalogue No: 276.

Item: Singer sewing machine.

Date of Manufacture: Circa 1920.

Significant Accession Details: Abigail Faragher, Earystane, Colby.

Description: A treadle operated Singer sewing machine on a cast iron stand. The sewing machine sits on a mahogany top and is covered by a green baize lined mahogany hood when not in use. The machine is operated by a foot-treadle, which rotates a string around the drive wheel and enables variable speeds to be regulated by the user's foot power. This leaves the hands free to guide and regulate the fabric being sewn. The underside of the machine's top holds a mahogany drawer with an integral turned knob, to hold small sewing items.

Woods: *Primary*: Mahogany.

        Secondary: Cast iron base. Green baize lining to hood.

Applied Surface Finish: Varnished wood. Black painted metal.

Dimensions: 96.5 h 64.5 w 41.5 d.

Noteworthy Construction Details: Hood is wood-pegged.

Catalogue No: **277.**

Item: Fire screen.

Date of Manufacture: Circa 1850.

Description: A mahogany framed fire screen, carved in the rococo manner. A glazed oval panel of woolwork embroidery depicts a floral spray. Screens of this kind were popular in fashionable households from about 1830 until the late - 19th century. Of the four designers of this type of furniture during the mid-19th century, Henry Wood, John Taylor, Henry Lawford and W. Thoms Wood (1848), all illustrated screens which are closely similar to this example. Wood, of Percy Street, London, who called himself a 'decorative draughtsman' was particularly intent on designing pieces to be upholstered in Berlin woolwork. This kind of work, introduced from Germany, had become increasingly popular since the beginning of the century as it could be done cheaply at home. Housewives bought patterns on squared paper and coppied them stitch by stitch in coloured wools onto square-mesh canvas. The fashion was at its height between about 1820 and 1860. Wood published *Eighteen Plates of Berlin Woolwork*, and other pattern books on the subject, all undated but probably between 1840 - 50. His *Cheval and Pole Screens* reminds us of the universal use in Victorian times of this type of furniture, now obsolete, for keeping the heat of large coal fires from becoming too uncomfortable for those sitting near them, and for stopping ladies' complexions from being coloured.

Woods: *Primary*: Mahogany.

  Secondary: Porcelain castors. Glazed panel.

Dimensions: 104 h 67 w 46 d.

Damage/Repairs/Replacement: Back paper very fragile.

Catalogue No: **278.**

Item: Artist's easel.

Date of Manufacture: Circa 1900.

Significant Accession Details: From the studio of J. M. Nicholson, Well Road Hill, Douglas.

Description: An adjustable artist's easel made of oak, with a steel and brass mechanism to alter the height and holding capacity for different canvas sizes. This well made easel, manufactured by Winsor & Newton, London, displays high technical qualities in its manufacture, with precise jointing and wood finishing throughout. It probably represented the most advanced easel available to artists at the time.

Woods: *Primary:* Oak.

Applied Surface Finish: Varnished.

Dimensions: 207 h 89.5 w 71 d.

Notworthy Construction Details: Woodwork through morticed and tenoned at many joints. High quality cabinet making throughout.

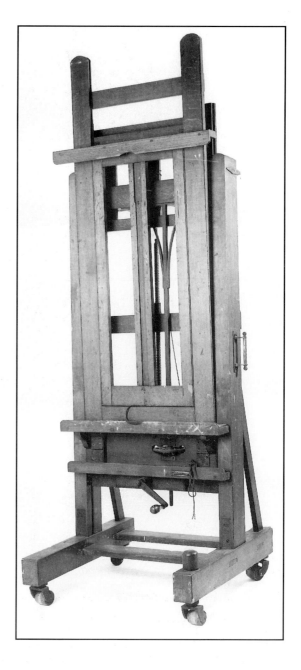

Catalogue No: **279.**

Item: Artist's workstand.

Date of Manufacture: Circa 1900.

Significant Accession Details: From the studio of J. M. Nicholson, Well Road Hill, Douglas.

Description: An oak artist's table or compendium of drawers, with a folding top which opens to provide a working surface or palette. Below this is a well to hold paints and other artist's materials. There are three drawers with wooden knob handles. The base has four castors which enable the table to be wheeled to the canvas. This well-made piece is a companion to the easel, No. 278, and was used in the late - 19th and the first part of the 20th century. It is made with high technical standards throughout, with fine dovetails to the drawers.

Woods: *Primary*: Oak.

      Secondary: Pine drawer linings.

Applied Surface Finish: Varnished.

Dimensions: 78 h 76 w 35.5 d (opened 53 d).

Noteworthy Construction Details: Drawers with fine dovetails at back and front.

LATE ADDITIONS

Catalogue No: **280.**

Item: Oak chair.

Description: Solid panel-back oak chair, with '17011' and elaborate initials carved across the top rail. Turned front stretchers and front legs, straight back legs. Reinforcing metal brackets on seat and stretchers. Rockers are later additions.

Dimensions: 120 h 63 w 65 d.

Catalogue No: **281.**

Item: Chest of drawers.

Description: Three large drawers and two small drawers. Pine, stained/painted light mahogany red on visible surfaces. One replaced handle. Brass locks and escutcheons. Made by Hugh Kaighen, joiner of Kerrowglass - see Hugh Kaighen essay.

Dimensions: 113 h 116 w 52.5 d.

Catalogue No: **282.**

Item: Table.

Description: Round topped three-legged table with triangular shaped shelf; legs rhomboid in section. The top is unpolished pine while the shelf and legs are painted dark brown.

Dimensions: 71 h 75 diam.

Catalogue No: **283.**

Item: Bed.

Description: Solid wood head and footboards with turned uprights - all with scumble finish. Pine cross pieces fit into slots on frame to support the mattress. Said by donor (in 1938) to be over 100 years old: originally owned by donor's great-grandfather, John Cowell, blacksmith.

Dimensions: 199 h 196 w 138 d.

Catalogue No: **284.**

Item: Bed.

Description: Harry Kelly's bed; traditionally said to have come from the farmhouse on the Calf of Man and to have been cut down from a full tester bed to fit into Harry Kelly's cottage. It is of all wooden construction with nine cross pieces fitted into slots on the frame to support the mattress. Each corner post has been cut down.

Dimensions: 118 h 197 w 137 d.

The Grove Rural Life Museum : Ramsey

DOWNSTAIRS HALLWAY

G. 1 OAK CHEST. 76 h 116 w 48 d.

Circa 1790. Made to hold linen, this generic form of chest is of Welsh origin. It has four flat panels to the front, two to each side, and three at the back. The board lid now hinges on 19th century metal strap hinges. Originally, two wooden strips were fixed to the underneath of the top, which located into square holes in the rear edge. This created a hinging mechanism of a type commonly found in chests of Welsh origin.

G. 2 HAT STAND. 172.5 h Base 32.5 x 45.

Circa 1860. Made with a solid mahogany stem and spindles, the base is beech with mahogany veneers. This item was intended to stand in a hallway. The central turned column has turned branches obliquely morticed into it to hang hats and coats on (one of them is a later replacement). The central stem has a turned screw which unites it with the base. The stem is assymetrically positioned on the base so that it can stand more closely to the wall.

G. 3 TWO HALL CHAIRS. 83 h 41.5 w 36 d.

Circa 1850. Made in mahogany with a beech seat frame, which is veneered on the outer edges with mahogany. Chairs of this kind were common in genteel households. Their original use, of providing austere seating for waiting servants or tradesmen, gradually declined during the 19th century and their functions became largely symbolic and decorative. See Loudon, 1833, for further references to chairs of this type.

MIDDLE LANDING

G. 4 LONG CASE CLOCK. 239 h 52.5 w 25 d.

This long case clock, dated *circa* 1780, has an oak case which is veneered with mahogany. Crotch mahogany was especially selected for the door front. The reeded columns are made of solid mahogany and are tapered from top to bottom. The framing wood inside the case is pine. The movement is of eight-day duration. The brass/silvered dial has a brass plate rivetted to it which bears the name Wm. Lassel of Toxteth Park, (Liverpool). A written biography of Wm. Lassel is fixed inside the case. However, the plate bearing his name may well be an addition to the clock.

UPPER LANDING

G. 5 CARVED OAK CHEST. 87.5 h 52.5 w 51.5 d.

An oak chest with the date 1667 carved on the front. The chest is made in two parts, the upper one from panelled sections which derive from at least two different sources. The front, which has marquetry and parquetry inlays of coloured woods, was probably made as a tester bed head or an over-mantle. The side and rear panelled sections are probably constructed from parts of an original chest. The exterior of the chest has applied geometric mouldings which are later

additions. The lid, made of thin boards, has replacement strap hinges, and three pairs of holes are evident which originally held staple hinges. Internally, the right side shows evidence of a till, with small drawers below which are now missing. The base is a fabrication, made to support the upper chest, and carved with similar forms to simulate compatibility of design.

DRAWING ROOM

G. 6 BAMBOO STAND. 39 h 30 x 30.

A low bamboo stand with a ceramic top, *circa* 1900. Furniture of this type, made of bamboo and fitted together with thin metal joints, was fashionable in the late - 19th and early - 20th centuries. Imports from China and home produced bamboo furniture were both available in Britain. This stand was made in Britain, and has four brass ferrules terminating its feet which bear the inscription 'W. F. Needham's Patent Metal Jointed Bamboo Furniture.'

G. 7 DISPLAY CABINET. 91.5 h 166 w 40.5 d.

Glazed display cabinet or credenza, *circa* 1820. This cabinet was made to display fragile and precious objects. It is made of the highest quality materials, with the outer case having solid rosewood mouldings and veneers of rosewood on the front and sides over a pine carcass. The interior has pine shelves and back, painted in matt black. The fronts of the shelves are veneered in rosewood. The doors are rosewood veneered over mahogany framing.

G. 8 CORNER WHATNOT. 88 h 47.5 w 38 d.

Circa 1850. This piece of furniture was intended to stand in the corner of the room, to display decorative objects. It has three triangular shaped shelves which are serpentine shaped to their fronts. These are separated by decoratively turned spindles, and there is a fretted gallery around the two sides of the top. The two lower shelves are in plain mahogany, and the top is made from crotch sawn timber.

G. 9 SIDE CHAIR. 92 h 51.5 w 46 d.

Circa 1840. This chair is one of a group of five similar chairs located variously in the sitting room, sewing room and drawing room. They are made in mahogany, painted to simulate rosewood, and have loose upholstered seats. This fashionable style of chair dates from the reign of William IV and has many of the neo-classical features associated with chairs of this period which were particularly influenced by the designs of Thomas Hope.

The Grove Drawing Room

G. 10 POLE SCREEN. 151 h 38 x 31.

Circa 1860. Made in mahogany and decorated with a black lacquer. Finials are missing from the top and bottom of the central pole. Screens of this type are adjustable so that the heat of the fire could be screened from the sitter's face. Alternatively, it may be that it was also used to shield the sitter from the direct rays of the sun. This is highly probable in this case, since the pole has marks indicating that the round screen was on occasion set at the highest level on the pole, in a position which would have been effective in screening the sun.

G. 11 FIRE SCREEN. 109 h 65.5 w.

A square fire screen with a central needlework panel, under glass, *circa* 1860. The frame of this screen is made of solid rosewood and carved in the fashionable manner of drawing room furniture of the high Victorian era. The embroidered panel has a coral and water-lily design. Its function was to provide an attractive screen to the fireplace when no fire was burning.

G. 12 FIRESIDE OR SEWING CHAIR. 98 h 56 w 47 d.

Circa 1850. This upholstered chair has a visible mahogany frame. The 'knees' of the front cabriole style legs are decoratively carved, as are the back and the under-seat frieze. There is a break to the right hand lower arm area. The chair has been re-upholstered in red material over a sprung base. Chairs of this kind were common in genteel households during the 19th century; they were used as occasional easy

chairs in bedrooms as well as sitting rooms, where the use of castors allowed such chairs to be moved around easily.

G. 13 WORK TABLE. 72 h 57 w.

A work table on a central pedestal, *circa* 1860, with a three-lobe shaped top, decorated with stencilled fern and leaf patterns in yellow, and with an inlaid edge in stained woods. Such pieces were known as fern or gipsy tables, and the firm of William Corris of Seel St., Liverpool, specialised in making items of this kind during the 19th century. The top has a needlework compartment below, which rests on a decoratively turned column. The table has a base which has an upper surface veneered in burr walnut. One foot is damaged.

G. 14 FIRESIDE OR LADY'S EASY CHAIR. 94 h 53.5 w 56 d.

This chair has front and rear legs, as well as the front under-seat frieze, made of solid rosewood. There is a fracture to the right rear leg which has a metal repair. The chair probably had castors originally, which are now missing. It has been re-upholstered in a blue fabric, *circa* 1970. Chairs of this type were common in genteel households during the second half of the 19th century, where they could be used as occasional chairs in bedrooms, and in sitting rooms where their mobility allowed them to be moved around easily.

G. 15 OCCASIONAL TABLE. 52 h 47 diam.

A small occasional table, *circa* 1860, made of ash. It has a circular top supported on three turned simulated bamboo legs. These are united below with a further turned circular wooden shelf, which shows evidence of the lathe stock marks underneath.

G. 16 PATENT READING TABLE or EASEL. 65 h 37 diam.

This patent table has a cast iron base with a vertical stem of gilt over brass, and a canted mahogany reading shelf above. The table is adjustable to suit different reading heights, from 67 hh to 49hh. In addition to adjustable height, the reading platform also swivels on a metal joint. The stand has a descriptive legend inscribed on it. 'Reading Easel. May be applied to any chair, bed, or sofa. Made by E. P. North. Birmingham. Manufacturer. Can be used in any position.'

G. 17 LACQUERED GAMES TABLE. 78 h 50 x 60.5.

Circa 1870. Made in the manner of Chinese export furniture, with exaggerated carved paw feet, and a decorative black lacquered surface and relief decoration overall. The top has a sliding lid, with a backgammon board in the well and a chequer board on the under-surface of the top. A round wooden washer between the stem and the top is an addition.

G. 18 X-END OCCASIONAL TABLE. 61.5 h 58 w 37 d.

A painted X-end occasional table, *circa* 1880. This table is made with cross ends of turned ash, joined by a turned cross stretcher, also in ash. Both the cross ends are intersected by roundels bearing the Three Legs emblem of the Isle of Man. The table has a thick pine top and was probably intended to support a tray. It is painted in matt black with decoratively painted turned nodal rings and Manx emblems.

G. 19 UPRIGHT PIANOFORTE. 188 hh 125.5 w 65 d.

This piano, *circa* 1840, has a (visible) mahogany carcass, inlaid at the front with fretted brass. The upright internal framing is in beech, and the keys are ivory and ebony. The front cover to the metal stringing is in pink pleated silk (replacement). Made by John Broadwood & Sons – a plaque near the keyboard declares them as 'Makers to His Majesty and the Princesses, Great Pulteney Street, Golden Square, London.'

G. 20 SOFA. 86 h 174 w 62 d.

This upholstered sofa, *circa* 1880, has a mahogany carved frame and turned feet. The upholstery is horsehair internally, and there is replacement fabric over this.

G. 21 SUTHERLAND TABLE. 73.5 h 89 w 14 d (folded) 96 d (extended).

A decorative folding table, *circa* 1870, made of walnut, with two hinged flaps which can be raised and supported on hinged supports. The feet have white china and metal castors, emphasising that this is a mobile table which could be wheeled into place when needed, perhaps to serve food on, and could be extended when in use. The narrow top when folded is a feature of Sutherland tables, and makes for minimum use of floor space when the table is not in use.

G. 22 FOLDING SCREEN. 167 h 63.5 w.

A three section folding screen made with a bamboo frame and covered with fabric. Screens of this type were intended as draught excluders, and commonly as decorative items of furniture which could be used to create private spaces in a room, or to conceal unsightly areas.

G. 23 CANTERBURY. 51.5 h 34.5 w 11 d.

A late - 19th century canterbury made of pine. This small music/newspaper rack is painted black and partially covered with embroidered fabric. This example was intended to hang on the wall, and a small part of the hanging section is missing.

G. 24 GAMES TABLE. 75 h 61 x 38.

This games table, *circa* 1840, has a rectangular top secured to a turned base stem. The table is veneered in rosewood over a pine frame, with mahogany feet which terminate in metal castors. The top has an inlaid chequer board formed from rosewood heartwood and satinwood, with surrounding stringing inlays or ebony. The top also opens and swivels to create a card table with a green baize surface. It has three drawers below, with two small outer drawers which pull out on opposite sides. The drawers have pine fronts veneered in rosewood, and with quarter sawn oak linings. The top is connected to the base stem with a metal bolt. A small piece of veneer is missing from the top front edge.

G. 25 WINDOW SEAT. 44.5 h 108 w 63 d.

This low upholstered window seat, *circa* 1870, has wooden X-ends in the neo-classical manner, and is made of mahogany with an internal pine frame. The top is upholstered, with a replacement *petit point* fabric which covers a similar, earlier, cover. The upholstery is supported over a webbing and hessian base. The stool has brass and ceramic castors.

DINING ROOM

G. 26 BUFFET. 117 h 122 w 56 d.

A mahogany buffet, *circa* 1870. Storage pieces of this type were used to place tableware and food on prior to bringing them to the table. This example has three shelves supported on two vertical side supports which stand on carved paw feet, fitted with castors. The outer supports are fitted with a system of pulleys which allow the upper shelf to be lowered to a more convenient height for serving.

G. 27 'LAZY SUSAN'. 18 h 64.5 diam.

A low revolving circular table on a round base. This item could be placed in the centre of the dining table, and could be revolved in order that diners could have access to its contents. It is made with a mahogany top and turned beech base.

The Grove Dining Room

G. 28 TWO CIRCULAR UPHOLSTERED
FOOTSTOOLS. 15.5 h 42.5 diam.

These footstools, *circa* 1870, have solid rosewood frames and
feet and pine bottom boards. Internally, solid wooden walls
extend to the top of the stools, and are covered with hand
worked *gros point* fabric which extends over the upholstered
top and sides. The rosewood base frame is made of six
segments in laminated form, and turnery marks on the pine
base board suggest that this acted as a face plate for the
turnery process involved in turning the rosewood edge
moulding and solid sides.

G. 29 BOOKCASE. 229 h 158.5 w 31 d.

This bookcase appears to be made in two parts, with an
upper bookcase which stands on a lower base of shelves.
However, it is made in one piece, in oak with pine shelves
faced with oak strips, which also hold leather shelf frills in
place. The backboards are spruce, and are constructed in
sections with a central mounting. The four shelves above the
base are adjustable on narrow wooden cut-out strips.

G. 30 TEA TABLE. 74.5 h 92 w 46 d.

A mahogany folding tea table, *circa* 1840, standing on four
fluted legs with finely carved paterae above. The top is made
of two highly figured solid mahogany leaves. The frieze and
supporting brackets are made in beech, with mahogany
veneers to the frieze. The two rear legs are pivoted to swing
outwards to support one of the leaves. A section of moulding
is missing around the right back leg.

G. 31 TWO TURNED FIRESIDE ARM CHAIRS.
98.5 h 50.5 w 63 d.

These chairs, *circa* 1880, are made with decoratively turned
beech frames and back spindles, and display residues of the
original rosewood simulation. The seats are made from cane,
and one chair has an additional pine slat support nailed to
the front seat stretcher. The arms have upholstered pads
fixed to them, and the backs and seats have loose cushions.

G. 32 BUTLER'S TRAY. 75 w 50 d.

This butler's tray, *circa* 1870, is a folding occasional serving
tray which could be brought to the table when required for
serving. This item has a typical shallow mahogany tray (with
a fracture and metal repair to one corner) which rests on a
folding X-shaped base with webbing straps.

G. 33 SIDEBOARD. 142.5 h 186.5 w 61.5 d.

An imposing sideboard, *circa* 1870, with a carcass of pine and
thick mahogany veneers. The ornately carved backboard is of
solid mahogany, and the four door panels are of crotch sawn
mahogany cut from the same section of wood. The three
upper drawers intended to hold cutlery have shaped fronts
and are lined with green baize. The cupboards below have
central shelves and are also baize lined. The right hand
cupboard has a cellarette.

The Grove Kitchen

G. 34 EXTENDING DINING TABLE.
75 h 148 w 132 d.

A mahogany oval ended dining table, *circa* 1860, with a heavily moulded edge around the top, supported on heavily carved legs which terminate in brass and white ceramic castors. The under-top framing is made in ash with a mahogany cross frame. This is constructed with a metal screw mechanism, to allow the base to be wound outwards so that up to four extra leaves could be inserted to lengthen the table.

G. 35 UPHOLSTERED SUITE.
SOFA. 94 h 201 w 65.5 d.
SIDE CHAIRS. 90.5 h 51 w 41 d.
ARM CHAIRS. 91.5 h 57.5 w 46 d.

This suite, comprising a sofa, six side chairs, and two arm chairs, dates from *circa* 1840. The frames are made of mahogany, and the secondary wood which forms the under-seat framing is beech. The corner blocks are also mahogany, and the outer surfaces of the seat frames are veneered in the same wood. The seats of the chairs are removable. They have wooden (beech) frames upholstered in cross webbing with hessian, and are stuffed with horsehair under fabric covers. The sofa has a separate seat cushion and end bolsters filled with horsehair stuffing. The seat cushions and sides are supported by beech cross slats and webbing supports.

The overall design of this suite reflects a neo-classical interpretation, probably inspired by Thomas Hope's designs which were highly fashionable in the Regency period. However, the suite was made a little later than Hope's

designs, and incorporates the use of turned front legs which were fashionable from the mid-1830s and throughout the 19th century. The heavily carved crest rails and the generally heavy frames are suggestive of fashionable chairs made within the Scottish tradition, *circa* 1850, and it is probable that this suite originates from there.

KITCHEN

G. 36 WINDSOR SIDE CHAIR. 85 h 39 w 35.5 d.

This Windsor side chair, *circa* 1890, is made in beech with an elm seat. The rear of the seat is stamped 'JD 25,' the initials of the chair assembler and the number of the chair in a batch being made. This chair was made in the Chilterns area of Buckinghamshire, probably by one of the High Wycombe chair manufacturers.

G. 37 BAR TOP LADDER-BACK CHAIR.
96 h 65 w 51 d.

This ladder-back chair, *circa* 1840, is made of ash and stained with a dark stain. It was made in the North-West of England, probably in Lancashire, now has a webbing seat which replaces its original rush seat. The chair's feet have been removed, and it is now fitted on later rockers.

G. 38 LOW STOOL. 30 h 43.5 w 22 d.

Circa 1850. This stool is carpenter-made in pine, with five sections of wood nailed together. The flat end boards have simple feet formed by a V-shaped cut out, and a piece of wood is nailed to each end to strengthen it. The top board has an S-shaped hand grip cut into it. The side boards form robust supports for the stool. The end supports are mahogany stained.

G. 39 STOOL. 25.5 h 24.5 x 22.

A stool made in an unidentified hardwood, *circa* 1880. The rectangular top is chamfered on its lower edges and supported on four turned legs, one of which is a replacement.

G. 40 CLOTHES HORSE. 91 h 60 w 5 d (closed).

A large three-fold clothes horse, *circa* 1900, made of pine with webbing hinges. The tiers of four cross rails are morticed through the uprights.

G. 41 KITCHEN TABLE. 73.5 h 115 w 76 d.

A square-form kitchen table, *circa* 1880, made in pine with four planks to the top which are tongue-and-grooved together. The top is scrubbed and fixed to a base of four square legs, joined by under-top stretchers. The base is mahoganised and is without a drawer.

G. 42 FIXED FOLDING TABLE.
91 h 75.5 x 158. Fixed strip 16.

A pine flap table, *circa* 1860, which folds down from a wall fixing. One end of the top is rounded on its outer corner; the other end has a pine cleat. Two simple square-form leg supports pivot to hold the top when in use. The base is painted brown and the top is scrubbed.

G. 43 IRONING BOARD. 124 long 28.5 w 2.5 d.

An oak shaped board without legs or supports, *circa* 1900, which was evidently placed on another surface to iron linen on.

G. 44 LINEN PRESS. 114 h 73.5 w 22.5 d.

A free standing linen press with a screw mechanism, *circa* 1780. The two pressing boards are of cedar and the cross bars and uprights are of oak. The screw is made of mahogany. The press, which is badly eroded on its top surface, stands on a base made of pine, which was made for other purposes than that for which it is now used.

G. 45 WALL CLOCK. 43 diam.

An ebonised, round faced wall clock made by Litherland, Whiteside & Co., Liverpool (*fl.* 1800 - 1816). The movement is by J. Gonliffe of Liverpool, and the dial and dial plate are by Wilkes & Son, Birmingham.

G. 46 DRESSER. 243 h 186.5 w 53 d.

This joiner-made dresser is made in pine, *circa* 1840. It has several coats of paint on its base and shelves, the most recent being brown gloss paint. It is the major storage piece in the kitchen, and has a base consisting of three drawers above two cupboards. The open rack above has three shelves. The thin top of the base is scrubbed. This dresser was crudely adapted to its position in the kitchen: the sides of the rack, which were probably continuous with the sides of the base, were cut off flush with the top of the base and moved backwards to fit to the wall, and a moulding was nailed to the ceiling to hold it

in place. The base has planks of wood roughly fitted to the back to fill the space between itself and the wall. The three drawers are dovetailed, with five joints to the front and four to the rear. The central drawer is divided front to rear, and the right hand one from side to side.

SCULLERY

G. 47 LOW PLATFORM. 7.5 h 33.5 w 35 d.

A low platform made in pine, *circa* 1900, which was used to stand on to raise a worker's feet off the stone floor.

G. 48 PLATE DRYING RACK. 76 h 107 w 23.5 d.

Circa 1900. Made of a rectangular frame supporting pine dowels to hold plates whilst they were drying. This rack could accommodate thirteen plates in each of two rows.

G. 49 LAUNDRY OR IRONING TABLE.
82 h 171.5 w 51 d.

An unusual form of table, *circa* 1880, which may have been made as a stand for washing tubs, the raised edges stopping water from dripping onto the feet of the laundress. With a cloth pad, it could also have been used as an ironing table. Made of pine, the one piece top has raised edging strips nailed around the edge with flooring nails. The base is made with chamfered cross-ends, and supported by a centre stretcher. The base is mahoganised, as is the under-surface of the top.

G. 50 LAUNDRY OR IRONING TABLE.
88.5 h 201 w 50 d.

An unusual form of table, *circa* 1880, which may have been used as a laundry table to stand the washing tubs on, the edging strip preventing water from dripping onto the laundress's feet. With the addition of a cloth pad it could also have been used as an ironing table. Made of pine, the one piece top has raised edging strips, nailed around the edge with flooring nails. The base is made with chamfered cross-ends, and supported a centre stretcher. There are paint residues below the top and on the rim. A label below the top states 'Carriage Paid. Gibb. The Grove. Ramsey'.

G. 51 JOINED ARM CHAIR. 110 h 61.5 w 47 d.

A panel-back chair, *circa* 1750, of a generic type associated with Scots/Irish/IOM design. This chair is made of oak and has two Scots pine panels in the back. The seat is a replacement, and the bottoms of the legs are shortened. Originally stretchers connected the legs, and remnants of these are visible. The oak arms mortice into the back uprights, and the top cross rail is made of cleft oak.

G. 52 RECTANGULAR TABLE. 74 h 147 w 78 d.

This table, *circa* 1880, is of an unusual design and was evidently made for a specialised use; exactly what is unclear, but it was probably related to the laundry. The base has two horizontal slats enclosing three sides of its upper part. Mortice and tenon remains show that others also enclosed the fourth side. Mortices indicate that the enclosed area had a floor of nine slats. The function of this may have been to hold laundry, but if this is so, the thick pine top now nailed to the top of the frame is evidently a later addition.

G. 53 RECTANGULAR TABLE.
71.5 h 167 w 64 d.

Made of pine, *circa* 1880, this table has square tapered legs and a deep under-top frieze, which precludes sitting at it. This suggests that it was a table at which people stood to work. The top is made of four planks and fixed to the base.

G. 54 ROUND TOPPED TABLE. 66 h 70 diam.

This table, *circa* 1880, is made of pine, and has a round top fixed to a base comprising three turned legs which are joined by a triangular shaped frieze. The bottoms of the legs have been lowered. The table originally had a mahoganised base with a scrubbed pine top. It is now crudely painted with green paint.

MAIN BEDROOM

G. 55 TESTER BED. 243.5 h 231 w 195.5 d.

An imposing tester bed, *circa* 1870, made with an ornately carved mahogany foot board and posts, and with a pine, mahogany stained, head board and square posts. A square wooden frame connects the top of the uprights and a fabric tester covers this. The tester is surrounded by a moulded mahogany cornice (badly fitting at the bottom left corner). Below this, a surround of embroidered fabric with a fringe provides a frieze. The side stretchers supporting the mattress are made of mahogany and have cross slats of pine joining them. The bed has metal screws uniting the lower sections, hidden behind fascia boards on the uprights which can be slid off.

G.56 STOOL OR BED-STEP.
22 h 48.5 w 38.5 d.

Circa 1870. Made in mahogany with a drop-in top, now covered with a piece of carpet. This stool was used as a step to get into the tester bed. It is made in a Gothic revivalist manner, with stylised chamfered Gothic arches to the wooden frame.

G. 57 SIDE CHAIR. 113 h 50 w 48.5 d.

Circa 1870. An upholstered bedroom chair of decorative design. The carved frame is made of solid rosewood with an upright back and low seat, supported on short cabriole legs one of which is damaged and has a clumsy repair. The back and seat are upholstered.

G. 58 BED-TABLE. 76 h (lowest) 82 w 46 d.

Circa 1880. This patent table has an ornate cast iron base with acanthus leaf and claw feet castings. The front feet alone have castors, to aid stability. The metal stem terminates in a metal capstan wheel device which supports and allows the plywood top to swivel into position. The table has the information on it: 'Foots Patent. J. Foot & Son. 171 New Bond St. London W.'

G. 59 TAPESTRY FRAME. 122 h 89 w 41 d.

Circa 1840. An adjustable mahogany stand made to hold a stretched section of canvas for embroidery. The turned frame which holds the fabric is adjustable both top and bottom on outer screw-turned supports, and it can be inclined to suit the sitter. All the parts composing this item are also turned.

G. 60 CHEVAL MIRROR. 61.5 h 83 w 57.5 d.

Circa 1880. A large free-standing dressing mirror made entirely in mahogany, with turned outer uprights joined by two turned cross stretchers, and standing on two carved feet with castors. The frame surrounding the mirror is made of mahogany veneered onto solid mahogany. The rear of the mirror is composed of four panels of unstained mahogany, which fit tightly into the frame, and have no further fixing. The name 'Cope & Austin Patent' is stamped on the back hinge fixing.

G. 61 BIDET. 46 h 55.5 w 38 d.

Circa 1880. This shaped metal bidet with a concave bottom is held in an outer case of mahogany supported on four turned feet. A mahogany lid slips over both base and bidet.

G. 62 TOWEL RAIL. 60 h 71.5 w 34 d.

Circa 1870. A mahogany towel rail with one upper and two outer turned rails. One lower cross rail is supported between two flat end supports which are fretted and shaped with stylised tulip motifs.

G. 63 COMMODE CHAIR. 70 h 55.5 w 47 d.

Circa 1840. A commode chair made in mahogany and inlaid with ebony. This is a specialised item of bedroom furniture, with flat outer sections which partially enclose the seating area. The ceramic commode is covered with a hinged seat cover, and the pot is held in a pine frame below this. The pot has a circular mahogany cover. The front of the commode is made of pine with decorative veneers of mahogany, and inlaid with ebony stringing to the front.

G. 64 OTTOMAN. 44 h 70 w 52 d.

Circa 1880. An upholstered ottoman or storage box. The box is made in pine with an upholstered top and a fabric (chintz) cover on the outside. It is lined with waxed fabric. The castors on which the box can be moved are made of metal and lignum vitae.

G. 65 BED TRAY. 24 h 60.5 w 37.5 d.

Circa 1870. A shallow mahogany tray which has a low surrounding frieze on three edges, and fretted hand grips to each side. The tray is intended to provide a table for a person lying in bed to eat from, and has four turned feet which raise it over the reclining body.

G. 66 COAL BOX AND SHOVEL. 37 h 33 w 46 d.

Circa 1880. A carved mahogany coal box with brass handles and shovel. The base is made of pine and there is an internal metal liner to hold the coal in the box.

G. 67 WHIP AND BOOT STAND.
121 h 72 w 43 d.

Circa 1860. A fruitwood (pear or cherry-wood) stand with a lower rack to hold inverted riding boots and pegs above to hang riding whips. Alterations have been made to this stand; the top shelf is an addition in mahogany and now covers the whip hooks which have had their tips broken off. One boot hanger is also a replacement in mahogany.

G. 68 WARDROBE. 200 h 139 w 67 d.

Circa 1880. A mahogany wardrobe made with high cabinet making specifications. The design is in the restrained classical arcadian style, standing on a plinth and with two plain doors below a simple cornice. The solid door panels are made of burred and figured mahogany, and the case of the wardrobe is made of spruce with, again, highly figured mahogany veneered onto this. Internally, the left side has seven turned mahogany pegs for hanging clothes. To the right, three sliding trays are fitted. These have birch fronts and are lined with oak. A mahogany shelf also forms part of this storage area, below which one short and one long drawer are fitted. This wardrobe is reputed to have been made by a Kilmarnock cabinet making firm, but no confirmatory evidence is apparent.

G. 69 TRUNK. 42.5 h 76 w 48.5 d.

Circa 1880. A storage trunk made of pine and covered with American oil-cloth, with leather edging to the lid. The base has protective metal corners and brackets riveted to the wooden frame. Internally, the trunk is covered in fabric and fitted to hold hats and other articles of clothing.

G. 70 TEA TABLE. 74 h 91.5 w 45 d.

Circa 1820. A mahogany *demi-lune* folding tea table with a leaf which can be supported on two rear legs, wooden-hinged to fold outwards and with metal brackets to hold them in place. The top sections are located together with three peg joints when opened. The frieze is veneered in panels of highly figured mahogany over blocked pine. The tapered legs are made of solid mahogany, and have stringing at the top composed of bands of holly and ebony.

G. 71 DOUBLE WASH STAND. 95.5 h 92 w 45 d.

Circa 1870. A mahogany wash stand with splash boards around the sides and back of the top. This has two circular holes to accept ceramic washing bowls. The turned legs support a lower shelf which has a single shallow drawer below it.

G.72 DRESSING TABLE. 95 h 114.5 w 50 d.

Circa 1870. A mahogany dressing table made to high cabinet making specifications. The top of the table has surrounding edge boards, and two shallow drawers with further drawers with black painted knobs and oak drawer linings fitted beneath. It is supported by two outer uprights which are joined by a decoratively turned cross rail. The side supports and other parts of the carcase are made of pine with mahogany veneers.

G. 73 TOILET MIRROR. 59.5 h 55 w 26.5d.

Circa 1870. A mahogany toilet mirror made to high cabinet making specifications. The carcase of the mirror is made of pine with mahogany veneers. The feet, drawer knobs, and the two mirror supports are made of solid mahogany. The three drawers are concave to the front and have fronts of pine, veneered in mahogany and finely lined in oak. The mirror frame is made of pine with concave veneers.

SEWING ROOM

G. 74 PRESS CUPBOARD. 220.5 h 135.5 w 63 d.

Circa 1790. The carcase of this press cupboard, which is made in two parts, is of spruce veneered externally with mahogany. The doors are made of solid mahogany panels inset with decorative central oval mahogany veneers which

have a highly figured grain, and ebony and boxwood stringing. The escutcheons are inlaid bone or ivory. The brass handles are replacements. Internally, the cupboard has five full width sliding trays to hold linen. The base has two short and two long drawers, lined with oak, and with five dovetails joints to front and rear. The drawer fronts are made of spruce with mahogany veneers. The press rests on bracket feet and has a cornice above.

G. 75 CHEST OF DRAWERS. 77 h 66.5 w 39.5 d.

This chest of drawers, in its present altered form, dates from *circa* 1920. It is made of mahogany, with black and white stringing to the drawer fronts. The drawers have oval handles dating to the first twenty years of the 19th century, and replaced escutcheons. The backboards are missing. The design of the chest suggests its period of manufacture to be *circa* 1780. However, it is probable that the chest was originally a commode, with *faux* drawers which have been converted to full drawers at a later time, probably in the 20th century.

G. 76 TOILET MIRROR. 46.5 h 19 d 44.5 w.

This toilet mirror, made *circa* 1880, has solid mahogany uprights, securing knobs, and feet. It has a pine base, veneered with mahogany, and the outer frame edge of the mirror is also veneered in mahogany over pine.

G. 77 HANGING WALL SHELVES. 67 h 34.5 w 17 d.

A mahogany decorative tier of three graduated shelves, separated by ornately turned spindles which are screwed through each shelf. The lower spindles could form feet, and allow the shelves to stand on a flat surface.

G. 78 TREADLE SEWING MACHINE.
91.5 h 66.5 w 48.5 d.

A treadle sewing machine with no maker's mark evident. The base is made of cast iron, with a treadle, fly-wheel and belt providing motive power to the sewing machine which rests on a mahogany bed above. A covering case of mahogany can be fitted over the machine when it is not in use, and in the drawer are many of the sewing accoutrements for use with the machine.

G. 79 PEMBROKE TABLE.
67 h 55.5 w 38 d (folded) 68 (extended).

A Pembroke table, made *circa* 1840 in solid mahogany. This table has two flaps which can be supported on two swivelling wings which are knuckle jointed to fold under the top side frieze. One wing is absent. The legs terminate abruptly, and it is probable that the bottoms of the legs have been lowered, or its feet totally removed. It is likely that it was originally fitted with castors.

G. 80 CHEVAL MIRROR. 159 h 77.5 w 45.5 d.

A large free-standing dressing mirror, *circa* 1860, made in solid mahogany with the mirror frame made of veneered mahogany onto pine. It has decoratively 'ball' turned outer mirror supports, and an elaborately moulded mirror frame.

Child's Bedroom at The Grove

G. 81 OCCASIONAL OR LADY'S SEWING CHAIR.
86.5 h 59 w 46 d.

A low upholstered occasional chair made with a walnut frame which has decoratively shaped and carved cabriole front legs and frieze. The Berlin woolwork upholstery cover may be a later replacement. Chairs of this type were common in genteel households during the second half of the 19th century, where they could be used as occasional chairs in bedrooms, and in sitting rooms where their mobility allowed them to be moved around easily.

G. 82 LOO TABLE. 73 h 138 x 103.

A loo table made with ornately carved central walnut pedestal and cabriole supporting legs with porcelain castors. The top is now oval and made of pine. Evidence from the scarified surface and the crude edge cutting marks indicate that this may be the original top from which the original veneers have been removed, and its shape altered. The edging surround below the top is a later addition. The top in unstable on the base.

CHILD'S BEDROOM

G. 83 TEA TABLE. 72.5 h 91 w 45.5 d (folded).

A folding semi-circular tea table, *circa* 1790. The solid

mahogany top sections have a curved frieze which is veneered with mahogany onto a pine base. This is made in the stacked block manner, with four glued juxtaposed sections which have opposing grain. The tapered legs are made of solid mahogany. Two legs swivel to the rear to support the top, which folds in half. The frieze has classical style painted decoration, and the legs have lining in gold, which may be additions applied in the 19th century.

G. 84 DOLL'S CRADLE. 47 h 61.5 w 29d.

This doll's cradle, made in pine, is carpenter-made using nailed construction throughout. The surface is painted and grained to simulate mahogany, and has decorative black lines.

G. 85 CHEST OF DRAWERS. 107.5 h 128.5 w 54.5 d.

Made in pine, this chest is made to high cabinet making specifications. It has two small drawers and three long drawers below, and stands on turned feet. The drawers are jointed with dovetails to the front and the rear, and the intervals between the drawers have full dustboards. The drawers have turned and black japanned knobs, fitted with metal bolts and screwed to the rear. The surface of the chest was originally filled with whiting or gesso, painted and grained to simulate oak, with the drawer fronts alternately grained as quarter sawn and transverse sawn grain. The chest front is also lined out in red/brown paint, and the kite shaped escutcheons are painted in brown paint (some now worn away).

G. 86 TOILET MIRROR. 64 h 59 w 26.5 d.

A free-standing toilet mirror, *circa* 1880, with a solid mahogany base and uprights. The edges of the base and the mirror surround are veneered in mahogany onto a pine substrate.

G. 87 HANGING SHELVES. 65 h 59 w 15 d.

A small set of hanging shelves with cupboards below, *circa* 1880. Made of pine and stained to simulate mahogany, this hanging shelf and storage item has decoratively shaped sides, a shelf above and a cupboard with two chamfered panelled doors below. Hanging shelves and cupboards of this kind were popular during the 19th century, and were commonly used for display and to provide more private storage.

G. 88 SIDE CHAIR. 75.5 h 39 w 35 d.

Circa 1900. Made in mahogany with bone inlays, and stained brown over-all. The legs of this chair are joined by replacement dowels.

G. 89 WARDROBE. 227 h 131 w 58 d.

This wardrobe is made in pine, *circa* 1880, and painted and grained externally to simulate oak. The upper section has two round arched doors, which open to reveal, to the right, three fixed shelves with two sliding trays fitted between them. A large drawer is fitted below the shelves. To the upper left side of the cupboard, pegs are fitted for hanging clothes, and a lidded shoe or hat box is fitted below this. The cornice is removable, and the cupboard sits on a plinth. See Loudon, 1833, for further discussion of wardrobes of this type.

G. 90 WASH STAND. 72 h 92 w 49d.

This wash stand, *circa* 1880, has a birch base stained to simulate mahogany. The drawers have birch fronts and ash linings, which are also stained with mahogany stain. The top is composed of one section of Sicilian marble.

G. 91 HALF TESTER BED.
216.5 hh (bed head 119.5 h) 198.5 w 108.5 d.

A half tester bed, *circa* 1860, made of cast metal painted black with coloured floral decoration. The metal frame supports the decorative head and base, and the tester fits into the bed head. The half tester is hung with fabric, and a fabric frieze reaching to the floor is fixed with tapes to the bed frame.

G. 92 SCREEN. 152.2 h 60.5 w.

A three-fold screen, *circa* 1890, with a fabric covered pine frame. The frame has pictures glued to it to form a collage of images taken from various sources, including advertisements as well as book and magazine illustrations.

G. 93 OTTOMAN. 41 h 108 w 36 d.

This upholstered ottoman, or storage box, is made of pine and covered with fabric, and more recently upholstered on its top. It has a decorative fabric lining which is probably original to the box.

STORED ITEMS

G. 94 CANTERBURY. 51 h 39 w 25 d.

A cane canterbury, *circa* 1880, with later black paint over the original natural bamboo. The tops of the legs terminate with buttons of turned bone, and the centre of each side has a rectangular lacquered plaque with foliar decoration.

G. 95 STAND. 86 h 76 w 25 d.

A stand made of mahogany, with dark varnish over this, *circa* 1900. The function of this stand is not clear. It may have been intended as an umbrella stand, or as a rail for clothes or towels.

G. 96 WALL SHELVES. 91 h 74 w 22 d.

A three tiered wall shelf or 'whatnot', made in mahogany *circa* 1860. Shelves of this type were made to display items of virtue in fashionable Victorian households. This example has barley twist turned supports on the front only, and screw turned supports on the back. These have turned ends which screw onto the shelves, and decorative wooden screw terminals on the top shelf.

G. 97 THREE SIDE CHAIRS. 84 h 43 w 43 d.

Three lightly framed bedroom or fancy chairs of slightly different designs from each other, *circa* 1870. Made with beech frames, they originally had cane seats. Chairs of these designs were made in large quantities by chair manufacturers in High Wycombe, Bucks, during the 19th century. Manufacturers also produced cheap pressed and drilled seats which could be nailed over broken cane seats, as is the case with these chairs.

G. 98 FOLDING SEAT. 71 h 54 w 31 d.

A folding seat, *circa* 1900, made from square sections of pine, pinned through the joints with metal bars which allow the seat to be folded or opened. Seats of this form were known in classical antiquity, and it is this source which provides the design impulse for this example.

G. 99 CONSERVATORY CHAIR. 100 h 74 w 80 d.

A conservatory chair, *circa* 1920, made with a bamboo frame, and decoratively woven with sea-grass (coir) thread.

G. 100 WINDSOR CHAIR. 86 h 40 w 45 d.

A Windsor side chair, *circa* 1880. This chair is painted with 20th century gloss paint which completely obscures the woods. However, the design of the chair indicates that it was made in the High Wycombe, Bucks, tradition, and the use of beech with an elm seat was conventional for chairs of this type.

G. 101 WINDSOR CHAIR. 84 h 44 w 36 d.

A Windsor chair, *circa* 1880, made in beech with an elm seat. The turnery devices on the back outer spindles suggest that this chair was made by one of the High Wycombe, Bucks, chair manufacturers; the rear of the seat has the chair framer's initials, C.K. stamped on it. This chair was originally finished with a walnut staining varnish, which is now eroded.

G. 102 BEDROOM CHAIR. 83 h 38 w 36 d.

A single bedroom chair made with a beech frame and a pressed plywood seat, *circa* 1910. The surface has several layers of 20th century paint.

G. 103 SIDE CHAIR. 90 h 48 w 50 d.

A mahogany side chair, painted to simulate rosewood *circa* 1840. This is one of a group of six side chairs, the other five dispersed throughout the main house. For a full description, see the Drawing Room entry for chair G 9.

G. 104 HOOP BACK WINDSOR CHAIR. 100 h 43 w 38 d.

A Windsor side chair, *circa* 1880, made with an ash hoop, hand-shaped spindles, and a birch seat. Three of the legs are replacements in pine, as is the cross stretcher which is oak. The fourth (original) leg is in beech. The chair has traces of green paint with later brown paint over this.

G. 105 WINDSOR CHAIR. 78 h 62 w 46 d.

A smoker's bow or office chair, made in elm, *circa* 1880. This chair was probably made in the High Wycombe, Bucks, tradition of chair making, and carries its framer's mark D.P. on the rear of the seat.

G. 106 SIX BALLOON BACK CHAIRS. 88 h 48 w 45 d.

A set of six balloon-back side chairs, made in mahogany, with beech seat rails, *circa* 1860. These elegant chairs have their original loose seats, made with pine frames, covered with webbing and hessian. Over this is a layer of horsehair covered with hessian, and the original green leather covers which although damaged, are rare survivals of this type of seat cover.

G. 107 COMMODE. 98 h 53 w 52 d.

A birch commode arm chair, *circa* 1900, made with a caned and hinged seat which covers a white glazed pottery pot and cover. The design of this chair, particularly the use of reeded cross splats and uprights in the back, is reminiscent of chair designs made by John East & Co. of Dundee during the second half of the 19th century, and into the 20th.

G. 108 SNAP-TOP OR TILT-TOP TABLE. 72 h 52 w 38 d.

A mahogany tilt-top or snap-top table, *circa* 1815, with a rectangular top and a brass locking device below to hold or release the top into an upright position. The pintles or wooden hinges on which the top should hinge are broken, and later steel hinges are fitted, as is a replacement block in oak. The slender turned column with multiple ring turnings and curved feet are typical of tables made in the Regency period.

G. 109 BAMBOO TABLE. 71.5 h 29.5 diam.

A lacquered stand, *circa* 1880, made with four bamboo legs and round lacquered shelves which have black lacquered pine edges. The top is divided into three decoratively painted sections. The tops of the legs have turned ebony 'buttons' to seal them, and 'U' shaped bamboo staples are fitted to the upper legs. The exact purpose of these is unclear, but they were probably to hang decorative items from. Bamboo furniture of this kind was popular in the second half of the 19th century, and was imported from China as well as being made in England.

G. 110 TRIPOD TABLE. 43 h 63 diam.

An oak pedestal table, *circa* 1850. The top has a brass band around its edge which extends above the level of the table top, perhaps to stop glasses or other objects from falling off. This feature may indicate that it was made for use on board ship, although the brass and porcelain castors would make it unstable in such a setting. The three curved feet are decoratively gouge carved. The top is made from three sections of quarter sawn oak.

G. 111 TILT-TOP TABLE. 74 h 65 w 48 d.

A mahogany tilt-top or snap-top pedestal table, *circa* 1815, made with a rectangular top and a slender turned support. The top has a brass clip below, to lock it in place when folded down. The three shaped feet are reinforced underneath, with a steel support.

G. 112 CHEST OF DRAWERS. 94 h 110 w 53 d.

A mahogany, oak and pine chest of drawers, *circa* 1810, with two small drawers above three long ones. The chest has ogee shaped feet. This piece is made to high cabinet making specifications, with a pine case veneered with mahogany. The back is made of pine boards. The three long drawers are made with pine fronts which are veneered with mahogany and lined with quarter sawn oak, apart from the drawer backs which are also pine. The top small drawers have solid mahogany fronts, and linings similar to those employed in the long drawers. The brass handles are original to the piece.

G. 113 LINEN CHEST. 155 h 125 w 47d.

A pine linen chest, *circa* 1850, with one long drawer below a cupboard with two doors. The interior of the cupboard is fitted with shelves on which linen could be stored. The exterior is painted yellow and the doors and drawer fronts are decoratively lined with red paint.

G. 114 CHEST OF DRAWERS. 118 h 121 w 52 d.

A mahogany chest of drawers with two small drawers at the top and four long ones below. The turned wooden handles and escutcheons are original to the piece. The drawers are lined with cedar, an aromatic wood used to pleasantly scent stored clothes or linen. The chest is supported on turned feet.

G. 115 WARDROBE. 207 h 197 w 70 d.

A mahogany wardrobe, *circa* 1850, made to high cabinet making specifications, with a solid mahogany front, sides and cornice, and spruce used for the back. The doors have simple Gothic arch mouldings. The interior has, to the left, a hanging space with gilt hanging pegs each side and a deep hat drawer below. The right hand side is fitted with four upper sliding trays to hold linen. Below these are three long drawers, with mahogany fronts which have original gilt brass handles in rococo style.

BENTWOOD CHAIRS

A collection of bentwood chairs is variously distributed throughout The Grove. These chairs represent designs pioneered by Michael Thonet, 1796 - 1871, the Austrian furniture designer. Some chairs in this group have paper labels or brands which variously advertise makers in Austria, Poland, and Czechoslovakia. These labels indicate chairs made variously during the 1920s when the Thonet factory formed associations with other companies in Europe.

The Grammar School : Castletown

GS. 1 DESK. 113.5 h 82 w 69 d (117 w extended).

A teacher's desk, *circa* 1910, made in Scots pine and raised on four turned legs. This general form of desk was made by many suppliers of school furnishings, including the North of England School Furnishing Co. Ltd., Darlington; a similar desk is illustrated in their catalogue of 1905. The centre stretcher has a metal strip screwed to it to protect it from footwear. See No. 207 for a similar desk in the reserve collection.

GS. 2 TEACHER'S CHAIR. 107 h 4 6 w 67 d (inc. step).

A specialised form of Windsor chair, made *circa* 1880, for use with a high desk. Made in beech with an elm seat and birch foot rest. This chair was probably made in one of the High Wycombe, Bucks, manufactures, originally finished with walnut or mahogany stain, and varnished over this. The surface finish is now eroded. See No. 72 A & B for two similar chairs in the reserve collection.

GS. 3 SCHOOL DESKS WITH BENCHES.
A. 64 h 186 w 57 d.
B. 67.5 h 186 w 57 d.
C. 55 h 186 w 57 d.
D. 55 h 186 w 57 d.

Four school integral desks with benches, *circa* 1900. Made with pine tops and seats and cast iron frames, which have decorative trefoil apertures in their bases in the Gothic manner. The upper wooden desks are screwed to ratchet devices which enable the slope of the desk to be adjusted. Below the ratchets are flat metal supports, with holes onto which a shelf could be mounted under the desk. The two taller benches were made for older children to sit at, and one of these has a rail with spaces to hold slates, and holes for inkwells. Each desk seats five pupils. Desks of this type were made by the North of England School Furnishing Co. Ltd., Darlington, 1905.

The Nautical Museum : Castletown

NT. 1 DESK ON STAND WITH CABINET ABOVE. 223 h 96 w 88 d.

A mahogany and pine desk located on a separate stand, and with a cupboard above now containing pigeon holes. The original desk, stand, and top cupboard date from *circa* 1790. The pigeon holes in the top were fitted later, to act as a filing system for the owner George Quayle who traded as a banker in the first half of the 19th century. The stand is made with mahogany front legs and connecting rail, and the rear legs, side and back stretchers are made of stained pine. The desk has a bank of interior drawers and pigeon holes, the drawers being lined in pine. The rear section of the top of the desk has been added later, and the top cabinet originally fitted into this space. The cabinet now has two replacement lower side sections, made from the same timber as the additional back section of the desk top. The interior pigeon holes in the top are a later fixture. The lower moulding, which is now fitted to the base of the cabinet, is also a replacement and suggests that at some point the cupboard has stood independently from the desk.

NT. 2 ARM CHAIR WITH UPHOLSTERED SEAT. 92 h 46 w 46 d.

A low mahogany arm chair, *circa* 1790. This chair was probably made by a joiner, and the exposed arm support tenons and the general massiveness of the parts supports this belief. The back has horizontal cross rails and a shaped top rail. The seat is stuffed over with a replacement leather cover. The back right leg has a metal repair, and the original castors are now missing.

NT. 3 FOUR SIDE CHAIRS. 97 h 49 w 40 d.

Four similar side chairs made of oak, *circa* 1790. These chairs are in the style of 18th century fashionable chairs, more usually made in mahogany, and have top rails which are reminiscent of those adopted by Thomas Chippendale and other designers from the mid-18th century. The fretted splats display a stylised wheatsheaf motif, and the wooden seats are nailed to the frames. The back legs are generously curved, and the surface was originally stained red to simulate mahogany. The chair is glue-jointed, without pegs.

NT. 4 PEMBROKE TABLE. 72 h 84 w 48 d.

A mahogany Pembroke table, *circa* 1780. This table has two side flaps which can be raised and supported on two mahogany wing supports each side, knuckle jointed to the frame. The square tapered legs have restrained gouge carving, and are supported on brass castors. One end frieze has a false drawer. At the other is an oak lined drawer which opens to reveal parts of two tea caddies and the frame into which they fitted. The top is now screwed down with various modern screws.

T.E. Brown Room : Manx Museum

MD. 1 CREDENZA. 108 h 150 w 45 d.

A credenza, *circa* 1850, made with a softwood carcase and veneered with complex parquetry and foliate designs in both exotic and indigenous woods. It has ormolu grotesque mounts and borders of classically inspired gilt brass mouldings. The shaped front has a curved glazed door fitted each side of a large central glazed door. Credenzas were intended for the display of precious, and often fragile, items and the doors have locks to protect the contents. The predominant veneer on the outer carcase of the top, doors, and base plinth, is burr walnut. Elsewhere on the top and front, diamonds of burr walnut and holly are bordered with box and ebony stringing. Stylised flowers of kingwood are inlaid at cross points in the mahogany. The panels are bordered in kingwood veneers.

MD. 2 HIGH DESK. 135 h 83 w 59 d.

High desk, *circa* 1850, made of pine, and stained with a pale yellow staining varnish. This high desk was used by the Manx poet and teacher, T.E. Brown (1830 - 1897). It was made to stand at, or to sit at with a tall chair, and has a hinged lid with the remains of a blue leather writing surface. The interior has pigeon holes labelled to accommodate Brown's personal business and pupils' accounts. A lockable, and perhaps later, drawer fits below the top, and two shelves are fitted below this. The legs are chamfered at the corners in the manner of designs popularised by A.W.N. Pugin in the first half of the 19th century, which continued to be followed throughout the 19th century.

MD. 3 OAK DINING TABLE. 71 h 141 w 141 d.

An oak dining table, *circa* 1890. This table was made to extend in order to take an additional central section. It is supported on four massive chamfered legs and under-top framing, decorated with black painted grooved lines and other fashionable motifs in the manner promulgated by A.W.N. Pugin (1812 - 1852). The legs originally had castors, and the table is now around 5 cms. lower than it was intended to be. It was originally stained with a yellow varnish which is now largely worn from the top. Pugin's designs were very influential in the first half of the 19th century, and his work *Gothic Furniture in the Style of the Fifteenth Century*, published in 1835, was widely used by architects and furniture makers at that time. Revivalist furniture inspired by this work was made into the late - 19th century, and this table dates from that period.

MD. 4 SEMI-GRAND PIANO. 93 h 123 w 224 d.

A mahogany semi-grand piano, *circa* 1835, made by John Broadwood & Sons, London. The case is made with specially selected figured mahogany which has now faded. The tapered octagonal faceted legs have neo-classical carvings at their tops in the Egyptian taste, and the ends of the keyboard have acanthus leaf carvings in the same manner. The lid can be hinged at the front or side. There is a lyre-shaped framework to support the tone pedals below the keyboard.

MD. 5 LONG CASE CLOCK. 218 h 54 w 26 d.

An oak long case clock, *circa* 1850, with an eight day movement and arched painted dial signed J. Muncaster, Douglas, on the dial. Although restrained for a case of this type, it has features of those made in the north of England, particularly Yorkshire, and was probably imported to the Island from there, then fitted with a mass produced Birmingham made movement. The case is made from quarter sawn oak throughout, apart from a pine back. John Muncaster is recorded as working as a watch and clockmaker between 1841 and 1852, at 13, Factory Lane, Douglas, at which time he had two employees.

MD. 6 OAK BOOKCASE. 225 h 144 w 56 d.

An oak bookcase, *circa* 1890, made by Radcliffe of Douglas, which belonged to T.E. Brown, the Manx poet. This bookcase is made to high cabinet making specifications in oak, and with fashionable engraved gilt brass handles dating from the late - 19th century. The upper case is glazed, and has internal adjustable bookshelves. The lower section has two drawers above two lower cupboard doors. The bookcase rests on a plain plinth.

MD. 7 FIVE UPHOLSTERED ARM CHAIRS.
121 hh 79 h 63 w 61 d.

Five fashionable upholstered chairs of a style which was widely interpreted by furniture manufacturers during the last quarter of the 19th century and into the first decade of the 20th. The chairs are made with oak frames, and the under-arm areas have decoratively carved oak panels of highly skilled execution. The upholstery is composed of a system of metal springs sewn between webbing framework, covered with hessian and padding, with imitation leather over this. Three other chairs from this suite of chairs are included in the reserve collection, Catalogue No. 95 A - C.

MD. 8 SQUARE PIANO. 84 h 174 w 69 d.

A mahogany square piano with wooden frame, *circa* 1830, labelled on an ivory plaque, John Broadwood, London. The carved and fretted panel above the keyboard is rosewood.

The turned legs, terminating in brass castors, can be removed to transport the instrument. A tone control foot pedal is fitted to the centre rear of the piano.

MD. 9 SETTLE. 140 hh 38 h 152 w 57 d.

An oak settle, *circa* 1870, with pine bottom boards. This settle is made with a panelled back and front. The box-shaped seat has a hinged lid, with an enclosed storage space below. The four vertical lower back panels are carved with a linenfold design, and the upper panels with a quasi-17th century stylised motif. The three flat panels in the base are without embellishment, and the settle is constructed with pegged joints throughout.

Military Cases : Manx Museum

MD. 10 CHEST OF DRAWERS. 94.5 h 90 w 46 d.

Three large and two small drawers, made in two parts. Brass bound mahogany with oak drawer sides and back. 'WR' on locks probably indicates a William IV date. This type of object was used as cabin or campaign furniture.

MD. 11 CIRCULAR TABLE. 73 h 62 d.

Three legs radiating from a central turned spindle. Possibly oak, painted to appear as mahogany.

Internee's Bedroom : Manx Museum

MD. 12 DRESSING TABLE.
135 hh (inc. mirror) 82 h 91 w 45 d.

Two large and two small drawers. Oak faced with a plywood base and softwood sides and back. Brass handles (two replaced) and escutcheons, ceramic rollers in metal fittings as castors. Mirror and frame not original.

MD. 13 WARDROBE. 188 h 93 w 41 d.

Central door with bevel edged mirror; carved panels to either side. Loose drawer underneath, with metal fittings, imitating copper/bronze. Made completely in oak, including the drawer sides.

MD. 14 SINGLE BED. 92 h 193 w 93 d.

Matching light oak head and foot boards, metal frame. Bed heightened for display purposes.

APPENDIX II
Catalogue Numbers & Museum Accession Numbers

When an item arrives at the Manx Museum it is allocated a unique number - its 'registration' or 'accession' number. Each item in this catalogue has an accession number which is different from the catalogue number allocated to it in this publication. The correlation between these two numbers can be found in the following pages.

The Museum accession number gives an approximate guide to when an item came into the Museum. A simple running number was used between 1922 and 1955 and a year prefix after that date. A five figure running number denotes a loan.

Items prefixed with 'G' are part of the collections at The Grove Rural Life Museum in Ramsey.

Items prefixed with 'GS' are located in the Grammar School, Castletown.

Items prefixed with 'NT' are located in the Nautical Museum, Castletown.

Items prefixed with 'MD' are additional display items within the Manx Museum, Douglas.

Catalogue No.	Accession No.		Catalogue No.	Accession No.		Catalogue No.	Accession No.
			59	61 - 22		105	88 - 1716
JOINED CHAIRS						106	60 - 129
1	1260		**WINDSOR CHAIRS**			107	67 - 234
2	4621		60	6499		108	67 - 191
3	6555		61	68 - 266		109	R151
4	R53		62	3567		110	77 - 2
5	675		63	3375		111	79 - 76
6	5713		64	84 - 214		112	88 - 1703
7 & 7 A	3473 & 3474		65	68 - 1			
8	21330		66	3656		**ECCLESIASTICAL CHAIRS**	
9	76 - 54		67	65 - 72		113	21653
10	6789		68	5955		114	81 - 33
11	R137		69 A & B	91 - 75 & 91 - 76			
12	R138		70	73 - 217		**STOOLS & BENCHES**	
13	72 - 12		71	63 - 135		115	R133
14	676		72 A & B	57 - 53 & 91 - 79		116	55 - 244
15	6062		73	86 - 153		117	R166
16	55 - 337		74	91 - 63		118	61 - 23
17	4467		75	76 - 4		119	55 - 229
18	R55		76	91 - 62		120	83 - 146
19	59 - 145		77	73 - 202		121	73 - 166
20	4850		78 A & B	91 - 77 & 91 - 78		122	7537
21	6778 B		79	3010		123	62 - 431
22	6778					124	65 - 34
23	74 - 269 A		**FASHIONABLE CHAIRS OF THE 18th CENTURY & REGENCY PERIOD**			125	4780
24	5273					126	69 - 2
25	1676					127	60 - 432
26	1262		80 A - C	6634 A - C		128	55 - 230
27	91 - 74		81	55 - 161		129	3625
28 A - C	55 - 246 A - C		82	69 - 1		130	4463
29 A & B	R54 A & B		83	3852		131	88 - 463
30	5954		84	57 - 69			
31	5953		85	5715		**SETTLES & SOFAS**	
32	7242					132	R130
33 A - D	R52 A - D		**CORNER CHAIRS**			133	4870
34	65 - 185		86	57 - 18		134	69 - 154
35	72 - 168		87	78 - 29		135	R134
36	6556		88	62 - 47		136	91 - 143
37	65 - 68					137	88 - 1713
38	3851		**19th CENTURY CHAIRS**				
39 A - D	63 - 78 A - D		89 A - F	70 - 120 A - F		**TABLES**	
40 A & B	88 - 1688 & 1689		90	1214		138	R132
41	6828		91	55 - 336		139	55 - 245
42	55 - 250		92 A - F	55 - 335 A - F		140	R161
43	6592		93	7664 A		141	R129
44	R56		94	7689		142	6788
45	56 - 121		95 A - C	88 - 14 A - C		143	69 - 153
46	55 - 307		96	88 - 1702		144	85 - 289
47	84 - 284					145	R140
48	R141		**HALL CHAIRS**			146	55 - 247
49	55 - 242		97	57 - 26		147	58 - 66
50	55 - 245					148	69 - 152
51	4975		**20th CENTURY CHAIRS**			149	80 - 314
52 A - C	85 - 290 A - C		98	88 - 1715		150	60 - 430
53	3894		99	88 - 1707		151	R185
54 A & B	21662 A & B		100	88 - 1706		152	R200
55 A & B	7241		101	88 - 1708		153	R156
56	55 - 346		102	88 - 1709		154	R162
57	74 - 269 B		103	90 - 235		155	88 - 1725
58	7390		104	88 - 459		156	69 - 237

Catalogue No.	Accession No.
DRESSERS	
157	55 - 267
158	4542
159	88 - 1732
CUPBOARDS	
160	1194
161	55 - 318
162	5718
163	R159
164	69 - 236
165	5767
CHESTS OF DRAWERS	
166	R160
167	88 - 1707
168	88 - 1706
169	88 - 1708
170	88 - 1730
171	88 - 1731
CHESTS & STORAGE BOXES	
172	5326
173	3472
174	1195
175	R157
176	R201
177	R202
178	61 - 137
179	83 - 265
180	21289
181	R154
182	R155
183	73 - 62
184	87 - 580
185	88 - 1726
186	88 - 1712
187	66 - 254
188	55 - 285
LONG CASE CLOCKS	
189	6637
190	88 - 1709
191	6508
192	67 - 199
193	7579
194	R168
195	59 - 138
196	71 - 277
197	63 - 67
198	55 - 248
199	76 - 31
200	59 - 224
WRITING FURNITURE	
201	R155
202	83 - 179
203	5711
204	6635

Catalogue No.	Accession No.
205	56 - 320
206	60 - 237
207	R158
BEDS AND BEDROOMS	
208	88 - 1733
209	88 - 2051
210	88 - 1727
211	88 - 1728
212	88 - 1729
213	88 - 1717
214	88 - 1721
215	88 - 1722
216	88 - 1718
217	88 - 1720
218	88 - 1719
219	72 - 54
WOODEN CRADLES	
220	6116
221	4605
222	2875
223	6779
224	6922
225	62 - 134
226	5185
227	6420
228	55 - 252
229	57 - 14
230	58 - 53
231	73 - 157
232	66 - 379
SPINNING WHEELS & WINDERS	
233	R153
234	R205
235	712
236	5956
237	4006
238	80
239	5448 A
240	5825
241	5967
242	6076 A
243	6344
244	6448
245	6483
246	6583
247	6843
248	7493
249	7503
250	7547
251	7820
252	59 - 133
253	63 - 84
254	67 - 161
255	87 - 1724
256	1677
257	21273

Catalogue No.	Accession No.
258	65 - 61
259	6955
260	5448 B
261	4828
262	6951
263	5968
264	687
265	3974
266	4956
ORGANS & HARMONIUMS	
267	1348
268	R163
269	R164
270	R165
271	57 - 83
PRISON FURNITURE	
272	90 - 102
273	90 - 103 A
MISCELLANEOUS	
274	R167
275	55 - 338
276	88 - 1723
277	55 - 309
278	73 - 201
279	73 - 203
LATE ADDITIONS	
280	92 - 70
281	92 - 177
282	61 - 202
283	4471
284	55 - 249

THE GROVE RURAL LIFE MUSEUM, RAMSEY

DOWNSTAIRS HALLWAY	
G1	76 - 1437
G2	76 - 1521
G3	76 - 1466 A & B
MIDDLE LANDING	
G4	76 - 1628
UPPER LANDING	
G5	76 - 1438
DRAWING ROOM	
G6	76 - 1486
G7	76 - 1470
G8	76 - 1479
G9	76 - 1441
G10	76 - 148
G11	79 - 68
G12	76 - 1471
G13	76 - 1477

Catalogue No.	Accession No.
G14	76 - 1473
G15	76 - 1485
G16	76 - 1476
G17	76 - 1480
G18	76 - 2072
G19	76 - 1436
G20	76 - 1487
G21	76 - 1446
G22	76 - 2107
G23	76 - 2100
G24	76 - 1495
G25	76 - 1478

DINING ROOM

G26	76 - 1443
G27	76 - 1465
G28	76 - 1452
G29	76 - 1448
G30	76 - 1445
G31	76 - 1453
G32	76 - 1522
G33	76 - 1447
G34	76 - 1440 A
G35	76 - 1441 A
	1442
	1444

KITCHEN

G36	70 - 80
G37	76 - 1914
G38	76 - 2121
G39	76 - 2122
G40	76 - 2123
G41	76 - 2124
G42	76 - 2125
G43	76 - 2126
G44	76 - 2127
G45	76 - 2128
G46	76 - 2129

SCULLERY

G47	76 - 2130
G48	76 - 2131
G49	76 - 2057

CELLAR

G50	76 - 2132
G51	76 - 2133
G52	76 - 2134
G53	76 - 2135
G54	76 - 2136

MAIN BEDROOM

G55	76 - 1500
G56	76 - 1509
G57	76 - 1473
G58	76 - 1538
G59	76 - 2109
G60	76 - 1506

Catalogue No.	Accession No.
G61	76 - 1505
G62	76 - 1510
G63	76 - 1504
G64	76 - 2110
G65	76 - 2111
G66	76 - 1533
G67	76 - 2112
G68	76 - 1501
G69	76 - 1498
G70	76 - 1539
G71	76 - 1503
G72	76 - 1502
G73	76 - 2113

SEWING ROOM

G74	76 - 2115
G75	76 - 2116
G76	76 - 2117
G77	76 - 1514
G78	76 - 2118
G79	76 - 1515
G80	76 - 1513
G81	76 - 2119
G82	76 - 2120

CHILD'S BEDROOM

G83	76 - 1519
G84	76 - 1524
G85	76 - 1531
G86	76 - 1512
G87	76 - 1527
G88	76 - 1526
G89	76 - 1530
G90	76 - 1525
G91	76 - 1517
G92	76 - 2114
G93	76 - 2053

STORED ITEMS

G94	76 - 1520
G95	76 - 1541
G96	76 - 1514 A
G97	76 - 2137
G98	76 - 2138
G99	76 - 1540
G100	76 - 2140
G101	76 - 2052
G102	76 - 2114
G103	76 - 1441
G104	76 - 2142
G105	76 - 2143
G106	76 - 1708
G107	76 - 2144
G108	76 - 2145
G109	76 - 2146
G110	76 - 2147
G111	76 - 2148
G112	76 - 2149
G113	76 - 2150

Catalogue No.	Accession No.
G114	76 - 1537
G115	76 - 1439

THE GRAMMER SCHOOL, CASTLETOWN

GS1	58 - 62 A
GS2	58 - 62 B
GS3	R186 A - D

THE NAUTICAL MUSEUM, CASTLETOWN

NT1	5716
NT2	5714
NT3	R187 A - D
NT4	5712

MANX MUSEUM, DOUGLAS : DISPLAY ITEMS

T. E. BROWN ROOM

MD1	R173
MD2	R172
MD3	R170
MD4	R171
MD5	R174
MD6	R177
MD7	R188
MD8	R178
MD9	65 - 163

MILITARY CASES

MD10	76 - 1518
MD11	3877

INTERNEE'S BEDROOM

MD12	R189
MD13	R190
MD14	R191

GLOSSARY OF TERMS

Auger - a basic boring tool, used for boring large holes by hand.

Backstool - a term current in the 17th and 18th centuries for an upholstered single chair.

Ball and claw foot - found at the bottom of the leg, representing an animal's paw or a dragon or bird's claw, clutching a ball.

Baroque - a flamboyant style, prevalent in the first half of the 18th century; can also mean whimsical or irregularly shaped.

Bevel - sloping edge; also a joiner's tool for adjusting angles.

Blind fretting - interlaced work.

Braganza feet - scroll-like feet; a style introduced during the Restoration period.

Caqueteuse - a conversational chair, adopted in Scotland from France in the late - 16th century, with a triangular seat, narrow back and spreading arms; a woman's chair.

Cabriole leg - a leg curved outwards at the knee and returning in an inward curve.

Chamfered - a surface or edge which has been smoothed off and cut away from the square.

Cleat - a block of wood attached to one member and locating or fixing another.

Cleft - split as opposed to sawn.

Cock beading - small mouldings applied to the edges of drawer fronts.

Cornice - The uppermost moulding or a horizontal moulded projection which crosses a piece of furniture.

Dovetail joint - see diagram, p. 284.

Draw knife - a flat or curved blade, fitted with wooden handles; used for removing surplus wood and for rounding and chamfering.

Escutcheon - shield shaped ornament, for example over a key-hole; can also refer to the central motif of the pediment of a cabinet.

Fielded panel - a panel with bevelled edges, enclosing a flat central section.

Fretted - decorated.

Frieze - strictly speaking that section between the architrave and cornice, but commonly any horizontal broad band.

Gesso - plaster of Paris, gypsum; originally used as a grain filler, but developed into a substance which could be carved in low relief and gilded.

Graticule - a design or plan divided into squares to facilitate its proportionate enlargement or reduction.

Heartwood - the wood at the centre of the tree, providing a solid core (no longer carrying sap).

Japanned - lacquered (varnished); japan lacquer gives a very hard, black, glossy finish.

Joints - see diagrams, p. 284.

Lap joint - see diagram, p. 284.

Loper - the sloping flap of, for example, a writing bureau, rests on two sliding pieces, traditionally called 'lopers'.

Marquetry - inlaid work; the most common form of floral marquetry incorporates the use of leaves, vines, flowers, all set in panels and incorporating a number of woods.

Medullary rays - rays which radiate outwards from the centre of the tree trunk.

Mitre joint - see diagram, p. 284.

Mortice - a hole in a piece of timber, cut to allow the tenon of another timber to slot into it - see diagram, p. 284.

Muntin - central vertical piece between two panels.

Nulling - (gardooning) - carved ornamental edging of repetitive form, concave or convex, upright or twisted.

Ormolo - gold coloured alloy used for decoration.

Parquetry - a mosaic of woods, often in the form of an inlay; can also describe any veneering where pieces of wood of contrasting colours are cut and laid so as to form a geometric or symetric pattern.

Patera - a flat, round or oval disk, applied or carved as ornament, or painted as low relief.

Pediment - the triangular part crowning the front of a building or, as in this case, a piece of furniture.

Peg - a short length of wood, driven into a bored hole to draw together and secure joints. Through-peg - a peg running through a joint.

Pintle - a bolt or pin, especially on which something turns; sometimes wholly of wood in Manx joinery.

Plinth - a foundation supporting the body of a piece of furniture.

Rabbett - an open sided groove cut along only one edge of the piece of timber - see diagram, p. 284.

Retarditaire - looking backwards for inspiration.

Rhomboid - lozenge or diamond shaped.

Rococo - a very florid style, with a multiplication of ornamental details; popular in the middle of the 18th century.

Scarf joint - see diagram, p. 284.

Scumble - a thin coat of coloured glaze, in this context used to simulate grain.

Shellac - a form of varnish; lac is melted and run into plates (*laq* is a dark red incrustation produced on certain trees by the puncture of an insect and used in the Far East as a scarlet dye).

Side axe - an axe whose cutting edge is bevelled on one side only.

Spindle - a rounded rod tapering towards each end.

Splat - the vertical or member, generally shaped or pierced, contained between the uprights of the chair back.

Stile - the vertical or upright section of a framed, panelled chest, door etc (cf. 'rail' = the horizontal or cross section).

Stretcher - a horizontal bar uniting and strengthening the legs of a chair, table etc.

Tester - canopy, particularly over a bed.

Tenon - that part of the end of a timber, shaped to fit into a corresponding hole (mortice) in another, see diagram, p. 284.

Through and through sawn - sawn with a very rough surface.

Vasiform - shaped like a vase.

Wainscot - panelling; can also refer to imported oak of fine quality.

Diagram to show common jointing techniques

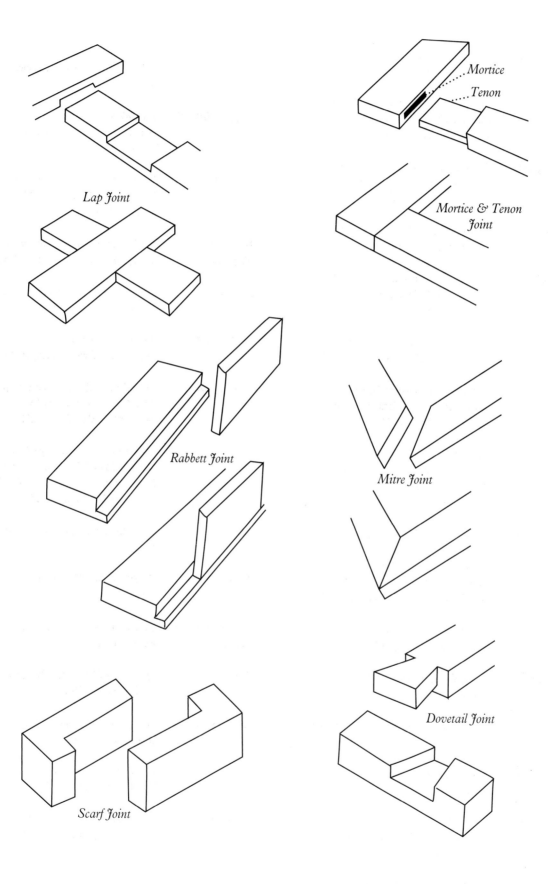

Lap Joint

Mortice

Tenon

Mortice & Tenon
Joint

Rabbett Joint

Mitre Joint

Scarf Joint

Dovetail Joint

BIBLIOGRAPHY

Airey, R. ed., *Feltham's Tour though the Isle of Man,* (Manx Society, Vol VI, 1861).

Anon. 'Unpublished Documents in the Manx Museum', *Journal of the Manx Museum,* Vol II, No. 38, 1930 - 34.

Edward, J. ed. *Pictorial Dictionary of British 19th Century Furniture Design* (Antique Collector's Club, 1977).

Chinnery, V. *Oak Furniture, The British Tradition* (Antique Collector's Club, 1979).

Chippendale, T. *The Gentleman and Cabinet Maker's Director,* 1762 (Dover Publications Reprint, 1966).

Cotton, B. D. *The English Regional Chair,* (Antique Collector's Club, 1990).

Cottage and Farmhouse Furniture in East Anglia (Exhibition Catalogue, Norfolk Rural Life Museum, 1987).

Crellin, J. C. 'Ballachurry, Kirk Andreas', *Isle of Man Natural History and Antiquarian Society Proceedings,* Vol IV, No. 4, 1962-64, pp. 255 - 262.

Crossley, F. R. *English Church Furniture,* (1917).

Cubbon, A. M. 'A Wattle Chimney Canopy from Kirk Andreas', *Journal of the Manx Museum,* Vol. VIII, No. 85, 1980, pp. 28 - 30.

Curtis, L. J. *Lloyd Loom Woven Fibre Furniture,* (Salamander Books, 1991).

Davenport, E. *Your Handspinning,* (Sylvan Press, 1953).

Fayles, D. *American Painted Furniture,* (New York, 1972).

Fleming, J. and Honour, H. *Penguin Dictionary of Decorative Arts,* (Viking, 1979).

Gilbert, C. G. *School Furniture in the Vernacular Tradition,* (Exhibition Catalogue, Temple Newsham, 1978).

English Vernacular Furniture 1750 - 1900, (Yale Press, 1991).

Harrison, W. ed., *A Description of the Isle of Man,* by G. Waldron gent, (Manx Society, Vol XI, 1865).

Hepplewhite, G. *The Cabinet Maker and Upholsterer's Guide,* 1794 (Dover Publications Reprint, 1971).

Hope, T. *Household Furniture and Interior Decoration 1807,* (Dover Publications Reprint, 1971).

Ince and Mayhew *The Universal System of Household Management* (Tiranti Reprint, 1960).

Kenyon, J. S. *The Gibbs of the Grove,* (Manx Museum and National Trust, 1979).

Killip, C. A. *A Book about the Manx,* Preface by John Berger, (The Arts Council, 1980).

Killip, I. M. 'Mrs Gilrea of the East Nappin', *Journal of the Manx Museum,* Vol VI, No. 81, 1957 - 1965, plate 277, p. 232.

'Thie Thooit Lesh Maidjyn Ayn - A Note on Manx Thatching Methods', *Journal of the Manx Museum,* Vol VII, No. 86, 1966 - 1976, pp. 157 - 160.

The Folklore of the Isle of Man, (Batsford, 1975).

Kinvig, R. H. *The Isle of Man,* (Liverpool University Press, 1975).

Kniveton, G. and Goldie, M. *Tholtans of the Manx Crofter,* (Manx Experience, n. d.).

Leadbeater, E. *Spinning and Spinning Wheels,* (Shire Publications, 1979).

Loomes, B. *Lancashire Clocks and Clockmakers,* (David and Charles, 1985).

Grandfather Clocks and their Cases, (David and Charles, 1985).

Loudon, J. C. *Encyclopaedia of Cottage, Farm and Villa Architecture,* (Longman, 1833).

Megaw, B. 'An Old House in Ballaugh: a Type of Rural Building', *Journal of the Manx Museum*, Vol IV, No. 63, 1938 - 40, p. 209.

'Life on a Mountain Farm: the Deserted Homestead of 'Iliam y Close', *Journal of the Manx Museum*, Vol V, No. 66, 1942 - 56, pp. 63 - 65.

Morrison, S. *Manx Fairy Tails*, (Morrison, Peel, 1929).

Moore, A. W. *The Folklore of the Isle of Man*, (Brown and Son, Isle of Man, 1891).

A History of the Isle of Man, (Manx Museum, 1976).

Quayle, G. 'Folklore of the Lezayre Tops', *IOMNHAS Proc.*, Vol 5, No. 4, 1946 - 50, pp. 26 - 43.

Quilliam, G. 'The Manx Museum Folk Life Survey', *IOMNHAS Proc.*, Vol V, No. 4, 1942 - 56, pp. 399 - 410.

'A Simple Cottage Home Place, Glimpses of the Folk Life Survey', *Journal of the Manx Museum*, Vol VI, No. 75, 1957 - 65, pp. 58 - 59.

'Stiff Carts and Spinning Wheels - Some Notes on Two Country Crafts', *Journal of the Manx Museum*, Vol VI, No. 77, 1957 - 65, pp. 116 - 120.

Roe, F. *A History of Oak Furniture*, (Connoisseur, 1920).

Ancient Church Chests and Chairs, (Batsford, 1929).

Salaman, R. A. *Dictionary of Woodworking Tools c. 1700 - 1970*, (Unwin Hyman, 1989).

Sheraton, T. *The Cabinet Maker's and Upholsterer's Drawing Book*, 1793 - 1802, (Dover Publications Reprint, 1972).

Stenning, E. H. *Portrait of the Isle of Man*, (Robert Hale, 1978).

Stevenson, M. 'Clock and Watchmakers of the Isle of Man, 1785 - 1850', *Journal of the Manx Museum*, Vol IV, No. 63, 1938 - 40, pp. 211 - 214.

Williamson, K. 'Characteristics of the Chiollagh - Dominant Types and their Distribution', *Journal of the Manx Museum*, Vol IV, No. 54, 1938 - 40, pp. 23 - 28.

———————— *Regional Furniture* Volumes I-IV (The Journal of the Regional Furniture Society), 1987 - 1992.